A Dictionary of
Card Games

DAVID PARLETT

*'I look upon cards in general as a rational amusement...
and while they amuse also supply matter for the exercise
of genius.'*   'Q. Quanti' (1822)

'Play smart, act dumb'
       Anon.

Oxford   New York

OXFORD UNIVERSITY PRESS

OXFORD
UNIVERSITY PRESS

Great Clarendon Street, Oxford OX2 6DP

Oxford University Press is a department of the University of Oxford.
It furthers the University's objective of excellence in research, scholarship,
and education by publishing worldwide in

Oxford New York

Auckland Bangkok Buenos Aires Cape Town Chennai
Dar es Salaam Delhi Hong Kong Istanbul Karachi Kolkata
Kuala Lumpur Madrid Melbourne Mexico City Mumbai Nairobi
São Paulo Shanghai Taipei Tokyo Toronto

Oxford is a registered trade mark of Oxford University Press
in the UK and in certain other countries

Published in the United States
by Oxford University Press Inc., New York

© David Parlett 1992

The moral rights of the author have been asserted
Database right Oxford University Press (maker)

First published 1992 as an Oxford University Press paperback
Reissued in new covers 1996

British Library Cataloguing in Publication Data

Data available

Library of Congress Cataloging in Publication Data

Data available

ISBN 0-19-869173-4

13 15 17 19 20 18 16 14 12

Printed in Great Britain by
Clays Ltd, St Ives plc

OXFORD PAPERBACK REFERENCE

A Dictionary of
Card Games

David Parlett is a games writer and consultant of
international repute. He is the author of many game
books, including *The Guiness Book of Word Games*. He
also advises on card-playing sequences in film and
television and acts as a consultant to playing card
and computer companies. He is a South-Londoner
by birth, domicile, and inclination.

Oxford Paperback Reference

The most authoritative and up-to-date reference books for both students and the general reader.

*forthcoming

To the
International Playing-card Society
and especially
John McLeod and Michael Dummett

Acknowledgements

As always, I am glad to acknowledge the kindness of Dan Glimne, John McLeod, Andrew Pennycook, and Arthur Taylor in helping weed the text of errors, omissions, and ambiguities. If any remain, they are all my own work.

Contents

Introduction

This book tells you how to play almost any card game you are likely to find current today, or mentioned as popular in the past, in Europe, the Americas, and the Western world in general. Though complete in itself, it is in fact a companion volume or supplement to *The Oxford Guide to Card Games*, whose nature and content were more clearly indicated by the title *A History of Card Games* under which it was reprinted in paperback. As it would have been distracting and uneconomical to give detailed rules of play for every game mentioned in such a book, it was obvious that a second volume would be needed to fulfil this function and so complete the survey.

The supplement is called a *Dictionary* because, after much thought, I decided to follow the unusual practice of arranging the games in alphabetical order rather than family by family or according to numbers of players. Besides making it easier to find any given game, this also means that games of radically different types may be found in one another's accidental company on the same page, and this in turn will (I hope) encourage players to go exploring in the realm of card games. One hobby-horse of mine is that too many players know only one or two games, and so deprive themselves of a good deal of potential enjoyment. It is not enough to play just Bridge, or Poker, or Crib, to consider yourself an educated card-player. Anybody worthy of the name should have at least five good games at their fingertips: one for two players, one for three, one for four as individuals and another for partnerships, and a round game for up to six or seven. Ten or fifteen would be better still, allowing for different *types* of game for each number. By way of encouragement, a breakdown of games by number and type will be found under 'Recommendations' immediately before the first entry in the book.

The present anthology aims to be a treasury of great and interesting card games of the Western world. Besides the obvious international favourites like Bridge, Poker, Hearts, and Rummy, it also includes major national card games such as Cribbage (Britain), Belote (France), Skat (Germany), Scopa (Italy), Tute (Spain), Jass (Switzerland), and Ulti (Hungary), as well as classic games formerly occupying either of the above positions, such as Piquet, Bezique, Hombre (Ombre), Trappola, and Boston Whist. Also included are several Tarot games. The Tarot tradition still flourishes in many parts of Europe, and in some is even on the increase. Besides French Tarot, entries will be found for Scarto (Italian) and Tarock (Austrian). Players wishing to delve more deeply into these ancient and fascinating games should refer to Michael Dummett, *Twelve Tarot Games* (London, 1980). That still leaves other games of unusual interest or eccentric habits which it would have been a shame to omit, such as Cucumber, Durak, Le Barbu, Phat, Sedma, Spite and Malice, Trouduc, Vint, Watten, and others you will discover while browsing.

It may be helpful to indicate what I have omitted or only summarily dealt with.

Of several hundred games for one player, I have selected only a handful of the most representative, and slotted them into the single entry 'Patience'. Curiously, there seems to be little overlap between Patience players and players of competitive card games, and a book that devoted equal space to both would therefore probably satisfy no one. A Patience enthusiast myself, I hope the few examples described will encourage players to explore this realm from books devoted to the subject (such as my *Penguin Book of Patience*).

Only limited coverage is given to gambling games involving little or no intelligent card-play, such as Faro and Baccarat, though I have been more generous with those that have been socially fumigated and thus become popular as children's games, like Go Fish and My Ship Sails. It seems to me that there is as little overlap between serious card-players and mere gamblers as between card-players and Patience-players, and (again) that no one would be satisfied by a book that devoted equal space to both.

I have largely avoided proprietary and one-off games by known inventors, apart from some half a dozen that can reasonably be described as breaking new ground (Calypso, Concerto, Eleusis, Ninety-Nine, Quinto, Zetema).

While I have entirely omitted games requiring special cards not widely obtainable, such as Aluette and Gnav, I have nevertheless included many games normally played with one of the standard national packs (see table opposite). It is always possible to play such games with the British 52-card French-suited pack used for interna-

| Italian: | swords | batons | cups | coins |

| Spanish: | swords | clubs | cups | coins |

| Swiss: | acorns | escutcheons | flowers | bells |

| German: | acorns | leaves | hearts | bells |

| French: | trèfle | pique | coeur | carreau |
| English: | clubs | spades | hearts | diamonds |

Major European suit systems showing possible lines of evolution from earliest and most complex to latest and simplest.

Nation	Length	Courts			Numerals
Italian	52, 40	King	Cavalier	Soldier	(10 9 8) 7 6 5 4 3 2 1
Spanish	48, 40	King	Cavalier	Valet	(9 8 7) 6 5 4 3 2 1
Swiss	48, 36	King	Over	Under	Banner 9 8 7 6 (5 4 3) Deuce
German	36, 32	King	Ober	Unter	10 9 8 7 (6) Deuce
French	52, 32	King	Queen	Jack	10 9 8 7 (6 5 4 3 2) Ace

tional card games, stripping out the lower numerals where necessary. In the main entries I have stated where a game is normally and properly played with a local pack, but have then described the game as if played with international cards. Such cards are widely used and easily obtainable in their countries of origin. German-suited cards are also used in some eastern European countries, and Spanish-suited cards are the norm throughout Latin America.

Why so many card games?

Several hundred games are described in this book. The figure is imprecise, as it is not always possible to draw a hard and fast line between different games and variants of the same game. Names are nothing to go by: most games have alternative names, which may or may not imply variations in play, and some quite unrelated games may share the same name. California Jack and Shasta Sam sound like different games, but are virtually identical; Polish Bezique sounds like a minor variant of Bezique, but, in practice, feels entirely different.

People often ask why there are so many different card games. The simple answer is that so many different card games are possible. A pack of cards in itself does not imply any particular way of playing: it is not self-evidently 'a game', but a piece of equipment for playing different types of game, and will therefore be used in different ways by different types of player according to temperament, intelligence, tradition, and fundamental motivation for playing. A card game is a way of playing cards characteristic of a particular group of people living in a particular country at a particular time in history. Games therefore vary from place to place—not just from country to country, but also between regions or towns within the same country. In a given area they also vary according to social context. Thus we may distinguish such genres as children's games, drinking games, casino games, commuter games, club games, men's games, women's games, and games favoured by particular professions, age ranges, ethnic groups, and so on. They vary, yet again, according to the number of players involved. Two-hand games differ in kind from three-handers, three-handers from partnership games, partnership games from round games. Finally, of course, they vary in time:

Contract Bridge developed from Auction Bridge, Auction from Bridge-Whist, Bridge-Whist from Whist, Whist from Ruff-and-Honours, Ruff-and-Honours from Trump.

Games vary quickly and easily because, as we have said, cards are adaptable by nature. When a game gets played so extensively that the same situations and outcomes begin to appear with monotonous regularity, it often takes only a slight alteration or addition to the 'rules' (the 'mechanics', more accurately) to open up new vistas of challenge and calculation. Naturally, the deepest games offer the greatest inherent variety, and tend to remain stable over longer periods of time.

The ready adaptability of card games has another notable consequence. It is that very few of them are played so widely, or for so long, as to acquire a corpus of definitive or 'official' rules from which there is no apparent deviation. In this respect, the relative fixity and invariability of Contract Bridge is itself the exception that tries the rule. Many national games, such as Skat in Germany, are governed by a code of rules observed in official tournaments, but in domestic and informal play are otherwise subject to a range of minor variations not always recorded in the textbooks. In fact, the vast majority of card games are folk games, with all the liveliness and variability implicit in the word 'folk'. This makes it difficult to record them all accurately and authentically, and it is regrettable that so few people have the time, money and expertise to keep up to date with field research into what is actually being played at any given time or place.

Necessarily, most of the games described in this book are based on records made by one or more other authorities in other books. (Where there is only one main source, I have cited it.) It must be understood that the very appearance of a game in a book tends to impart to it a sense of timeless fixity quite contrary to the progressive fluidity it actually enjoys; one must therefore not be surprised to find it, in real life, played with differences ranging from the trivial to the substantial. For this reason I have not hesitated to record variations and even the occasional suggestion for variation. Games should be tailored to the needs of the players, not vice versa. Partly for the same reason, I have not gone deeply into advice on strategy. The strategy of a game varies with its content, and is therefore equally fluid. In the section headed 'Notes' at the end of most entries, I do little more than outline what I see as the strategic 'point' of the game.

What's in a game?

We can see how rich the realm of card games is by essaying a classification of them, and may usefully start by surveying the basic elements of the pack.

A typical pack contains fifty-two cards divided into four sets of thirteen. The sets are called 'suits' and are identified by names and symbols, spades and clubs being black (♠ ♣), hearts and diamonds red (♥ ♦). Each set contains thirteen cards theoretically numbered one to thirteen. In fact, only two to ten are so numbered. Cards eleven to thirteen are illustrated with medieval characters known respectively as Jack (originally Knave), Queen, and King. These are called face-cards, court cards, or, as I prefer, 'courts'. The numeral 'one' has the special name 'Ace', and in many games ranks above the King as the highest card in its suit. Each card in the pack therefore has a unique identity composed of its rank and suit—Ace of spades, Queen of hearts, and so on. (To complete this survey, it should be added that the Joker is a highly specialized Jack devised in the nineteenth century for American Euchre. It does not derive from the 'Fool' in Tarot packs, as sometimes stated. Jokers would probably now be extinct were it not for their persistent and extensive use in Rummy games.)

All card games hinge on the fact that a card has two sides, one of which *reveals* its identity (Ace of spades, Queen of hearts, etc.), while the other *conceals* it, being indistinguishable from the reverse of any other card in the pack.

A game begins with one player, the dealer or banker, randomizing the pack by holding it face down and shuffling the cards, so that no one knows in what order they lie. In simple gambling games, reduced to their barest essentials, a banker merely turns cards up one by one, and collects or repays wagers made by punters as to which cards will turn up in what order. In more strategic games, they are distributed amongst the players and held in such a way that each can identify his own cards but not those of anybody else.

This element of secrecy puts cards into the category of 'games of imperfect information', by contrast with board games such as

Chess, in which each player always knows exactly what his opponent's resources are. Some games do not progress beyond this point: they may offer no choice of play, in which case the outcome is entirely determined by chance; or, if they offer a choice of moves, the skill involved in selecting one move over another is largely that of playing 'with the probabilities', that is, with an intuitive or calculated sense of what play will, more often than not, produce the best result from a given situation. In the deepest games, play can be directed towards the eliciting of information as to the lie of cards in adverse hands, and control exerted over the subsequent course of events so as to profit from that information while enough time or material remains in which to make informed strategic choices. Generally, the most advanced games—Bridge, Piquet, Stud Poker, to name but a few—reveal a lot of information early in the play. Very few, however, apart from some forms of Patience, reveal everything. This suggests that 'information' and its acquisition are what card games are all about, and that those involving perfect information from the outset, such as Svoyi Koziri, are rare because they feel unnatural—because perfect information contradicts the very nature of the equipment.

To get an overall picture of the variety of card games, it is theoretically helpful (though in practice not very easy) to classify them. One way of doing so is to note three basic ways of relating cards to one another as follows:

Superiority. One card beats or captures another by outranking it, as in trick-taking games.

Similarity. Cards are formed into matched sets ('melds'), as in Rummy or Bezique, or are played to a matching sequence, as in Newmarket.

Numericity. Play involves adding together cards' numerical values, as in Cribbage and Pontoon.

But this classification is rather academic, and too small to be useful. It may be better to take games as they stand and try to separate along more natural lines of demarcation.

In the following attempt, the first three groups may be described as technically 'gambling games', in that cards are staked upon, or provide eventualities upon which wagers may be made, *but are not themselves the instruments of play*—that function being assigned, in effect, to the stakes placed on them. The fourth is rather miscellaneous, but most of the remainder are technically 'strategic games', in that cards are actively and purposefully played with a view to engineering a winning situation.

1. *Games of chance.* Gambling games whose outcome depends entirely upon chance. There is no significant card-play, but skill may consist in matching one's stake to the relevant probabilities. Many children's games are basically gambling games shorn of real pecuniary interest (Beggar my Neighbour).

2. *Banking or casino games.* Gambling games in which one player, or 'the house', plays an essentially two-hand game of chance against a single player, a group of players acting as one, or a simultaneous series of non-interacting players (Pontoon, Blackjack).

3. *Vying games.* Gambling games in which the pot is won by the player who either has the best hand when it comes to a showdown or, by skilfully persuading others that he has the best hand ('bluffing'), forces them to withdraw before any showdown is reached.

4. *Testing games.* Games, mainly for children, that test skills other than those normally understood by the term 'card sense'. (Snap tests reaction speed; Pelmanism tests memory; I Doubt It tests bluffing power.)

5. *Ordering or Patience games.* The aim is to work cards drawn at random from the shuffled pack into complete suit sequences or other ordered patterns. They are typically, but not necessarily, solitaires or one-player games.

6. *Collecting games.* Players collect cards that match one another by rank or suit. The aim may be to collect the most valuable set (Commerce), or to be the first to match all one's cards (My Ship Sails).

7. *Rummy games.* A subset of collecting games played by 'draw and discard'. Again, the aim may be to collect the highest-scoring sets (Canasta), or to be the first to match all one's cards (Gin). Matched sets are called 'melds'.

8. *Going-out games.* Players discard to a common wastepile, complying with certain rules of matching or beating the previous discard, with a view to being the first to play out all one's cards. (Rolling Stone, Switch, Durak).

9. *Stops games*. A subset of going-out games characterized by the fact that certain cards are left undealt and so stop the sequence from being continued. (Newmarket.)

10. *Adding-up games*. Players discard to a common wastepile and announce the cumulative face value of the cards so far played, making scores or penalties for reaching or exceeding certain totals. (Jubilee.)

11. *Fishing games*. Cards are played from the hand to capture, by matching or addition, 'pool' cards lying open on the table (Cassino).

12. *Trick games*. The largest and most varied group requires separate consideration.

Trick-playing games

Most Western card games, and especially the deepest, are based on trick-play.

One person leads a card by playing it face up to the table. Each in turn contributes a card. The cards so played constitute a trick, which is won by the player of the best card to it. The trick-winner squares it up, places it face down on the table before him, and leads to the next trick.

Normally, the 'best' card is the highest card of the suit led. A card played from a different suit cannot take the trick, no matter how high its rank. Even the lowest card of a suit will win the trick if it is led and no one can match it ('follow suit'). Because it is usually advantageous to lead, the privilege of doing so is conferred as a reward upon the winner of the previous trick.

This principle is enlivened and deepened by the introduction of trumps (originally 'triumphs'). Typically, a given suit is designated trump. If a plain (non-trump) suit is led, it can be beaten by playing any trump. Even the lowest-ranking trump beats the highest-ranking plain card. In trick-and-trump games, therefore, *the trick is taken by the highest card of the suit led, or by the highest trump if any are played*. This simple device, unique to Western card games, adds a significant dimension to the strategy of play.

Although it is an almost invariable rule that the leader to a trick may play any card, different games have different rules governing what cards may be played by those who follow to it. Given that the possibilities are to follow suit to the card led, to play a trump (if different from the lead), or to renounce (play from a different non-trump suit), the commonest rules, from laxest to strictest, are:

1. Any card may be played without restriction (as in the first half of trick-and-draw games like Bezique and Sixty-Six).
2. Follow suit or trump, as preferred, but only renounce if unable to follow suit (All Fours, Pitch, etc.).
3. Follow suit if possible, otherwise play any card (Whist, Bridge, etc.).
4. Follow suit if possible; otherwise trump if possible; otherwise play any card (typical of Tarot games).
5. Follow suit and head the trick if possible—i.e. play higher than any other card so far played of that suit. If unable to follow, trump (and overtrump) if possible (Écarté).

The Whist rule, (3), is by far the commonest, as it is neither so strict as to nullify strategic choice nor so lax as to confound the drawing of positional inferences. Other variants may be encountered, and the situation is sometimes further complicated by appointing a particular rank or ranks as trumps as well as a given suit.

Independently of these 'rules of following', trick games also vary according to their principle objective. There are three main types:

Plain-trick games. The outcome depends solely on the number of tricks taken, regardless of the cards comprising them (Whist, Nap, Solo, Euchre, Bridge).

Point-trick games. The outcome depends wholly or largely on the total point-value of individual cards contained in won tricks (All Fours, Manille, Skat, Tarot).

Trick-avoidance games. The object is to avoid winning tricks, whether for themselves alone, or for the avoidance of certain penalty cards contained within them (Hearts, Black Maria, Reversis).

Any of these may also belong to one or more of the following types:

Trick and bluff games. A hand is won by the player who either wins most tricks or, by raising the stakes, forces opponents to concede before all tricks are played (Put, Truc).

Trick and meld games. Scores are also made for declaring melds (combinations of matched cards) which may be dealt (Belote), drawn (Bezique), or won in tricks (Klaverjas).

Auction (or contract) games. In older games, a trump is selected at random and the objective is statutory and invariant—e.g. in Whist, to win seven or more tricks. In auction or contract games (e.g. Bridge, Skat, Solo) both the trump and the objective are variable. Players bid for the right to name trumps by raising the number of tricks they offer to win in exchange, or by offering to achieve some special feat such as to lose every trick. The proposed objective and trump constitute a 'contract'.

Notes on the 2001 reprint

I have taken advantage of this reprinting to incorporate changes that have been made since 1992 to the International Laws of Contract Bridge and to the International Laws of Skat (*die Skatordnung*). I have also revised, in the light of new discoveries and developments, the introductory passages to Catch the Ten, Eleusis, Preference, Schafkopf, and Svoyi Koziri, and have corrected some errors in Don and Hearts.

Since this book was first published a great deal of information on card games has been available through the growth of the Internet. The best source of authoritative and up-to-date information is John McLeod's web site, <http://www.pagat.com>. Some games of my invention are to be found at my own site, <http://davidparlett.co.uk>, where I also intend to post any further corrections or revisions that may come to light. I will be grateful for any notifications and contributions sent to me via this site.

David Parlett, London, June 2001

Good practice

Many rules and procedures are not specific to particular games but serve as a general code of good practice over the card-table. Their purpose is to keep things running smoothly and fairly and to obviate disputes, so that nobody's enjoyment of the game is marred by embarrassment, ill behaviour, or time-wasting. The following points are worth taking into account.

Cards. Regular card-players prefer standard packs with sober back designs rather than packs with novelty faces and garish advertisements. Always have fresh cards handy for replacement. A sloppy old pack encourages sloppy old habits, and cards should be abandoned when they get sticky or when any of them are so worn with use as to be identifiable from the back by a stain, fold, or tear. It is good practice to alternate two packs of similar back design but contrasting colour, one of them being thoroughly shuffled for the next deal while the other is being dealt out for this. That cards sometimes run unfavourably to a particular player for a long time is not a superstition but an observable fact. By tradition, anyone may call for new cards at any time in the session (but—also by tradition—at their own expense).

Cutting. Cards are cut to decide choice of seats, who partners whom, who deals first, etc. The cut is made by lifting the top portion of the pack and turning it up to show its bottom card. For this purpose cards normally rank in their 'natural' order from Ace low to King high. If two or more cut equal ranks, they cut again, but only to break the tie between themselves. Instead of cutting, players may draw a card at random from the whole pack shuffled and spread face down on the table.

Partners. In a fixed-partnership game, players may wish to select partners at random. This may be determined by cutting or drawing, the two highest ranks playing the two lowest, and having first choice of seats.

Seating. The order of seating around the table may be randomized by cutting, with highest cut conferring first choice of seat, and so on. This practice is rooted in superstition, the aim being to prevent players from fighting over 'lucky' seats or positions. There is, however, also a practical reason for it. Experienced players who know the company well can often adjust their play according to who is sitting on either side of them, and it is therefore only fair to randomize their relative positions.

Rotation. In some games, the turn to play passes to the left (clockwise around the table as seen from above); in others, it passes to the right. Different countries have different traditions, and which way round a game is played often indicates its country of origin. Of course, it makes no practical difference which way round a game is played; but, since neither is more logical or convenient than the other, one might as well follow tradition. In this book the rotation is stated as part of the rules of play.

Dealer. Unless tradition or book-rules decree otherwise for a particular game, and for a sensible reason, the turn to deal passes from person to person in the same order as the turn to play. The first dealer may be selected by cutting or drawing the lowest (or highest) card. Normally, though not invariably, it is for the player next in rotation from the dealer—'eldest hand'—to play, bid, or bet first.

Shuffle and cut. Unless it is specifically agreed otherwise beforehand, or otherwise stated by the rules of the game, the pack should always be shuffled and cut between deals. Any player who wishes to may shuffle, but dealer has the right to shuffle last. If you can't shuffle well, practise; and if this doesn't help, get someone else to do it. The important thing is the randomization, not the performance. Cutting is done as follows. Dealer places the pack face down on the table; the player at his right (in a clockwise game, otherwise vice versa) lifts the top portion and places it face down on the table; dealer then completes the cut by placing the previously lower half on top of it. There should be at least five cards in the smaller half of the cut.

Dealing. Unless otherwise agreed or specified, cards are dealt face down in rotation around the table, one at a time, starting with eldest and finishing with the dealer. In some games cards are dealt not singly but in batches of three or four at a time. This is not designed to produce 'more interesting hands' so much as to save time and effort. Custom should always be followed in this matter, as the dealer who fails to do so may be suspected of nefarious motives, not to mention bad manners.

Play. It is bad manners to pick your cards up before the deal is complete. (It may put the dealer off his stroke, or cause a card to be faced, which is a waste of time and effort.) In play, restrict conversation to that necessary to the game—gossip can be left to between deals. Make bids clearly and audibly. Play cards smoothly rather than histrionically, decisively rather than hesitantly. If you have to stop and think, do so before touching a card in your hand, as the act of touching first one and then another may be construed as signalling to a partner, which is illegal. Don't criticize anyone for their play, especially a partner, or brag about or justify your own. If the rules of the game do not demand that players show the cards they have won, played, or discarded, don't insist on seeing them.

These procedures are open to relaxation in informal play, for example among close friends who are not playing seriously for money and know one another well enough to follow an intuitive code of behaviour. But it is as well to know and follow them, especially when a newcomer joins the group.

Scoring. An exciting characteristic of card games is that they rarely produce a simple 'win/lose' outcome like that of Chess. In most of them you win or lose *a greater or lesser amount* depending on the outcome of the game. Exactly what you win or lose may be measured in what I call 'hard' or 'soft' score.

Hard score means an immediate cash settlement, or an exchange of tokens representing pay-off values. Typically, such settlements are made at the end of each deal, so that, in effect, each deal is a game in itself resulting in a 'zero-sum' transaction (as it is called in Game Theory)—i.e. the total values entered at start of play remain unchanged at the end, having been merely redistributed amongst the players, so that all the gains and all the losses cancel out to zero.

Soft score means a record of game-points made in writing or with mechanical markers such as a Cribbage board. Typically, a soft-score game is structured into a number of separate deals, with points scored cumulatively by each player until the whole game reaches a previously agreed ending, at which point the winner is (usually) the player with the highest score. Since all players can finish with a positive score, a game played in this form cannot be described as 'zero-sum'. For example, in a three-player game starting from a universal score of 0 (no handicap being given) Abel might finish up with 40 points, Baker with 75, and Charlie with 100; and these, clearly, do not sum to zero. If, however, the players have previously agreed to play for money, then they can easily translate the final, notional point-score into a zero-sum transaction. This is done by each person's paying to any player with a higher score a 'hard' amount equivalent to the difference. In this case, supposing it was agreed to play for a penny a point, Abel pays Baker 35 and Charlie 60, and Baker pays Charlie 25, thus turning it into a zero-sum transaction as shown here.

Abel	Baker	Charlie	
− 35	+ 35		(B's 75 *less* A's 40)
− 60		+ 60	(C's 100 *less* A's 40)
	− 25	+ 25	(C's 100 *less* B's 75)
− 95	+ 10	+ 85 = 0	

There is another way of reducing a set of scores to zero-sum format for settling-up purposes, which may be easier to calculate when there are more than three players:

(*a*) Sum the scores of all the players. In the above example, A's 40 + B's 75 + C's 100 = 215.

(*b*) Multiply each player's score by the number of players. Thus: A 120, B 225, C 300.

(*c*) A player whose multiplied score is less than the total pays the difference into a pool, and one whose multiplied score exceeds the total draws that difference from the pool, as shown here.

$$
\begin{array}{ll}
A & 120 - 215 = -95 \\
B & 225 - 215 = +10 \\
C & 300 - 215 = +85 \\
& = 0
\end{array}
$$

(An alternative to (*b*) is to divide the total by the number of players. The results are proportionally identical, though different in absolute terms.)

Whether a game is played for hard or soft score depends sometimes on the game and sometimes on the players. The advantage of hard score is that each deal is complete in itself, and players can cut in and out at any time between deals without disturbing the progress of play. The advantage of soft score is that it occupies less table space, requires less equipment, and takes less time to record.

Most gambling games are played for hard score, since cash, not cards, is the instrument of play, and the pay-offs are variable rather than fixed. A written record of transactions at Poker is theoretically possible, but ridiculous in practice. At the other extreme, a strategic game like Bridge has a multi-deal structure and a complex point-scoring system which is much easier to record in writing than to convert into hard score as you go along.

At end of play the final soft score can easily be converted into a hard-score settlement by any of the means described above. It is, however, a measure of a game's depth that players may be more interested in the play than in the pay-off, and will not bother to make a monetary settlement out of it.

Many games can be played either way. Solo Whist, for instance, is normally played for hard score, but, as it has a fixed schedule of pay-offs, it may be found more convenient to use the schedule as a soft-score system. In this event, note that it is *not necessary* to record the result of each deal as a zero-sum transaction. If, for instance, Abel wins a contract worth 12, it is sufficient to write '12' in Abel's column without also bothering to write '−12' in everyone else's. The final result can always be turned into a zero-sum transaction as demonstrated above.

The scoring of a soft-score game (pencil and paper) should be entrusted to the player most reliable as to neatness, numeracy, and objectivity—but keep an eye on it all the same, as no one is infallible. In a two-sided game, it is helpful to follow Contract Bridge practice whereby each side keeps a scoresheet recording both sides' current scores. If playing *for* money, ensure that everyone agrees the final basis of settlement in advance and that it is not increased in mid-play. If playing *with* money, or its equivalent, make provision for players to retire when they have had enough. To end a game in real embarrassment is not only stupid: it also devalues the moral integrity of play as a form of social intercourse.

Recommendations

Many games are designed for a specific number of players, and nothing is gained, though much may be lost, by adapting them for the wrong number. Many others work best for a specific number, but with slight modifications can be played reasonably well by one more or less. Quite a few, known as 'round games', are playable by any small group from about three to seven. The following games are solely or best suited to the number of players stated:

Games for two

Plain tricks: Écarté, German Whist, Put, Truc.

Point tricks: All Fours, Auction Pitch, Bohemian Schneider, California Jack, Elfern, Sedma.

Trick and meld: Belote, Bezique, Bondtolva, Briscan, Imperial, Klaberjass, Marjolet, Piquet, Sixty-Six, Tausendeins, Trappola, Tute.

Rummy: Conquian, Gin.

Fishing: Cassino, Scopa, Tablanette.

Other: Costly Colours, Cribbage, Durak, Gops, Svoyi Koziri, Quinze, Spite and Malice.

Games for three

Plain tricks: Bismarck, Five Hundred, Hombre, Ninety-Nine, Preference, Put.

Point tricks: Auction Pitch, Bavarian Tarock, Mariáš, Reunion, Sheepshead, Six-Bid Solo, Skat, Spanish Solo.

Trick and meld: Auction Pinochle, Belote, Jass, Terziglio, Tyzicha, Ulti, Zwikken.

Tarot: Scarto, Tapp Tarock, Tarot (French).

Trick avoidance: Black Maria, Hearts, Knaves.

Rummy: Oklahoma.

Fishing: Scopa, Tablanette.

Other: Zetema.

Recommendations

Games for four (solo)

Plain tricks: Boston, Brandle, Dutch Whist, German Solo, Mauscheln, Ninety-Nine, Nomination Whist, Oh Hell!, Pirate Bridge, Quadrille, Solo Whist
Point tricks: Auction Pitch, Schafkopf, Sheepshead, Špády.
Trick and meld: Bondtolva, Pandur, Pinochle.
Tarot: Tarot (French).
Trick avoidance: Bassadewitz, Hearts, Le Barbu, Polignac, Reversis, Slobberhannes.
Rummy: Kaluki.
Fishing: Tablanette.
Vying: Bouillotte, Primiera.
Other: Trouduc, Neuner.

Games for four (partnership)

Plain tricks: Bridge, Calypso, Cayenne, Contract Whist, Euchre, Five Hundred, Norwegian Whist, Put, Vint, Watten, Whist.
Point tricks: Cinch, Don, Doppelkopf, Manille, Phat, Quinto, Sedma, Sueca.
Trick and meld: Belote, Bondtolva, Gaigel, Jass, Klaverjass, Pinochle, Tressette.
Rummy: Canasta, Persian Rummy.
Fishing: Scopone, Tablanette.
Other: Concerto.

Games for five

Tricks: Five Hundred, Hearts, Nap, Oh Hell!, Pip-Pip, Quintille, Slobberhannes, Spoil Five, Yukon.
Other: Poker.

Games for six

Tricks: Sixte, Sizette, Slobberhannes, Spoil Five.

Round games (3 to 6 or more)

Plain tricks: Julep, Knockout Whist, Loo, Nap, Oh Hell!, Rams
  (Rounce), Spoil Five.
Point tricks: Briscola, Catch the Ten, Manille, Pip-Pip, Yukon.
Trick avoidance: Black Maria, Hearts, Polignac.
Rummy: Kaluki, Kings and Queens, Rummy, Vatican.
Adding-up games: Hundred, Jubilee, Obstacle Race, Twenty-Nine.
Stops games: Epsom, Pink Nines, Michigan, Newmarket, Pope
  Joan, Spinado.
Going-out games: Eleusis, Go Boom, Go Fish, Neuner, Switch.
Gambling games: Blackjack, Brag, Commerce, Matrimony, Poch,
  Poker, Pontoon, Primiera.
Others: Chase the Ace, Cucumber, Rolling Stone, Sift Smoke,
  Zetema.

Abbreviations

2p, 3p, 4p (etc.) denotes the possible number of players. '4pp' means 'four players in 2×2 partnerships', and 'Np' means 'any number of players'—typically 3 to 7.

52c, 32c (etc.) indicates the number of cards required. A doubled pack is indicated '$2 \times 52c$' rather than '104c'.

'T' stands for the card numbered 10, as in (for example) 'Cards rank A K Q J T 9 8 7 6 5 4 3 2'.

Technical terms used in card games are listed in the Appendix.

Adding-up games

Each in turn plays a card to a common wastepile, announces the total face value of all cards so far played, and earns a score or penalty for making or exceeding certain totals. Such games are uncommon in Western Europe, apart from the play up to 31 of Cribbage. See Fifty-One, Jubilee, Ninety-Nine, Obstacle Race, One Hundred, Twenty-Nine.

All Fours

Point-trick game: 2–4p, 52c

An English tavern game from the late seventeenth century, possibly of Dutch origin, and the one responsible for attaching the name 'Jack' to what was formerly just a knave. In nineteenth-century America it was called Seven Up and gave rise to Pitch, Cinch, and California Jack. Modern descendants include Don and Phat.

Traditionally, 2 players each receive 6 cards dealt in 3s from a 52-card pack ranking A K Q J T . . . 2. The next is turned for trumps: if it is a Jack, Dealer scores a point.

The aim is to win as many as possible of the four points: High, Low, Jack, and Game.

High scores to the person dealt the highest trump in play.
Low goes to the player capturing the lowest trump in play.
Jack goes to the player capturing the Jack of trumps (if it is in play).
Game scores to the player taking, in tricks, the greater value of card-points, counting each Ace 4, King 3, Queen 2, Jack 1, and Ten 10.

Elder may accept the turned suit as trump by saying 'I stand', or reject it by saying 'I beg'. If he begs, Younger may accept the trump, in which case Elder scores 1 point for 'gift', or 'refuse the gift', thereby rejecting the trump. If Younger refuses, the cards are 'run' as follows: 3 more are dealt to each, the next is turned for trump and placed on top of the previous turn-up. If it is the same suit as the first, it is turned down, each discards the three he was just dealt, and the cards are run again. This continues until a new suit is turned, which automatically becomes trump. Whenever a Jack is turned,

1

Dealer's hand   Turn-up   Non-dealer's hand

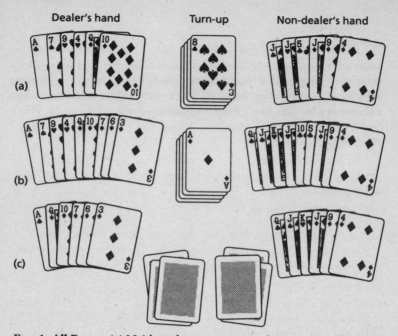

FIG. 1. **All Fours.** (*a*) Neither player accepts spades as trump. (*b*) Cards are 'run', and Dealer accepts the newly turned suit of diamonds. (*c*) The hands after discarding. Dealer scored for high, low, and game, but did not win the Jack.

Dealer scores a point. Turned cards are not dealt. If cards run out, there is a new deal by the same dealer.

If cards were run, both reduce their hands to six. Non-dealer leads first. Second to a trick may follow suit or trump as preferred, but may only renounce if unable to follow suit. The trick is taken by the higher card of suit led, or the higher trump if any are played, and the winner of each trick leads to the next.

Players sort through their won cards and score 1 for the highest trump, 1 for the lowest, 1 for the Jack, 1 for most card-points (no score if tied). Game is 7 up. If both reach it on the same deal, priority goes in order to high, low, Jack, game.

3–4 players

As above, but only Dealer and Eldest hand accept trumps or call for cards. If cards are run, all receive 3 more. All Fours is played as a partnership game on a league basis in parts of Lancashire, with rules of trick-play reflecting those of Whist—i.e. follow suit if possible, otherwise play any card. See also Auction Pitch.

All Fives

Two-hand variant in which each player makes an additional score immediately upon capturing each of the following trumps: Ace 4, King 3, Queen 2, Jack 1, Ten 10, Five 5. Points for high, low, Jack, and game are scored as normal. Game is 61 up, a Cribbage board being used for keeping count.

California Jack (Shasta Sam)

Two-hand trick-and-draw variant. Deal 6 each in 3s, turn the next for trumps, bury it in the pack, and stack the undealt cards in a squared-up pile either face up (California Jack) or face down (Shasta Sam). Non-dealer leads. Follow suit if possible, otherwise play any card; the privilege of trumping when able to follow does not here apply. The trick is taken by the higher card of the suit led, or by the higher trump if any are played. The winner of each trick draws the top card of stock, waits for his opponent to draw the next, then leads to the next trick. Score one game each for high, low, Jack, and game—'game' being 41 or more card-points. Play ceases the moment either player reaches a total of 7 game-points, or whatever other number is agreed. California Jack may also be played with the scoring of All Fives (above).

Alliance games

Same as Solo games: those in which each plays for himself in the long run, but at each deal the highest bidder may play in alliance with a temporary partner.

As Nas

Old Iranian card game once considered ancestral to Poker. Four or five players receive 5 cards each from a pack of 20 or 25 cards, and play as at Poker but without a draw. Only ranks count, there being four or five of each. The valid combinations are one pair, triplets, full house, fours, and five alike.

Auction Bridge

See Bridge.

Auction Forty-Fives

See Spoil Five.

Auction Pinochle

Point-tricks and melds: 3p, 2 × 24c

Pinochle (q.v.) is one of America's great national games. Of many forms, Auction Pinochle is a great three-hander by any standard of judgement. The following is typical of several varieties differing only in detail.

Forty-eight cards (double-24) rank as follows and bear either modern American or traditional European point-values as preferred:

	Mod.	Trad.
Ace	10	11
Ten	10	10
King	5	4
Queen	5	3
Jack	0	2
Nine	0	0

Deal 15 cards each in 3s. After the first 3, lay 3 aside, face down, as a *widow*.

Eldest bids first; the minimum bid is three hundred (variable by agreement); each in turn must raise by a multiple of ten or else pass, and, having passed, may not come in again. The highest bidder aims to score at least as many as he bid by (*a*) scoring for melds, and then, if necessary, (*b*) clearing the deficit by winning counters in tricks.

The bidder turns the widow face up and announces trumps. From the eighteen cards in his possession he shows and scores for as many as possible of the following melds:

Flush (A T K Q J in trumps)	150
Royal marriage (K Q in trumps)	40
Plain marriage (K Q in non-trump suit)	20
Hundred Aces (four Aces, one per suit)	100
Eighty Kings (four Kings, likewise)	80
Sixty Queens (four Queens, likewise)	60
Forty Jacks (four Jacks, likewise)	40
Pinochle (♠Q ♦J)	40
Dix ('deece') (trump Nine)	10

(If any of these appear twice—the pack being doubled—both count. If a flush is declared, the royal marriage it contains may not be scored separately.)

If the bidder has already fulfilled his bid, there is no play and he scores the value of his game (see below). If not, and he doubts whether he can, he may concede immediately. He then loses only his game value (*single bête*), as opposed to twice that amount for playing and failing (*double bête*).

To play, the bidder takes all eighteen cards into hand and discards face down any three which have not been used in melds. Any counters among them will count in his favour at end of play. He then leads to the first trick. On a plain-suit lead, follow suit if possible, otherwise trump if possible. On a trump lead, follow suit and head the trick if possible. A trick is taken by the highest card of the suit led, the highest trump if any are played, or the first played of two identical winning cards. The side winning the last trick scores 10.

If successful, the bidder scores or receives from each opponent an agreed game value related to the size of the bid; if not, he loses or pays it double. A game valuation scheme might be 1 unit or game-point for a bid of 300–40, 2 for 350+, 3 for 400+, 5 for 450+, 7 for 500+, and so on.

(a)

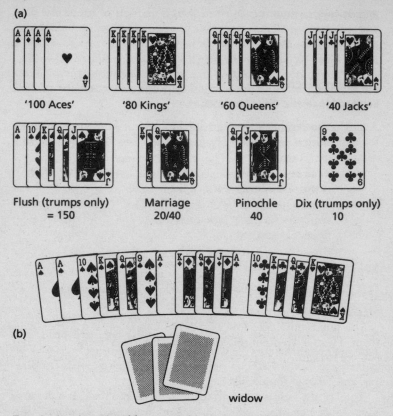

'100 Aces'   '80 Kings'   '60 Queens'   '40 Jacks'

Flush (trumps only)   Marriage   Pinochle   Dix (trumps only)
= 150   20/40   40   10

(b)

widow

FIG. 2. **Auction Pinochle.** (*a*) Melds and scoring factors. (*b*) As dealt, this hand already melds 210 (80 Kings, pinochle, royal marriage, two common marriages, dix) and should certainly be bid up to 350. As any one of five cards in the widow will improve the melding value by anything up to 150, a bid exceeding 400 is not out of the question.

All scores are doubled when spades are trump; many schools also rate hearts triple. Some also award side-payments for special melds, such as 5 for a 'roundhouse' (four marriages, one in each suit), flush 4, double pinochle 2, hundred Aces 2, four different Kings 1, likewise Queens or Jacks.

Auction Piquet

See Piquet.

Auction Pitch

Point-trick game: 2–7p (4 best), 52c

A nineteenth-century American development of All Fours, which see for explanation of terms *high*, *low*, *Jack*, *game*. For a partnership version, see Cinch.

Deal 6 each in 3s from a 52-card pack ranking A K Q J T 9 8 7 6 5 4 3 2. Starting with Eldest, each in turn may pass or make a higher bid than any so far made. Bids range from 1 to 4, representing the number of points for high, low, Jack, and game which the bidder offers to win in return for choosing trumps.

The highest bidder starts play by pitching (leading) any card, the suit of which automatically becomes trump. Players may follow suit or trump, as preferred, but may only renounce if unable to follow. The trick is taken by the highest card of the suit led, or by the highest trump if any are played.

The points for high, low, Jack, and game go to whoever wins them. There is no point for Jack if the trump Jack wasn't dealt, nor is there for game if players tie for taking the most card-points. If the pitcher fails to score as many as he bid, his bid is deducted from his score (he is 'set back').

Game is 7 or 11 up, as agreed. If two or more reach the target in the same deal, the pitcher wins if he is one of them; if not, the winner is the first to reach seven on the basis of counting points strictly in order (high, low, Jack, game). The winner receives 1 unit from everyone else, or 2 from whoever scored less than one.

Variants. 1. Dealer may become the pitcher by equalizing the last bid made. If all pass, however, he must bid at least one. 2. A player with a negative cumulative score may 'smudge' — i.e. bid four and, if successful, thereby win the game outright. This may not be taken over by Dealer. 3. 'Racehorse Pitch' is Auction played with a 32-card pack, Seven low.

Notes. If four play, the chances are slightly better than evens that the King will be the highest of its suit in play or the Three the lowest,

Auction Solo

and slightly worse that the Jack will be in play at all. Three trumps should suffice to assure the point for game.

Auction Solo

See Solo Whist.

Baccara
Casino game

Spelt 'Baccarat' in Britain and Las Vegas, this is a more up-market but less intelligent version of Pontoon (Blackjack). It first appeared in nineteenth-century France and may be of Oriental inspiration.

Play involves three or six 52-card packs shuffled together and is essentially two-handed between a banker and a punter, though the punter may be any one of a table of players. Counting numerals at face value and courts 0, the punter's aim is to receive cards totalling closer to 9 than the banker's, for which purpose 10 or more counts only as its last digit.

The banker deals 2 cards to the punter and to himself. If either has a point of 8 or 9 he turns them face up. With under 5, the punter must call for a 3rd card, dealt face up; with more than 5 he must stand; with exactly 5 he may do either. The banker must draw to a point under 3, stand with a point above 6, and may do either with a point of 3 to a punter's 3rd-card 9, or 5 to a punter's 3rd-card 4. Otherwise, he must draw or stand as dictated by the most favourable odds.

In basic Baccara, the house is the bank. In Chemin de Fer, or 'Chemmy', the bank passes from player to player. In Punto Banco, it appears to pass from player to player, but is actually held by the house.

Banking games

Gambling games typically played in casinos. They are essentially two-handers, in that one player, the banker, plays against one or more punters on an individual basis, there being no interaction between the punters themselves—who may, indeed, collectively constitute the banker's opponent. As the banker deals and usually has an inbuilt advantage, the bank is held in casinos exclusively by a house representative; otherwise, it passes from player to player by rote, by purchase, or by the occurrence of a winning hand. See Baccara, Basset, Faro, Lansquenet, Pontoon (Blackjack), Thirty-Five.

Barbu

See Le Barbu.

Bassadewitz

Trick-avoidance game: 4p, 32c

First recorded in the early nineteenth century and still played as a family game in parts of German-speaking Europe, Bassadewitz (or Bassarovitz) is a neat little member of the trick-avoidance group. Rules vary; the following are typical.

Dealer puts up a pool of twelve chips and deals 8 cards each from a 32-card pack ranking and counting as follows:

A	K	Q	J	T	9	8	7
11	4	3	2	10	0	0	0

Eldest leads to the first trick and the winner of each trick leads to the next. Suit must be followed if possible. The trick is taken by the highest card of the suit led. There are no trumps.

Whoever takes fewest card-points wins 5 chips, second fewest 4, third fewest 3. Ties are settled in favour of the elder player, but a player taking no trick beats one who merely takes no card-points.

A player winning every trick is paid 4 each by the others; a player taking 100 or more card-points but failing to win every trick pays 4 each to the others. In these cases the pool remains intact and the same dealer deals again, as also if all four take the same number of card-points.

Variant. Ace counts 5 instead of 11, and each player adds 1 per trick to his total of card-points. (This may be an earlier form of the game.)

9

Basset
Gambling game

A notorious Italian gambling game recorded from the mid-fifteenth century onwards, and a favourite of Charles II's favourites, Basset was overtaken by its simpler descendant Faro in the eighteenth century.

Each punter has a layout of thirteen cards in front of him and lays stakes on one or more ranks. The banker starts by turning up the bottom card of his pack and winning all the stakes placed on cards of the same rank in the layouts. He then deals cards face up from the top of the pack alternately to two piles. After each two he receives all stakes wagered on the rank of the first of them, and pays out matching stakes to all those wagered on the second. His last card, like the first, wins all stakes on the corresponding rank. Upon winning a stake, a punter may decline it and bet on the same rank again, as indicated by turning up one corner of the appropriate card and leaving his stake intact. This bid, called *sept-et-le-va* from the fact that it pays seven times the stake made, can in theory be repeated three more times, another corner being turned for each, and the respective payments being 15, 30 and 60 times the amount staked—thus accounting for the game's extraordinary popularity with the mindless rich. (On a bid of 60, or *soixante-et-le-va*, the dealer is, of course, obliged to gather the pack in and deal again, as it contains only four cards of each rank.)

Battle
Children's game: 2p, 52c

An early nineteenth-century French game (Bataille), resembling but simpler than Beggar my Neighbour. Each player holds half the pack face down and at each turn plays the top card face up. Whoever plays the higher card, regardless of suit, wins and places both cards at the bottom of his pile. If both tie, they are laid aside and taken by the winner of the next untied pair.

Bavarian Tarock

Point-trick game: 3p, 36c

One of several German varieties of a game obviously based on true
Tarock but dispensing with the special trump cards. This version
dates from the 1930s.

Players start by contributing 100 units each to a pot. A game ends
when the pot is empty.

Deal 11 cards each in batches of 4 3 (3) 4, the bracketed 3 going
face down to the table as a widow. Cards rank and count as follows:

A	T	K	Q	J	9	8	7	6
11	10	4	3	2	0	0	0	0

Each in turn, starting with Eldest, may pass or say 'Play'. 'Play' is an
offer to take at least 61 of the 120 card-points in tricks after naming
trumps and playing alone against the other two. If not overcalled, he
declares whether he will play a 'pick-up' or 'hand' game. 'Pick-up'
means he will take the widow and discard three unwanted cards
before announcing trumps; 'hand' means he will play the hand as
dealt. In either case, any card-points contained in the widow will
count at end of play as if he had won them in tricks.

If he says 'Play', the next in turn (or, if he passes, the third player)
may try to take the game off him by bidding 'hand'. The first bidder
may then pass, or assert priority by bidding 'hand' himself. The
latter may be contested by raising the amount bid in successive
multiples of five ('And five', 'And ten', etc.; no jump-bidding permitted), until one of them passes. If the third player has yet to speak, he
may bid the next higher multiple of five; and so on.

Eldest leads to the first trick. Follow suit and head the trick if
possible, otherwise trump if possible. A trick is taken by the highest
card of the suit led or by the highest trump if any are played.

The plus value of a game won by the soloist is a basic 5 units, plus
5 per whole or part of every 5 points he took in excess of his
contract. If he loses, the minus value is 5 units per whole or part of
every 5 card-points by which he fell short of it. (Example: In a basic
contract, the value is 5 for taking 61–5, 10 for 66–70 etc, or minus
5 for 56–60, etc. In a 66-contract, it is 5 for taking 66–70, minus 5
for 61–5; and so on.)

For winning a pick-up, the soloist takes the appropriate amount from the pot; for winning a hand game, he receives the appropriate amount from each opponent, plus 10 units for each additional 5 points by which he raised his contract above 61.

For losing a pick-up, he pays out of pocket to one opponent, the other taking that amount from the pot; for losing a hand game, he pays it to each opponent instead.

The game ends when the pot is empty. If the last soloist wins, and the amount due from the pot is more than it contains, he can take only what is there. But if he loses, and the amount due from him is more than the pot contains, he need not pay one player more than the other can take from the pot.

Variant. If an opening bid is uncontested, and the bidder announces a hand game, he may raise the amount of his contract by any multiple of five.

Beggar my Neighbour
Children's game: 2p, 52c

An extension of Battle, also called Beat your Neighbour out of Doors. Each receives 26 cards and stacks them face down on the table. Each in turn plays the top card of his stack to a common pile. When one of them plays a Jack, Queen, King, or Ace, the other must play (respectively) one, two, three or four cards immediately to the top of the pile. If they are all numerals, the pile is won by the other player and placed face down beneath his stack. If one of them is a pay card, however, the tables are turned, and the other must pay the appropriate number of cards. Whoever captures all 52 cards wins.

Belote
Point-tricks and melds: 2–4p, 32c

The French national card game, a variety of Klaberjass, first reached France in about 1914.

Belote for two

Lower draw deals first; thereafter, the winner of each hand deals to the next. Deal 6 each in threes and turn the next for trump. Cards rank and count thus:

Trumps	Jack	Nine	A	T	K	Q	—	—	8	7
Non-trumps	—	—	A	T	K	Q	J	9	8	7
Point-value	20	14	11	10	4	3	2	0	0	0

The winner is the first to reach an agreed target (e.g. 1000) over as many deals as necessary. Points are scored for declaring melds and winning card-points in tricks. Whoever determines trumps is expected to score more than the other, and will be penalized for failing to do so.

Elder may accept the turned suit as trump, or pass the choice to Younger. If Younger also passes, Elder may turn it down and propose another suit; if he does not, Younger may do likewise. If both still pass, there is no play and Elder makes the next deal.

Trumps selected, Younger deals 3 more cards apiece and turns the bottom card of the stock face up (for information). If the original suit was accepted, either player holding the Seven may exchange it for the trump turn-up. This must be done before any melds are declared.

Upon leading to the first trick, Elder announces the highest he has (if any) of the following melds:

Quartet of	Jacks	200
	Nines	150
	Aces	100
	Tens	100
	Kings	100
	Queens	100
Sequence of five or more		100
	four	50
	three	20

A sequence is three or more cards of the same suit forming part of the sequence A K Q J T 9 8 7. A longer sequence beats a shorter; if equal, a higher beats a lower; if still equal, a trump sequence beats a plain; if still equal, Elder's wins. When first announcing a sequence, Elder need only identify as much of it as is necessary to determine whose is better.

If Younger cannot beat the declared meld, he says 'Good', whereupon Elder scores for it and any others he may have and is willing to show. If he can beat it, Younger in replying to the trick

13

declares his best combination and scores for it and any others he may have and is willing to show.

Belote is the King and Queen of trumps in the same hand. Its holder scores 20 upon playing either of them to a trick and announcing *belote*. Later, on playing the other, he must announce *rebelote*, otherwise the 20 is annulled.

The second to a trick must follow suit if possible, otherwise trump if possible, otherwise play any card. To a trump lead, the second must play higher if possible. The trick is taken by the higher card of the suit led or the higher trump if any are played. The winner of the last trick scores 10 for last (*dix de der*), or 100 for *capot* if he won all nine.

Both players then declare their respective totals for melds and card-points. The trump-maker's opponent always scores what he makes. If the trump-maker took more, he also scores what he makes; if less, his score is added to the opponent's; if equal, it is held over and counts to the winner of the next deal.

Optional rules. 1. A player dealt all four Sevens may annul the deal. His opponent then deals to the next. 2. If previously agreed, the game may cease in mid-play the moment either player claims to have reached the target score. The claimant must have won at least one trick before claiming. An incorrect claim loses the game. 3. Bids of *sans atout* and *tout atout* may be admitted, as in the partnership game (below).

Belote for three

As above, but: the deal and the turn to play pass always to the right. If a plain suit is led which neither opponent can follow, and the first of them plays a trump, then the other need not also trump but may renounce. If one player wins no trick, the others score 50 each for capot; if two take none, the third scores 100.

Partnership Belote

Four may play Belote solo or in one of several partnership forms. In Belote Coinchée (or Contrée), bids are raised by stating the number of points one contracts to win with one's partner. Belote Bridge ranks the suits in Bridge order for bidding purposes, producing a hybrid concoction rightly eschewed by players of taste and refinement. Basic Partnership Belote runs as follows.

Two new bids overcall a bid in the turned suit, as follows:

In *sans atout*, or 'no trump', the cards of every suit rank A 11, T 10, K 4, Q 3, J 2, 9 8 7 zero. A quartet of Aces counts 200, Tens 150, Kings, Queens, or Jacks 100 each. No recognition is accorded to either a quartet of Nines or a belote.

In *tout atout*, or 'grand', the cards of every suit rank Jack 20, Nine 14, A 11, T 10, K 4, Q 3, 8 7 zero. All the usual melds are recognized, and there are four possible belotes, one in each suit. This is the highest possible bid.

The turn to deal, play, and bid passes always to the right. Deal 5 each (3 + 2) and turn the next for trump. There may be one or two rounds of bidding. Eldest starts. On the first round, each in turn may pass, name the turned suit as trump, bid no trump, bid grand, double an opponent's bid, or redouble one's partner's bid if it has been doubled by an opponent.

If a bid is doubled and redoubled, the contract is established and the auction ends. If not, each in turn may bid again, provided that each bid, including the first, is higher than any which has gone before. In this case, however, a simple trump bid may no longer be made in the suit of the turn-up, but only in a suit of one's own choice. Bidding ends when a bid has been redoubled, or when three players successively pass. No player may raise his own bid. If all four pass, the deal is annulled and the next in turn to deal does so.

The undealt cards are then dealt 3 to each player, the turn-up going to the player who named the contract. Eldest leads first. Each in turn, on playing to the first trick, announces his highest meld (if any). At the end of the trick, the player announcing the best meld shows and scores for it and any others he is willing to show; his partner also may show and score for any melds he has.

To a plain-suit lead, players must follow suit if possible, otherwise trump if possible. To a trump lead, players must follow suit and head the trick if possible, even if one's own partner is winning it. At no trump, all leads are plain. At grand, logic demands that all leads count as trump; but this rule is variable and should be settled beforehand.

The last trick counts 10 to the side taking it, or 100 in case of capot. If the contracting side scores more than the other, both score what they make; if equal or less, the other side scores both totals. This also applies in a redoubled contract, but not in a contract doubled once only. Equality here entitles the contracting side to score its points, as the double is construed as an undertaking by the other side to take a majority of points. Whatever the outcome, the score is doubled at no trump, or tripled at grand.

The game is won by the first side to reach 3000 points (or, since scores are usually recorded in tens, 300).

Bezique

Trick and meld game: 2p, 2 × 32c

A nineteenth-century French game derived from Mariage (via Briscan) by the addition of more scoring features—notably a peculiar liaison between ♣Q and ♦J under the names *bésigue*, *binokel*, *pinochle*, etc., according to country. Originally a 32-card game, its rapid popularity engendered elaborations involving anything up to eight such packs shuffled together. In the twentieth century it has lost much ground, probably to Gin Rummy. Bezique survives as the following classic two-hander still cherished by card connoisseurs. Other varieties, now virtually museum pieces, include: (*a*) Cinq Cents, using one 32-card pack, (*b*) four-pack Rubicon or Japanese Bezique, (*c*) six-pack or Chinese Bezique, (*d*) eight-pack Bezique, and (*e*) Polish Bezique, or Fildinski, in which combinations are made not from cards in hand but from those won in tricks.

Two players each receive eight cards (3 2 3) from two 32-card packs shuffled together, ranking A T K Q J 9 8 7. The next card is turned for trumps and placed under the stock, face up and slightly projecting.

The winner is the first to reach 1000 points over as many deals as necessary, the players dealing alternately. Points are scored partly for capturing *brisques* (Aces and Tens) in tricks, but mainly for acquiring and declaring any of the following features:

Trump sequence (A T K Q J)	250
Marriages (K Q of same suit)	
Trump	40
Plain	20

Beziques (♠Q + ♦J)	
Single	40
Double	500
Quartets (four of a kind)	
Aces	100
Kings	80
Queens	60
Jacks	40
Dix (trump 7)	10

Non-dealer leads first. Second to a trick may play any card. A trick is won by the higher card of the suit led, the higher trump if any are played, or the first played of two identical cards.

Winning a trick entitles its winner to declare a scoring combination. More than one may be declared upon winning a trick, but only one may be scored at a time. Any others must be scored one at a time for each subsequent trick won, and only so long as they remain intact. The appropriate cards are taken from the hand and laid face up on the table, where they remain until played to tricks. Declarer then draws the top card of stock, waits for the other to draw, and leads to the next trick.

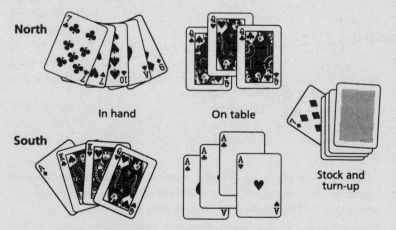

Fig. 3. **Bezique.** A hand in progress. North has scored 60 Queens and an earlier bezique, having since played the Jack; South has scored 100 Aces and 10 for exchanging the trump Seven, and has a marriage to score upon winning a trick.

The player who wins the last trick before the stock is emptied may make one declaration before drawing the penultimate card. When both last cards have been drawn, no more declarations may be made, and each player takes all his cards back into hand. In playing the last eight tricks the second must follow suit if possible, win the trick if possible, and trump if unable to follow. Combinations are no longer declarable. The winner of the eighth trick scores 10 for last.

Each player finally adds 10 for each Ace and Ten he has taken in tricks. If neither has yet reached 1000, a new deal is played.

Special rules. Accounts differ: the following are typical:

A card once declared may later be combined with one or more others from hand or table to form a different combination, but it may not be used twice in the same combination. Thus, the Queen in a spade marriage may not be remarried to the other King, but may later be counted in a bezique or a quartet of Queens. Similarly, with 'eighty Kings' and 'sixty Queens' declared, each possible marriage may be scored on subsequent tricks so long as valid pairs remain intact. It is not (as sometimes claimed) illegal to make a meld entirely from cards already on the table, so long as it is different.

If you score a trump sequence, you may not subsequently score the marriage it contains; but you may count the marriage first, and include it in a scoring sequence upon winning a subsequent trick.

You may declare double bezique by laying out all four cards at once, or by adding a second bezique to a single bezique already scored and still on the table; but if you score for two singles, you may not count the double as well.

Holding a Seven of trumps, you may, upon winning a trick, declare it for 10 points and exchange it for the turn-up. This counts as a declaration (unless otherwise agreed—authorities are unclear about it).

Variants. 1. Instead of turning a card, start at no trump and entrump the suit of the first marriage declared. 2. If spades or diamonds are trump, bezique may be redefined as ♣Q ♥J.

Notes. The main point of the game is to judge which cards to collect for possible melds and which to throw to tricks, especially when the hand consists entirely of meldable cards. It is important to remember which cards are not available because declared by the opponent or previously played to tricks. Win tricks with Tens wherever possible, as they have no melding value but score 10 each. Lead Aces and Tens to tempt out trumps if weak in trumps yourself. Win tricks only if they contain brisques, or if you have something to declare, or if you think the opponent has something good to declare.

Fildinski (Polish Bezique)

Play as above, but with the following differences. Cards held in the hand may not be melded. Instead, those won by each player are left face up on the table before him. Either or both cards of a won trick may be used to form and score for a meld in conjunction with one or more cards already won. More than one meld may be scored at a time, provided that each incorporates a card won in the trick just played, and that no card is used simultaneously in different melds.

Multi-pack variants

Bezique may be played with four, six or eight 32-card packs shuffled together. (Four is called 'Rubicon' or 'Japanese' Bezique, six is 'Chinese'.) The following general rules apply to all; see Table 1 for other scores and details.

Cards dealt. See Table 1. No card is turned for trump, and no score or significance attaches to the trump Seven.

Carte blanche. Except in eight-pack Bezique, a player dealt no court may show the hand and score for *carte blanche* (see Table 1). Thereafter, so long as the card he draws from stock after each trick fails to be a court, he may show the card and make the score again.

Trump suit. Play starts at no trump. The first marriage (or sequence) declared establishes a trump suit, which remains unchanged throughout.

Bezique. If agreed, bezique may be redefined as the Queen of trumps and the appropriate Jack of opposite colour—spades with diamonds, clubs with hearts. In this case, the trump may be established as that of the Queen if a bezique is declared before a marriage. Also, the same suit may not be entrumped twice in successive deals. The score for a multiple bezique only obtains if all cards involved are on display at the same time.

Additional melds. Sequences may be declared in plain suits as well

Bezique

TABLE 1. *Four-, six-, and eight-pack Bezique features*

	Four	Six	Eight
Deal to each	9	12	15
Carte blanche	50	250	—
Sequences			
Trump sequence (A–T–K–Q–J)	250	250	250
Non-trump sequence	150	150	150
Royal marriage (trump K–Q)	40	40	40
Common marriage (other K–Q in suit)	20	20	20
Quartets, quintets			
Any four Aces	100	100	100
Any four Kings	80	80	80
Any four Queens	60	60	60
Any four Jacks	40	40	40
Four trump Aces	—	1000	1000
Four trump Tens	—	900	900
Four trump Kings	—	800	800
Four trump Queens	—	600	600
Four trump Jacks	—	400	400
Five trump Aces	—	—	2000
Five trump Tens	—	—	1800
Five trump Kings	—	—	1600
Five trump Queens	—	—	1200
Five trump Jacks	—	—	800
Beziques			
Single	40	40	40
Double	500	500	500
Treble	1500	1500	1500
Quadruple	4500	4500	4500
Quintuple	—	—	9000
Winning last trick	50	250	250
Rubicon	1000	3000	5000
Add for game	500	1000	1000
Add for rubicon	500	Loser's total	Loser's total

as trumps. In six- and eight-pack Bezique, trump quartets are declarable as shown in the table.

Re-forming melds. A meld that has been broken up by the play of one or more cards to a trick may be re-formed and scored again by the addition of matching replacements.

Brisques do not count in multi-pack variants, except to break ties in the four-pack game.

Game score. Final scores are rounded down to the nearest 100 and the winner scores the difference, plus a bonus if the loser fails to 'cross the rubicon'—that is, fails to reach the target score specified in the table for that purpose.

Bid Euchre

See Five Hundred.

Binocle, Binokel

See Pinochle.

Biritch

Plain-trick game: 4pp, 52c

The earliest form of Bridge first published in English was described in 1886 by an unidentified 'John Collinson' in a four-page leaflet spuriously entitled *Biritch, or Russian Whist*, from which the game later called Bridge-Whist differs only in minor details.

Play like Whist, but without a trump turn-up and with these modifications:

Dealer must either announce trumps or pass this privilege to his partner, who must then exercise it. Whichever of them declares may either nominate a suit or announce *biritch*, making it no trump. Either opponent may double (*contre*); declarer or partner may redouble (*surcontre*), and such doubling and redoubling can go on indefinitely. The player at Dealer's left leads; Dealer's partner then lays his hand face up on the table, and Dealer plays from both hands throughout. Consultation is not allowed.

A rubber is the best of three games. A game is won by the first side to reach 30 points in play, irrespective of honours. Each trick taken over six scores, according to the trump suit: spades 2, clubs 4, diamonds 6, hearts 8, biritch 10. There is a bonus of 40 for 'grand slam' (taking every trick), or 20 for 'petit slam' (taking all but one).

Winning the rubber carries a bonus of 40 for 'consolation'. All but the rubber scores are affected by any doubling that took place.

Points not scored towards game, but recorded separately and contributing to the final margin of victory, are made for 'honours' and various other features as follows. All remain unaffected by doubling.

At biritch the only honours are Aces. Three held score the equivalent of 3 tricks, four of 4 tricks, four in one hand of 8 tricks. In trumps, the honours are A, K, Q, J, T. Three held ('simple honours') score as for 2 tricks; four as for 4 or, in one hand, 8; five as for 5, or, in one hand, 10. A hand without trumps when any are declared is called *chicane*. It entitles the holder to add the value of simple honours to any other honour score his side may make—or, if none, to deduct it from the opponents' honour score.

Bismarck

See Dutch Whist.

Black Jack

See Eights.

Blackjack

See Twenty-One.

Black Maria

Trick-avoidance game: 3–7p, 52c

A derivative of Hearts (q.v.) perfected by Hubert Phillips in the 1920s, and now well established as the British member of the trick-avoidance family.

The fewer the players, the more skilful the game. Three is ideal. Unless four play, start by stripping from the 52-card pack as many of the following cards as necessary to ensure that they will go round evenly: ♣2, ♦2, ♠2, ♣3.

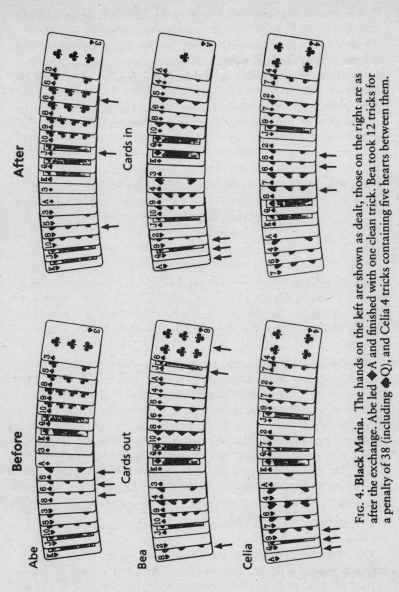

FIG. 4. Black Maria. The hands on the left are shown as dealt; those on the right are as after the exchange. Abe led ♦A and finished with one clean trick. Bea took 12 tricks for a penalty of 38 (including ♠Q), and Celia 4 tricks containing five hearts between them.

The turn to deal and play passes to the left. Deal all the cards out one at a time. The aim is to avoid winning tricks containing hearts or any of the three highest spades—or, if the hand is strong enough, to win *all* such penalty cards.

Each player first passes three cards face down to his right-hand neighbour and receives the same number from his left. If more than four play, only two are passed.

Eldest leads first and the winner of each trick leads to the next. Suit must be followed if possible; if not, any unwanted or penalty card may be thrown without restriction. The trick is taken by the highest card of the suit led. There are no trumps.

At end of play each player scores penalty points for cards taken in tricks as follows:

Each heart	1
Spade Ace	7
Spade King	10
Spade Queen	13

A player taking all penalty cards deducts 43 points from his current penalty score.

The winner is the player with fewest points after an agreed number of deals, or when one player reaches an agreed limit, such as 100 points.

Notes. In passing cards on, try to void a suit if possible, so that dangerous cards may be thrown as soon as it is led. If cards of that suit are then received from the left, remember that that player may throw penalty cards as soon as that suit appears. High hearts or spades should not necessarily be passed: they can be safely kept if guarded by a sufficient number (related to the number of players) of low cards in the same suit. Never pass low hearts or spades. In play, take the tricks you must as early as possible, hopefully before penalties can be discarded to them. When unable to follow, throw potentially dangerous trick-takers before bothering to load the trick-winner with penalties.

Black Peter

See Old Maid.

Blackout

See Oh Hell!

Bohemian Schneider

Plain or point-trick game: 2p, 32c

Evidently related to Elfern (q.v.), this is a good game for children but not without potential interest to adults.

Deal 6 cards each in 3s from a 32-card pack ranking A K Q J T 9 8 7. The aim is to win a majority of honours, i.e. Tens or higher. Elder leads. Suit need not be followed; there are no trumps; and a trick can only be taken by the next higher card of the suit led (♥7 by ♥8, ♣J by ♣Q, etc.). The trick-winner draws from stock, waits for the other to do so, and leads to the next trick. Taking eleven or more honours wins a single game, sixteen or more double, all twenty treble.

Variants. 1. An Ace, normally uncapturable, may be taken by a Seven. 2. Cards count A 11, K 4, Q 3, J 2, T 10, others 0. Play as above, but a trick is taken by any card exactly one rank higher than that led, regardless of suit. A single game is won by taking 61 or more card-points, double for 91 plus, treble for all 120.

Bolivia

See Canasta.

Bondtolva

Point-trick game: 2–4p, 24c

A traditional Swedish game evidently related to Sixty-Six, but with a curious resonance of All Fours. The simplest version is for two:

Deal six each in threes from a 24-card pack ranking A T K Q J 9. Turn the remainder face down as a stock. The winner is the first to reach 12 points over as many deals as necessary, each dealing in turn. Points are scored for declaring marriages, for winning the most 'matadors' (Aces and Tens), and for winning the last trick.

Elder leads to the first trick. Suit need not be followed. A trick is taken by the higher card of the suit led, or, when trumps have been made, by the higher trump. The trick-winner draws the top card of stock, waits for the other to draw, and leads to the next.

The leader to any trick may declare a marriage by showing a King and Queen of the same suit and leading one of them. The first marriage, called 'trump', scores 2 points and establishes trumps for the rest of the deal. A subsequently declared marriage scores 1 point, but does not change the trump suit.

When the stock is empty no more marriages may be declared. Second to a trick must then follow suit if possible, head the trick if possible, and trump if unable to follow.

The winner of the last trick scores 1 point, as does the player who took a majority of Aces and Tens. If equal, that point goes to the player who took most card-points, reckoning each Ace 4, King 3, Queen 2, and Jack 1. If still equal, neither scores it.

Optional rule: A player must attain exactly 12 points to win. If the number he gains in a deal would take him over 12, that number is deducted from his current total.

Three or four players. The cards are all dealt out, and the rules of trick-play are those applying to the two-hander when the stock is empty, except that marriages are declarable throughout.

The four-hander is played in partnerships. Before trumps are established, the leader to a trick may do one of the following:

(a) If holding a marriage, show and lead from it. This scores 2 and fixes the trump suit.

(b) If not, ask if partner holds a marriage. If so, partner shows it for 2 and this establishes trumps. Any card may then be led.

(c) Holding one card of a marriage, ask if partner can pair it, by saying (for example) 'Hearts?'. If partner says 'Yes', the trump is established for 2 points and the qualifying King or Queen must be led. If 'No', any card may be led of that suit, but no other.

Note that only one marriage query may be made on the same turn. Given a negative to (b) or (c), the asker must win a trick and be on lead before asking again.

Subsequent marriages score only 1 each and do not change the trump. Upon leading, you may:

(a) declare a marriage yourself by showing and leading from it; or

(b) ask if your partner has one. If so, you must lead the stated suit in order to score the point; or

(c) lead a King or Queen and ask if your partner can wed it. If so, the marriage partner must be shown, but need only be played to the trick in order to comply with the rules of following—i.e. head the trick if possible, and trump if unable to follow suit.

Footnote: The first marriage is called a 'trump' for obvious reasons, and each subsequent marriage a 'score' (tjog). The latter reflects its original score of 20 points, as in Sixty-Six, Bezique, and related games.

Booby

Plain-trick game: 3p, 52c

An adaptation of Contract Bridge for three (see also Towie), invented by Hubert Phillips. The general idea is that each player receives 17 cards and the last is left face down on the table to start the 'booby'. After examining his hand, each player discards four cards face down to the booby, thus reducing his hand to thirteen cards. An auction follows, after which declarer turns the booby face up and plays it as a dummy hand.

Boston

Plain-trick game: 4p, 52c

This great nineteenth-century card game, once played throughout the Western world apart from Britain, forms an evolutionary link between Hombre and Solo Whist. Though appropriately named after a key location in the American War of Independence, it was probably devised in France in the 1770s, combining the 52-card pack and logical ranking system of partnership Whist with a range of solo and alliance bids borrowed from Quadrille. It soon gave rise to countless variants—Maryland, Boston de Nantes, Boston de Lorient, Russian Boston, etc.—and inventive bids with titles amounting to variations on a theme—*indépendance*, *souverain*, *concordia*, and suchlike. Described below is the highly developed version called Boston de Fontainebleau. As no two accounts are identical, the following rules can only be described as 'typical'. In particular, I have translated the hard-score into an equivalent soft-score system. As originally played, Boston required several thousand chips or counters, hundreds of which could be involved in complicated transactions between various players at the conclusion of every hand. Players nowadays are unlikely to have that many counters lying around, or tables big enough to accommodate them, or the patience to be forever fiddling about with bits of plastic.

Four players each receive 13 cards from a 52-card pack ranking A K Q J T 9 8 7 6 5 4 3 2. Eldest bids first and the highest bidder becomes the soloist, playing alone against the other three unless one of them bids to be an ally. Eldest leads first. Follow suit if possible, otherwise play any card. A trick is taken by the highest card of the suit led, or by the highest trump if any are played.

The contracts. Each in turn may bid or pass. A bid states the name of the proposed contract plus the suit of the proposed trump. Each bid must be higher than the preceding one in accordance with the schedule below, or equal in height but in a higher suit. For this purpose, suits ascend in the order spades, clubs, diamonds, hearts.

Although misère bids are actually played at no trump, a nominal suit must be stated for each one, as it can only overcall the positive bid ranking immediately below it if made in an equal or higher suit. For example, while 'six diamonds' may be overcalled by seven or more in any suit, a petite misère will only overcall it if said to be in diamonds or hearts. The nominal suit of a misère bid also governs the amount it wins or loses.

A player having once passed may not come in again, except to support a bid of from five to eight tricks, provided that it has not been overcalled. To support a bid means to ally oneself with the main bidder, thereby sharing in his win or loss.

The schedule of bids and values runs as follows:

1. *Five.* A bid to win at least five tricks with the named suit as trump. If supported, the ally must win at least three. Base value 4 (+1 per over/undertrick).
2. *Six.* To win at least six tricks with the named suit as trump. If supported, the ally must win at least four. Base value 6 (+2 per over/undertrick).
3. *Petite misère.* To lose every trick after making one discard face down and playing to twelve tricks at no trump. Base value 16.

4. *Seven.* To win at least seven tricks with the named suit as trump. If supported, the ally must win at least four. Base value 9 (+3 per over/undertrick).

5. *Piccolissimo.* To win exactly one trick at no trump. Base value 24.

6. *Eight.* To win at least eight tricks with the named suit as trump. If supported, the ally must win at least four. Base value 12 (+4 per over/undertrick).

7. *Grande misère.* To lose all thirteen tricks at no trump. Base value 32.

8. *Nine.* To win at least nine tricks with the named suit as trump. Base value 15 (+5 per over/undertrick).

9. *Four-ace misère.* Though holding four Aces, to lose all thirteen tricks at no trump, but with permission to revoke once in the first ten tricks. Base value 40.

10. *Ten.* To win at least ten tricks with the named suit as trump. Base value 18 (+6 per over/undertrick).

11. *Petite misère ouverte.* To lose every trick at no trump after making one discard face down, exposing one's hand on the table, and playing to twelve tricks. Base value 48.

12. *Eleven.* To win at least eleven tricks with the named suit as trump. Base value 21 (+7 per over/undertrick).

13. *Grande misère ouverte.* To lose all thirteen tricks at no trump, after laying one's hand face up on the table. Base value 56.

14. *Twelve.* To win at least twelve tricks with the named suit as trump. Base value 24 (+8 per over/undertrick).

15. *Boston.* To win all thirteen tricks with the named suit as trump. Base value 100.

16. *Boston ouvert.* The same, but with one's cards face up on the table. Base value 200.

Note. In any ouvert, the hand is exposed before the opening lead. In petite misère, only the bidder makes a discard, and only twelve tricks are played.

Scoring. In an unsupported contract, the amount won or lost by the soloist is found by taking the base value stated in the schedule above and increasing it as follows:

1. Except in misères and Bostons, add the stated 'overtrick' value

for each trick taken in excess of the contract (or, if lost, for each trick short of the contract requirement.)

2. Except in misères and Bostons, add the equivalent of two over-tricks if the bidder held three honours, or four overtricks if he held all four. The honours are Ace, King, Queen, Jack of trumps.

3. Multiply the result by two if the bid was made in clubs, three if diamonds, four if hearts.

In a supported contract,

if both players either make or fail their individual contracts, each one's win or loss is calculated exactly as described above, but is then halved before being recorded. (For a supporter, an overtrick or undertrick is that in excess of, or short of, the three or four he personally contracted to win.)

if only one succeeds, he scores zero. The other loses half the value of his lost contract plus half the value of his ally's won contract. (This correctly reproduces the equivalent payment in counters, but points up its unfairness. It would seem preferable for the successful ally to win half the value of his contract, leaving the other to lose half the value of his own.)

Note. French schedules include an apparent contract of *Boston à deux* ranking between bids of five and six tricks, but do not state how it arises. We may assume that it is not a bid but a premium score applied when, in a supported game, each makes his contract and both take all thirteen tricks between them. The base value is 50 – i.e. half the value of a Boston contract played alone.

Bouillotte

Vying game: 4p, 20c

A game of the French Revolution, based on Brelan. It achieved some popularity in nineteenth-century America before being ousted by Poker.

Four players use a 20-card pack ranking A K Q 9 8 in each suit. Each starts with a *cave* of 30 chips, five each of reds and whites, a red being worth five whites. The deal and turn to bet pass always to the right. Deal 3 cards each in ones and turn the next face up.

Dealer opens the pot for a previously agreed amount. Each in turn may then drop out, straddle, or make an opening bet. To straddle is to pass the responsibility of making an opening bet to the next in turn to play, but without dropping out. It is done by paying in the amount paid by the dealer or previous straddler, plus one white chip. If all four pass, the pot is carried forward and there is a new deal by the same dealer. If a straddle is followed by three passes, the straddler wins the pot without further play. If the dealer straddles, Eldest must open or drop out. If he drops, the next in turn has the same option; and so on.

A player opens by staking any amount up to the limit of his *cave*. Each in turn must then either drop out or match the previous bet to stay in. If he matches, he may also raise the amount required to stay. When only two remain, either may call for a showdown. Otherwise, when all bets are equalized, the player to the right of the previous raiser is always entitled to raise again. Play continues until all but one drop out, in which case the last in wins, or when one of two players left in calls, or no one is willing to raise, in which case there is a showdown.

The best hand is a *brelan* (three of a kind). If more than one player has a brelan, the best is one that matches the rank of the turn-up (a *brelan carré*, or 'squared-up brelan'). If none matches, that of highest rank wins. Any player with a brelan receives a side-payment of one chip—two, if it is a carré—from each opponent.

If there is no brelan, the winning hand is that containing the best *point*, determined as follows. All hands are turned face up, including those of players who dropped. The face values of all these cards are totalled for each suit, counting Ace 11, courts 10, numerals face value. The 'best suit' is the one with the highest visible total, and the player holding the highest card of it wins the pot—provided that he has not previously dropped. If he has, the winner is the player counting the greatest face value of cards in any other suit.

Brag

Vying game: 3–7p, 52c

One of several ancestors to Poker, and the British national representative of the vying or 'bluffing' family of gambling games. It derives from the Elizabethan game of Primero and formed the subject of a treatise by Hoyle in 1751. Many different versions have been played throughout its long history. All they have in common is the fact that they are based on three-card hands—as opposed to the four of Primero and five of Poker—and that the highest is three of a kind, though many also feature wild cards called 'braggers'.

Brag is played with a 52-card pack basically ranking A K Q J T 9 8 7 6 5 4 3 2, and recognizes the following range of 'Brag hands', from low to high:

Pair. Two cards of the same rank, the third unmatched.

Flush. Three non-consecutive cards of the same suit.

Run. Three consecutive cards, not flush. (As a deliberate oddity, 3 2 A beats A K Q, and the lowest is 4 3 2.)

Running flush. Three consecutive cards of the same suit. (Again, 3 2 A is best.)

Prial. Three cards of the same rank. (As a deliberate oddity, the highest is a prial of Threes, followed by Aces, Kings, etc.)

A higher combination beats a lower. If equal, that containing the highest top card wins, or second highest if equal. A hand containing one or more wild cards loses to a hand of the same type containing fewer wild cards, regardless of rank (e.g. 4 4 4 beats 5 5 W beats 6 W W). Nowadays Deuces may be wild, or the Joker added as a wild card. But they are often omitted altogether.

Several typical versions are described below, all individual rules being variable by agreement. Each can involve as many players as there are cards to go round. All are hard-score games, requiring coins or counters.

Basic Brag

The turn to deal passes to the left. A game ends at any time that everyone has made the same number of deals. Cards are shuffled before the first deal, but thereafter not between deals until a hand has been won on a prial. Before the deal, players may be required to ante one chip each (desirable if fewer than five play). It may be previously agreed to place a limit on the amount that may be bet at each turn. Deal 3 cards each, in 1s, face down.

Each in turn, starting with Eldest, may drop out or make a bet by pushing one or more chips into the kitty. The number bet must be not less than that bet by the previous player, nor more than any

Highest

Prial

Running flush

Run

Flush

Pair

Lowest

FIG. 5. **Brag.** Excluding hands containing no combination, the lowest Brag hand is a pair of Twos, the highest a prial of Threes.

limit that may have been previously agreed. (There is no need to equalize bets as in Poker, unless it has been agreed to follow Poker-style betting.)

Play continues until all but two have dropped out. The two remaining continue betting until either one drops out, whereupon the other wins the kitty without showing his hand, or one 'sees' the other by paying twice the amount legally required to stay in, whereupon both hands are revealed and the higher one wins.

The next dealer then gathers in all the hands, including those that have been dropped, and stacks them at the bottom of the pack without mixing them up. Only if the kitty was won on a prial does he shuffle them before dealing.

Betting blind. A player may leave his hand face down, untouched, and 'bet blind' for as long as he likes. So long as he does so, he need only add half the amount staked by the previous player, while any raise he makes must be doubled by those who follow. If *one* of the two final players is betting blind, the other may drop out but may not 'see' him until the blind bettor looks at his cards.

Covering. A player who runs out of chips but wishes to stay in the game may 'cover the kitty' by laying his hand face down on top of it. Subsequent players start a new kitty and continue playing for it. When one of them wins, his hand is compared with that of the covering player, and the better of them wins the original kitty.

Five-Card Brag

As above, but each receives 5 cards and discards two face down before play begins. A prial of Threes ranks between Deuces and Fours, but, by agreement, the top hand is a prial of Fives.

Seven-Card Brag

All contribute equally to a kitty and receive 7 cards face down. Anyone dealt four of a kind wins the kitty and there is a new deal. Otherwise, each discards one card face down and forms the other six into two Brag hands, laying the higher of them face down on his left and the lower face down on his right.

To play, Elder turns up his left hand. Each in turn thereafter may pass, or turn his left hand face up if it beats the highest hand showing. Whoever is showing the best hand then turns up his right hand. Again, each in turn thereafter either passes or turns his hand up if it beats all other right hands.

The kitty goes to a player winning on both hands, or winning one and tying for best on the other. In the unlikely event of two players tying for best on left and right, it is divided between them. Otherwise, the kitty is not won but is carried forward to the next deal.

A prial of Threes counts between Deuces and Fours, the unbeatable top hand being a prial of Sevens.

Nine-Card Brag

As Seven-Card, except that each receives 9 cards and arranges them into three Brag hands, which must be exposed in order from highest to lowest. All three must win (or at least tie for best) for a player to sweep the pool. The best hand is variously set at a prial of Threes or Nines.

Crash

A Lancashire game briefly outlined by Arthur Taylor in *Pub Games* (St Albans, 1976). Four players each receive 13 cards and arrange them into four Brag hands, ignoring the odd card. Each lays his hands out in a row face down before him. (It is not stated whether they need be in order of superiority.) The hands are revealed strictly in order from left to right, the winner of each marking one point. The kitty is won by the first to reach seven over as many deals as necessary, but a player receiving four of a kind in one deal wins the game outright.

Bastard (Stop the Bus)

A cross between Brag and Commerce or Whisky Poker. Deal 3 cards each and a spare hand of 3 face up to the table. Each in turn must exchange one or more cards with the same number on the table. (In a particularly frustrating variant, a player may exchange one card or three, but never two.) Play continues until someone knocks, whereupon the others may—but need not—make one more exchange. Best hand wins the kitty, or worst hand pays a forfeit, or whatever.

Three-Stake Brag

Still recorded in books, but probably now defunct. Each player puts up three stakes and receives 3 cards, two face down, one face up. The first stake is won for the best up-card, or, if equal, by the elder of two tied players. The second goes to the winner of a round of bragging (betting, raising, etc.). All hands are then revealed, and the third goes to the player whose cards total closest to 31 without exceeding it. For this purpose Ace counts 1 and courts 10 each, and one or more additional cards may be drawn until a player is either bust or satisfied.

Classical Brag

An eighteenth-century version, but not according to Hoyle. Only prials and pairs are recognized. There are three wild cards or 'braggers': ◆A, ♣J, ◆9. A hand containing a wild card beats a like hand without; two braggers beat one; and the top hand is all three.

Brandle

Plain-trick game: 4p, 28c

An old German game related to Nap and Euchre, played with a Piquet or Skat pack lacking Eights. Rules vary; the following are typical.

Cards rank A K Q J T 9 7, but in trumps J 7 A K Q T 9. Deal 7 each in batches of 2 3 2. The bids are:

Brandle (3 tricks)	1 point
Four	2
Five	3
Six	4
Bettel (none)	5
Mord (all 7)	6
Herrenmord (7 NT)	7

Bettel and Herrenmord are no-trump games; in others, the bidder names trumps before leading.

Each in turn, starting with Eldest, may pass or bid. A player who has passed may not come in again. If all pass, there is no play and the deal moves round. Each bid must be higher than the previous one, but an earlier (elder) player may 'hold' the bid of a later one, thus forcing the latter to pass or go higher. The highest bid is *Mord* ('Death'): *Herrenmord* is not an overcall, merely a Mord played at no trump.

The soloist announces trumps (if any) and leads to the first trick. Follow suit if possible and head the trick if possible. If unable to follow, trump or renounce as preferred.

If successful, the soloist receives the value of his bid from each opponent, or scores the appropriate amount. There is no bonus for overtricks. If unsuccessful, he pays it to each opponent, or deducts it from his score.

Brelan

Famous French vying game from the seventeenth to nineteenth centuries, but nowhere clearly described. It was played by three or more with a 32-card pack (or fewer); each received 3 cards and a fourth was turned from stock. The best hand was a *brelan carré*, or four of a kind made with the aid of the turn-up, followed by a simple *brelan* or prial.

Bridge

Plain-trick game: 4pp, 52c

Bridge arose in the last third of the nineteenth century as one of several attempts to turn partnership Whist into a game with 'bidding' and 'suit hierarchy' like Boston. Other solutions included Cayenne Whist (q.v.) and the Russian game of Vint (q.v.); but what made Bridge unique was the additional feature, lacking from Boston, of the 'dummy', which, once the bidding is over, in effect turns Bridge into a three-player game. Although tradition places the origins of Bridge in the Levant, the dummy feature should probably be credited to the French. Whether or not they invented it, it was certainly in the Parisian clubs that Dummy Whist enjoyed its greatest popularity.

The game's first description in English appeared under the spurious title 'Biritch, or Russian Whist' in 1885. By 1900, as

Bridge-Whist or simply Bridge, it had almost completely ousted Whist as the high-class club game of Europe and America. By 1905 it had been replaced by Auction Bridge, in which all four could bid instead of just the dealer's side. Contract Bridge, first developed in France (again!) under the name Plafond during the First World War, came into its own in the early 1930s, following the application of technical improvements by millionaire Harold S. Vanderbilt and a world-wide publicity campaign engineered by Ely Culbertson.

As no one now plays Auction, the following outline is restricted to Contract; and as there is no shortage of books, clubs and classes for those wishing to learn more than the basic essentials, only the basic essentials are given below. Contract is played in several different formats: 'rubber Bridge', the traditional domestic and informal game; 'Chicago', an American variation increasingly popular in Britain; and 'duplicate', the tournament game. (For adaptations for other numbers of players, see Booby, Towie, and Honeymoon Bridge.)

Rubber Bridge

Partners sit opposite each other. They are agreed in advance or decided by drawing cards, the two highest playing against the two lowest. The scoresheet is divided into two columns, one for each side, and into an upper and lower half by a horizontal line. Scores for tricks contracted and won are recorded below the line; extras, overtricks, and penalties are recorded above it. A game is won by the first side to score 100 or more points 'below the line', over as many deals as it takes. When a game is won, another line is drawn beneath it across both columns, and the next game scored (from zero) below it. A rubber is won by the first side to win two games. A side that has won one game is described as 'vulnerable', which makes it subject to higher scores for success and penalties for failure. The turn to deal, bid, and play passes to the left.

Deal 13 cards each, singly, from a 52-card pack ranking A K Q J T 9 8 7 6 5 4 3 2.

Play is preceded by an auction. Its main purpose is to decide what contract will be played and by whom, but it also enables partners to exchange information as to the lie of cards by means of conventions encoded in the bidding system being followed.

Each in turn, Dealer first, must either pass (saying 'No bid'), or

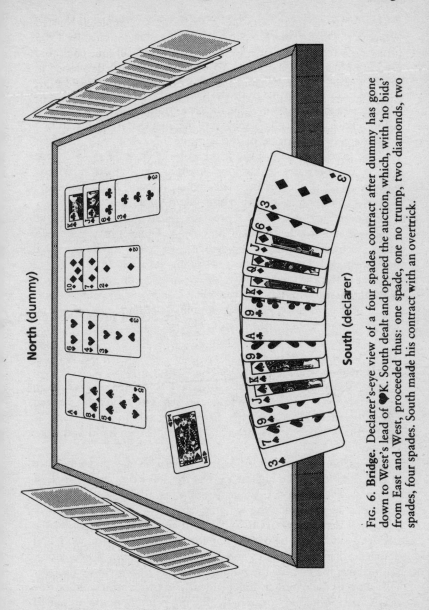

North (dummy)

South (declarer)

FIG. 6. **Bridge.** Declarer's-eye view of a four spades contract after dummy has gone down to West's lead of ♥K. South dealt and opened the auction, which, with 'no bids' from East and West, proceeded thus: one spade, one no trump, two diamonds, two spades, four spades. South made his contract with an overtrick.

bid, double, or redouble. A pass does not prevent one from bidding next time round. If all pass immediately, the deal is annulled and a new one made by the next dealer.

A bid states the number of tricks above six which the bidder proposes to win from his partnership's two hands, and the suit he proposes as trump for the purpose. The lowest bid is 'one club'—an offer to win at least seven of the thirteen tricks played with clubs as trumps. Each bid must be higher than the last: that is, it must offer a greater number of tricks, or the same number but with a higher-ranking trump. For this purpose the order is ♣ ♦ ♥ ♠ NT. 'One club' is therefore overcalled by 'one' anything else, but 'one no trump' only by 'two clubs' or higher. The highest possible bid is 'seven no trump'—an offer to win a no-trump 'slam' of all thirteen tricks.

A player may 'double' the previous bid if it was made by an opponent and no other bid has intervened. A player may 'redouble' the previous double if it was made by an opponent and no other bid has intervened. Doubling and redoubling respectively double and quadruple the eventual score if the proposed contract is actually played, but are automatically cancelled if followed by a higher bid.

The auction ends when a bid, double, or redouble has been followed by three consecutive passes. The last named bid is the 'contract'; whoever of the contracting side first named its suit is the 'declarer'; and the two opponents are the 'defenders'. The opening lead is made by the player at Declarer's left, e.g. West if Declarer is South. As soon as West has led, North lays his hand of cards face up on the table as a 'dummy', the four suits separate and each arranged from highest to lowest. North thereafter takes no active part, as South (the declarer) plays alternately from his own hand and from dummy.

Players must follow suit if possible, otherwise may play any card. A trick is taken by the highest card of the suit led or by the highest trump if any are played. When South wins a trick, he leads from whichever hand yielded the winning card.

Scoring details appear in Table 2. If the contract is made, the declaring side scores below the line for each trick bid and won, and above the line for overtricks and other bonuses. If not, the defenders score above the line for the number of tricks by which the declarer falls short of the contract. Independently of the contract, either side may score for holding (or, strictly, having held) 'honours' in one of

TABLE 2. *Scoring at Contract Bridge*
(D = if doubled, R = if redoubled, V = if declaring side vulnerable)

Contract made: contractors score

Below the line, for each contracted trick:

With minor suit trump (♣, ♦)	20 (D 40, R 80)
With major suit trump (♥, ♠)	30 (D 60, R 120)
At no trump: for 1st trick	40 (D 80, R 160)
... for each subsequent trick	30 (D 60, R 120)

Above the line, for each overtrick:

With minor suit trump	20 ⎱ D 100, DV 200
major suit or no trump	30 ⎰ R 200, RV 400

Above the line, bonuses for making:

A (re)doubled contract	50
A small slam	500 (V 750)
A grand slam	1000 (V 1500)

Contract failed: defenders score

Above the line, for each undertrick:

If not doubled	50 (V 100)
If doubled, 1st undertrick	100 (V 200)
... 2nd and 3rd undertricks	200 (V 300)
... 4th–7th undertricks	300 (V 400)
If redoubled, 1st undertrick	200 (V 400)
... 2nd and 3rd undertricks	400 (V 600)
... 4th–7th undertricks	600 (V 800)

Bonus to either side, regardless of contract:

5 trump honours in one hand	150
4 trump honours in one hand	100
At NT, four Aces in one hand	150
Rubber won in 2 games	700
Rubber won in 3 games	500
Rubber unfinished: 1 game won	300
Rubber unfinished: part score	50

---

their two hands before play began. The five top trumps (Ace to Ten) are honours, as are the four Aces in a no trump game.

Chicago or Four-Deal Bridge

This alternative structure is designed to speed the game up. A rubber is four contracts. (In effect, four deals; but if a deal is passed out, it does not count, and the same dealer deals again.) These are conducted on the following basis:

1. Neither side vulnerable.

2 and 3. Non-dealer's side vulnerable, dealer's not.
4. Both sides vulnerable.

If and when either side wins a theoretical 'game' by making 100 points below the line, it adds an above-line bonus of 300, or 500 if vulnerable on the deal on which that total was reached. A new line is then drawn, and both sides start counting again (from zero) towards game.

If at the end of the fourth deal either side has a part-score (more than zero but less than 100 below the line), it adds a bonus of 100 above the line.

Various other scoring refinements may be applied.

Duplicate Bridge

A tournament system designed to increase the superiority of skill over chance in determining the overall outcome. Basically, four hands dealt randomly at one table are duplicated deliberately at another. If played on a team basis, two partnerships sitting at different tables but belonging to the same team receive not the same but the complementary hands of their fellow partnership.

Notes. Bridge is unique in that the auction is at least as weighty as the play—almost a game in itself. Bidding serves two purposes: to enable each side to work towards its highest and safest contract, and to exchange as much information as possible as to the lie of cards before play. For the second purpose, a strong hand will not necessarily be opened at a high level or in its best suit, as this would waste valuable 'bidding space' from which more detailed information could be gleaned about the complementary hand. The more progressively a contract has been worked towards, the higher and more accurate it is likely to be. The same purpose has also encouraged the growth of 'conventions', by which a particular bid may be made not as a serious suggestion for a contract but as a device for requesting or conveying information. It is illegal in tournament play, and bad practice in home play, for partners to use systems or conventions unknown to the other side, and each side must state at the outset what system it is using. Of many systems that have been devised, that most used by British players is 'Acol', on which the following brief and elementary notes are based.

Assessing the hand. Hands are assessed by a point-count system originally devised by Milton Work. Each Ace held counts 4, King 3, Queen 2, Jack 1 'strength point'. There being 40 points altogether, the minimum requirement for a bid of 'one'—which assumes four tricks by oneself and three from one's partner—is a hand worth at least 12 and preferably 13 points (because $4/13 \times 40 = 12 \cdot 3$). Points may be added for an unbalanced distribution between the four suits. A balanced or 'flat' hand, in which they fall 4 3 3 3 or 4 4 3 2, has nothing extra to offer in this regard; but an unbalanced hand may be upgraded by the addition of one point for each card above four in any suit, or, in responder's hand, below three in a side suit when trumps have been agreed. Generally, a hand counting 13 or more justifies an opening bid, and since an opening 'one' in a suit may be made on anything up to 21 points, the partner may respond positively to it on as few as 6 points.

Another measuring device is 'quick tricks'. For this purpose, a suit headed

> A K   counts 2 quick tricks
> A Q, or K Q J $1\frac{1}{2}$
> A, or K Q   1
> K x, or Q J $\frac{1}{2}$

Outlined below are very general procedures for opening bids, responses to them, further rebids by either player, and 'defensive' bids that intervene between the bids of the opposing side. Except where otherwise stated, and for very specific purposes, they should be regarded as guidelines rather than rules to be followed slavishly. Much depends on the current score, whether or not you are vulnerable, whether you were first to speak or your opening bid was preceded by one or more passes, and so on.

Opening one in a suit. An opening bid is the first one made, whether or not preceded by one or more passes. Open 'one' in a suit if you have 13–20 strength points and at least two quick tricks. You also need a sensible rebid—not necessarily in the same suit—in case your partner makes an encouraging response. Of two biddable suits, bid the longer, or, if they are equally long, the higher-ranking — unless both are black, in which case bid clubs. Don't forget to use your discretion. A hand worth 10 could be worth opening; one worth 14 could be better passed.

In response to an opening 'one' in suit, pass on a hand counting 5 or less. With four or more of the same suit, rebid it; with a balanced hand reply in no trumps; with neither, but a good suit of your own (at least five), bid it at the lowest possible level. With 6–9 points, rebid two of partner's suit or one no trump. These are 'limit bids' and will discourage partner from bidding further unless he has additional strength. With 10–12, bid three in suit or two no trump; with 13–15, four in suit or three no trump. With 13–15 you may 'jump bid' a good six- or seven-card suit of your own by bidding it at a higher level than needed to show it. With 16 or more, a jump-bid in your own or partner's suit is expected, and demands further exploration.

Opening no trumps. Open 'one no trump' on a balanced hand within an agreed range of strength points. This requires agreement before play. Some play a 'weak no trump', opening 1 NT on 12–14 points (or 13–15, if agreed); some play a 'strong no trump', opening on 15–17 points (or 16–18, if agreed). A popular system is 'variable no trump'—i.e. open strong when vulnerable, otherwise weak.

With 20–22 or more on a balanced hand, bid 2 NT, inviting partner to show a strong suit or support the no-trump bid.

With 23 or more, don't bid no trump immediately. If NT is the right contract, it can be reached via two in a suit, as explained below.

With 25 or more, bid 3 NT if all your suits are stopped (headed Ace, or K x . . . , or Q x x . . .). This strongly invites your partner to keep the bidding open.

Two in a suit. Two in a suit other than clubs may be opened on a hand worth 17 or more and capable of winning at least eight tricks. It is regarded as forcing for one round, requiring partner to bid his best suit, or to indicate no best suit with a conventional 2 NT.

An opening of 'two clubs' is a convention with a highly specialized meaning. It denotes a strong, balanced hand worth 23–5 and is forcing to game. (From a zero score the bidding must be kept open until a contract is reached worth at least 100 below the line, i.e. at least five in a minor suit, four in a major, or three at no trump.) If partner has nothing to offer, he returns an equally conventional 'two diamonds', leaving you to rebid 'two no trumps' with relative safety. Otherwise, he should show his best suit at level 2 if major, 3 if minor.

Three in a suit. This bid may be made on an unbalanced hand containing a six- or seven-card suit and hence probably only good for one thing. It is described as a pre-emptive or 'shut-out' bid, its main value being to prevent the other partnership from establishing communications at a low level. As you will need to win at least nine tricks if everyone passes, you should be sure of at least six in your own hand before making it. Seven is better. Eight would rate an opening bid of four.

Defensive bids are those made by the other side when one side has seized the initiative of opening. Accurate defensive bidding requires skill, judgement, and experience and is not easily reduced to rules. It is especially important to listen to all the bids and passes that precede your own, and to draw inferences from them as to the distribution of suits and strength points. Generally, your first defensive bid should be made from length rather than strength, and should be one you can actually expect to win if landed in it by three promptly consecutive passes. If the opening is one in a suit, and you have the normal opening requirement for one no trumps, you may still use it, provided you are not excessively weak in the suit first named. If you have what seems a remarkably strong hand, you can force your partner to show his best suit by yourself bidding in the suit named by the opposition. This is known as a cue-bid. Since it obviously cannot be taken literally, your partner dare not pass for fear of dropping you in an unplayable contract. Another option is to make a conventional rather than a serious double, thereby requiring partner not to pass. A double will normally be understood as conventional if neither partner has yet made a positive bid.

Slam bids. The large bonuses for slams makes it important to reach high bids at all costs provided they can be made safely. Safety depends on conveying useful information accurately. The most popular of various conventions devised with this in mind is that named after Easley Blackwood. The partners having decided on a trump suit, one of them initiates Blackwood by bidding four no trumps. This asks partner how many Aces he holds. The response 'five clubs' indicates all or none, 'five diamonds' one, 'five hearts' two, 'five spades' three. The continuation 'five no trumps' similarly asks how many Kings are held, and the same code is used in response, except that 'six clubs' denotes none and 'six no trumps' all four.

Play. The defenders' play generally follows principles applicable to Whist or any other plain-trick partnership game, but with potentially greater accuracy because of the relatively great degree of information available as to the lie of cards, derived from both the auction and the visible dummy hand. It is the dummy, however, which makes Bridge virtually unique among partnership games in that the declarer is not involved in partnership play but occupies a playing position rather resembling that of a soloist in three-hand games. His first task when the dummy goes down is to pause and calculate how the contract can be won from the two visible hands, leaving overtricks (if any) to take care of themselves. The aim is to decide which of the twenty-six cards should be trick-winners, and how those that must be lost can be lost in such a way as to ensure that declarer gets back into his own or dummy's hand as required. Working out how to weave back and forth between the two hands to ensure that each can benefit from its strong points without being blocked or held up by the other is rather like getting a bird's eye view of a maze before plunging into it at ground level.

Generally, declarer should concentrate on drawing trumps if all three side suits are strong or well guarded between the two hands, but not if any one of them is markedly weak. With a short side suit in either hand, the aim is to work towards a situation in which one hand can lead it for the other hand to trump. In the ideal case, declarer sets up a different void suit in each hand so that each can lead into that of the other for a bout of 'cross-ruffing'.

For such techniques as unblocking, squeezing, and finessing, see Appendix.

Bridge-Whist

The earliest form of Bridge, so called from about 1900. Virtually identical with Biritch (q.v.).

Briscan

Point-tricks and melds: 2p, 32c

Or Brisque: a late eighteenth-century French relative of two-hand Bezique, with a vast range of scores and declarations.

Deal 5 each from a 32-card pack and play as at Bezique. Game is 600 points, scoring as follows:

Dealer scores 30 for turning an Ace as the trump card, 10 for turning any other card higher than Nine.

For sequences, Ten counts in normal position between Nine and Jack. Quint to the Ace 300, King 150, Queen 100, Jack 50; quart to the Ace 100, King 80, Queen 60, Jack 40, Ten 30; tierce to the Ace 60, King 50, Queen 40, Jack 30, Ten 20, Nine 10. All these are doubled in trumps. A longer sequence is not scorable if any of its cards has already been scored in a shorter. (*Example*: Having declared 9 T J for 30, you can't add Queen for 40 or Eight for 30.)

For a quartet of Aces 150, Tens 100, Kings 80, Queens 60, Jacks 40.

For a marriage 20, in trumps 40. Also scorable for a *mariage de rencontre*, i.e. taking a Queen in a trick with the King of the same suit.

For a hand composed entirely of courts (*carte rouge*) 20, of numerals (*carte blanche*) 10. Each score is repeated each time the hand is re-formed by the draw of another matching card.

The trump Seven may be exchanged for the turn-up at any time before the stock is exhausted, but attracts no score. For taking the last card of stock, score 10. For a hand composed entirely of trumps when the last card has been taken, 30. For winning the last five tricks, 30. For winning nine or more in all, 10. Taking all sixteen wins the game outright.

Finally, score for each Ace captured in tricks 11, each Ten 10, King 4, Queen 3, Jack 2.

Briscola

Point-trick game: 2–5p, 40c

One of Italy's most popular games (with Scopa and Tressette), Briscola is a little-changed descendant of Brusquembille, the ancestor of Briscan and Bezique. It is known as Brisca in Spain.

Briscola

All forms of the game are played with the Italian 40-card pack, cards ranking and counting as follows:

Ace	11
Trey (Three)	10
King (*Re*)	4
Queen (*Cavallo*)	3
Jack (*Fante*)	2
7 6 5 4 2	0 each

When three play, a Deuce is omitted from the pack. The following description is for two, three, and partnership four.

The player cutting the lowest card deals first. The turn to deal and play passes to the right. Deal 3 cards each face down, turn the next card for trumps, and slide it face up and partly projecting from beneath the face-down stock. Eldest leads to the first trick. The winner of each trick draws the top card of the stock, and waits for the other(s) do to so in turn before leading to the next.

Suit need not be followed so long as any cards remain in the stock. A trick is taken by the highest card of the suit led or by the highest trump if any are played. Suit must be followed in the play of the last three tricks.

The game is won by the player or partnership taking most of the 120 card-points, the hands being played right through. A rubber is the best of five games (first to three). 60–60 or 40–40–40 is a stand-off. So, presumably, is a two-player tie when three play.

In the four-hander, partners may communicate certain trump holdings to each other by means of the following facial signals, preferably without being spotted by the opponents:

Ace	Go tight-lipped.
Trey	Twist mouth sideways.
King	Raise eyes heavenwards.
Queen	Show tip of tongue.
Jack	Raise one shoulder.

They may also secretly show each other their final hand of three cards when the last card is taken from stock.

Briscola Chiamata

A modern alliance game for five (or, less happily, four). Deal 8 cards each in 4s, or 10 each (4 2 4) if four play. An auction follows to decide who will play against the others, either alone or with a secret partner. A bid is made by naming a card by rank only, the intention being that the holder of that card in trumps will become the bidder's partner when the trump suit is announced. Thus, a bid of 'Ace' means 'If I become the declarer I will name the trump suit, and the holder of the trump Ace will be my partner'. A bidder may name a card in his own hand if he thinks himself strong enough to play solo. Any bid can be overcalled by naming a lower-ranking card, Ace being followed by Trey, and so on down to Deuce. The player naming the lowest rank becomes the soloist and announces trumps. The holder of the called card may not reveal himself except through the play.

Eldest leads. Follow suit if possible, otherwise play any card. A trick is taken by the highest card of the suit led, or by the highest trump if any are played. The winner of each trick leads to the next.

If the declarer played alone and took 61 or more card-points, he scores 4 game points. If he and an ally took 61 or more between them, he scores 2 and his ally 1 point. Each opponent loses 1 point. These scores are doubled for winning every trick, and reversed if the declarer loses. The overall winner is the first to reach 11 game points.

Variant. A Deuce bid may be contested by raising the minimum number of card-points required to win, e.g. '66', '71'.

Briscolone

Two-hand Briscola with five cards each and no trumps. Theoretically, suit must be followed throughout; but, as the rule cannot be policed, players may agree to ignore it.

Brusquembille

Probable French ancestor of this family; played like Briscola but with a 32-card pack ranking A T K Q J 9 8 7.

Bulka

See Trappola.

Calabresella

Or Terziglio: see Tressette.

California Jack

See All Fours.

Calypso

Tricks and melds: 4pp, 4 × 52c

An interesting hybrid of Whist and Rummy, invented by R. W.
Willis of Trinidad, polished by Kenneth Konstam, and promoted—
unsuccessfully—by British playing-card companies in the 1950s as a
cross between Bridge and Canasta. Newcomers to this highly original game take to it either immediately or never.

Use four 52-card packs, preferably of identical back design and
colour, and certainly all the same size, weight, and finish. Shuffle
them together very thoroughly before play. Cards rank A K Q J T 9
8 7 6 5 4 3 2.

The players cutting the two highest cards are partners against the
two lowest, and sit opposite each other. Whoever cut highest deals
first and has the choice of seats, thereby determining his own and
everyone else's personal trumps (Fig. 7).

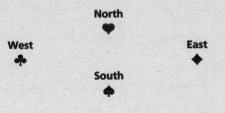

Fig. 7.

Deal 13 cards each face down in 1s, and stack the remainder face
down to one side. These will gradually be used up in subsequent
deals. A game consists of four deals, one by each player, the turn to
deal passing to the left.

A calypso is a complete run of cards in one suit from Ace down to Two. Each player's aim is to build calypsos in his personal trump suit, to assist his partner in building calypsos in his own suit, and to hinder his opponents from building those in theirs. The cards from which they are built come from cards won in tricks, not directly from the hand. The catch is that calypsos must be completed one at a time. That is, a player may not begin a second calypso until he has completed his first. If any cards won in a trick duplicate those already in a calypso under construction, they cannot (with one slight exception) be retained for future calypsos. It is therefore practically impossible for anyone to complete all four possible calypsos, and even three will be something of a feat.

Eldest leads to the first trick, and the winner of each trick leads to the next. Follow suit if possible, otherwise play any card.

If the leader leads his personal trump, then the trick is taken by the card led, regardless of rank, or by the highest personal trump if any are played (by anyone who cannot follow suit).

If the leader leads from any other suit, then the trick is taken by the highest card of the suit led, or by the highest personal trump if any are played.

If the trick is being taken by two identical cards, or by personal trumps of different suits but equal rank, then the first such card wins.

Note. If the suit led is another player's personal trump, then that player cannot 'trump' it: he can only follow suit, and hope to win by playing the highest card.

The winner of a trick takes from it any cards needed towards the building of his current calypso, and passes to his partner any needed for his. The remainder are stacked face down on a pile of won cards belonging to his partnership, only one such pile being needed for each. These cards will be either of the opponents' suits, or of one's own but unusable because they duplicate cards already contained in the calypso under construction.

A completed calypso is immediately bunched together and stacked face up on the table in front of its builder. Its owner may then start building a new one, and for this purpose may use any valid cards in the trick just taken.

When thirteen tricks have been played, the next in turn to deal

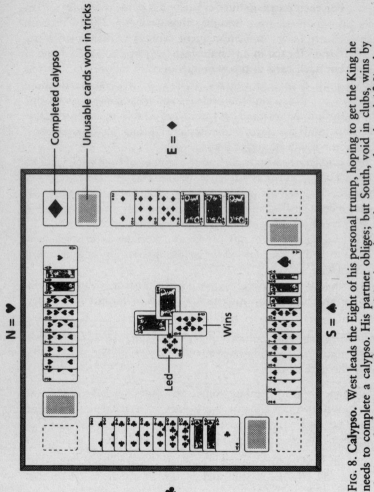

Completed calypso

Unusable cards won in tricks

N = ♥

E = ♦

S = ♠

W = ♣

Led

Wins

Fig. 8. **Calypso.** West leads the Eight of his personal trump, hoping to get the King he needs to complete a calypso. His partner obliges; but South, void in clubs, wins by playing a higher personal trump (♠9) than the only one so far played (♠8), thus completing his own calypso.

does so, and this continues until four deals have been played. Each
side then scores as follows:

For each partner's first calypso	500
second calypso	750
subsequent calypso	1000
For each card in an unfinished calypso	20
For each card in the winnings pile	10

Notes. Beginners should resist the temptation to lead personal
trumps at every opportunity for the novelty of winning easy tricks.
Opponents can easily thwart this approach by throwing to tricks
cards which duplicate those in the leader's current calypso and must
therefore be lost for ever. In the worst possible case, if as North you
lead ♥6 and everyone else plays ♥6 (your opponents deliberately,
your partner having no other card of the suit led), then you will
clearly be unable to build more than one calypso in the whole game.

Canasta

Rummy game: 2–4pp, 2 × 52c + 4 Jokers

Canasta (Spanish for 'basket') evolved in Uruguay and Argentina in
the mid-1940s, became an American fad game around 1948, and a
British one from 1950. An elaboration of Rummy, it is the only
partnership member of that family to have achieved the status of a
classic. It makes a good two-hander and is playable by up to six; the
2 × 2 version probably won out because of its appeal to Bridge-
players. It is no longer a fad game, and its even more elaborate
descendants, Samba and Bolivia, have not survived the parent. The
following 'book rules' are subject, in practice, to local variations.

Preliminaries. Use two 52-card packs and four Jokers, 108 cards in
all. It doesn't greatly matter if the backs are of different colours.
Partners, decided by any agreed means, sit opposite each other and
play alternately. Game is 5000 points, which usually takes several
deals.

Deal. After thorough shuffling, deal 11 each in 1s and stack the rest
face down. Turn the top card of stock and lay it beside stock to form
the first card of the wastepile. This pile is known as 'the pack', and
its top card as 'the upcard'. If the turned card is a Joker, a Two, or a

red Three, cover it with the next card turned from stock. Keep doing so, if necessary, until it is some other card. Anyone dealt one or more red Threes must, on his first turn to play, lay them face up before him and draw replacements from stock.

Object. A meld is three or more cards of the same rank (other than Jokers, Twos, and Threes). A canasta is a meld of at least seven such cards. Each partnership's aim is to make melds and build them up into canastas. Melds and canastas made by a single partnership belong equally to either partner. When a partnership has made at least one canasta it may end the game by 'melding out'.

Card values and uses. Individual cards score as follows:

Red 3s	100 each
Jokers	50
Ace, Deuce	20
K Q J T 9 8	10
7 6 5 4 black 3	5

Threes have special uses, and are not normally melded together. All Jokers and Twos are wild, counting as any desired rank except Threes. A meld must always contain at least two 'natural' cards (non-wild), and may never contain more than three wild ones. A canasta must contain at least four natural cards but may contain any number of wild ones.

Play. The player at Dealer's left goes first and the turn to play passes to the left. Each player in turn

1. must draw,
2. may meld,
3. must discard,

in accordance with the following rules.

Drawing. You may always draw the top card of stock. Alternatively, you may take the pack, in which case you must take the whole of it, and must use the upcard immediately. Furthermore:

If the pack is frozen, you may only use the upcard to start a new meld with at least two natural cards from your own hand. The pack is frozen to your own partnership until either of you has made an opening meld, and to both partnerships whenever it contains a wild card or red Three.

If the pack is unfrozen, you must still use the upcard, but may merely lay it off to an existing meld. This still prevents you from taking the pack if the upcard is a black Three, as they cannot be melded.

Note. Red Threes are simple bonus cards. If you draw one from stock, lay it face up next to your melds and draw the next card as a replacement. If you are the first player to take the pack, and it includes a red Three, lay it out. Subsequent packs will not include red Threes, as they may not be discarded.

Melding. A new meld is made by laying face up on the table three or more cards of the same rank, of which at least two must be natural and not more than three wild. The first meld made by either side must consist of cards whose combined values reach a minimum requirement. This requirement depends on that partnership's current score, as follows:

Current score	Minimum value
Less than 0	Any
Less than 1500	50
1500 or more	90
3000 or more	120

(At the start of the game, therefore, the minimum requirement is 50.)

Once a meld has been made, either partner may extend it in his proper turn to play by laying off to it one or more cards of the same rank, or one or more wild cards. When a meld contains seven or more cards, it becomes a canasta, and is squared up into a pile with a red card on top if it consists entirely of natural cards, otherwise a black one. (If a wild card is subsequently laid off to a 'red' canasta, it becomes a 'black' canasta, and its top card must be changed accordingly.)

A player may make as many melds and lay-offs as he can and wishes. In doing so, however, he may not reduce his hand to less than two cards unless he is legally entitled to meld out. No wild card may be shifted from one meld to another, and no one may lay off to a meld belonging to the other side.

Discarding. A turn is completed by making one discard face up to the top of the pack. Any card may be thrown. If it is a black Three, it prevents the next in turn from taking the pack. If it is a wild card, it should be placed sideways across the pack so as to project from it when subsequent discards are made. This shows that the pack is frozen.

Melding out. A player goes out by playing the last card from his hand, whether as lay-off or discard. All play then ceases immediately. In order to meld out, however:

1. His partnership must have made at least one canasta, and
2. He must have asked, and received, his partner's permission to go out. Permission may be asked before or after the draw.

A player cannot go out if he holds two black Threes and nothing else. With just one, he can go out by discarding it. With three or four, he may go out by melding them. Wild cards may not be included in such a meld.

A player with just one card in hand may not go out by taking the pack if the pack also contains only one card (unless the stock is empty: see below.)

There is a bonus for going out 'concealed'—that is, by melding all eleven cards (or ten and a discard) without having previously made any melds or lay-offs. The hand must include a canasta, and no lay-off may be made to any meld made by the partner.

End of stock. The stock very occasionally empties before anyone has gone out. If the last card drawn is a red Three it automatically ends the game, except that the player drawing it may first make as many melds and lay-offs as possible. (He may not discard.) If it is not a red Three, play continues without a stock. Each in turn must then take the upcard if he can meld or lay it off, and end his turn by discarding or melding out. This continues until someone either goes out or cannot use the previous player's discard. All play then ceases.

Score. Each side scores the total value of all cards it has melded, plus any of the following bonuses that may apply:

For each natural canasta made	500
For each mixed canasta	300
For going out	100 (200 if concealed)
For each red Three declared	100 (200 each if all four held)

Subtract from this the total value of cards left in both partners' hands. If the partnership has failed to make any meld, subtract also 100 per red Three possessed (or 800 for all four). Carry the score

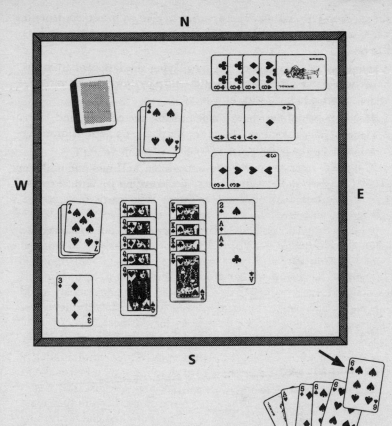

FIG. 9. **Canasta.** South has just drawn ♣6 from stock and will, if his partner agrees, go out by melding three Sixes, laying off the Ace and Joker to the meld of Aces, and discarding ♦5. N–S will score 300 for the mixed canasta (Sevens), 50 for Queens, 40 for Kings, 130 for the Ace meld, 15 for the Sixes, 100 for the red Three, and 100 for going out, total 735, less whatever remains in North's hand. W–E have 90 for the Eight meld, 60 for the Aces, and 200 for the red Threes, total 350, less whatever remains in both hands.

forward, and cease play if either side has reached or exceeded 5000. The winning margin is the difference between the two side's final scores.

Penalties. The commonest penalties are the loss of 500 for holding an undeclared red Three, 100 for trying to go out without permission, 100 for being unable to go out after receiving permission to do so, 50 for taking the upcard when unable to use it legally.

Notes. Canasta is essentially a point-scoring game. Generally, you should keep the game open as long as possible by taking the pack frequently, freezing it to your opponents, and not reducing your hand too early in the game. Aim to go out when you are well ahead, or if you can do so before the other side has melded, or as a defensive measure if the other side is doing too well. Use wild cards to freeze the pack when the other side is well ahead, or has made an initial meld before you have. Discard a black Three to 'stop' the pack to your left-hand opponent, especially when your right-hand opponent has just made their side's opening meld.

Canasta for three

Deal 13 cards each and play as above, but without partnerships.

Canasta for two

Deal 15 cards each and play as above.

Variants. (1) A player requires two canastas to go out. (2) Two cards are drawn from stock instead of one. Recommended for players with large hands.

Samba

The earliest of several variations giving credit for suit-sequences (*sambas*). Use three packs and six Jokers; deal 15 cards each; at each turn draw two from stock and discard one. The pack, whether frozen or unfrozen, may not be taken to start a sequence meld. A sequence meld is three or more natural cards in suit and sequence (Ace high, Four low). More may be added until it contains seven, whereupon it becomes a samba. No meld may contain more than two wild cards; sambas and sequence melds may not contain any.

Two canastas are required to go out, for which purpose a samba counts as a canasta.

Game is 10,000. At 7000 the minimum opening meld requirement is 150. There is a bonus of 200 for going out (open or concealed), and of 1500 for each samba made. Red Threes count 100 each, or all six 1000.

Bolivia

As Samba, but with additional scores for purely wild-card melds of three or more. A *bolivia* is a meld of seven wild cards; it is stacked with a Joker on top and may not then be extended. A seven-card suit-sequence is called an *escalera* ('ladder'). Black Threes left unmelded in hand count minus 100 each.

Canfield

See Patience.

Casino games

Mostly gambling games of the 'banking' variety, played between 'the house' on one side and one or more punters on the other.

Cassino

Fishing game: 2–4p, 52c

This Italian game of the Scopa family is the only one to have penetrated the English-speaking world, via Italian immigrants to America. First recorded just before 1800, it seems to have been heavily elaborated in nineteenth-century American practice. It is mostly played by two, but works well for three. Four play in partnerships.

From a 52-card pack, deal, 2 at a time, 4 cards face down to each player and 4 face up to the table. When everyone has played their four cards the same dealer deals 4 more each, but none to the table. Similar deals ensue, the game ending when no cards remain in stock or in anybody's hand.

The aim is to capture table cards with cards played from the hand. The eventual scores will be:

For taking most cards	3 points
For Big Cassino (◆T)	2
For Little Cassino (♠2)	1
For taking most spades	1
For each Ace captured	1
For each sweep made	1

('Most cards' is 27 or more when two individuals or partnerships play, or more than either opponent when three play.)

Each in turn plays a card to the table, thereby either capturing one or more table cards, or building a combination with one or more table cards for capture on a subsequent turn. Captured cards, together with the card they were taken with, are stored face down in front of the player taking them.

A 'sweep' is the capture of all the table cards in one turn. As this is a scoring feature, it is indicated by storing one of the cards face up instead of down.

A player unable to capture or build can only 'trail'—that is, play a card to the table, where it becomes just another table card. When a player makes a sweep, the next in turn to play can only trail.

On your turn to play, take a card from your hand and (unless forced to trail) do one of the following with it:

1. Capture one or more cards of the same rank as itself. Example:

Table	A 3 7 Q
Hand	3 5 Q K

Capture the Three with your Three or the Queen with your Queen.

2. If the played card is one of a pair in your hand, build it on a table card of the same rank, with a view to capturing both on your next turn. You must announce 'Building Aces' (or 'Twos', 'Kings', etc., whatever the rank may be).

Table	3 5 Q K
Hand	4 5 5 J

Play a Five to the Five, announce 'Building Fives', capture both on your next turn.

3. Capture two or more numerals that sum to the value of the played card. The latter may simultaneously capture any number of single or combined cards equal in face value to itself. Example:

Table   A 2 4 7
Hand   7 8 9 J

Play 7, capture A 2 4 by combining and 7 by pairing, thus also making a sweep. Courts cannot be so used, as they have no counting value.

4. Build it on one or more table numerals to produce a total which you can capture with a single card that you already hold. Example:

Table   2 3 8 J
Hand   4 9 Q K

Put 2 3 together, add your 4, announce 'Building nine', and capture it with the 9 on your next turn.

5. Increase a build with it, provided that you already hold the capturing card. Example

Table   (2 3 4) 8 J
Hand   A 10 Q

Play the Ace to the (2 3 4), announce 'Building ten', capture with the 10 on your next turn.

A build may not count more than 10, as no numeral card can capture it. The cards of a build cannot be taken individually by pairing, as the build itself counts as a single card.

Multiple builds—that is, more than one totalling the same amount—may not be increased individually: they can only be captured with a card of the same value. Example:

Table   (2 5) (3 4) 7
Hand   2   7 7 9

You can't play the Two to capture the Two, as the latter is part of a build. You can't play the Two to build nines on one of the seven-builds, as each is part of a multiple build. You may play a Seven and capture the two builds and the Seven, thereby making a sweep. Better, you may play one Seven, announce 'Building sevens', and sweep on your next turn.

A build may be captured by another player, whether opponent or partner. In the partnership game, you may increase builds made by your partner without yourself holding a capturing card, provided that it is evident from his announcement that he can capture on the next turn. (*Example*: He plays a Four to a Three and announces 'Building seven'. You may play a Seven and announce 'Building sevens', even if you do not hold another Seven yourself.)

A player who makes or increases a build on one turn must either capture or increase it on his next. He may not trail, unless the build he was making has meanwhile been captured by somebody else.

When the last deal is played, the player who made the last capture adds to his won cards all the untaken table cards, but this does not count as a sweep unless it is one by definition.

Players then sort through their won cards and score as shown above. The game ends at the end of the deal on which a player or side reaches a previously agreed target score, typically 11 or 21.

Variants. (1) When two play, sweeps are sometimes ignored. (2) Some players allow a court card to capture only one card by pairing, or one card or three but not two. This is because, if two are cap-

On table

In hand

FIG. 10. **Cassino.** This player can sweep the board with a Seven. Better still, he can play a Seven to the Seven, announce 'Building Sevens', and sweep the board on his next turn—provided his opponent does not himself hold a Seven with which to sweep it first. He cannot increase the 2–5 or 4–3, as they form a multiple build.

tured, the fourth will be impossible to capture when it becomes a table card, thus preventing sweeps from being made. (If sweeps are not counted, there is no point in restricting court captures.) (3) It may be agreed that play ends the moment someone makes a capture that brings his score to the target.

Notes. Concentrate always on the objectives: to capture most cards, most spades, Aces, the ♦10, and the ♠2. Avoid 'trailing' any of the latter, and work on builds rather than individual cards. Beware of capturing a court if this leaves only numerals on the table, as it is impossible to make a sweep so long as it remains. Do so only when you have a good chance of making the sweep yourself.

Catch the Ten
Point-trick game: 2–8p, 36c

First described in *The American Hoyle* of 1880, Catch the Ten is an old Scottish game also called 'Scotch Whist'. Dr Johnson's Scottish biographer, Boswell, refers to it in 1766 as 'Catch-Honours'.

Cards rank A K Q J T 9 8 7 6 except in trumps. If five or seven play, omit a Six; if eight, omit all Sixes, or (better) add the Fives. Four, six, or eight may play in partnerships as arranged by agreement.

Deal all the cards out one at a time, turning the last for trumps. If two or three play, deal (respectively) three or two 6-card hands face down to each. Each hand is picked up and played separately, the others remaining face down until the previous hand has been played out.

The aim is to win tricks, especially those containing any of the top five trumps, which rank and count as follows:

Trump Jack	11
Ace	4
King	3
Queen	2
Ten	10

(Players accustomed to Continental games may prefer Ace 11, King 4, Queen 3, Jack 2, Ten 10. It makes no difference to the play, and is easier to remember.)

Cayenne

Eldest leads to the first trick and the winner of each trick leads to the next. Follow suit if possible, otherwise play any card. The trick is taken by the highest card of the suit led or by the highest trump if any are played.

Each player scores the point-value of any top trumps won in tricks, plus 1 point per card taken in excess of the number originally held. Game is 41 points. If previously agreed, play ends when anyone reaches 41 by winning a counter; otherwise, play the last hand out.

French Whist

Similar, but played with 52 cards. Score 10 extra for capturing ◆10, nothing for non-counting cards. Game is 40 points, the maximum available.

Cayenne

Plain-trick game: 4pp, 52c

One of the most interesting nineteenth-century variations on a theme of Whist, and in some respects a forerunner of Bridge. It first appeared in the 1860s and takes its name from the capital of French Guyana. Whether or not it has any connection with the penal settlement established there in 1854 is not recorded, but the date suggests it might have.

Players sitting opposite each other are partners. Deal 13 cards each in batches of 4 4 5. A suit called *cayenne* is chosen by cutting another pack (or by any agreed means if a second is not to hand). This establishes the following suit hierarchy:

If cayenne is	♥ ◆ ♣ ♠
then second colour is	◆ ♥ ♠ ♣
third colour is	♣ ♠ ♥ ◆
fourth colour is	♠ ♣ ◆ ♥

Dealer announces either a trump suit, or 'grand', or 'nullo', or passes the choice to his partner, who may not refuse. In a trump game (specified by announcing 'cayenne', 'second', 'third', or 'fourth') the aim is to win seven or more tricks. Grand is the same, playing at no trump. Nullo is to win as few tricks as possible, also at no trump.

Eldest leads to the first trick, and the winner of each trick leads to the next. Follow suit if possible, otherwise play any card. The trick is taken by the highest card of the suit led or by the highest trump if any are played. At nullo, each Ace counts as the *lowest* card in its suit, unless its holder declares it high immediately upon playing it.

Score. At grand, the side taking most tricks scores 8 per trick taken in excess of six. At nullo, the side taking fewest scores 8 per trick taken in excess of six by the opposing side. In a trump game, the side taking most tricks scores the number of tricks taken in excess of six, multiplied by

> 4 if cayenne was the trump suit
> 3 if second colour
> 2 if third
> 1 if fourth

In addition, winning a slam (all thirteen tricks) carries a bonus of 6, and a small slam (twelve tricks) a bonus of 4.

The side originally dealt a majority of honours (A K Q J T of trumps) scores 2 for each honour dealt in excess of two, and this also is multiplied by the trump suit factor.

The side first reaching 10 points wins a game. This may not be done by honours alone. If the side scoring honours does not also score for tricks, then (*a*) they score nothing if the other side reaches 10; (*b*) if not, and if honours would bring them to 10 or more, their score remains pegged at nine.

Points made by the winning side in excess of 10 are carried over to the next game, with an additional

> 4 if opponents have no score
> 3 if they have 1–3
> 2 if they have 4–6
> 1 if they have 7–9

The other side is then set back to zero for the next game.

The first side to win four games wins the rubber and gets a bonus of 8.

Challenge

See Svoyi Koziri.

Chase the Ace

Gambling game: 3–10p, 52c

A primitive gambling or children's game, called Cuckoo in most European countries, though recorded in Cornwall as Ranter-go-Round. Much played in Scandinavia with specially designed cards (Gnav, Killekort, etc.).

Players deal in turn. Deal 1 card each face down from a 52-card pack ranking A 2 3 4 5 6 7 8 9 T J Q K. The aim is to avoid holding the lowest card at end of play. Suits are irrelevant; Ace is always low.

Each in turn, starting with Eldest, may either keep his card (and must turn it face up if it is a King), or demand to exchange it with that of his left-hand neighbour. The latter may only refuse if he holds a King, which he must then show (saying 'Cuckoo!', in some versions).

The dealer, on his turn, may either stand pat or reject his card and cut a replacement from the pack. The cards are then revealed, and the player with the lowest (Ace low) loses a life. Players tying for lowest all lose one.

Variants. If Dealer rejects his card, and then cuts a King, it counts lowest of all, and only he loses a life. Some do not cut, but take the top card of the pack. Some have a rule that a player passing an Ace, Two, or Three to his right-hand neighbour must announce that fact.

Cheat

See 'I Doubt It'.

Chemin de Fer

Or Chemmy: see Baccara.

Children's games

This is not a technical classification, as much depends on the child. Any game with easily grasped rules is suitable for children. See, in particular: Adding-up games, Battle, Beggar my Neighbour, Dudak, Elfern, Fishing games, Going-out Games, I Doubt It, My Ship Sails, Old Maid, Pelmanism, Rummy games, Slapjack, Snap.

Chinese Whist

Plain-trick game: 2–4p, 52c

Nineteenth-century Whist-players became fascinated with exposed hands, or 'dummies', which increased skill and calculation at the expense of chance and estimation. One outcome was the development of Bridge from Dummy Whist. This more lightweight derivative recalls a period when the epithet 'Chinese' was attached to any unusual or eccentric variation on an otherwise commonplace theme. The partnership version is described first.

Players sitting opposite each other are partners. Each receives 6 cards, and, without examining them, lays them face down in a non-overlapping row. Six more are then dealt face up across the same row, so that each of the 6 pairs consists of a down-card partly covered by an upcard. The 4 remaining cards are dealt 1 to each hand.

The dealer, after examining his hand-card and upcards, announces a trump suit (without consulting his partner.)

Eldest leads to the first trick, and the winner of each trick leads to the next. Each may play his hand-card or any upcard at any time, but must follow suit to the led card if possible. The trick is taken by the highest card of the suit led or by the highest trump if any are played. At the end of each trick, any down-card uncovered by the play of an upcard is itself turned up.

Each side scores 1 point per trick taken above six. Play up to any agreed target.

Three players

They use a pack from which a Two has been omitted. They receive 8 cards face down, 8 face up, and 1 in hand.

Cinch

Suggested variations. Use a full pack and turn the last for trump, without dealing it to anyone. Score for each trick taken above five.

Two players

Each player receives 12 face down, 12 face up, and 2 in hand. Score for each trick taken above thirteen.

Cinch

Point-trick game: 4pp, 52c

A descendant of All Fours and Pitch, Cinch originated in Denver, Colorado, around 1885 and was a popular club game until the advent of Auction Bridge.

Cards rank A K Q J T . . . 2, except that the Five of the same colour as trumps ('Left Pedro') ranks immediately below the trump Five ('Right Pedro'), thereby extending trumps to fourteen cards and reducing one plain suit to twelve.

Deal 9 each in 3s. Starting with Eldest, each in turn may pass or make a higher bid than any so far made. The possible bids range from one to fourteen, representing the number of points the bidder offers to win, with his partner, in return for choosing trumps. The 14 points accrue for winning certain trumps in tricks, namely:

Ace	1	R. Pedro	5
Jack	1	L. Pedro	5
Ten	1	Two	1

If all pass, dealer declares trumps, but this does not constitute a bid and hence there are no penalties for failure.

Declarer having named trumps, each in turn, starting with Eldest, discards from his hand all cards which are not trumps and is promptly dealt as many more as necessary to restore his hand to six. (Anyone dealt seven or more trumps must reduce his hand to six, discarded trumps being shown for information.) When the first three have been dealt with, dealer then 'robs the pack' by (in effect) adding the undealt cards to his hand and discarding down to six. The net result is that all fourteen trumps will be in play, and only ten plain cards.

Declarer leads first. Players may follow suit or trump, as preferred, but may only renounce if unable to follow suit. The trick is taken by the highest card of the suit led or by the highest trump if any are played.

Game is 51 up, or 61 if a Cribbage board is used. Scoring methods vary. For instance:

1. If the bidding side fulfils its contract, each side scores what it took in tricks. If not, the bidding side deducts from its score 14 plus the number of points it did take. If both sides reach the target on the same deal, the bidding side wins. Or:
2. If the bidding side fulfils its contract, it scores the difference between the number of points taken by each side. If not, the other side scores what it made plus the amount of the bid. This makes the game longer and prevents both from reaching the target simultaneously.

Notes. This is the most skilled member of the All Fours family, largely because all the trumps are in play, they account for 56 per cent of the cards held, and the number of discards made by each hand gives some indication of its strength. Bidding conventions may be devised, such as starting with a bid of five to show that a Pedro is held. To 'cinch' a trick is to play in such a way as to prevent an opponent winning it with a Pedro—a key feature of the game, and hence the origin of its title.

Cinq Cents

1. A one-pack form of Bezique, played with 32 cards.
2. Swiss variety of Klaberjass.

Clobbiosh

Or Clob, or Bella: Anglo-Jewish variety of Klaberjass.

Collecting games

Games in which the aim is to collect matching cards. The ultimate aim is usually to go out first by matching all one's cards, in which case they are better classed as Going-out games. Rummy is a major example.

Comet

Stops game: 2–5p, 52c

An ancestor of the Newmarket or 'Stops' family of gambling games, originally called Manille, which now denotes a different game. Very popular at the court of Louis XIV, but first recorded under its new name in England shortly after the 1682 appearance of Halley's Comet—possibly from the fancied resemblance of its layout to a comet's tail. The following is one of several different versions.

Use a 51-card pack lacking ◆8. Two to five players contribute equally to a pool and receive (respectively) 20, 14, 11 or 9 cards each, the rest being left out of play. The aim is to run out of cards before anyone else, thus winning the pool.

Eldest starts by playing any card face up to the table and adding to it as many cards as he can in ascending numerical sequence, regardless of suit. If he reaches a King he continues Ace, Two, etc. When he gets stuck, the next in turn continues the sequence from the next higher rank, and so on.

The ◆9, or 'Comet', is wild, being playable at any time. It is followed by the next above the rank it represents, or by a Ten, but a Ten ends one's turn. When no one can continue, the current player starts a new sequence.

If previously agreed, anyone holding the Comet when someone else goes out pays a fixed sum to the winner, and anyone going out by playing the Comet receives a bonus from everyone else.

Commerce

Gambling games: 3–10p, 52c

Several similar games conveniently congregate here. Commerce itself is a nineteenth-century French game, akin to Thirty-One and perhaps ancestral to Whisky Poker and Bastard Brag. Trade and Barter, sometimes also called Commerce, has the same combinations but a different way of acquiring them, and (to my knowledge) appears only in English books. Trentuno applies basically the the same method of play to slightly different combinations; while Trade and Barter, the English equivalent, has the same combinations as

Commerce (by which name it is also recorded) but a different way of acquiring them.

Commerce

Use a 52-card pack ranking A K Q J T 9 8 7 6 5 4 3 2. Players contribute equally to a pool. The aim is to finish with the best three-card combination. Traditionally, the turn to play passes to the right.

Deal 3 each and a widow of 3 face up to the table. Before play, the dealer may exchange his hand for the widow. Thereafter, each in turn, starting with eldest, exchanges a hand card for a card in the widow. A player who is satisfied with his hand knocks on the table instead of playing, and play ceases as soon as two have knocked. The best hands are, from high to low:

Tricon. Three of a kind. Aces best, and so on down.

Sequence. Three cards in suit and sequence. Best is A K Q, lowest 3 2 A.

Point. The greatest value of cards in any one suit, counting Ace 11, courts 10 each, numerals at face value. If equal, a three-card beats a two-card flush. If still equal, the winning equal hand is that of the dealer if he is involved, otherwise that of the first in order of play after the dealer.

Trentuno (Thirty-One)

Use a 40-card pack lacking Eights, Nines, and Tens, and play (to the right) as above. The best hand when someone knocks is that containing cards of the same suit totalling 31 or the nearest below it. Three of a kind is a special hand ranking between 30 and 31.

Trade and Barter

From a 52-card pack deal 3 each (to the right) but no widow. The aim is to have the best Commerce hand (tricon, sequence, point) at a showdown. Each in turn, starting with Eldest, must exchange one card by announcing 'trade' or 'barter'. If he says 'trade', he passes a card face down to the dealer and receives the next one from the stock, paying the dealer one chip for this privilege. If he says 'barter', he exchanges one card with his right-hand neighbour, sight unseen and without payment. Play continues until someone knocks.

Commit

See Comet.

Concerto

Matching game: 4pp, 52c

This game of my own invention merits inclusion partly because it is unlike any other and partly because many years of extensive play have not exhausted its interest. The version described below is an improvement on that first published in Parlett, *Original Card Games* (London, 1977).

Preliminaries. Four players sit crosswise in partnerships. Choose first dealer by any agreed means; thereafter, the turn to deal and play passes to the left. Deal 13 each, in 1s, from a 52-card pack ranking A K Q J T 9 8 7 6 5 4 3 2 (A).

A game is four deals or 100 points, whichever is reached sooner. In each deal, each side's object is to make four five-card Poker hands, and to avoid finding any Poker combination in the six cards left over.

Play. Each partnership in turn plays one hand while the other partnership looks on. The player at Dealer's left leads to the first hand: he may not pass the lead. His partner may then add a card to it or pass. Play continues with each in turn either adding a card or passing. This continues until five cards have been played. If these form a Poker combination, the partners score as follows:

1 pair	1	(2 of same rank, 3 unmatched)
2 pairs	2	(2 pairs, 1 unmatched)
Triplet	3	(3 of same rank, 2 unmatched)
Straight	5	(5 in sequence; Ace counts high or low)
Flush	6	(5 of a suit, not in sequence)
Full house	8	(1 triplet plus 1 pair)
4 of a kind	12	(4 of same rank, 1 unmatched)
Straight flush	15	(5 in suit-sequence; Ace counts high or low)

The hand remains face up on the table in front of its leader so that everyone can see which cards are no longer in play. The player at leader's left then leads the first card to his own side's first hand. This continues, with each player in turn having the opening lead, until each side has made four hands.

Special rules. The first card to each hand must be played by the player to the left of the previous leader: he may not pass the lead.

Not more than two passes may be made in succession. For example, if North passes and South immediately passes, North must then play. But there is no restriction on the total number of passes that may be made in making one hand.

A player entitled to pass may instead say 'Play'. This means he will play no more cards to that hand, which must be completed by his partner. (If his partner hasn't enough cards for the purpose, the first player must play all he has and let his partner complete it; but the hand is thereby annulled and scores nothing.)

Score. The side scoring the greater total over four hands may claim a bonus for 'left-overs'. The bonus is 10 times the value of the best Poker hand they can make from the six cards left over by the losing side—one pair 10, two pair 20, etc. If no scoring hand can be made there is no bonus. If both sides equalize over four hands, the bonus goes to whichever of them can make the higher Poker hand from the other side's left-overs. For this purpose, equal combinations are decided by the highest top card (as at Poker).

Each side's score for hands and left-overs is carried forward to the next deal. Play continues until one side has made 100 or more points, or four deals have been played. The winners count a double game or stake if they have at least 100 and the losers have less, and treble if this is achieved in under four deals. A three-deal tie is decided by a fourth deal. A four-deal tie wins for the side that scored more for 'left-overs' overall.

Notes. The leader should start play from a straight flush or four of a kind if he has one, otherwise from three or more cards belonging to the same straight flush. Second to play should normally pass (unless he can himself complete a straight flush), to see what sort of hand the leader is playing from. At any given point in play there is always a theoretical 'best hand' that can be made. Normally, the player whose turn it is should play if he can contribute to that best hand, and pass if he cannot, leaving his partner to downgrade it if necessary. Much of the fun and skill of Concerto lies in the development of signalling systems to indicate what sort of hand is being played from. Suppose, for instance, leader starts by playing ♠5 and his partner passes. If leader's second card is ♠9, this tells his partner to keep passing (or say 'Play'), as he has a complete straight flush. Similarly, ♠8 would show a sequence of four, asking partner to play the Four or the Nine if possible; ♠A would show four to a straight flush requiring the Two, Three, or Four to complete it; another Five would show he is playing from four of a kind; a pass would show he has nothing better than another Five in hand.

Conquian

Rummy game: 2p, 40c

The earliest true Rummy, a kind of proto-Gin, seems to have been first played in Mexico and bordering American States, especially Texas, from the mid nineteenth century. It was first described as 'Coon Can' in 1887 and as 'Conquian' in 1897.

Two players each receive 10 cards dealt singly from a 40-card pack ranking A 2 3 4 5 6 7 J Q K, the rest being stacked face down. The aim is to be the first to go out by melding *eleven* cards, including the last one drawn. Melding means laying them down in sets of three or more matched cards, each consisting of three or four cards of the same rank, or from three to eight cards in suit and sequence.

It is impossible to meld eleven in sequence, as there are only ten per suit. The longest possible is therefore eight, the other three forming a separate meld. Because Ace is low and Seven and Jack consecutive, both A 2 3 and 6 7 J are valid, but Q K A is not.

Non-dealer starts by facing the top card of stock. He may not take it into hand, but must either meld it immediately (with at least two hand-cards) or pass. If he melds, he must balance his hand by making a discard face up. If he passes, Dealer must either meld it himself, leaving a discard face up in its place, or else also pass by turning it face down. In the latter event it becomes his turn to draw from stock.

Play continues in the same way. Whoever turns from stock has first choice of the card turned, and must either meld it, extend one of his existing melds with it, or pass. If both pass, the second turns it down and draws next.

In melding, a player may 'borrow' cards from his other melds to help create new ones, provided that those thereby depleted are not reduced to less than valid three-card melds. After melding, the player's discard becomes available to the opponent, who may either meld it himself or turn it down and make the next draw.

The game ends when one player melds both the faced card and all cards remaining in his hand, whether by adding to existing melds, making new ones, or both.

If a player declines a faced card which can legally be added to one of his existing melds, he must meld it if his opponent so demands. In this way, it is sometimes possible to force a player into a situation from which he can never go out—a point of much interest to the strategy of play.

If neither is out when the last available card has been declined, the game is drawn and the stake carried forward.

Continental Rummy

See Contract Rummy.

Contract Bridge

See Bridge.

Contract Rummy

Rummy game: 3–8p, 2–3 × 52c + Jokers

A group of Rummy games with a variety of names (Combination R., Hollywood R., Joker R., King R., Liverpool R., Progressive R., Shanghai R., Zioncheck, etc.), dating from the Contract Bridge boom of the 1930s. They were later swept aside by Canasta. Typically, a game is several deals, in each of which the first meld anyone can make—the initial meld or 'contract'—gets progressively larger. The following rules assume a knowledge of basic Rummy, and many variations will be found.

Three or four players use 105 cards (2 × 52 + Joker), five or more use 158 (3 × 52 + 2 Jokers). Cards rank 2 3 4 5 6 7 8 9 T J Q K A. The aim is to be the first to go out by melding all one's cards.

Other players are penalized for cards remaining unmelded in hand, counting numerals at face value, courts 10 each, Aces and Jokers (or other agreed wild cards) 15 each.

The turn to deal and play passes to the left. A game is seven deals, the first four of 10 cards each, thereafter 12, dealt face down and 1 at a time after very thorough shuffling. Deal the next card face up to start the wastepile, and lay the rest face down as a stock beside it.

Each deal imposes the following requirement as to what every player must meld first before making any other play:

1st	2 sets
2nd	1 set + 1 sequence
3rd	2 sequences
4th	3 sets
5th	2 sets, 1 sequence
6th	1 set, 2 sequences
7th	3 sequences using all cards held

A set is three or more cards of the same rank, regardless of suit. A sequence is three or more cards in suit and sequence. Ace normally counts high in sequences. If it is agreed to count it low as well, it is permissible to make a fourteen-card sequence using it in both capacities. Jokers are wild, and so are Deuces if agreed. Where two or more sequences are required, none may be consecutive and in the same suit. Thus ♠2 3 4, 6 7 8 is valid, but ♠2 3 4 5 6 7 counts as one sequence, not two.

Eldest plays first. Each in turn draws the top card of the stock or wastepile, may meld or lay off as the rules direct, and ends with a face-up discard to the wastepile.

If the player in turn does not want the upcard, each other player in turn from his left may take it instead, but whoever does so must also draw the top card of stock, without discarding, before the player in turn does so.

Each player's first meld must be as directed in the schedule above. In later turns he may then lay off one or more matching cards to any meld or melds on the table, whether his own or someone else's, but may not start a new one.

Wild cards represent any desired card in a set or sequence, but only in sequences may they be replaced by the natural cards they represent. In this case the holder of the natural card may substitute it for the Joker, and either take the Joker into hand or shift it to one end of the sequence. In the latter case, it must stand for a real card with which it can be replaced to produce a valid meld. A player able to substitute a natural for a wild card may do so at any time (not necessarily in turn), provided that he has made his requisite initial meld(s). If two players are able, priority goes to whichever is next in turn to play. It may be agreed to limit the maximum legal size of sets to eight if two packs are used, twelve if three, whether or not including wild cards.

Play ceases as soon as any player goes out by laying off or discarding his last card. In the seventh and last deal a player may only go out by melding his whole hand (with or without one discard) in one go, and making at least three sequences. The others are penalized by the value of cards remaining in hand, and the overall winner is the player with the lowest score at the end of the last deal.

Continental Rummy

A relative of Contract Rummy, equally obsolete, played by three or four with two 53-card packs, by five or more with three, by eight or more with four. Ace high, Jokers wild (sometimes also Deuces). Deal 15 each. Play as basic Rummy—but collecting only suit-sequences, not sets—until someone ends the game by melding all 15 cards in any of these sequence patterns:

(*a*) 3 3 3 3 3 (*b*) 4 4 4 3 (*c*) 5 4 3 3

No cards may be laid off or naturals exchanged for wild cards. The winner receives from (or scores off) each opponent 1 for going out, 2 per Joker melded, 1 per Deuce melded if Deuces wild. Other possible bonuses include 10 for going out without having drawn a card, 7 for having drawn only one, 10 for having melded only natural cards, 10 for melding 15 cards of one suit.

Contract Whist

Plain-trick game: 4pp, 52c

Perfected by Hubert Phillips around 1932, Contract Whist is a deliberate cross between ordinary Whist and Contract Bridge, made by eliminating dummy play and considerably simplifying the scoring schedule. It is ideal for players looking for something deeper than Whist or Solo, but who dislike the dummy feature of Bridge, or for those wishing to graduate from Whist to Bridge.

Four players form two partnerships, with partners sitting opposite each other. Deal 13 cards each, 1 at a time, from a 52-card pack ranking A K Q J T 9 8 7 6 5 4 3 2. There is an auction to determine the declarers and their contract. The contract is an undertaking made by the declaring partnership to win at least a certain number of tricks using a given suit (or none) as trump. For each side, a horizontal line is drawn half way down the scoresheet. A side scores points below this line for winning the contracted number of tricks, and above it for winning any overtricks and other bonuses. A game is won by the first side to reach 10 points below the line. The rubber is won by the first side to win two games.

Starting with the dealer, each in turn may pass, bid, double the previous bid, or redouble the previous double. Passing does not prevent a player from speaking next time round. The auction ends when a bid, double, or redouble is followed by three consecutive passes.

A bid states the number of tricks above six which a player proposes his partnership to take, and the suit proposed as trump. The lowest bid is 'One club' — an undertaking to win at least seven of the thirteen tricks with clubs as trump. Each bid must be higher than the last. A bid is higher if it raises the number of tricks contracted, or if it involves the same number but in a higher trump. For this purpose clubs are lowest, followed by diamonds, hearts, spades, no trump. Thus there are thirty-five possible bids, ranging from 'one club' to 'seven no trump'.

Instead of bidding, a player may 'Double' the previous bid, or 'Redouble' the previous double, if the previous announcement was made by an opponent and no other bid has intervened. A double or redouble is cancelled if followed by another bid.

Following three consecutive passes, the last bid named becomes the contract. The opening lead is made by the player to the left of that member of the contracting side who first named the trump involved. Follow suit if possible, otherwise play any card. The trick is taken by the highest card of the suit led or by the highest trump if any are played, and the winner of each trick leads to the next.

If the contract is made, the contracting side scores as follows:

	Basic	Doubled	Redoubled	
Per contracted trick at NT	4	8	16	below
in trumps	3	6	12	below
Per overtrick (trump or NT)	2	5	10	above
Bonus for winning doubled contract		5	10	above

If it is defeated, the other side scores (above the line) 10 per trick by which the declarers fell short of the contract, or 20 if doubled, 40 if redoubled.

Winning the rubber carries a bonus of 50.

Notes. Although Bridge-players may follow their normal bidding practice for Contract Whist, caution should be exercised in respect of conventional or artificial bids, as their significance in Bridge often only becomes clear when the dummy is exposed. There being no dummy, such bids may give information more useful to the opponents than to one's partner.

Coon Can

See Conquian; also an obsolete double-pack Rummy known as 'Colonel' in Britain.

Coquimbert

Or 'Qui gagne perd' (English 'Losing Loadam'), a 16th century ancestor of Reversis and the Hearts family.

Costly Colours

Add and match game: 2p, 52c

This fascinating relative of Cribbage was first described in Cotton's *Compleat Gamester* and is occasionally mentioned as a regional game in the eighteenth century. The following description comes from an edition of *Shropshire Folklore* of 1874, itself partly based on a booklet entitled *The Royal Game of Costly Colours* published in Shrewsbury in 1805.

Cards rank A 2 3 4 5 6 7 8 9 T J Q K. Numerals count face value, courts 10 each, Ace 1 or 11 as its player declares. Deal 3 each in 1s and turn the next for trumps. This is called the 'deck card'. If it is a Jack or a Deuce, Dealer pegs 4 'for his heels'.

Mogging. The players may now 'mog'. This is done by each passing a card from his hand face down to the other. If either refuses to do so, the other pegs 1 point for the refusal. If a player gives away a Jack or a Deuce, he may first peg 2 points for it (4 if in trumps). If he neglects to do so, the other may score for it when the final declarations are made.

Play. Each in turn, starting with non-dealer, plays a card face up to the table in front of himself, announcing the cumulative face value of cards played as they go along. In play, scores are pegged for making sequences and points, at the rate of 1 per card.

A sequence is three or more cards in ranking order (Ace low). Example: Abel plays Eight, Baker plays Six, Abel plays Seven and pegs 3 for the sequence. If Abel then plays Five or Nine, he pegs 4.

The points are 15, 25, 31, the last known as the 'grand point' or 'hitter'. A player making any such total pegs as many points as cards involved. Example: 7 4 4 scores 3 for the 15. If the next adds a court or a Ten, he pegs 4 for the 25; and if the next plays a Six, he pegs 5 for the 'hitter' or 'grand point' of 31.

The count may not exceed 31. The first player unable to play without busting says 'Go!', whereupon the other may add as many more cards as he can without busting. The last to play scores 1 for the go, plus 1 per card if he hits 31 exactly.

If any cards remain in hand, those so far played are turned down, and whoever scored the previous 'go' begins another series as before.

Hand scores. The players then reveal their cards and score for any of the following features they can make. Non-dealer counts first. Each player's hand is considered to consist of four cards, i.e. his own three plus the deck card.

> *Points*
> 15   1 per constituent card
> 25   1
> Hitter (31)   1
> *Jacks and Deuces*
> Jack or Deuce of trumps   4 'for his nob'
> Any other Jack or Deuce   2

Pairs and prials

Pair (two of same rank)	2
Prial (three alike)	9
Double prial (four alike)	18

Colours

Three in colour	2
Three in suit	3
Four in colour, two in suit	4
Four in colour, three in suit	5
Four in suit	6 for 'Costly Colours'

As in Cribbage, the same card may be used in as many combinations as possible, provided that no combination is made by rearranging exactly the same set of cards. However, it is not permitted to score separately the constituent pairs of a prial, or the prials of a double pair royal. There is no score for runs.

Examples.

◆5 + ♥Q ♥K ♥5 pegs fifteen 2, 4, 6, 8; twenty-five 3, 6; pair 2; colours 5: total 21.

◆5 + ♥J ◆J ♣J pegs fifteen 2, 4, 6; twenty-five 3, 6, 9; Jacks 4 (matching the deck card), 6, 8; prial 9; colours 2: total 34.

♠A + ♣2 ◆2 ♣Q pegs fifteen or twenty-five 4 (Ace counts 1 or 11, but not both); Deuces 4 (matching the deck-card), 6; pair 2; colours 4: total 16.

Play up to 121 (twice round the board).

Note. Four may play in partnerships. Each player mogs with his partner, and the dealer, if refused, may mog alone by taking the card below the deck-card and substituting a card he does not want.

According to the Shropshire source, 'his nob' denotes the Jack or Deuce of a suit *other* than trump. I query this, and have here followed Cribbage terminology. In Salopian dialect, a score of zero in a single hand (known as a 'nineteen' in Cribbage because it is impossible to score exactly 19) is called 'a cock's nist'.

Crapette

Or Cripette: See Spite and Malice.

Crash

See Brag.

Crazy Aces

And Crazy Eights: see Switch.

Cribbage

Add and match game: 2–4p, 52c

English national card game apparently derived from Noddy (q.v.) by the addition of the lay-away, box, or 'crib'—an invention traditionally ascribed to Sir John Suckling (1609–42). Considered royal and aristocratic until the mid-eighteenth century, it became a club game in the nineteenth and is nowadays mostly played in pubs. By the early twentieth century the old five-card game had been supplanted by the present six-card form described below. It is properly a two-hander, with variants for three or four. See also Costly Colours.

Two players use a 52-card pack ranking A 2 3 4 5 6 7 8 9 T J Q K. The aim is to be the first to score 121 over as many deals as necessary. Scores are best recorded by moving pegs round a Cribbage board ('pegging').

The deal. The player cutting the lower card deals first (Ace lowest), after which the deal alternates. Deal 6 cards each in 1s.

The discard. Each player discards two cards face down to form a 'crib' of four cards. Their aim in discarding is to keep a hand of four cards which form scoring combinations. The four-card crib eventually scores for combinations in favour of the dealer, but must not be looked at yet.

Combinations. The combinations and their scores are:

1. *Fifteen* (2): two or more cards totalling 15 in face value, counting Ace 1, numerals as marked, courts 10 each.
2. *Pair* (2): two cards of the same rank.
3. *Prial* (*pair royal*) (6): three of the same rank.

4. *Double pair royal* (12): four of the same rank.

5. *Run* (1 per card): three or more cards in ranking order.

6. *Flush*: Four cards of the same suit in one hand.

Starter. Non-dealer lifts the top half of the undealt pack, the dealer removes the top card of the bottom half and places it face up on top as the starter. If it is a Jack the dealer pegs 2 'for his heels', provided that he remembers to claim it before any card is played.

Play. Starting with non-dealer, each in turn plays a card face up to the table in front of himself and announces the total face value of all cards so far played by both.

A player making it exactly 15 pegs 1 point. Each must play if able to do so without going over 31. A player unable to do so says 'Go'. The other then adds as many more cards as possible without exceeding 31 and scores 1 for the go, or 2 for making 31 exactly. If any cards remain in hand, the cards played so far are turned face down, and the next in turn to play begins a new series. When one player runs out of cards, the other continues alone.

Points are also pegged for pairs and runs made by cards laid out successively in the play. A card matching the rank of the previous one played scores 2 for the pair; if the next played also matches, it scores 6; and the fourth, if it matches, 12.

If a card just played completes an uninterrupted run of three or more in conjunction with the cards just played, the run is scored at the rate of 1 per card.

Example. Abel plays 5, Baker 7, Abel 6 and pegs 3 for the run. If Baker then plays 4 or 8 he pegs 4. If he played 2 he would peg nothing, having broken the sequence; but Abel could then play 3 and re-form it for 6.

(Flushes are ignored in the play to 31. Some wrongly believe that runs also don't count in the two-hand game. They may be confused by the fact that a run is broken by the interruption of a paired card. For example, in the consecutive play of 6 7 7 8, the second Seven breaks the run, which therefore doesn't count.)

The show. Each player, starting with non-dealer, picks up his four hand cards and spreads them face up. Counting these and the starter as a five-card hand, he then scores for any and all combinations it may contain—fifteens, pairs, prials, runs, and flushes. A given card

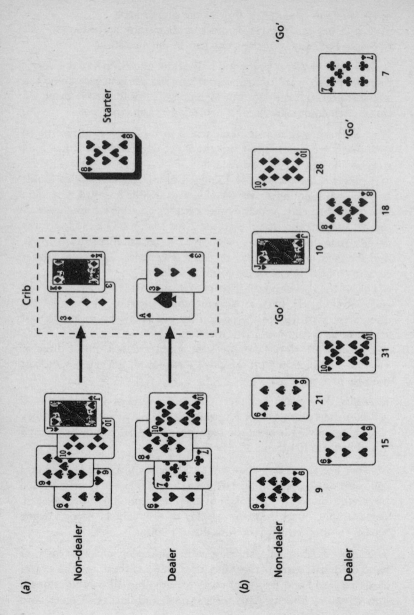

FIG. 11. Cribbage. (a) The players each discard two to the dealer's crib and a starter is turned from the pack. (b) How the hands might be played. (c) The score. Non-dealer pegged in play 2 for the second Six and 1 for a go; in hand fifteen 2 (6 + 9), 8 9 T J, and 1 for his nob (♥J), total 3 + 7 = 10. Dealer pegged in play fifteen 2, thirty-one 2, and 1 for the last go; in hand fifteen 2, fifteen 4 (for the Seven and each Eight), 2 for a pair (Eights), and 6 7 8 twice for 6; in the crib fifteen 2 (8 3 3 A) and a pair 2; total 5 + 12 + 4 = 21.

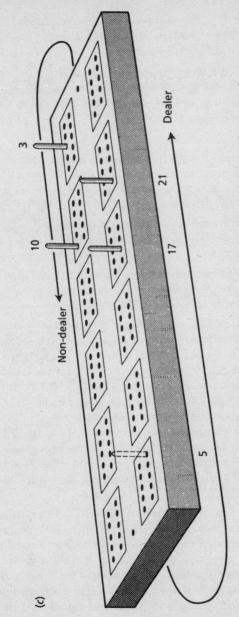

Fig. 11. Cribbage. (a) The players each discard two to the dealer's crib and a starter is turned from the pack. (b) How the hands might be played. (c) The score. Non-dealer pegged in play 2 for the second Six and 1 for a go; in hand fifteen 2 (6 + 9), 8 9 T J, and 1 for his nob (♥J), total 3 + 7 = 10. Dealer pegged in play fifteen 2, thirty-one 2, and 1 for the last go; in hand fifteen 2, fifteen 4 (for the Seven and each Eight), 2 for a pair (Eights), and 6 7 8 twice for 6; in the crib fifteen 2 (8 3 3 A) and a pair 2; total 5 + 12 + 4 = 21.

may be used in more than one combination. It may even be used more than once in the same combination, provided that at least one other associated card is different each time.

Example. ♠6 ♥7 ♣7 ♦8 ♠9 scores 2 for each distinct card combination counting 15 (♠6 ♠9, ♥7 ♦8, ♣7 ♦8) 2 for the pair of Sevens, and 4 for each run of four (♠6 ♥7 ♦8 ♠9, ♠6 ♣7 ♦8 ♠9). The score is announced thus: 'Fifteen 2, 4, 6; pair 8; fours 16'.

A flush in the hand counts 4, or 5 if its suit matches the starter's. A player holding the Jack of the same suit as the starter also pegs 1 'for his nob'. (If the starter is a Jack, neither player reckons for his nob, as it is overridden by the 2 'for his heels'.)

Counting the crib. Finally, dealer turns the crib face up and pegs for it as a five-card hand exactly as above, except that a flush only counts if all five are in suit.

Muggins. A player who notices that his opponent has failed to declare a scoring feature may point it out ('Muggins!') and peg it himself. This optional rule is nowadays often ignored.

Score. Play ceases the moment either player 'pegs out' by reaching the target score, no matter what stage of the game has been reached. If the loser has less than 91 he is whitewashed (or 'lurched', or 'in the lurch'), and loses a double game or an agreed additional stake. Also by agreement, game may be set at 61 (lurch 31) or 181 (lurch 121). It is customary to play for a fixed amount per game and on-the-spot side payments for extras such as dozens and nineteen in the box. 'Dozens' means a player gets, say, a penny for scoring 12 in hand or crib, two for 24, or three for 29, the highest possible. 'Nineteen in the box'—a crib worth nothing—is so called because 19 is the lowest count it is impossible to get in one hand (other impossibilities are 25, 26, 27).

Notes. Surprisingly, for so arithmetical an exercise, Crib yields less to calculation than to intuition born of experience. Skill consists largely in recognizing hands from previous experience and knowing automatically how best to play them, making it truly a game of speed and card-sense. In discarding, it is obviously the dealer's aim to lay to the crib cards best able to make scoring combinations, especially Fives, Tens or courts, and pairs, and equally the non-dealer's to discard unrelated and unpromising cards, especially two lying three or more ranks apart, in order to prevent a run. If in doubt, non-dealer should generally keep whichever four cards score highest for him, unless this gives the dealer a Five, a Ten or court, a fifteen, or a pair. A flush is relatively unimportant and can often be ignored. Keep hold of one if the four it counts is the best scoring feature available, but don't bother about a flush in the crib. In play, avoid starting with a Five, Ten, or court and avoid bringing the count to 21. A card below Five is a good lead, as the dealer cannot immediately fifteen it. At the other extreme, low cards are good for goes and thirty-ones.

Cribbage variants

Five-card. The original game, usually played up to 61. At start of play, non-dealer pegs '3 for last' as compensation for dealer's having the first crib. Deal 5 each, discard two. Play up to 31 once only: any unplayed cards remain unplayed. A flush in hand counts 3, or 4 with the starter. In the crib, only a 5-point flush counts.

Seven-card. Deal 7 each, discard two. Game is 181. Rarely played.

Auction Cribbage. (By Hubert Phillips.) Before the starter is turned (see note on starter above), each in turn, Dealer first, states how many points he will pay (deduct from his score) in return for the privilege of the crib. The higher bidder promptly subtracts that amount, and play proceeds as in any of the above games as if he were the normal dealer.

Three-hand (Cut-throat). Deal 5 cards each and 1 card face down to the crib, to which each then discards another one, making four in all. Player at dealer's left plays and counts his hand first; dealer plays and counts his hand and crib last. Each player scores for himself.

Three-hand (Solo). The dealer's two opponents play as a partnership. Deal 5 each and 6 to the dealer. The partners pass one card each to the dealer, who from his hand discards four to the crib. Play as above, except that each partner scores the total made by them both.

Four-hand (Partnership). Deal 5 each, discard one each to the crib. Player at Dealer's left has first lead and show. Pegging is done by

Cuckoo

Dealer's and leader's partners. Each partnership scores the amount made by both its members.

Cribbage Patience. Deal 16 cards face up to form a square of four rows and columns, placing each new card adjacent to any previous one. Turn the 17th up as a starter. Score for each row and column as for a five-card hand including the starter. Win if you make at least 61.

Cuckoo

Or Cuccù: see Chase the Ace.

Cucumber

Quasi-trick game: 3–8p, 52c

Called Gurka in Swedish and Ogórek in Polish, both meaning 'cucumber', this Baltic gambling game need not be taken too seriously, and can be played for a simple point-score.

From three to eight players contribute equal stakes to a pot and receive 6 cards, each dealt singly from a 52-card pack ranking 2 3 4 5 6 7 8 9 T J Q K A. The aim is to avoid being left with the highest card at end of play.

Eldest leads any card. Each in turn must play a card equal to or higher in rank than the previous card played, regardless of suit. Anyone unable to do so must play the lowest he has. Whoever plays the highest card—or the last played of equally highest—removes the 'trick' and leads any card to the next. When five tricks have been played, everyone reveals their last card. The player with the highest card (or each of tied players) scores penalty points equal to its face value, counting Ace 14, King 13, Queen 12, Jack 11, numerals as marked.

A player reaching 30 minus points is a 'cucumber' and drops out of play. He may buy himself back into the game for a new stake, but must restart with the same number of minus points as the player with the next highest total. No one may buy in more than once.

When only three players are left, buying in is barred, and play continues until one of them is sliced (or cucumbered). The pot then goes to the player with the lowest total.

Czech Rummy

Rummy game: 2–5p, 2 × 52c

A relative of Contract Rummy with an interesting twist, in that different players may have different initial meld requirements at the same time. A knowledge of basic Rummy is assumed.

The aim is to make melds in order to avoid being left with counting-cards in hand, which score against. Each player drops out of the game on reaching 300 penalty points, and the winner is the last one left.

The turn to deal and play passes to the left. Deal 12 cards each from a 108-card pack (2 × 52 plus Jokers). Stack the rest and turn the top card face up to start a wastepile. Each draws the top card of stock or wastepile, melds or lays off subject to the rules below, and discards one to the wastepile. It is forbidden to draw and discard the upcard on the same turn.

Cards count as follows: Joker 25, King 13, Queen 12, Jack 11, numerals face value. Ace counts 1 point and is always low, forming a sequence only with 2 3 . . . etc.

A meld is three or more cards of the same rank or in suit and sequence. A Joker represents any desired card. Each player's first meld must be worth a minimum amount. At start of play it is 15. In subsequent deals, the player with the highest penalty score must start with a meld of at least 15, the second highest with 20, the third with 25, and so on in increments of five. If two players have the same total, their requirement is the same, but the next increment is omitted.

Example. At the end of the first deal Abel counts 0 against, Baker 28, Charlotte 72, Dora 28. In round two Charlotte may start with a sequence worth at least 15 (e.g. A 2 3 4 5, 4 5 6). But Baker and Dora must meld at least 20 and Abel at least 30 to start.

Having made an initial meld, a player on subsequent turns may meld new sets or sequences of any value and lay off individual cards to any melds of his own. He may also take a Joker from any meld on the table in return for any card that leaves it legally intact.

Play ceases the moment someone plays or discards the last card from his hand. The others are then penalized by the face values of all cards left in hand, even if they form valid melds. There is no plus score for melds lying face up on the table.

Dealer's Choice

If the stock runs out, leave the upcard intact but shuffle the wastepile below it and turn it face down as a new stock.

Dealer's Choice

Method of playing Poker whereby the version played at each deal or round of deals is chosen by the current dealer.

Demon

Or Canfield: see Patience.

Don

Point-trick game: 4pp, 52c

A game of the All Fours family, generally called Nine-card Don, also Big Don, Long Don, Welsh Don. See also Phat.

Four players sitting crosswise in partnerships receive 9 cards each from a 52-card pack. The aim is to win counting cards in tricks. Game is 91 up, scores being pegged on a Cribbage board.

Cards rank and count as follows:

rank	in trumps	in plain suits
Ace	4	4
King	3	3
Queen	2	2
Jack	1	1
Ten	10	0
Nine	9	0
8-7-6	0 each	0 each
Five	10	0
4-3-2	0 each	0 each

Eldest leads. The suit he plays establishes trumps. Others must follow suit if possible, otherwise may play any card. The trick is taken by the highest card of the suit led or by the highest trump if any are played. Each trick-winner leads to the next.

During play, each side pegs immediately the value of any trump counters and Fives taken in tricks. After play, the side that took a majority of card-points (by the traditional count of each Ace 4, King 3, Queen 2, Jack 1, Ten 10) pegs an additional 8, but neither does so if equal. This makes the total peggable for the whole deal 52.

Doppelkopf

Point-trick game: 4p, 2 × 24c

A north German four-hand alliance game related to Skat. It is always played for hard score (coins or counters) and acknowledges no authoritative code of practice, being subject to a wide range of variant bids and elaboration. Beginners to point-trick games should approach it via Sueca and Schafkopf.

Cards. 48, a double 24-card pack with Nine low, as for Pinochle. All Queens, Jacks and diamonds are permanent trumps, ranking and counting from high to low as follows:

♣Q	♠Q	♥Q	♦Q	♣J	♠J	♥J	♦J	♦A	♦T	♦K	♦9
3	3	3	3	2	2	2	2	11	10	4	0

Plain suits rank and count Ace 11, Ten 10, King 4, Nine 0. Note that trumps account for half the pack (twenty-four cards), and that the total value of all counters is 240.

Start. Everyone starts with the same number—at least ten—of coins or gaming chips. The turn to deal and play passes to the left. Deal 12 cards each in 4s.

Aim. The holders of the two club Queens are secret partners, their partnership being discovered only from the play. Their object is to take at least 121 card-points in tricks.

Various options are open to a player dealt both club Queens. He may either seek someone with whom to take at least 121 card-points in partnership, or else play solo and aim to take at least 121 playing alone against the other three. Typically, he may:

1. Call for a partner by declaring a 'wedding' (*Hochzeit*). The first opponent to win a trick automatically becomes his partner. *Or*
2. Call for a partner by naming a card not in his own hand, typically a plain-suit Ace. Whoever first plays that card to a trick (there being two of them, remember) automatically becomes his partner. *Or*
3. Say nothing, and play a secret solo. *Or*

4. Declare a trump solo by naming as trumps a suit other than diamonds. In this case Queens and Jacks are still top trumps, followed by the eight cards of the nominated suit, but diamonds count as an ordinary plain suit.

Doubling. If a solo is announced, an opponent who thinks the contract will fail may double the amount being played for. The soloist, if confident he can win, may then redouble.

Play. Eldest leads first. Follow suit if possible, otherwise play any card. The trick is taken by the highest card of the suit led or by the highest trump if any are played. Of identical cards, the first played beats the second. Each trick-winner leads to the next.

Settlement. When two play two, each member of one partnership pays one member of the other. The amount paid depends on how many card-points they took between them—the fewer they took, the more they pay.

If the Queen partners win, they get 5 if the losers took no trick, 4 if they took less than 30, 3 if less than 60, 2 if less than 90, 1 if less than 120. (The method of announcing is 'No tricks, no 30, no 60, no 90, no 120, total five'; or, if they took (say) 58, 'No 60, no 90, no 120, total 3'; etc.)

If the Queen partners lose, the other side counts in the same way but with an extra point for playing 'against the Queens'. Thus, if they took only 89, the others would count 'No 90, no 120, against the Queens, three'. (Note that 120 is a loss for the Queen-players, even though announced as 'No 120'.)

Solo games are reckoned in the same way, except that if the three partners win they do not count an extra chip for playing against the Queens. If the soloist wins, each opponent pays him the relevant amount; if not, he pays that amount to each opponent.

Notes. In the orthodox game (as distinct from the 'free' game involving variants described below) the Queen-holders will quickly seek to find each other out by leading, playing, or inviting the play of a club Queen as soon as possible. If one of them has the opening lead, a trump Ace or Ten will serve this purpose while gaining some high card-points. Once partnerships are known, players will be alert to the possibility of 'fattening' tricks being won by their partners by throwing the high-counting Aces and Tens to them.

Variations. An advanced form of the game promotes certain cards to trumps ranking above the black Queens. The top two are the diamond Nines, referred to as Jokers. (If real Jokers are used, remove both diamond Nines from the pack.) These are followed by both heart Tens, called *die Tollen*, 'the loonies'. This has the curious effect of shortening the red plain suits and increasing trumps to twenty-eight. In play, it inhibits a black-Queen partner from discovering his ally by leading an Ace, as an opponent may now win the trick with a Joker (worth 0 card-points) or a loony (worth 10).

By agreement, an additional unit may be paid as between each partner and one opponent, or the soloist and each opponent, for

(*a*) capturing a trump Ace (a 'fox') played by an opponent;

(*b*) winning a *doppelkopf*—a trick consisting of four 'big 'uns' (Aces and Tens);

(*c*) winning the last trick with a club Jack (*Karlchen Müller*, or 'Charlie Miller').

Each of these is settled independently of winning or losing the main game.

Variant solo bids include a 'Jack solo', in which only Jacks are trumps and plain suits rank A T K Q 9, and a 'Queen solo', in which only Queens are trumps and plain suits rank A T K J 9. In the more off-beat solo bids it may be agreed to disregard Jokers and loonies, leaving those cards in their normal positions.

Draw Bridge

See Honeymoon Bridge.

Drinking games

Simple gambling games producing not a winner but a loser, whose penalty is to buy the next round of drinks. Many children's games, such as Cuckoo and Old Maid (q.v.) are old drinking games from which the drinking element has been removed.

Dudak

Going-out game: 2–4p, 32c

This Czech game, whose name means 'bagpipe', is related to Russia's Durak (q.v.) and Svoyi Koziri (q.v.), and said to be much played by children.

Four players (the best number) each receive 8 cards from a 32-card pack ranking A K Q J T 9 8 7 in each suit. The aim is to play out all one's cards. The last player left with cards in hand is the loser.

Eldest starts by playing any card face up to the table to start a wastepile. Each in turn thereafter may, if possible, play two cards to the wastepile. The first must be a higher card of the same suit as the top card of the pile, and the second may then be any card at all.

A player unable or unwilling to beat the top card must take it and add it to his own hand, and must keep doing so until he uncovers a card which he is able and willing to beat. He does so, adds any second card, and play continues as before. If, however, he thereby takes the whole pile, his turn ends, and the next in turn starts a new pile with a single card.

The game gets interesting when trumps are declared. Any player, on his turn to play, may announce any suit and say 'That's my trump'. Thereafter, the first of his two discards must be either a higher one of the same suit as the top card, or any card of his personal trump suit. Typically, each player will choose a different suit; however, it is allowed, and can be tactically interesting, for two or more players to choose the same trump.

A player who has once declared a trump is subject to the following rules. First, he may not cancel or change his suit for the rest of the game. Second, whenever he finds himself unable or unwilling to beat the top card, he may not remove cards one by one but must take the whole pile into hand. A new one is then started with a single card by the next in turn to play.

When a player plays his last card to the pile, he drops out of play, and the others continue from the next in turn. If the player who went out did so by playing two cards, play continues exactly as before. If, however, he had only one card at the start of his last turn, and so went out by beating the top card, then the current wastepile is turned face down and put to one side. The next in turn then starts a new wastepile by playing one card only, and play continues as before.

The overall winner is the one who loses fewest of an agreed number of games. Alternatively, it is the one who has not lost a game when everyone else has lost at least one.

Lacking rules for fewer players, I suggest three receive 10 each from a 30-card pack made by removing the black Sevens, and two 12 each from a 24-card pack with Nine low.

Durak

Going-out game: 2p, 36c

A popular Russian game related to Dudak and Svoyi Koziri. Other relatives are played throughout Eastern Europe and Scandinavia. The two-hand version runs as follows.

Deal 6 cards each, in 3s, from a 36-card pack ranking A K Q J T 9 8 7 6. Stack the rest face down, then turn the top card for trumps and slip it under the pack, face up and half exposed.

A game consists of several bouts, each followed by a draw of fresh cards if necessary. The aim is be first out of cards when the stock is exhausted. The loser is *durak* — 'a fool'.

In each bout, one player attacks and the other defends. Non-dealer attacks first; thereafter, the winner of each bout attacks in the next. Each bout proceeds as follows:

Attacker leads any card. Defender must respond with a higher card of the same suit, or any trump if a non-trump was led. Attacker continues with any card of the same *rank* as either of the first two, and, again, defender plays higher or trumps. This continues till all twelve cards are played, or one player can't or won't make a legal continuation. Note that the two follow different requirements: the attacker's lead must always match the rank of any card so far showing, the defender's reply must always be higher in suit or a trump.

If all cards are played out, the attacker draws six cards from stock, waits for the defender to do likewise, then starts a new bout with any desired lead.

But a bout more commonly ends because one player fails to play the next card. If the attacker fails, he concedes the bout by turning the played cards face down and pushing them to one side, where they remain out of play for the rest of the game. He then becomes the defender in the next bout.

If the defender fails, he does so by gathering up all cards so far played to the bout and adding them to his hand. He will continue to defend in the next bout.

Before the next bout begins, each player (starting with the attacker) must, if necessary and if he can, restore his hand to six cards by drawing from stock. The last card drawn from stock will be the turned trump, after which play continues without further drawing until one player goes out.

Dutch Whist

Plain-trick game: 3–4p, 52c

Light-hearted Whist variant with a different rule of play on each deal. The three-hander is called Bismarck. Both are subject to variation.

Four players, in two partnerships, receive 13 cards each from a 52-card pack ranking A K Q J T 9 8 7 6 5 4 3 2.

First deal. The last card is turned for trump. The side taking most tricks scores 1 point per trick taken above six.

Second deal. No card is turned, and the game is played at no trump.

Third deal. No card is turned, and eldest hand announces trumps on his opening lead.

Fourth deal. Trumps are established by cutting the pack before the deal.

Bismarck

Three players each deal four times in succession, making twelve deals in all. Dealer takes the top four cards himself, then deals 16 cards to each player one at a time (including himself), then discards any four unwanted cards from his own hand.

First deal. Play at no trump. Dealer scores 8 less than the number of tricks he took, and each opponent 4 less.

Second deal. As before, but with a trump selected by cutting the pack before dealing.

Third deal. As before, but with trumps announced by the dealer before Eldest leads.

Fourth deal: misère. No trump; aim to lose tricks. Dealer scores 4 less the number of tricks he took, each opponent 6 less the number he took.

Earl of Coventry

See Snip-Snap-Snorem.

Écarté

Plain-trick game: 2p, 32c

Fast, skilful, classic two-hander derived from fifteenth-century Triomphe or 'French Ruff'. Much played in nineteenth-century clubs and casinos but now restricted to connoisseurs.

Two players each receive 5 cards (3 + 2) from a 32-card pack ranking K Q J A T 9 8 7. The next is turned for trump and placed under the stock. If it is a King, Younger (Dealer) scores a point. The aim is to win at least three of the five tricks played, using the turned suit as trump.

Players may draw fresh cards to improve their hands before starting, provided that both agree to do so. Elder, first, must either lead to the first trick or 'propose' (an exchange of cards). If he proposes, Younger either accepts the proposal, or refuses it by saying 'Play'.

If the proposal is accepted, each in turn, starting with Elder, discards at least one and up to five cards and is dealt the same number from the stock. Elder then again either leads or proposes; and so on until either bars the exchange.

Note. The trump turn-up may not be taken, and neither player may call for more cards than remain face down. When five or fewer remain, Elder may call for them all. If no cards remain to draw, the player who should have drawn is obliged to play.

The holder of the King of trumps may show it and score 1 point, but must do so before playing to the first trick.

. Elder leads first and the winner of each trick leads to the next. The

Elder **Younger**

(a) Proposes . . . accepts

(b) Proposes . . . accepts

(c) Plays . . . wins !

FIG. 12. Écarté. (*a*) With diamonds trump, neither player is willing to play as dealt. 'X' marks their respective discards. (*b*) A second round of discarding is agreed. (*c*) Elder chances his arm with two trumps and two Kings, but, in the event, cannot by any play beat Younger's three trumps and one King.

other must follow suit if possible, win the trick if possible, and trump if unable to follow.

Score 1 point for taking three or four tricks, or 2 for the vole (all five). If no cards were exchanged, and the refuser loses, the other scores 2 invariably.

The game is five points, and is not played out if this is reached by scoring 1 for the King. By agreement, the game counts double if the loser scores less than 3, treble if he scores none.

Optional rule. Traditionally, the leader to a trick announces the suit he is leading. If he announces it wrong, the other may demand that it be withdrawn and a card of the announced suit played, if possible, or else may play to the suit led exactly as if it were the suit announced.

Notes. Experience tells, both in judging when and when not to exchange, and in playing the hand. 'Strict' rules of following are not as restrictive as they sound: they release valuable information as to the lie of cards, and give the leader to a trick considerable control over subsequent play. A hand is normally playable if it contains three or more power factors, a power factor being a trump, a King, a guarded Queen, or a good three-card plain suit. It usually helps to lead the longest plain suit in order to draw trumps.

Eights

See Switch.

Eleusis

Going-out game: 3–8p, 52c

Invented around 1960 by American gamesman Bob Abbott, Eleusis could be described as a simulation of the type of inductive thinking which underlies scientific investigation and hypothesizing. Fortunately, it is also fun to play. The latest version of Eleusis can be found at its inventor's web site http://www.logicmazes.com/games/index.htm.

Remove from the 52-card pack a number of cards related to the number of players as follows: three players 1, four 0, five 3, six 1, seven 3, eight 2. The cards omitted should be of different ranks and suits.

A game consists of as many rounds as there are players, each in turn acting as the umpire. The umpire deals all the cards around evenly until only one remains, which he places face up on the table as a starter.

The aim is to be the first to play off all one's cards to a sequence following on from the starter in accordance with a particular rule of matching. The rule of matching differs from deal to deal, being invented in each case by the umpire before play begins. The primary object, therefore, is to discover the umpire's rule of following. This is done by formulating and testing hypotheses as to what the rule might be, by observing the results, and by drawing inferences from them. The umpire's object is to devise a rule that is neither too easy nor to hard to deduce, since his score is based on how many players succeed in discovering the rule and how fast they do so.

A typical elementary rule is: 'If the last card is red, the next card played must be an even number; if black, the next must be odd.' (It is an invariable rule that, where face values are significant, Ace = 1, Jack = 11, Queen = 12, King = 13.)

Each in turn, starting with Eldest, plays a card to the sequence. If it properly follows the previous card in accordance with the umpire's rule, he says 'Right' and it is the next one's turn to play. If not, he says 'Wrong', and the player retrieves his card and places it face up in a reject pile in front of himself. The cards of this pile, as it builds up, must be spread slightly so that all are identifiable, and must be kept in order so that players can see exactly which cards did not follow the rule at which point in the sequence. On subsequent turns cards must be played from the hand, not from the reject pile. Players may not pass, even if they think the card they play will be wrong.

Phase 1 ends when no one has any cards left in hand. At this point the umpire scores as follows. Whoever has the fewest reject cards before him is called the leading player. (If two have the same number, choose either one of them.) The umpire's score is the number of reject cards made by the leading player, multiplied by the number of other players in the game, and subtracted from the total number of rejects in front of all players other than the leading one.

Example. Suppose there are four players other than the umpire, and their rejects are

$$A \quad B \quad C \quad D$$
$$4 \quad 7 \quad 8 \quad 4$$

Call A or D the leading player. The umpire scores $(7 + 4 + 8) - (3 \times 4) = 7$.

Phase 2 is played like Phase 1, except that cards are played directly from the reject piles, and, if rejected again, are simply put back. None are turned face down or taken into hand. Players need no longer keep their rejects in any particular order, but may rearrange them in whatever way they find most helpful. It is not permitted to attempt to play the same reject twice in succession to

What next?

FIG. 13. **Eleusis.** The secret rule by which one card legally follows another in sequence renders only one card playable from this five-card hand. Which? (See end of Appendix for solution.)

the same sequence card (no one else having successfully placed a card since the previous turn).

Play continues until (*a*) one player has played his last card to the sequence or (*b*) the umpire can see that no more cards are legally playable, in which case he must call a halt.

Each player now gets a score found by multiplying the number of rejects he has left by the number of other players, and subtracting this from the total number of rejects remaining before the other players. A 6-point bonus goes to the player who went out first, or, if no one did, to the player left with the fewest rejects. If tied, it is divided between them. Minus scores are rounded up to zero.

Example.

  A (2 left) scores $(3 + 5 + 0) - (3 \times 2) = 2$
  B (3 left) scores $(2 + 5 + 0) - (3 \times 3) = -2$, call it 0
  C (5 left) scores $(2 + 3 + 0) - (3 \times 5) = -10$, call it 0
  D (0 left) scores $(2 + 3 + 5) - (3 \times 0) = 10$, plus 6 bonus = 16.

If a rule is not meaningful until two or more cards are down (for example, 'If the two previous cards are the same colour, play a face card, otherwise a numeral'), any cards played before it takes effect must be accepted.

Elfern

The rule must be one which, on average, and certainly to start with, would give a card played at random at least a one-fifth chance of being acceptable. (This is the inventor's rule. I strongly recommend adding the words 'or unacceptable', remembering the experience of my wife's brilliantly sabotaging a game by permitting every second card played to be anything you like.)

Beginners should keep rules simple to start with. It is fatally easy to be too clever too soon. If you play regularly, it is worth keeping a notebook of rules devised and their relative success rate.

Elfern

Simple trick-play: 2p, 32c

An old German card game suitable for children and beginners, especially those intending to graduate to Bezique. Elfern means 'making elevens'. Its alternative title, Figurenspiel, means 'the honours game'. See also Bohemian Schneider.

Deal 6 each from a 32-card pack ranking A K Q J T 9 8 7 and turn the rest face down as a stock. The aim is to capture, in tricks, at least 11 of the 20 honours, namely, all Aces, Kings, Queens, Jacks, and Tens.

Eldest leads first. Suit need not be followed. The higher card of the suit led wins the trick. The trick-winner draws the next card from stock, waits for the other to draw, and leads to the next.

When no cards remain in stock, suit must be followed if possible in the play of the last six tricks. Count a single win for taking eleven to fourteen honours, double for fifteen to nineteen, treble for all twenty.

Variant. Before play, the top card of the stock is turned to establish a trump suit, and is slipped under the pack so as to be taken by the loser of the sixth trick. A trick can then be taken by the higher trump if any are played. In the last six tricks, a player unable to follow suit must trump if possible.

Elimination games

See Going-out games.

Enflé

See Rolling Stone.

Epsom

Stops game: 3–6p, 52c

A relative of Newmarket, as suggested by the hint of turf in its title.

Prepare a staking layout consisting of an Ace, King, Queen, and Jack from another pack, or a piece of paper so marked. These are called 'boodle' cards.

Deal the same number of cards to each player, as many as will go round, leaving any remainder face down, out of play.

Each player, after examining his hand, stakes five counters: one for 'game', the other four distributed as he pleases amongst the boodle cards. The aim is to play the fourth Ace, King, Queen, or Jack, and to be the first out of cards.

Eldest starts by choosing any suit and playing face up to the table the lowest card he has of that suit. This starts a sequence which will be made face up and slightly spread so that all its cards are visible. Each in turn thereafter must play *either* the next higher card of the same suit *or* a card of the same rank as any card already played. A card of matching rank does not start a new sequence: it merely interrupts the main sequence.

Example. The sequence starts ♥3, ♥4, ♣3. The next required card of the sequence is not ♣4 but ♥5, though any 3 or 4 may be played instead.

A player may only pass if unable to do either. The turn then passes to his left.

Whenever the fourth card of a given rank is played, the four are set aside face down and its player may start a new sequence, again from any suit, but again with the lowest he holds of it. If the fourth card is a Jack, Queen, King, or Ace, he wins the counters from the corresponding boodle card.

Play ceases when one player has played his last card. He thereby wins the stakes for 'game' and all remaining on the boodle cards.

Euchre

Plain-trick game: 4–6p, 24–32c

Euchre, the game responsible for introducing the Joker into modern packs, started life as Juckerspiel, a late eighteenth-century Alsatian derivative of Triomphe. It spread widely during the Napoleonic era, eventually becoming the great social card game of nineteenth-century America and Australia, rivalling in popularity the more upmarket Whist. Nowadays it is still much played in the south and west of England, especially Cornwall. The Joker was invented around 1860 to act as the top trump or 'Best Bower' (from German *Bauer*, 'farmer', denoting also the Jack at cards). Though constant in essentials, the game is played in many different formats for various numbers of players, and exhibits a bewildering range of superficial variations. The modern partnership game for four, which follows, differs from the classical textbook game in reducing the pack from 32 to 24 cards. See also Five Hundred.

Partners sit crosswise, and the deal and turn to play pass always to the left. A game is played up to five, seven, or ten game-points, as agreed, over as many deals as it takes.

Deal 5 each, in batches of 3 and 2, from a 24-card pack ranking A K Q J T 9 (except in trumps). Place the odd four face down to one side, with the top one faced to show a preferred trump suit.

In trumps, cards rank as follows:

1. Jack of trumps, or Right Bower,
2. Other Jack of same colour as trumps, or Left Bower,

followed by A K Q T 9. Note that this gives seven in trumps, five in the suit of the same colour, and six in each other plain suit.

Auction. There is an auction to determine which side will contract to win a majority of tricks (three or more) in exchange for choosing trumps. A bidder who thinks he can take three or more from his own hand may offer to play 'alone'.

Each in turn, starting with Eldest, must either pass or accept the turned suit as trump. (Eldest accepts by saying 'I order it up', adding 'alone', if applicable. Second hand says 'I assist' if he intends his partner to participate, otherwise 'I play alone'. Third hand and dealer may 'order it up', adding 'alone' if applicable.) As soon as a bid is made, the auction ends.

If the turned suit is ordered up, Dealer may exercise the privilege of taking the turn-up into his hand in exchange for any face-down discard (unless, of course, his partner is playing alone).

If all pass, the turn-up is turned down and a second round of bidding follows. Each in turn may now pass, or, if the previous player passed, offer another suit as trump. (Choosing the other suit of the same colour is to 'make it next'; choosing either of the other two is to 'cross it'.) As before, a bidder may offer to play alone.

The auction ends when someone bids or all four pass. If a bid is made, the dealer may not exchange a card, as there is no turn-up. If all four pass, the cards are thrown in and a new deal made by the next in turn to deal.

Play. In a lone bid, the loner's partner lays his cards face down before the opening lead, which is made by the player at loner's immediate left. Otherwise, the opening lead is made by Eldest hand. Follow suit if possible, otherwise play any card. The trick is taken by the highest card of the suit led or by the highest trump if any are played. The winner of each trick leads to the next.

Score. If successful, the contracting side scores 1 point, or 2 for the 'march' (all five tricks), or 4 for the march if played alone. If not, they are 'euchred', and the other side scores 2.

Optional Joker. A Joker may be added. It is called the Best Bower and ranks as the highest trump. In England, its place is taken by the ♠2, or 'Benny'.

Notes. Euchre is a game of skill, especially in the bidding, where decision-making is governed more by the state of the score than the constitution of one's hand, unless, of course, it is a self-evident loner. The first two should only 'order it up' if fairly confident of winning three tricks alone and not holding an outstandingly better trump for the second round of bidding. Third and fourth hands need even more confidence, since their partners have already suggested weakness. The advantage of the dealer's side—that Dealer can void a suit by the exchange and may therefore win an extra trick by trumping—is slightly offset by the fact that Eldest has the opening lead. In the second round of bidding it is normally expected that Eldest will make it next and Dealer's partner cross it, for reasons that will become obvious in practical play. Neither third hand nor Dealer should bid in the second round unless strong enough to play alone. Any of these general rules may be negated by the state of the score. For example, if Dealer's side needs 3 or 4 points for game and the other is 'at the bridge' (needing only 1), Eldest should almost invariably order it up. This prevents the other side from playing to win on a lone hand, restricts them to a 2-point win for a euchre if the contract fails, and wins the game if it succeeds.

The many varieties of Euchre developed in its American heyday — Two-handed, Three-handed, Auction Euchre, Blind Euchre, Railroad Euchre, etc. — are virtually obsolete but easily reinvented if required. Still worth retaining are Bid Euchre, now called Five Hundred (q.v.), and the following:

Call-Ace Euchre

Four, five, or six players use 24, 28, or 32 cards respectively (no Joker). Play as above, except that, before the first trick, the bidder names a suit other than trumps. The holder of the Ace of that suit thereby becomes the bidder's partner for that deal, sharing in any gain or loss he makes, but may not reveal himself except by the play. If the called Ace is in the bidder's own hand, he is in effect playing alone, but no-one else knows this. (If it is one of the undealt cards, he will not know it himself.)

Hasenpfeffer

Four-player partnership game using 24 cards plus Joker. Deal 6 each in 3s and lay the last face down to one side. Each in turn bids, without yet naming a trump suit, by stating how many tricks he undertakes to win with the aid of his partner. Each bid must be higher than the last. If no-one bids, the holder of the Best Bower is obliged to bid 'three', and if it then proves to be the card out of play, the deal is annulled. The highest bidder announces trumps before play. The bidder's side scores 1 point per trick won if this is not less than the bid, otherwise it loses 1 point per undertrick. Play up to 10 points. (American rules differ. In particular, they allow the bidder, just before play, to take the undealt card and make any discard face down in its place. This misses the point of the game.)

Faro

Casino game: Np, 52c

Or Pharaoh: the most widespread Western gambling game of the eighteenth and nineteenth centuries. There was a staking layout of 13 cards, punters bet on individual ranks to win or lose, and the outcome was basically determined by the banker's dealing cards alternately to a winning and losing pile. When only three cards remained, players could bet on the order in which they would appear.

Fifty-One

Adding-up game: 2–4p, 32c

A Central European game, like most of its type.

Deal 5 each from a 32-card pack and turn the next face up to start the count. Cards count as follows:

A	K	Q	J	T	9	8	7
1	4	3	2	−1	0	8	7

Each in turn plays a card face up to the table and announces the total value of all cards so far played, including the starter. Whoever raises the total above 50 is the loser.

Fildinski

See Bezique.

Fishing games

Four or so cards lie face upwards in a 'pool', and players try to capture one or more at a time by matching them with cards played from the hand. Cards that make no capture are simply added to the pool. There is usually a bonus for capturing all the pool cards in one sweep. Games of this type are common in China, where they are generically referred to as 'Fishing'. Western games of the family are played mainly in Italy and the Balkans. See Cassino, Pishti, Scopa, Scopone, Tablanette, Zwicker.

Five Hundred

Plain-trick game: 3–6p, 33–63c

Five Hundred was devised in America shortly before 1900 as a form of Euchre incorporating the basic principles of Bridge. Contract Bridge subsequently drove it out of favour in America, but it has since become the national card game of Australia. Australian '500' packs contain 63 cards, extended from 52 by the addition of a Joker, Elevens and Twelves in each suit, and two Thirteens (red suits). The full pack is only required for six players, however, and is stripped of various low cards for varying numbers of players, the basic principle being that there should be just enough for ten cards per player and three left over (or two if the Joker is omitted). Though usually played by four in partnerships, it is excellent for three or five.

Players. Three to six. Four and six play in partnerships, the latter in either two partnerships of three (sitting A B A B A B) or three of two (sitting A B C A B C).

Cards. Joker optional, plus,

if two play, 24 cards (A K Q J T 9);
if three, 32 cards (A K Q J T 9 8 7);
if four, 42 (A K Q J T 9 8 7 6 5 and red Fours);
if five, standard 52-card pack;
if six, full 62-card pack.

The basic ranking is A K Q (J) T 9 8 7 6 5 4, but top three trumps are:

1. Best Bower (Joker)
2. Right Bower (Jack of trumps)
3. Left Bower (other Jack of same colour),

followed by Ace (etc.) down.

Structure. Play ceases when one player or partnership reaches either 500 or *minus* 500 points over as many deals as necessary, the winner(s) being the player or side with the highest plus score. The deal and play pass always to the left.

Deal. Ten each, in batches of 3 4 3, with a 'kitty' of three dealt face down to the table immediately before the batch of four. (If two play, the Joker is omitted and the kitty contains four cards.)

Bidding. Each in turn, starting at Dealer's left, either passes or names a contract with a higher value than the preceding one. A player may not rebid having once passed. The contract states a proposed trump and the minimum number of tricks the bidder offers to win either alone (if three play), in partnership (four or six players), or with or without the aid of a temporary partner (five players). It may be named by suit and number (e.g. 'Six spades', the lowest possible bid) or by game value ('40', etc.), according to the following schedule:

Trump	Six	Seven	Eight	Nine	Ten
Spades	40	140	240	340	440
Clubs	60	160	260	360	460
Diamonds	80	180	280	380	480
Hearts	100	200	300	400	500
No trump	120	220	320	420	520

Misère (no trump, lose every trick): 250
Open misère (same, cards exposed): 520

Misère is overcalled by any bid of eight or more tricks; open misère overcalls everything.

The highest bidder becomes the declarer. If all pass without bidding, tricks are played at no trump and scored to the players or partnerships winning them.

The kitty. Declarer takes the kitty in hand and makes any three discards face down before play. If all passed, the kitty remains untouched.

Calling a partner. If five play, declarer either announces that he will 'go alone', or calls for a partner (except in misère) by naming any non-trump card lacking from his hand. The holder of that card immediately identifies himself.

Play. Declarer leads first, or, if everyone passed, the player at Dealer's left. (At open misère, the hand is spread face up before the opening lead.) Normal rules of trick-taking apply. The Joker is the highest card of the trump suit. At no trump, it is the only trump, and may be used to win the trick when its holder cannot follow suit to the card led. If led, its holder calls for a suit to be played to it, which may not be one in which he has already renounced.

Score. For a won contract, the bidding player or partnership (or, five-handed, each member of the temporary partnership) scores the value of the contract. There is no credit for overtricks, but winning all ten scores 250 if the contract value was less. For a lost contract, the declarer or declaring partnership deducts the contract value from their score. Whether won or lost, each opponent or opposing partnership scores 10 points per won trick. (At misère, they score 10 per trick taken by the declarer. Misères must therefore be played right through.) If no bid was made, each player or partnership scores 10 points per trick won individually. If two or more players or partnerships reach 500+ on the same deal, the declaring side wins.

Variants. Rules vary slightly from circle to circle. The Joker is often omitted in serious play, especially four-handed. In the original game, each player could make only one bid, and had therefore to bid the maximum immediately. This rule has been largely dropped from modern Australian play.

Forty-Five

See Spoil Five.

Four Jacks, The

See Polignac.

French Ruff

English name for Triomphe, the forerunner of Écarté (q.v.).

French Whist

See Catch the Ten.

Frog

See Six-Bid Solo.

Gaigel
Point-tricks and melds: 3–4p, 2 × 24c

A multi-player extension of Sixty-Six, much played in Württemberg, sometimes by three but mainly by four in partnerships. Described below is the core of the German game, from which the form described in American books ultimately derives. The modern versions lack an official standard and are subject to many local variations and extras.

Use two 24-card packs shuffled together, each consisting of Ace, King, Queen, Jack, Ten, Seven. (Gaigel was originally played with 32-card packs containing Eights and Nines. When it was speeded up by the suppression of worthless ranks, Sevens were kept because they have a significant role to play. But Nines will do if it is more convenient to use a Pinochle pack.)

Four players sit crosswise in partnerships. The turn to deal and play passes always to the right. The winning side is the first to claim (correctly) that it has reached 101 points, which usually happens before all cards have been played out. Points are scored for capturing counting-cards in tricks and for declaring marriages.

Cards rank and count as follows:

A   T   K   Q   J   7 (or 9)

11   10   4   3   2   0

Deal 5 each in batches of 3 and 2. Turn the next face up to establish trumps, and stack the rest face down partly covering it.

Eldest leads first. So long as cards remain in stock there is no need to follow suit: any played card is legal, and may not be withdrawn. When the stock is empty, the rules change: each in turn must, if possible, (a) follow suit, (b) head the trick, and (c) trump (and overtrump) if unable to follow suit.

A trick is taken by the highest card of the suit led, by the highest trump if any are played, or by the first played of two identical winning cards. Players must remember the cumulative value of counters their side has won in tricks, as it is not permissible to keep a written or mechanical tally.

The winner of a trick draws the top card of stock and adds it to his hand, waits for the others in turn do likewise, then leads to the next.

Upon playing to a trick, any player, provided that his side has taken at least one trick, may declare a marriage—King and Queen of the same suit—if he has one. This adds 20 to his side's count, or 40 if in trumps. Both cards must be shown, and one of them played. The rule about having first won a trick is relaxed to the extent that the marriage may be declared in the qualifying trick. (*Example*: The leader's side has not yet won a trick. Trump Ace is led. As this is bound to win, leader's partner may declare a marriage upon playing to it. The same principle may be extended to any other certain trick.) No player may declare more than one marriage in the same deal. A note may be kept of declared marriages to avoid argument.

A player holding a trump Seven ('*dix*') may 'rob the pack' by exchanging it for the turn-up. He may do so at any time, provided that his side has won at least one trick, and that cards still remain in stock. Alternatively, he may place his Seven under the turn-up, thus leaving it for his partner to take in case he should have the other Seven. In this event, his partner may either take the turn-up and give his partner the Seven, or keep the Seven and invite his partner to take the turn-up. The other side may not take the turn-up, and, if anyone plays the other Seven to a trick, the player who first declared it may promptly take the turn-up to restore his hand to the correct number. This must be done before the last draw of cards, and if the last draw includes a *dix* it may not be exchanged.

Play ceases when any player claims that his side has reached or exceeded 101 in counters and marriages, or that the other side has done so and failed to claim before leading to the next trick. If correct, his side wins a single game, or a double if the other has not yet won a trick. (Even if they were about to win the trick in which the winning side reached 101 by declaring a marriage.) If incorrect, the other side wins a double game, or *gaigel*. (Incorrectly claiming a win is called 'overgaigling', and incorrectly failing to do so 'undergaigling'.)

Elaborations. The above account, from Claus D. Grupp, *Schafkopf, Doppelkopf* (Wiesbaden, 1976), is of a version played in Remstal, which also includes the following local elaborations.

1. By agreement, the first trick in each deal (and *only* the first) is played as follows. If eldest leads a non-trump Ace, the opponents refrain from trumping, and his partner throws him a high-

counting card. Alternatively, he may 'dive', i.e. lead any non-trump card face down. The others also play face down; the played cards are faced; and the trick is taken by the highest card of the suit led, trumps being powerless. If he 'dives' one of two identical Aces, he must say 'Double Ace', and it takes the trick. On diving an unpaired non-trump Ace he says 'Single Ace'. If then its twin is also played, the latter takes the trick.

2. A player holding five Sevens, whether dealt or drawn, shows them and thereby wins for his side without further play. The same may be applied for holding five cards of the same suit.

3. An extension of the above is that a player holding four Sevens, or four of a suit, and waiting for the fifth, must announce 'I'm on Sevens' or 'I'm on a flush'. In this case, so long as cards remain in stock, he is not permitted to win a trick. Whatever he plays counts as a plain-suit Seven, even if it happens to be the Ace of trumps!

4. Some circles play with 'winking'—that is, conventional signals, such as nods, winks, and grimaces, to indicate to a partner the holding of certain cards or suits. Winks must be common and intelligible to both sides, the aim being to make them without being spotted by an opponent.

Gambling games

All games are gambling games in the sense that they may be used as a determinant of winning and losing money between players, and that bystanders may wager on the outcome. (See banking and casino games.) Some are technical gambling games in the sense that they cannot be played for a notional point-score but only for a 'hard score' of cash, or its equivalent in chips or counters. (See Vying games. In Poker, to take an extreme case, money, not cards, is the actual implement of play.) Others are 'gambles' in that their outcome is determined more by chance than by the application of skill—many children's games are gambling games at root. All card games reflect an origin in gambling games, but by definition are not gambling games if not played for money. Obviously, the deeper and more strategic the game, the more interest attaches to the play than to the outcome, and the less likely it is to be played for money.

German Solo

Plain-trick game: 4p, 32c

This classic German game, though defunct since the nineteenth century, makes a good introduction to Hombre, of which it is a tidy simplification. It also bears interesting resemblances to English Solo.

Solo is a hard-score game, using coins or counters. Play goes to the left.

Deal 8 cards each in batches of 3 2 3 from a 32-card pack basically ranking A K Q J T 9 8 7. Trumps, however, when established, rank

1. ♣Q (*spadille*)
2. Seven of trumps (*manille*)
3. ♠Q (*basta*)

followed by Ace, King, Queen (if a red suit is trump), Jack, Ten, Nine, Eight. Trumps therefore number nine if black, ten if red, while plain suits contain seven in black and eight in red.

There is a round of bidding to establish who will undertake to win five or more tricks, alone or with the aid of a partner, in return for naming trumps. A player dealt both black Queens is obliged to bid at least 'grand'. From lowest to highest, the bids are:

1. Call (*Frage*): The bidder will name trumps and call, as his partner, the holder of a card lacking from his own hand, usually an Ace.
2. Grand (*Großfrage*): The bidder, holding both black Queens, calls a partner, as above, but leaves the partner to name trumps.
3. Solo: The bidder, whether or not holding black Queens, announces trumps and goes for a five-trick solo.
4. Slam declared: As solo, but the bidder undertakes to win all eight tricks.

The auction goes as follows. Eldest says 'Pass' or names a bid. If he names a bid, the next in turn may name a higher bid, which the first player must either undertake himself or else pass. This continues until one of them passes, whereupon the next in turn may name the next higher bid, and so on. If everyone passes, the holder of *spadille* is obliged to 'call'.

If the contract is a Call, the caller says, for example, 'Spades trump; call the Ace of hearts'. (He may not call a trump.) The holder of the Ace of hearts thus becomes his partner, and leads to the first trick.

In a Grand, the holder of the called card himself announces trumps and leads to the first trick.

In a solo or declared slam, the soloist announces trumps and leads first.

It is obligatory to follow suit and head the trick, if possible, and to trump if unable to follow suit. The winner of each trick leads to the next.

If the soloist or contracting side wins the first five tricks straight off, they must either stop or else go for the slam. Leading to the sixth trick is automatically a slam bid, and if all eight are not then made, the whole contract is lost. (If, of course, the soloist declared a slam to start with, he may not stop at five.)

The suit of the first deal becomes the preferred trump for the rest of the session. In subsequent deals, a given bid is overcalled by the same bid 'in best', that is, in the preferred suit.

The pay-offs are Call 2, Grand 4, Solo 4, Slam 8, Declared Slam 16. These are doubled if the preferred suit was trump (except in the first deal). The stated amount is paid by each partner of the losing side to one partner of the winning side, or as between the soloist and each opponent as the case may be.

German Tarock

See Bavarian Tarock.

German Whist

Plain-trick game: 2p, 52c

Whist for two. But why 'German'?

Deal 13 cards each, stack the rest face down and turn the top card to determine trumps. Non-dealer leads first. Follow suit if possible, otherwise play any card. The winner of each trick draws the top card of stock, waits for his opponent to draw the card beneath, then turns the new top card of stock face up before leading to the next. This does not change trumps, but it may influence strategy, in that both know what card will be drawn by the winner of a trick, but only the drawer of the card beneath can see what he has got. When the stock is exhausted, continue play until all twenty-six tricks have been won.

The winner is the player taking a majority of the twenty-six tricks, or, if preferred, of the last thirteen tricks only. Better still, the first thirteen tricks score one point each and the last thirteen two each. Alternatively, it is the player who *loses* the majority of the last thirteen tricks.

Other variations are easily invented. As it is impossible in the first half of the game to police the obligation to follow suit, the following may be preferred. After dealing, turn the top card for eventual trumps and slip it half under the stock, then turn the next card of stock as before. Play the first half at no trump, without obligation to follow suit, then play the second half with trumps and obligation to follow.

Gin

Rummy game: 2p, 52c

A development of Conquian (q.v.) devised early in the twentieth century but achieving maximum popularity in the 1930s and 1940s, especially in Hollywood. There are numerous variations on the basic game, which is further confused by the fact that many people nowadays ignorantly refer to almost any form of Rummy as 'Gin' Rummy whether it is Gin or not. Real Gin is only properly playable by two, and is usually played as a gambling game, offering little else to engage the attention. The classic version runs as follows.

Two players each receive 10 cards dealt one at a time from a 52-card pack ranking A 2 3 4 5 6 7 8 9 T J Q K. The next is laid face up on the table to start the wastepile, the remainder stacked face down beside it.

The aim is to be the first to 'knock' by laying out all or most of one's cards in matched sets or melds. A meld is three or four cards of the same rank, or three or more cards in suit and sequence (Ace low only). A player may only knock if the total face value of unmelded cards left in hand is 10 or less, counting Ace 1, numerals face value, courts 10 each. A 'gin' hand is one in which all ten cards are melded, and scores extra.

To start, non-dealer may take the faced card in exchange for any card from his hand. If he declines, dealer has the same option. If he also declines, non-dealer must draw the top card of stock, add it to his hand, and throw one card face up to the wastepile. Each in turn thereafter may draw the top card of the stock or the wastepile and makes one discard to the wastepile. If he takes the top card of the wastepile he may not discard it in the same turn.

Play continues until one player knocks. He does this by making a final discard face down to the wastepile and spreading his cards face up, separated into melds and deadwood (unmelded cards). The other player then makes whatever melds he can, lays off any cards that match the knocker's melds—unless the knocker went out 'gin', when this is not permitted—and reveals his deadwood.

If neither has knocked by the time only two cards remain in stock, the result is a draw, and the next in turn to deal does so.

The knocker normally scores the difference between the values of both players' deadwood, plus a bonus of 25 if he went gin. However, if he didn't go gin, and if his deadwood equals or exceeds that of his opponent, then the latter scores the difference between the two, plus a bonus of 25 for the 'undercut'.

The deal alternates and scores are kept cumulatively. The winner is the first to reach or exceed a total of 100. Both players then add 25 for each hand they won, and the winner adds a further 100 for the game. The final pay-off is the difference between these end-totals. It is doubled for a 'blitz' if the loser failed to win a single hand.

Notes. Beginners should note that a hand often ends before half the stock has gone, sometimes after only half a dozen draws. This gradually increases the importance of discarding high unmatched cards rather than low ones, so as not to be left with too much deadwood. If your opponent hasn't knocked after seven or eight draws, it doesn't mean he can't: he may be going for gin, or hoping to undercut you. When you are in a position to knock it is usually worth doing so quickly, as the longer you leave it (in a perhaps vain attempt at gin) the more risk you may run of being undercut. Draw from the wastepile if this gives you a meld or a strong two-way part-meld. Thus a holding of ♠8 ♠9 ♥9 would make ♥8 worth taking early in the game. Otherwise, draw from stock rather than from the wastepile, as this keeps down the number of cards in your hand known to your opponent. If you draw a useless card from stock, don't discard it immediately. A better discard is always one which actually comes, or at least appears to come, from a strong part-combination. Never match your opponent's last discard—he may be playing from a different type of meld. For instance, the fact that he throws ♣9 doesn't just mean that he isn't collecting Nines—he may be wanting you to drop the Nine he needs for a sequence in another suit.

Oklahoma Gin

The same, except that the value of the initial upcard fixes the maximum amount of deadwood permitted to the knocker in that deal. For instance, if the upcard is a Seven he may not knock with more than seven. Furthermore, if it is an Ace, a gin hand is required.

Hollywood Gin

In effect, a method of playing several games simultaneously. Rule up as many 'boxes' (double columns, one for each player) as there are deals to be played. The score for the first deal is entered only in the first box. That in the second is entered at the top of the second box and added to the same player's score in the first. Similarly, each new deal is entered at the top of the next box and added to the score in all the previous boxes that are still open. A box is closed when either player reaches 100 in it, each one counting as a separate game.

Go Boom

Going-out game: 3–6p, 52c

A simple but interesting game recommended for lighter moments, such as after a heavy meal. Related closely to Rolling Stone and Sift Smoke, perhaps more distantly to Cucumber and Switch.

Deal 8 each (or 7 if five play, 6 if six) from a 52-card pack ranking A K Q J T 9 8 7 6 5 4 3 2, and stack the rest face down. The aim is to be the first to run out of cards by playing them to tricks, which have no value in themselves.

Eldest leads first. Everyone else must play a card of the same suit or rank as the card led. The player of the highest card, or of the first played of equally highest, turns the trick down and leads to the next.

Anyone unable to match the led card by rank or suit must draw cards from stock and add them to his hand until able to do so. When the stock is exhausted, a player unable to match merely misses a turn.

Play ceases the moment a player has played his last card. He then scores, or is paid, according to the number of cards left in the other players' hands.

Variants.

1. One or two Jokers may be added as wild cards, or Deuces treated as wild. Wild cards belong to any specified suit, but can never take the trick.
2. It may be agreed that players score negatively for the cards left over in hand, at the rate of 20 for a wild Deuce, 15 per Joker, 10 each for courts, others at face value. The winner is the player with the smallest total after an agreed number of deals, or when one player reaches an agreed 'bust'.

Go Fish

Going-out game: 3–6p, 52c

Even lighter than Go Boom, Go Fish is recorded as early as 1585 (in Italy, as *Andare à piscere),* though it may not be exactly the same game.

Deal 5 each from a 52-card pack and stack the rest face down. The aim is to be the first to run out of cards by laying them down in sets of four of a kind (four Aces, Tens, Jacks, etc.).

Eldest starts by pointing to a player and asking for a particular card by name. It must be one of which he holds at least one other of the same rank. (Thus, if he asks for ♥Q, he must already have a Queen in hand.)

If the requested player has the card required, he must surrender it in exchange for any one the questioner does not want, and the questioner gets another turn. If not, he says 'Go fish!' This forces the questioner to draw a card from stock and add it to his hand. It is then the other player's turn to ask someone for a card.

Whenever a player gets four of a kind he lays them face down on the table. Play continues until one player has run out of cards. If the stock runs out first, anyone told to 'go fish' merely ends his turn without drawing.

Going-out games

Games in which the object is to be the first to play out all one's cards, either by collecting and discarding them in matched sets (early forms of Rummy) or by playing them to a common wastepile in such a way as to match or beat the previous card (Dudak, Durak, Stops games, Switch, Trouduc).

Gops

Quasi-trick game: 2–3p (2 best), 52c

This curious game of unknown origin is said to be named from the acronym 'Game Of Pure Strategy'. A more accurate description would be 'Game of Psychological Strife', as the skill involved is more like extra-sensory perception than calculation.

The pack is separated into suits. Each player takes one complete suit in hand. The fourth suit—diamonds, for example—is thoroughly shuffled and stacked face down. The aim of the game is to win the greatest value of diamonds, counting face value from Ace to Ten, then Jack 11, Queen 12, King 13.

A game consist of thirteen turns. At each turn the top diamond is turned face up. The players then bid for it by choosing any card from their hand and laying it face down on the table. When both are ready, both are turned face up. The player of the higher-ranking card (Ace low) wins the diamond. The bid cards are then put aside, and the next turn played in the same way.

If both bid the same amount, the bid cards are put aside but the current diamond is held in abeyance and the next one turned as well. On the next turn, the maker of the higher bid wins both diamonds—or however many are currently in question.

The winner is the player with the higher value of diamonds. If the last card or cards are tied, they belong to neither player, unless it is agreed to credit them to the winner.

If three play, and two tie for best, the next diamond is turned, as usual, and won by whoever makes the highest bid. The previous card, however, is won by whichever of the two previously tied players bids highest, as the third player has no valid claim on it.

Hasenpfeffer

See Euchre.

Hearts

Trick-avoidance game: 3–6p, 52c

This classic trick-avoidance game has become a popular family and informal game throughout Europe and the USA, in which country it is first recorded as appearing in the 1880s. Though its immediate ancestry is unclear, it contains elements clearly deriving from Reversis and Polignac.

In its purest form, the aim is simply to avoid winning tricks containing hearts. Each player counts a penalty point for each heart taken in tricks, and the winner is the player with the lowest score after a given number of deals, or when one player reaches a given maximum. No one, however, plays the purest form. Described here is a current American variety (from J. Andrews, *Win at Hearts*, New York, 1983), derived from an early twentieth-century development called Black Lady Hearts. For the British equivalent, see Black Maria. Both are also variously known as Black Lady, Black Widow, Chase the Lady, Slippery Anne, Slippery Bitch, and probably even less salubrious titles.

The turn to deal and play passes to the left. Four players each receive 13 cards dealt one at a time from a 52-card pack. (See note below if other than four play.)

The aim is to avoid winning tricks containing hearts or ♠Q—or, if the hand is strong enough, to win *all* such penalty cards.

Each player first passes three cards face down to his left-hand neighbour and receives the same number from his right. On the second deal, cards are passed to the right and received from the left; on the third deal they are passed between players sitting opposite each other; and on the fourth there is no passing of cards. The same sequence is repeated thereafter.

Whoever holds ♣2 leads it to the first trick. Suit must be followed if possible. The trick is taken by the highest card of the suit led, and the winner of each trick leads to the next. A player unable to follow suit may throw any unwanted card, except that (*a*) you may not play a penalty card to the first trick unless you have no alternative, and (*b*) you may not lead a heart until at least one player has already taken a heart, or unless your only alternative is to lead the ♠Q.

At end of play each player scores 1 penalty point for each heart he has taken in tricks, and 13 for ♠Q. However, a player taking all penalty cards deducts 26 points from his current score.

The winner is the player with fewest points when one player reaches an agreed limit, such as 100 points.

Notes. The simplest way of coping with the odd number of cards if other than four play is to deal cards round as far as they will go. Those with one card extra then play two cards to the first trick. For notes on strategy, see Black Maria.

Hearts Variants

Auction Hearts. Played with chips or counters. Players bid for the right to name the penalty suit. The highest bidder leads to the first trick. Each player pays into the pool the amount of the bid multiplied by the number of cards he has taken of the penalty suit. The pool is divided evenly among those who took no tricks, or, if everyone took tricks, among those who took none of the penalty suit.

Cancellation Hearts. Two full packs are shuffled together and dealt round evenly as far as they will go. Any extras are left face down and go to the winner of the first trick, who may look at them privately. Normal rules apply, except that each trick is taken by the highest card of the suit led only if its twin is not played to the same trick. If it is, then the trick is taken by the next best card, or the next best if that is paired, and so on. If all cards of the suit led are paired, the trick is put to one side and goes to the winner of the following trick.

Domino Hearts. Players receive 6 cards each and the rest are stacked face down. A player unable to follow suit must draw from stock until he can. Only when none remain in stock may he discard at will. Players drop out when they run out of cards, the turn to lead passing to the left if necessary. The last player left in adds the cards he holds to those he won in tricks. Scores are then made, or the pool divided, in the usual way.

Draw Hearts. Two players receive 13 cards each and the rest are stacked face down. The winner of each trick draws from stock, and waits for his opponent to draw before leading to the next. Keep playing till none remain in stock or hand. (Most rules state that the second to a trick must follow suit if possible. As this cannot be policed, here is a suggested alternative. In the first 13 tricks the second to a trick need not follow suit, but can only lose it by playing a lower card of the suit led.)

Greek Hearts. The penalties are 50 for taking ♠Q, 15 for ♥A, 10 each per ♥K, Q, J, 1 each per lower heart.

Hearts and Flowers. All clubs count plus the same value as hearts count minus, so the overall scores in each deal cancel to zero. Game is normally 30 up.

Heartsette (Widow Hearts). Three or so cards are dealt face down as a widow and the rest are divided evenly among the players. The widow is added to the last won trick. In some circles it goes to the winner of the first trick, who may see what it contains without showing it to anyone else.

Omnibus (or Red Jack) Hearts. The ♦J (or ♦10) reduces by 10 points the penalty score of the player who wins it in a trick.

Pink Lady. Version of Black Maria in which ♥Q, or Pink Lady, also scores minus 13.

Spot Hearts. The penalty score for each heart taken is the same as its face value, with Jack 11, Queen 12, King 13, Ace 14 (maximum 101).

Hi-Lo

See Poker.

Hoc

Seventeenth-century ancestor of Comet, Newmarket, etc.

Hombre

Plain tricks: 3p, 40c

Hombre, Spanish for 'man', denotes the lone player in a game where the highest bidder chooses trumps and plays against the combined forces of his opponents. It is the oldest and most classic game of its type, directly ancestral to Boston, Solo Whist, and many others. Hombre swept Europe in the late seventeenth century, becoming 'Lomber' in German and 'Ombre' in English. Under the names Rocambor and Tresillo, it survived in Spain and South America into the twentieth century.

With its upside-down ranking in red suits, peculiar rules of 'reneging', and other complex idiosyncrasies, Hombre may be found too baroque for modern tastes. But it is a fascinating game of skill, and experienced card-players will find it well worth exploring once its basic essentials have become familiar. The following account assumes play with chips and counters, of which each player should start with at least thirty. A point-scoring variation is appended for those who prefer it.

Three players are active. If four play, the dealer sits out. Use a 40-card pack made by stripping out Eights, Nines, and Tens. The rank of cards in each suit depends on whether it is (*a*) black or red, and (*b*) trump or plain, as follows:

	Trump		Plain
Black	♠A tr2 ♣A	K Q J 7 6 5 4 3	K Q J 7 6 5 4 3 2
Red	♠A tr7 ♣A trA	K Q J 2 3 4 5 6	K Q J A 2 3 4 5 6 7

Note that:
1. The basic ranking of numerals is reversed in red (Seven low), and a red suit is always one card longer than a black suit of the same status (trump or plain).
2. The black Aces are permanent trumps, and the top three trumps, called matadors, are
   (*a*) ♠A (*spadille*)

(*b*) Black 2 or red 7 (*manille*)

(*c*) ♣A (*basto*)

3. In a red trump suit, the fourth highest trump is the Ace, or *punto*. It does *not* have the status of a matador.

The turn to deal and play passes always to the right. The dealer antes five chips to the pool, deals 9 cards each in 3s, and spreads the remainder face down in a row.

Whoever bids highest becomes Hombre, chooses trumps, and seeks to win more tricks than either opponent individually. Thus five or more always wins, and four wins if the others split three-two. The bids are, from lowest to highest:

1. Simple (*entrada*): Before play, Hombre announces trumps, discards any number from his hand, and draws replacements from the stock.
2. Vuelta (*voltereta*): Hombre turns the top card of stock face up to determine trumps, then discards and draws as before.
3. Solo (*sans prendre*): Hombre announces trumps but plays without discarding and drawing.

Each in turn may pass or bid, and, having passed, may not come in again. Each bid must be higher than the last. However, a player who has made a lower bid, and not yet passed, may raise his bid to equal that of the next to bid against him, thus gaining the contract (unless overcalled again) by virtue of prior position.

Unless playing solo, Hombre may make as many discards as he likes before drawing the same number from the top of the stock. Solo or not, both opponents may then discard and draw for themselves. As it is advantageous for one of them to have the stronger hand, they may agree between them as to which is to exchange first. Whoever does so may discard and draw any number (up to eight, under English rules). The other may, but need not, discard up to as many as are left. Rules vary as to whether any untaken cards are left down or turned face up, and the point should be agreed before play.

Eldest leads first and the winner of each trick leads to the next. The trick is taken by the highest card of the suit led or by the highest trump if any are played. The two opponents must not mix their won tricks together. Normally, suit must be followed if possible, otherwise any card may be played. Matadors, however, can only be forced out by higher matadors, not by lower matadors or trumps.

Fig. 14. **Hombre.** This hand is good for a club solo, the Two and Ace being respectively the second and third highest trumps.

That is: if a player's only trumps are matadors, he need not follow to a trump lead but may 'renege' (discard) instead. However, if a higher matador is led, and his only trump is a lower one, he is obliged to play it.

If Hombre takes the first five tricks straight off, he wins without further play. If instead he leads to the sixth, he thereby obligates himself to win all nine ('the vole'), thus increasing his potential winnings or penalties.

If Hombre thinks he cannot win, he may surrender at any time before playing to the fourth trick. He may not do this if playing a solo. In a vuelta, his surrender must be accepted by both opponents. In a simple game, however, either opponent may himself take over the role of Hombre and play the rest of the hand as if he had made the bid himself.

The possible outcomes are:

Sacada: Hombre wins.
Puesta: Hombre loses, tricks are tied.
Codille: Hombre loses, an opponent wins.

For a win, Hombre takes the contents of the pot and is paid by each opponent as follows: simple game 5, vuelta 7, solo 15, plus any of the following bonuses:

The vole (nine tricks)	25
Primeras (win first five and stop)	1
Estuches (top trumps)	1 each

Estuches are top consecutive trumps from ♠A downwards. If he had held (say) the top four, but not the fifth, he would gain 4 extra. The same applies if he had been playing without them. For example, if he had held *basto* but not *spadille* or *manille*, he would earn 2 for *estuches*.

If Hombre loses *puesta* (tricks are tied 4 4 1 or 3 3 3), he doubles the pool and adds to it five chips for each other player in the game.

If Hombre loses *codille* (an opponent takes an individual majority of tricks), he pays the same as for a *puesta*, but to the player who won instead of to the pot.

These penalties are further increased as described above for *primeras* (losing the first five tricks), and *estuches* (one per top consecutive trump held or not held).

If Hombre fails to win all nine after leading to the sixth, he pays 30 to each opponent, less 2 if he played vuelta or 10 if he played solo, less also the number of *estuches* applicable.

Optional extras. (1) A bid in diamonds overcalls the same in a different suit, and is won or lost double. (2) If all pass immediately, lower bids may be made. They include:

(a) *Gascarille*: Hombre discards and draws eight cards and then announces trumps. This has a value of 3 chips.

(b) *Contrabola* or misère: No one discards, Hombre announces a trump suit of which he holds at least one, and aims to lose every trick. If successful, he wins a simple game; if not, it counts as a *puesta*.

Notes. The usual requirement for a simple bid is five trumps including two matadors, or one matador and King, Queen. Vuelta is bid with a few high cards in all suits rather than with two or three long suits. In neither bid is it wise to exchange more than about four cards. Remember that the effect of the exchange, which is also open to the opponents, is that the twenty-seven cards in play will include all eleven or twelve trumps and probably eight top cards in plain suits. Solo needs a long, strong suit with at least one matador and a void suit, or one headed solely by top cards. After winning five tricks, do not attempt the vole if there is a matador out against you. Since higher matadors cannot be forced out by lower ones, it is a common ploy for an opponent to hold one back in order to defeat the bid in the last four tricks.

The opponents should aim first to ensure that at least one of them takes more tricks than Hombre. To this end it is quite legal for either of them, upon playing to a trick before the other, to say 'My trick', meaning 'Don't beat my card'. Only when Hombre has certainly lost is it desirable to play for a tie. An opponent with weak cards should avoid winning two tricks unless confident of winning a third, so as to prevent Hombre's winning by 4 3 2.

Point-score variant

The following point-score system works reasonably well and produces interesting results. Agree on the number of deals to be played, and play as described above but with these modifications. The bids and their basic scoring values are:

Obligation	1
Exchange	2
Turn-up	3
Solo	5

If all pass without bidding, Obligation must be played by whoever holds ♣A, or by Eldest if no one does. It involves discarding all but one card, drawing eight from stock, and then announcing trumps. 'Exchange' is equivalent to a simple game, 'turn-up' to vuelta.

The value of each game is doubled for each of the following feats:

1. *Cuatro*: winning by four tricks (4 3 2).
2. *Primeras*: winning the first five tricks and then stopping.
3. *The vole*: winning all nine. This is doubled in addition to *primeras*, i.e. quadrupled.
4. *Vole declared*: the game value is doubled again (octupled) if Hombre predicts before playing to the first trick that he will win all nine.

The value of a lost game is exactly what Hombre would have won had he succeeded, and is deducted from his current score. If he loses by *codille*, the same value is also added to the score of the player who beat him. If he loses by *puesta*, that value is also recorded in a separate column representing the pot. The pot-points are carried forward cumulatively and are eventually credited to the first player to win a solo or the vole. The pot is then reset to zero. If the pot is not empty when the last deal has been played, it goes to the winner of the last hand—or, if this also resulted in *puesta*, is distributed evenly between the opponents.

Honeymoon Bridge

Plain-trick game: 2p, 52c

Any form of Bridge for two, such as the following. (A knowledge of Bridge is assumed).

Deal 13 each and stack the rest face down. Phase 1 consists of thirteen tricks, each player drawing from stock after each trick. There is no trump, and suit must be followed if possible. The aim is to finish with a thirteen-card hand suitable for Phase 2, which begins when the stock is exhausted. There is an auction to establish a contract, to which the non-declarer leads. Play and score along Auction or Contract lines.

Hundertspiel

See Trappola.

Hundred

Adding-up game: 3–6p, 32c

See also Adding-up games.
Cards count as follows:

A	K	Q	J	T	9	8	7
11	4	3	2	10	9	8	7

Divide them equally amongst the players, leaving any remainder face up on the table to start the total. Each in turn plays a card to the table, adding its value to the previous total and announcing the new one. A player making the total more than 100 loses, but making it 100 exactly wins. It may be agreed to continue play with another scoring point at 200.

I Doubt It

Going-out game: 3–6p, 52c

A good game for children.

Deal all the cards out. It doesn't matter if some have more than others. The aim is to be the first to run out of cards.

The first player takes one, two, three, or four cards from hand and lays them face down on the table, saying 'Aces'. The second does likewise, saying 'Twos'; and so on up to 'Kings'. If not challenged, the cards so played are left in a pile on the table.

Anyone may challenge an announcement by saying 'I doubt it'. The cards just played are then turned up. If they are not all Aces (or whatever they were said to be), the person who played them must take all the cards in the pile and add them to his hand; otherwise, they must be taken by the challenger. Play does not then continue from the left, but is resumed by whoever won the challenge.

Cheat

Similar, but more long-winded. Each in turn lays *one* card face down on the table. The first may state any rank, for example 'Ten'; the second to play must then say 'Jack', the third 'Queen', and so on. Anyone may challenge by saying 'Cheat!', whereupon the last card is turned up, and the loser of the challenge takes all the cards in the played-out pile. The winner of a challenge plays next, and may call it any rank he likes, which then starts a new sequence to be followed by the others.

Imperial

Plain-tricks and melds: 2p, 32c

Also called Piquet Imperial, Trump Piquet, and Vingt-quatre, this sixteenth-century cross between Triomphe and Piquet remains a popular two-hander in the Midi and offers many points of interest to card-game explorers. Descriptions vary, and the main source for this entry (Frans Gerver, *Le Guide Marabout*, Verviers, 1966) seems deliberately vague on such matters as scoring for honours.

Two players use a 36-card pack ranking K Q J A T 9 8 7 in each suit. (But A K Q J T 9 8 7 can be substituted without changing any rules.)

Scores can be kept in writing, but counters are better. Each starts with five reds and six whites on his left, and passes one white from left to right for each point won in play. Six points make an imperial, indicated by moving a red to the right and returning six whites to the left. Game is 36 points, being won by the first to pass all eleven counters from left to right.

Deal 12 each in twos, threes, or fours. Turn the twenty-fifth for trumps, and place the rest face down across it. If the turn-up is an honour (K Q J A or 7), dealer scores a white. If it is a King or an Ace, and dealer holds the Seven, he may exchange it for the turn-up.

Each in turn, starting with elder, scores for any of the following imperials he may have been dealt. All scoring combinations must be shown, and they must be declared in this order:

1. K Q J A of trumps (*impériale d'atout*)	2 reds
2. K Q J A of non-trump suit	1 red
3. All four of K Q J A or 7 (*impériale d'honneur*)	1 red
4. No court cards (*impériale blanche*)	2 reds

Next, the player with the better point scores one white. 'Point' is the total face value of all cards held in any one suit, counting Ace 11, courts 10 each, numerals as marked. If equal, Elder scores.

Elder leads to the first trick, and the winner of each trick leads to the next. 'Strict' rules apply: follow suit and win the trick if possible; if unable to follow, play a trump if possible. Score one white for leading an honour to a trick.

At end of play, each scores one white for each honour (K Q J A 7 of trumps) he has taken in tricks. Next, if either player took a majority of tricks, he scores one white for each trick taken above six, or two reds for *capot* if he won all twelve.

Throughout play, whenever one player scores a red—whether for an imperial or by getting his sixth white across—his opponent's odd points are promptly annulled, and he must shift all his whites back to the left. The sole exception is the *impériale blanche*, which does not annul the odd points. With this exception, however, the rule is also applied at the start of the second and subsequent deals when reds are scored for imperials in hand. Hence it is important, especially near the end of a game, that scores be made strictly in order: turned trump, imperials in hand, *impériale blanche*, the point, leading and capturing honours, number of tricks taken.

Optional extras. Some players recognize two additional imperials, each of which earns one red but does not force the opponent to cancel his whites. An *impériale de retourne* occurs when a player has all but one card of an imperial, and the card missing is the trump turn-up. This counts immediately before the score for point. An *impériale de rencontre*, or *impériale tombée*, occurs when a player wins the four top trumps in tricks without having been originally dealt all four. This counts immediately before the score for honours.

Irish Loo

Three-card Loo played with five cards. See Loo.

Jass
Point-tricks and melds: 3–4p, 36c

'Jass' is the name of the highest trump, the Jack, in a family of related games most widely played in Switzerland, though actually of Dutch origin. It is also the name of the game and of the traditional 36-card, Swiss-suited pack with which it is played. By extension, it is often used of any game played in Switzerland with such cards, whether or not of the true family. The following entry gives *general* rules for all true Jass games played in Switzerland, followed by the additional *particular* rules for (*a*) Handjass, a good beginners' game for 2–4 players; (*b*) Schieber, the most popular four-hand partnership game; and (*c*) Pandur, the equivalent of Solo. Separate entries will also be found for the related (but not specifically Swiss) Belote, Klaberjass, and Klaverjas. None should be undertaken without prior experience of point-trick games such as Pinochle or Sixty-Six.

General rules

Jass is essentially a game of points. Points are scored for three features known as *Stöck, Wys, Stich*, 'marriages, melds, tricks'.

Marriages. A marriage is the holding in one hand of the King and Queen of trumps. Its holder claims it upon playing the second of them to a trick. Its score of 20 is recorded as if made *before* those for melds and tricks, even though it is not revealed until after melds have been declared.

Melds. A meld is a suit-sequence of three or more cards (running A K Q J T 9 8 7 6), or a quartet of Aces, Kings, Queens, or Jacks. They score as follows:

Four Jacks	200
Five or more in sequence	100
Four A, K, Q	100
Four in sequence	50
Three in sequence	20

A card may not be used in two melds at once (though the trump King or Queen may belong to a meld in addition to being married). For example, a player holding four Kings and a sequence of four to the Ace or King would count only 100 for Kings, not also 50 for the sequence.

Only the holder of the best meld may score for it, but (*a*) he may also score for any other melds he holds involving entirely different cards, and (*b*) in a partnership game, his partnership also scores for those held by his partner. The holder of the best meld is found in the following way as each player contributes a card to the first trick. The leader announces the value of his best meld. The next, upon playing his card, announces a higher value if he has one, or 'Good' if he cannot equal it. If he has one of equal value, he states the number of cards it contains. A longer meld beats a shorter, so the previous player then says 'Not good' if he can beat it, 'Good' if he can't, or 'Equal'. If equal, the next states its rank if a quartet, or its top card if a sequence. A higher rank beats a lower, and the previous player again says 'Not good', 'Good', or 'Equal'. Equality must mean a sequence is in question, which the second player can then only win by (truthfully) announcing 'In trumps'. Otherwise, all else being equal, the previous player wins by prior position. The next player in turn then competes, if he can, with the winner of the first contest. As before, the pecking order is: value, length, height, trump, position.

Tricks. Won tricks are scored according to the point-value of the cards composing them. The rank and value of cards differs as between trumps and plain suits as follows:

In trumps	J	9	A	K	Q	—	T	—	8	7	6
In plain suits	—	—	A	K	Q	J	T	9	8	7	6
Card-points	20	14	11	4	3	2	10	0	0	0	0

Jass

The trump Jack, or 'Jass', counts 20 and is the highest card in the pack. The trump Nine, or 'Nell', counts 14 and is the second best. Plain-suit numerals below Ten count nothing. The total value of all counters in the pack is 152, i.e. 62 in trumps plus 30 in each plain suit. Winning the last trick scores an additional 5 points. Hence the total possible for the third scoring feature, 'tricks', is normally 157.

Play. All play, including the deal and turn to deal, passes to the *right*. Eldest leads to the first trick and the winner of each trick leads to the next. The trick is taken by the highest card of the suit led, or by the highest trump if any are played. If trumps are led, suit must be followed if possible, except that a player whose only trump is the Jass need not play it but may discard instead. If a plain suit is led, players may follow suit or trump, as preferred, but any trump played must (if possible) be higher than any other already played to the trick. Only if unable to follow suit may anyone renounce.

Handjass

From two to four play, each for himself. Deal 4 hands of 9 cards each in 3s. If four play, the last card is turned for trump, and dealer does not take it into hand until about to play to the first trick. If two or three play, the top card of the first dead hand is turned for trump, and may be taken in exchange for the Six of trumps if anyone has been dealt it.

The aim is to score as much as possible for cards and melds. Each must first declare whether or not he is prepared to play the hand. If not, he turns it down and sits the deal out. If all pass, there is a new deal by the same dealer. If all but one pass, he wins without playing. Otherwise, tricks are played as described above.

Two game-points are awarded at end of play, one each to the players making the highest totals. If there is a tie for second, it is broken in favour of the player cutting the higher card from the pack. If only one stayed in, he scores them both, as does the better of two players if the other failed to make 21. Any player failing to make 21 scores a negative game point (written as a nought, though actually counting minus one). As each player reaches seven game points he drops out of play, and the last left in is the loser.

Schieber

Four players; partners sit opposite each other. Precise rules vary considerably from place to place.

Deal 9 cards each in 3s. Eldest may nominate a trump suit or *schieben*, i.e. pass that privilege to his partner, who must then exercise it. If eldest leads without making any announcement, whatever he leads is a trump.

Follow basic Jass rules as described above. A side taking all nine tricks scores 100 extra for the 'match'. Each deal from the second onwards is made by a member of the side that won the previous deal, so that the losing side has the advantage of making trumps and leading first. Play ceases the moment one side reaches 1000 points, for which purpose it is important to remember that scores accrue in order 'marriage, melds, tricks'.

Optional extras. By agreement, a meld of four Nines may be recognized. It ranks below four Jacks and counts 150.

Schieber is usually played with two additional bids, *Oben-abe*, and *Unden-ufe*, which may reasonably be translated respectively as 'tops-down' and 'bottoms-up'. Both are played at no trump, so there is no Jass or Nell, nor cards worth 20 and 14. Instead, all Eights count 8 points each when captured in tricks, thus maintaining the total of 157 for tricks, including 5 for last. In 'tops-down', cards rank from Ace high to Six low, as normal; in 'bottoms-up' their trick-taking power is reversed: Six is the highest in its suit, Seven the second highest, and so down to Ace, the lowest of all. (In some circles the point-value of 11 is transferred from the Ace to the Six. Players may or may not find this preferable, but to describe it as 'more logical' is patent nonsense.) Reversed ranking also applies to melds of equal length—for example, a sequence of 6 7 8 beats 7 8 9, four Kings beat four Aces, etc.; but four Jacks still count 200 and so beat all else.

When these variations are included, it is usual to double all scores made in contracts with shields or bells (spades or diamonds) as trump, treble contracts in tops-down, and quadruple those in bottoms-up. The game target may then be raised to 2500.

For more advanced partnership games, such as Sidi-Barrani and Molotov, see Gottfried Egg, *Puur, Näll, As* (Neuhausen-am-Rheinfall, n.d.).

Pandur

Four usually play, but only three are active, as each in turn sits out the hand to which he deals. The scorekeeper deals first.

Deal 8 cards each in batches of 4 from a 24-card pack made by stripping out all ranks below Nine.

In addition to the usual melds, a player may announce a sequence of six or a quartet of Nines, each counting 150. Only the soloist may score for melds, provided that he has the best: if an opponent has a better, it does not score itself but only prevents the soloist from scoring.

Each in turn, starting with Eldest, may bid or pass, and, having passed, may not come in again. The lowest bid is 100; higher bids must be multiples of 10. A numerical bid is the minimum amount the soloist undertakes to make (for marriages, melds, and tricks) in return for nominating trumps and leading to the first trick.

A bid of 200 is overcalled by misère, then trump misère, then 210, etc. In misère, the soloist must lose every trick, playing at no trump. In trump misère the suit of the card he leads is automatically trump. Players are still required to trump when unable to follow suit, but are not obliged to overtrump.

A bid of 250 is overcalled by Pandur, and 300 by trump Pandur. In Pandur, the soloist must win every trick, playing at no trump. In trump Pandur, the suit of the card he leads is automatically trump.

If successful, the soloist wins a number of game-points equivalent to the bid divided by 50 (maximum 6). Misères count 4, Pandur 5, trump Pandur 6. For a failed bid, the game value is credited to each opponent. Game is 15 points or any other agreed target. If four play, the dealer gets the value of a failed bid, but not if he stands at 13 or 14: his last point(s) must be made in active play.

Each player drops out upon reaching the target, the game being played by three, then by two. The last one left in loses.

Note. Trump misère is dangerous and must be made in a very short suit, typically in order to lose a card that would be even more dangerous at no trump. For example, with three safe suits and a singleton Queen, the soloist would announce 'trump' and lead the Queen. As the Jack and Nine are top trumps, this would only lose if one opponent held the Ten and the others were void. If played at no trump, there would be three cards lower than the Queen, making the bid very risky. When only two players remain, so that eight cards are out of play, any misère is riskier than usual, especially with a trump.

Jig

See Snip-Snap-Snorem.

Jo-jotte

A hybrid of Klaberjass and Contract Bridge devised in the late 1930s by Ely Culbertson and named after his then wife, Josephine Dillon.

Jubilee

Adding-up game: 2–7p (3 best), 61c

A Czech member of the Adding-up family.

Make a 61-card pack comprising a whole suit of hearts, two whole spade suits, two each of club numerals from Ace to Nine only (no Tens or courts), and four Jokers. Aces count 15 each, courts 10, other numerals at face value, Jokers zero. Hearts count minus these amounts, black cards plus.

Deal 8 each and stack the rest face down. Each in turn, starting with Eldest, plays a card face up to a common wastepile, announces the total value of all cards so far played, and draws a replacement from stock so long as any remain.

Eldest must start with a black card. No one may bring the total below zero. Anyone unable to make a legal play must show his hand and pass.

Anyone making the total an exact multiple of 25, whether by addition or subtraction, scores 10 for a 'jubilee', or 20 if it is also a multiple of 100. Anyone making the total 'jump' a jubilee, whether by addition or subtraction, instead of hitting it exactly, loses 5 points.

Keep going till the last card has been played. The final total should be 189.

Julep

South American game similar to five-card Loo, best for six players. Deal 5 each from a 40-card pack lacking Eights, Nines, and Tens, and turn a card for trump. Players may pass or play. Those who play must win at least two tricks, but may first discard and draw any number of replacements.

Jungle Bridge

See Oh Hell!

Kaiserspiel

See Karnöffel.

Kalabriasz

See Klaberjass.

Kaluki

Rummy game: 2–6p (4 best), 2 × 52c

It is a moot point whether this double-pack Rummy has a greater variety of spellings (Caloochie, Kaloochi, Kaloochie, Kalougie, Kalookie, etc.) or of rules. The following can only be described as 'typical'.

Use a double 52-card pack and four Jokers. Deal 15 cards each (13 if five play, 11 if six), face the next to start the wastepile, and stack the rest face down beside it.

The aim is to be the first to run out of cards by laying them down in melds, and by laying off individual cards to existing melds (own or others') whenever they match. A meld is three or four cards of the same rank, or three or more cards in suit and sequence. Sequence order is A 2 3 4 5 6 7 8 9 T J Q K A, Ace counting high or low but not both (K A 2 is illegal). A Joker may be used to represent any desired card. No meld may contain two identical cards, or simultaneously a Joker and the card it represents.

Each in turn draws either the top card of the stock or wastepile, makes any possible melds, and makes one discard face up to the wastepile. A player may only draw from the wastepile if he has made at least one meld, or can immediately use that card to make one. The first meld made by each player must comprise cards totalling at least 51, counting Ace 15, courts 10, numerals at face value, and Jokers as the cards they represent. Alternatively, the meld itself may be worth less, provided that he simultaneously lays off a card or cards to other melds which bring the total of cards played from his hand to 51 or more. Any player on his turn to play may take a melded Joker in return for the card it represents.

Play continues until one player goes out by melding, laying off, or discarding the last card from his hand.

If playing for points, each player is penalized by the total face value of cards left in his hand, Jokers counting 25. When someone loses by reaching an agreed target, such as 150, the winner is the player with the lowest penalty score.

If playing for hard score, the player who went out receives from each opponent an agreed stake for each card left in hand. Each Joker counts as two cards, and all stakes are doubled if the winner went 'Kaluki' by going out without having previously made a meld.

Karnöffel

Oldest identifiable European card game, first recorded in Germany in 1426. A derivative is still played in parts of Switzerland under the name Kaiserjass, though not a true variety of Jass. It is a five-card partnership game of which each deal is won by the first side to win three tricks.

Kings and Queens
Rummy game: 3–7p, 2 × 52c

Play as ordinary Seven-card Rummy (q.v.) with a doubled pack of 104 cards ranking A 2 3 4 5 6 7 8 9 T J Q K. A meld is three or more cards in suit and sequence (Ace low) or three or more of the same rank. Deuces are wild.

The aim is to be the first to go out by melding all seven cards in one go—or six, provided that the seventh is not higher than a Seven.

When one player melds out, the others also make whatever melds they can, and whatever remains in their hands count against them.

If, however, the player who went out first melded only six cards, anyone else with an unmelded card matching his seventh may lay it off, thus reducing his own penalty score and increasing that of the one who went out first.

Unmelded cards count against their holders according to their face value (Aces 1 each, courts 10). The overall winner is the last player to reach a total of 100 penalty points.

The point of the game, as indicated by its title, lies in the fact that players can reduce their penalty scores by melding Kings and Queens. Each King used in a meld reduces its holder's score by 5 points, each Queen by 3 points, and each Deuce representing a King or Queen by the appropriate amount.

Suggestions. It would be sensible to (*a*) restrict the number of Deuces in a meld by insisting that every meld contain more natural cards than wild ones, and (*b*) count each unmelded Deuce at least 10 points against.

Klaberjass

Point-tricks and melds: 2p, 32c

A major international two-hander known in England as Clobiosh, Clobby, or Clubby, in America as Klob (notably in the writings of Damon Runyon) or Kalabriasz, and in France—with distinct differences—as Belote (q.v.). A member of the Jass family (q.v.), it is characterized by the promotion of the trump Jack (*Jass*) and Nine (*Menel*) to topmost position. Klaberjass—which, like its Dutch relative Klaverjas, means 'clover Jack', i.e. 'Jack of clubs'—is a particularly Jewish game, more probably of Dutch, Flemish, or Alsatian origin than of the Hungarian provenance sometimes assumed from the suspect spelling 'Kalabriasz'.

Four can play Klaberjass, but a more authentic four-hander is Klaverjas (see next entry).

Preliminaries. The player drawing the lower card deals first, after which the deal alternates. Deal 6 each in 3s and turn the next for trump. Cards rank and count thus:

Trump:	Jack	Nine	Ace	Ten	King	Queen	—	—	Eight	Seven
Plain:	—	—	Ace	Ten	King	Queen	Jack	Nine	Eight	Seven
Value:	20	14	11	10	4	3		2	0	0	0

Object. Points are scored for declaring melds and winning card-points in tricks, and the winner is the first to reach 500 over as many deals as necessary. In each deal one player becomes the 'maker' by choosing trumps and thereby contracting to score more than the other.

Bidding. There is first a round of bidding to see if either player will accept the turned suit as trump. Elder may 'take it', 'pass', or '*schmeiss*'. The last is an offer to become the maker in the turned suit if Dealer insists, on condition that, if he does not, then both hands be abandoned and a new deal made (by Elder). If he passes, Dealer may also either take it, pass, or *schmeiss*.

If both pass, Elder turns the trump card down and may propose another suit as trump, or pass, or *schmeiss*, which is now an offer to name a suit or abandon the deal. If he passes, Dealer has the same options. If he also passes, the deal is annulled and Elder deals to the next hand.

Completion of deal. If trumps are made, dealer deals 3 more cards apiece, then turns the bottom card of the stock face up and places it on top. This card is for information only: it may not be taken, and plays no part in tricks or melds.

Dix. If the originally turned suit was entrumped, either player holding the trump Seven (called *dix* or 'deece') may exchange it for the trump turn-up, provided that he does so before melds are declared.

Melds. A score is available for holding a sequence of three or more cards in the same suit, sequential order being A K Q J T 9 8 7 in all four suits. A sequence of three counts 20, of four or more 50. Only the player holding the best sequence may score, but he may then also score for any other sequences he can and will declare. A longer sequence beats a shorter. If equal, the one containing the highest cards wins. If still equal, a trump sequence beats a plain. If still equal, neither player scores. (*Variant*: If still equal, Elder scores.)

To determine which player has the better sequence, Elder announces, on leading to the first trick, 'Twenty' if he has a sequence of three cards, 'Fifty' if four or more. In responding to the first trick, Dealer announces 'Good' if he cannot match 20 or 50, or 'Not good' if he can beat it. In case of equality, he asks first 'How many cards?', then, if necessary, 'How high?', then, if still necessary, 'In trumps?' At the end of the first trick, whichever player has the best sequence (if any) must show and score for his best sequence, and may show and score for any others also held.

Tricks. Elder leads first, and the winner of each trick leads to the next. The second to a trick must follow suit if possible, otherwise trump if possible. If a trump is led, the second must play higher if possible. The trick is taken by the higher card of the suit led or by the higher trump if any are played.

Bella. If either player holds both King and Queen of trumps, he scores 20 for the marriage upon playing the second of them to a trick and announcing '*Bella*'.

Last trick. Winning the last trick scores 10 points extra.

Score. Both players then declare their respective totals for melds and

Fig. 15. **Klaberjass.**
(*a*) Elder hand, left, bids *schmeiss*. Holding the Nine and having access to the Queen for *bella*, he is willing to try spades as trump but unwilling to turn another. Dealer (right) agrees to take him on, holding *Jass* and a heart sequence for 20 each, and a plain-suit Ace.
(*b*) Younger deals 3 more cards each, buries the Queen and turns the top card of stock for information only. Elder exchanges the *dix* (♠7) for the turned Queen, enabling him to count 20 for *bella* in play. Elder, as maker, lost. He took 38 in card-points, which, with *bella* and the last trick, brought him to 68. Younger took 66 in card-points, but counted 20 more for the heart sequence. It is a rare game that lacks the Ace and Ten of trumps, and Elder's bid was undoubtedly rash.

card-points. If the trump-maker made more points, both score what they make; if less (when he is said to 'go *bête*'), his opponent scores the total made by both players. If equal, the opponent scores what he took and the maker scores nothing. (*Variant*: the maker's points are held in abeyance and go to the winner of the next deal.)

The game ends at the end of the deal in which either player has reached or exceeded 500 points. (*Variant*: It ends as soon as either player correctly claims to have reached 500, the rest of that deal not being played out.) The higher total wins.

Notes. Scoring for sequences introduces an element of chance, especially since three more cards are dealt between bidding and playing, and the maker's opponent may do very well out of the draw. In the long run, this factor evens itself out, and it should not be taken too much into account when bidding. In particular, don't bid on the probability of filling a potential sequence. Bid primarily on the strength of the hand for tricks, on the certainty of *bella* if held, and on the probability that a four-card or high three-card sequence already held will prove to be the best.

To succeed, the maker must usually take about 60 card-points in tricks. When bidding, therefore, with only six of nine cards dealt, he must be able to see at least 40 secure. For this purpose it is better to hold the Jack of proposed trumps (Jass), or Nine, Ace, and another, than a long trump suit. The maker can go *bête* though holding four trumps if he lacks both Jass and Menel; alternatively, he can win on as little as Jass alone with two plain-suit Aces.

Do not exchange the *dix* for the turn-up unless it yields a good sequence, or bella, or a safe trump worth 10 or more. Do not *schmeiss* unless the hand is possibly playable in the turned suit but certainly unplayable in any other.

Klaverjas

Point-tricks and melds: 4pp, 32c

Dutch national card game, a neat member of the Jass family (q.v.) and an excellent introduction for beginners to point-trick as opposed to plain-trick games. It exhibits the unusual feature of scoring for melds made 'on the table' by the cards composing the current trick, instead of for melds merely dealt to players by chance as in related Swiss games.

Klaverjas

Four players sitting in crosswise partnerships are dealt 8 cards each (3 2 3) from a 32-card pack ranking and counting as follows:

In trump suit	J	9	A	T	K	Q	—	—	8	7
In plain suits			A	T	K	Q	J	9	8	7
Point value	20	14	11	10	4	3	2	0	0	0

The trump Jack is called 'Jas', the Nine 'Nel'.

The winning side is the first to reach an agreed target, such as 1500 points, over as many deals as necessary. Points are scored (*a*) for capturing counters in tricks, according to the above schedule, (*b*) 10 for winning the last trick, and (*c*) for winning any trick containing one of the following melds:

Four of the same rank	100 points
Four in suit-sequence	50
Three in suit-sequence	20
Stuk (K + Q of trumps)	20

Sequence order is A K Q J T 9 8 7 in every suit including trumps. If a sequence of three or four includes a *stuk*, both are counted. Four of a kind occurs so rarely as to be hardly worth remembering.

Each in turn, starting with Eldest, may name trumps or pass the choice to his left. If the first three pass, Dealer must name trumps. Naming trumps obligates one's partnership to take more points than the opposing side from counters and melds contained in tricks. An opponent of the trump-maker may double if he thinks the contract doubtful, and the trump-maker or his partner may then redouble. These respectively double and quadruple the score made by both sides at the end of the deal.

Eldest leads first, and the winner of each trick leads to the next. Follow suit if possible, otherwise play a trump if possible. Whenever a trump is played (whether led or played to a non-trump lead), each subsequent player of a trump must, if possible, play a higher trump than the previous one. (*Variant*: It is not obligatory to overtrump one's partner.) The trick is taken by the highest card of the suit led, or by the highest trump if any are played.

A meld contained within a trick must be claimed and noted by its winner before the next is led, otherwise it is lost.

If the trump-maker's partnership takes more points than the other, both sides score towards game the amount they have taken in tricks and melds. If not, they count nothing, and the other partnership scores 162 plus the value of melds made by both sides. Taking all 162 card-points in tricks earns a bonus of 100.

Play ceases at the end of the deal in which either side reaches or exceeds the target.

Notes. A biddable suit is one of which you hold both Jack and Nine, or one of these plus two lower trumps, or at least four trumps other than Jack and Nine. Side-suit support should include at least one Ace. In a suit lacking an Ace, it is generally safer to hold pointless cards rather than counters, the worst holding being a singleton Ten. In play, seek every opportunity to 'stuff' the tricks your partner wins by playing either cards of high value, especially Tens, or those contributing to a sequence. Note the discrepancy in ranking between trumps and plain suits. For instance, a trick consisting of J 9 T Q is won, if in trumps, by the Jack, thus yielding 47 for cards plus 50 for the sequence Q J T 9, total 97!

Holding the trump Jack, try to save it for winning a trick containing high counters or a meld. On your first lead you may signal possession of the trump Jack by leading a worthless card from a plain suit, a convention which asks partner to lead trumps as soon as he can. The conventional lead of a non-trump Ace indicates non-possession of the trump Jack. A strong trump holding—three or more—may be shown by leading a low trump. Leading the trump King shows possession also of the Queen.

Klob

See Klaberjass.

Klondike

See Patience.

Knaves

Partial trick-avoidance game: 3p, 52c

An interesting cross between Black Maria and Polignac, first described by Hubert Phillips and B. C. Westall, and probably invented by Phillips, combines the aim of winning tricks with that of avoiding Jacks as penalty cards.

Deal 17 each from a 52-card pack ranking A K Q J T 9 8 7 6 5 4 3 2 and turn the 52nd card for trumps. Eldest leads first, and the winner of each trick leads to the next. Follow suit if possible, otherwise play any card. The trick is taken by the highest card of the suit led or by the highest trump if any are played.

At end of play each player scores 1 point per trick taken, less penalty points for each Jack taken as follows: of spades 1, clubs 2, diamonds 3, hearts 4. The winner is the first to reach 20 points.

Knockout Whist

Plain-trick game: 2–7p, 52c

A popular British game of pub and playground, not recorded in books until—surprisingly enough—about 1980. It need hardly be added that no two schools play it exactly alike. The simplest rules are as follows.

Deal 7 cards each and turn the next for trumps. Dealer leads first, and the winner of each trick leads to the next. Follow suit if possible, otherwise play any card. The trick is taken by the highest card of the suit led or by the highest trump if any are played.

Anyone failing to take a trick is knocked out and takes no further part in the game.

Whoever took the most tricks gathers up the cards, shuffles them, deals 6 to each player, looks at his hand, announces trumps, and leads to the second round.

Play continues in this way, with those taking no tricks being knocked out, and the player taking most tricks dealing, choosing trumps, and leading to the next. In case of a tie for most tricks, the tied player cutting the highest card deals next.

The number of cards dealt decreases by one on each deal, so that only one is dealt on the seventh round—if it gets that far. The winner, of course, is the player left in when everyone else is out.

Of many staking methods, the simplest has each active player putting a chip in the pot at the start of each deal, and the winner taking the pot.

Lansquenet

Gambling game: Np players, 1 pack

Famous, romantic, inane sixteenth-century gambling game played by German mercenaries (*Landsknechte*), not to mention the Three Musketeers.

One or more players match a stake put up by the banker, who then deals the top card face up to his left and the next face up to his right. If they are of the same suit, he wins, and there is a new round with new stakes. If not, he continues dealing cards one at a time face up to the middle until one appears that matches the suit of either start-card. A left-card match wins for the banker, who may either continue banking or sell this privilege to the highest bidder. A right-card match wins for the punters, and the bank automatically passes to the next in turn.

Lanterloo

See Loo.

Le Barbu

Trick-avoidance game: 4p, 52c

A compendium game of the Hearts family, the deals constituting a set of variations on a theme of avoiding the winning of tricks or of particular penalty cards. It first became prominent among French Bridge-players in the 1960s. Several versions have appeared in print; the following is an arrangement based on typical features of them all.

Mark a scoresheet into four columns, one per player, and twenty-eight rows, one for each deal. The deal passes regularly to the left, each dealing seven times in all. Deal 13 each in 1s.

The player at dealer's left is automatically the declarer. He examines his cards and declares one of seven possible contracts which he has not chosen before. Of these contracts, listed below, all but Domino are trick-taking games, and all but Domino and Trump attract negative scores or penalty points.

Declarer leads first. Follow suit if possible, otherwise play any card. The trick is taken by the highest card of the suit led, and the winner of each trick leads to the next. There are no trumps, except in the sixth contract. The possible contracts are:

1. No tricks. Each trick taken scores −2 points.
2. No hearts. Each heart taken scores −2, the Ace of hearts −6.
3. No Queens. Each Queen taken scores −6.
4. No King. Taking the heart King (*le Barbu*) scores −20.
5. No last. Taking the last trick scores −20, the penultimate trick −10.
6. Trump. Each trick won scores +5 points. (Declarer chooses trumps.)
7. Domino. Declarer lays any card face up on the table. Each in turn must then, if possible, play a card so that it abuts at least one card already in position and contributes to the eventual construction of a layout consisting of four 13-card suit sequences (Ace high, Two low), with one row per suit and one column per rank. First out of cards scores +40, second +20, third +5.

Note that the plus-scores gained in the last two games exactly match the total of penalties scored in the previous five, thus producing a zero-sum result.

Lift Smoke

See Sift Smoke.

Lily Bridge

Variety of Auction Bridge, *c.*1910, in which spades, normally the lowest suit at 2 per trick, could be bid as 'royal spades', or 'lilies', then ranking as the highest at 10 per trick.

Linger Longer

See Sift Smoke.

Liverpool Rummy

See Contract Rummy.

Lodam

Or 'Losing Loadum' (variously spelt): a sixteenth-century presumed ancestor of Hearts.

Lomber

Or l'Hombre: see Hombre.

Long Whist

Whist played to 10 instead of 5 game points.

Loo

Plain-trick game: 3–8p, 52c

Loo, of which many varieties are recorded, belongs to a sprawling family whose more intelligent members include Nap, Euchre, Rams (Rounce), and Spoil Five. It dates from the seventeenth century, was much played by the idle rich in the eighteenth, and got itself a thoroughly bad name in the nineteenth. Enthusiasts are still occasionally met with. The main forms are Three-Card Loo, Five-Card Loo, and Irish Loo, which is Five-Card Loo played with three cards. Let Five-Card be taken as typical.

Everyone contributes five chips to a pool. Deal 5 cards each (3 + 2) and turn the next for trump. Everyone's aim is to win at least one trick, under pain of increasing the pool. For this purpose cards basically rank A K Q J T 9 8 7 6 5 4 3 2, but the ♣J or 'Pam' (short for 'Pamphilus') beats everything, including the Ace of trumps.

Before play, each in turn announces which of three things he will do:

1. Play with the hand as dealt.
2. Play after discarding any number of cards and drawing the same number from the top of the pack (which he does before the next in turn speaks).
3. Drop the hand and sit the deal out, thereby losing his stake but

avoiding any further penalty. (*Variant*: In some circles, this is not permitted when clubs are trump.)

If any player holds a flush, whether dealt initially or obtained by drawing fresh cards, he wins the deal outright, there being no play. A flush is five cards of the same suit, or four of a suit plus Pam. If more than one has a flush, the best is a flush with Pam; failing that, a flush in trumps; failing that, the flush containing the highest top card (or cards if equal). The holder of the winning flush wins the stakes of all other players, including those who dropped, but excluding those holding either Pam or a lower flush.

Strict rules of trick-play apply. Eldest leads. If he has the trump Ace (or King if the Ace is the trump turn-up), he must lead it. If not, he must lead a trump if he holds two or more, and it must be his highest trump if there is only one opponent.

Subsequent players must—so far as possible—follow suit, head the trick, or trump if unable to follow. The trick is taken by the highest card of the suit led or by the highest trump if any are played. The winner of each trick leads to the next, and must lead a trump if possible.

If the trump Ace is led, and its player says 'Pam, be civil', Pam may not be played to the same trick, unless its holder has no other trump.

Each player takes one-fifth of the pool for each trick he has won. A player who takes no trick is looed and adds five more chips to the current pool. (*Variant*: In Unlimited Loo, he doubles the pool. This is not recommended.)

Lowball

Any variety of Poker in which only the lowest hand wins the pot.

Macao

Variety of Baccara, possibly ancestral, in which only one card is dealt.

Manille

Alternative name for Comet.

Manille

Point-trick game: 3–7p, 32c

This classic French game derives from Spanish Malilla (Catalan Manilla), and is played mainly in the south-west of the country. Its spread to the rest of France in the early twentieth century was subsequently checked and reversed by the expansion of Belote. It forms a good introduction to point-trick games for players only accustomed to plain-trick games. Of many varieties for various numbers of players, the following are typical.

Manille muette

Four players; those sitting opposite each other are partners. The deal and play pass always to the right. Deal 8 cards each in 4s. Turn the last card (Dealer's) to establish trumps, leaving it face up until the first card has been led.

Cards rank T A K Q J 9 8 7 in each suit. The aim is to win a majority (35+) of the 68 points available for tricks and cards. Each won trick counts 1 point, the other 60 deriving from the capture of the following cards in tricks:

Each Ten (*manille*)	5
Each Ace (*manillon*)	4
Each King	3
Each Queen	2
Each Jack	1

Eldest leads to the first trick and the winner of each trick leads to the next. Follow suit and head the trick if possible; if unable to follow, trump, and overtrump if a trump has already been played. However, a player who can neither follow suit nor play a higher trump is not then obliged to trump at all, but may play any card. The trick is taken by the highest-ranking card, or by the highest trump if any are played.

A common game structure is that the overall winners are the side first winning two games. Alternatively, players may agree to play up to a target score—50, 100, etc.—over as many deals as necessary, crediting (by agreement) either each side with the number of points it makes at each deal, or just the winning side with the number made in excess of 34.

Manille parlée

A more popular variety permitting spoken communication between partners, as the name implies; but what may be said is subject to stringent rules. The leader to a trick, before leading, may give his partner a single piece of information about his own hand, or request information about his partner's, or may (instead) invite his partner either to do the same or to give him some instruction as to the card or suit to be led. Such information may relate to the number of cards held of a specific suit or rank, or whether a particular card is held. Question and answer must be succinct, explicit, intelligible to the opponents, and not replaced or accompanied by any non-verbal conventions. Questions must be answered truthfully, and instructions followed if possible.

Auction Manille (1)

From three to seven may play, each for himself. Deal out all cards but two or four (depending on the number of players), which constitute a widow. Eldest has first privilege of becoming the declarer; if he declines, it passes to the right until somebody exercises it. The declarer's object is to take at least 21 points in tricks and cards, or at least 15 if more than four are playing. Before play, the declarer may keep drawing cards from the widow until he is satisfied with his hand. Each drawn card must be followed by a discard (which may be the card just drawn) before the next is taken. When satisfied, declarer announces trumps and eldest hand leads.

The amount won by the declarer from each opponent if successful, or paid to each if not, varies with the number of cards exchanged—e.g. 1 2 3 4, 1 2 4 8, 1 3 6 10, as agreed.

Auction Manille (2)

Remove as many Sevens as necessary to enable every player to receive the same number of cards. Each in turn, starting with Eldest, may pass or bid. A bid states the number of points the bidder undertakes to make in exchange for choosing trumps. Each bid must be higher than the last, and a player who has passed may not come in again. The highest bidder announces trumps (or 'No trumps'), and Eldest leads to the first trick—unless the bid was to win every trick, in which case the declarer leads. The player scores the amount of his bid if successful, or loses it if not. The winner is the player with the highest score after any agreed number of deals, each having dealt the same number of times.

Auction Manille (3)

A number of cards is dealt to each player in a particular manner, and the rest are laid some face up and some face down on the table, as follows:

Players	Deal each	Remainder
3	9 (3 3 3)	3 down, 2 up
4	7 (3 2 3)	2 down, 2 up
5	6 (2 2 2)	1 down, 1 up
6	5 (3 2)	1 down, 1 up
7	4 (2 2)	2 down, 2 up

Play as in Version 2, above, except that the highest bidder may exchange cards with the widow before naming trumps. In some circles the score is doubled if the bidder undertakes to win every trick, or plays without exchanging. (If both apply, the score is quadrupled.)

Mariage

See Sixty-Six.

Mariáš

Point-tricks and melds: 3p, 32c

The Czech national card game derives from Mariage (Sixty-Six) and underlies the more elaborate Hungarian game of Ulti (q.v.). Other relatives include Tyzicha, Bezique, and Pinochle. Players unacquainted with point-trick games should find it fairly easy to follow as an introduction to that family, and may particularly enjoy the bid of 'Seven last' as a novel feature.

Mariáš is normally played with the 32-card German-suited pack headed Daus, King, Ober, Unter, but is here described for the French pack headed Ace, King, Queen, Jack. Of several versions, each with its own range of variations, the following is slightly simplified from that described in V. Omasta and S. Ravik, *Hráčy Karty*, *Karetní Hri* (Prague, 1969).

General idea. In each deal there is a declarer who plays alone against a temporary partnership of the other two. The thirty-two cards rank A T K Q J 9 8 7 in each suit. Aces and Tens captured in tricks count 10 each to the side taking them, as does winning the last trick, making 90 points available in all. In a basic game, each side's aim is to take most points—normally at least 50. However, the total available may be increased by scoring for marriages. Any player holding a King and Queen of the same suit may declare it for 20 points, or 40 in trumps. This could bring the total available to as high as 190 points. Whatever it is, each side's aim is to take more than the other, ties being impossible.

Deal. The turns to deal and play pass always to the left. The player at dealer's left is called Forehand, and at his right Middlehand. Deal 5 cards each face down in batches of 3 then 2, then two more face down to Forehand, so that he has 7. Deal 5 more each in 3s and 2s, keeping them separate from the first 5.

Bidding. Forehand is expected to choose trumps and play a basic game. He starts by examining his first seven cards, leaving his other five face down. If willing to entrump the suit of any of these seven, he lays it face up, on the table. If not, he picks one of his other five at random, turns it face up, and must accept its suit as trump. He then takes all his cards except the turn-up, and discards any two face down as a widow. They may not include an Ace or Ten, and if they include a trump, he must say so.

Forehand then asks the others—Middlehand first—if they will let him play a basic game. One of them can prevent it by offering to play either *betl*, a bid to play at no trump and lose every trick, or *durch*, a bid to win every trick after nominating any desired suit as trump.

If neither does so, Forehand is the declarer in a basic game, which he may now (if he wishes) augment with extra or alternative bids as follows:

1. *Seven Last*: An undertaking to win the last trick with the trump Seven. A bonus accrues for doing this anyway, but announcing it beforehand doubles it.
2. *Hundred*: An undertaking to take at least 100 points with not more than one marriage. (But subsequent marriages are scorable once this has been achieved.) A bonus accrues for doing this anyway, but announcing it beforehand doubles its value.
3. *Hundred and Seven*: Both the above bids combined.
4. *Double Seven*: An undertaking to win both the last trick with the trump Seven and the previous trick with any other Seven. If either part of this bid is lost, the other is deemed to have failed too.
5. *Betl*: A bid to lose every trick, playing at no trump. Cards rank A K Q J T 9 8 7, and there are no scores for Aces, Tens, marriages or last. Betl may be played open, with all players' hands exposed on the table, for double the score.
6. *Durch*: A bid to win every trick, playing with the turned suit as trump. (Unlike the others, Forehand is not allowed to name a different suit from that turned.) As in betl, cards rank A K Q J T 9 8 7; there are no scores for Aces, Tens, marriages, or last; and it may be played open, with all players' hands exposed on the table, for double the score.

Other announcements and doubles. If either opponent has the trump Seven, he may announce 'Seven last' and score for it independently if successful. (There is a penalty for playing the trump Seven to the last trick and losing it, whether announced or not.) Similarly, either opponent may himself make a side-bid to take 100 points with the aid of only one marriage.

It is possible to double the basic contract or the bid of Seven last, or both, and each may be doubled at a different level. The possible levels are:

Double	× 2
Redouble	× 4
Tutti	× 8
Retutti	× 16

Either opponent may double the basic contract; declarer may redouble; and so on alternately. As to the Seven, either player other

than its bidder may double; its bidder may redouble; and so on
alternately. It is necessary to specify what is being doubled. For
example, a round of bidding might proceed:

Forehand	Clubs, hundred
Middlehand	Double
Dealer	Seven last
Forehand	Redouble the game, double the Seven
Middlehand	Pass
Dealer	Tutti the game
Forehand	Pass

Concession. If a basic game is bid, and no extras are added or
doubles made, the game is considered not worth playing. Forehand
is instead deemed to have won, and scores accordingly.

Play. Declarer leads to the first trick. Players must follow suit if
possible and head the trick if possible. If unable to follow, they must
trump and overtrump if possible. The trick is taken by the highest
card of the suit led or by the highest trump if any are played, and the
winner of each trick leads to the next.

A player holding a marriage announces 'Twenty' or 'Forty' upon
playing either of the relevant cards to a trick. The cards of a marriage are not gathered into the trick but left face up on the table
before the player scoring them, for ease of checking afterwards.

In an open betl or durch, all hands are laid face up on the table at
the end of the first trick, and the partners may discuss with one
another how best to play.

Score. The basic scores for betl and durch are 5 and 10 respectively,
or 10 and 20 if played open, and may have been increased by
doubling. The appropriate amount is added to the declarer's score if
successful, or deducted from it if not.

The scores for a trump game are as follows. Note that all are
doubled if hearts were trump, and may also have been further
doubled or redoubled after the auction.

	Basic game	1
	plus	
	Seven last (silent)	1
or	Seven last (declared)	2
or	Double Seven	8

plus

	Hundred (silent)	2
or	Hundred (declared)	4

The relevant score for winning the last trick with the trump Seven goes to both partners if one of them makes it. Playing it to the last trick and failing to win it incurs a penalty point, or 2 if it was declared. If this happens to the partners, both pay that penalty even if one of them wins the trick to which the other played the Seven. If Seven last was bid, its holder may not play it to any earlier trick unless he is forced to trump and has no other.

Marjolet

Trick and meld game: 2p, 32c

A simpler relative of Bezique popular in south-west France, according to Frans Gerver (*Le Guide Marabout*, Verviers, 1966). The peculiar liaison of Jack and Queen, so characteristic of Bezique and Pinochle, appears here in an unusual form, perhaps suggesting an ancestral version of this feature.

Two players each receive 6 cards (in 2s or 3s) from a 32-card pack ranking A T K Q J 9 8 7 in each suit. The rest are stacked face down, and its top card turned for trump and slipped face up half under the pack. If it is a Seven, dealer scores 10 for it.

Game is 500 (or 1000) points over as many deals as necessary, each dealing alternately. Scores accrue for collecting and declaring melds, as detailed below, and for winning brisques (Aces and Tens) in tricks, these counting 10 each.

Elder leads any card to the first trick. Suit need not be followed. The trick is taken by the higher card of the suit led, or by a trump to a non-trump lead. The winner of a trick draws the top card of stock, waits for his opponent to do likewise, and leads to the next. Before drawing, the trick-winner may show and score for any of the following melds:

Four Aces	· 100
Tens	80
Kings	60
Queens	40
Trump marriage	40
Plain marriage	20

Matching games

There are two sorts of marriage:

1. King and Queen of the same suit (40 trump, 20 plain).
2. The trump Jack, called 'Marjolet', and any Queen (40 trump Queen, 20 plain).

Melds are left face up on the table and still form part of their owners' hand for the purposes of trick-play. Marjolet, if kept, may be married at different times to different Queens, and the same Queen may be married both to Marjolet and to her matching King. More than one meld may be scored at a time.

A player drawing or dealt the trump Seven may exchange it for the turn-up and score 10. He may only do so upon winning a trick and before making a draw. Whoever wins the tenth trick, so drawing the turned trump, scores 10 for it.

The stock exhausted, players take their melds into hand for the last six tricks. It is now obligatory, so far as possible, to follow suit, head the trick, and trump if unable to follow. The winner of the final trick scores 10, or 50 if he took all six. Each player then sorts through his won cards and scores 10 for each brisque he has taken.

The winner is the player with the higher score at the end of the deal in which either player reached the target. (By analogy with Bezique; source is not explicit on this point.)

Matching games

Each in turn plays to a common wastepile a card which in some specified way matches the previous discard. Players unable to do so miss a turn and may have to draw more cards. As the usual object is to be the first to play out all one's cards, most matching games are also Going-out or Elimination games. Examples include the Stops and Switch families.

Matrimony

Gambling game: 3–10p, 52 cards

A nineteenth-century family gambling game.

A large sheet of paper is marked with five staking compartments labelled Matrimony, Intrigue, Confederacy, Pair, Best. Players start with the same number of chips. The turn to deal and play passes always to the left.

The dealer first distributes any number of counters in any way he likes between these five compartments, so long as each contains at least two. Each player then takes from his own store one less than the dealer's chosen quantity and distributes them with equal freedom.

The cards shuffled and cut, deal one card face down to each player, followed by a second card face up. If anyone's up-card is ◆A, he sweeps all the chips on the layout, and the cards are thrown in for the next deal by the player on the present dealer's left.

Otherwise, each in turn, starting at Dealer's left, turns up his down-card, and wins the contents of the appropriate staking compartment if his two cards form one of the stated combinations, namely:

Matrimony	Any King and Queen
Intrigue	Any Queen and Jack
Confederacy	Any King and Jack
Pair	Two cards of the same rank.

The contents of *Best* go to the player with the highest card of the diamond suit (Ace high, Two low). Any stake not claimed is carried forward to the next deal.

Mau Mau

See Neuner.

Mauscheln

Plain-trick game: 3–4p, 32c

This popular German and Danish family game, best for four, is played for small stakes and may be regarded as a variety of Nap. The title means (1) to talk Yiddish, (2) to fiddle, in its non-musical sense. Where necessary, I will use 'diddle' as an English equivalent.

The dealer forms a kitty (*Pinke*) and deals 2 cards face down to each player, 1 face up to establish trumps, and 2 more each face down. Cards rank A K Q J T 9 8 7 in each suit. Each in turn has one opportunity to say 'I'll diddle', which is an undertaking to win at least two tricks. If no one will diddle, the cards are thrown in and the next in turn deals. Otherwise, everyone else must either 'Go along', which is an undertaking to win at least one trick, or 'Pass', in which case they take no part in the hand. If no one will go along, the diddler wins the kitty without having to play, and the cards are thrown in for the next deal.

Given two or more players, each in turn may either stand pat or discard from one to four cards face down from his hand, receiving the same number from the top of the pack. This may only be done once.

The diddler leads to the first trick. Subsequent players must, so far as possible, follow suit and head the trick, and trump if unable to follow (in which case it is not necessary to beat a previous player's trump). The trick is taken by the highest card of the suit led or by the highest trump if any are played, and the winner of each trick leads to the next.

Each trick won earns its winner one quarter of the kitty. A player winning no trick, or the diddler if he wins only one, pays the amount of the kitty into the kitty for the next deal. If the diddler wins none, he is a 'diddle-twit' (*Mauschelbete*), and pays double that amount.

Optional extras include making ◆7 ('*Belli*') the second-highest trump.

Maw

A Scottish game played at the Stuart courts; the ancestor of Spoil Five.

Michigan

The earliest (1920s) example of a Rummy game in which players aim to score plus points for melds as well as to win by going out first. For more advanced versions, see Oklahoma and Persian Rum.

Michigan

Stops game: 5–8p, 52c

A sociable and family gambling game; the American equivalent of Newmarket.

A staking layout is made from four 'boodle' cards from another pack: Ace, King, Queen, Jack, all of different suits. Each player starts with the same number of chips, not fewer than 20. The turns to deal and play pass always to the left. As the deal is an advantage, the game should end whenever all have dealt the same number of times.

Dealer starts by staking two of his chips against each boodle card, and everybody else stakes one. (*Variant*: Dealer's eight and others' four chips may be distributed ad lib between the boodle cards.) Deal the cards round one at a time as far as they will go, but to one more hand than there are players. The odd hand is called the widow. It doesn't matter if some players have one more card than others.

If dealer does not like his hand, he may discard it face down and take the widow instead. If he keeps it, he may sell the widow (sight unseen) to the highest bidder. Whoever takes the widow must then use it as his playing hand.

Eldest starts by playing a card face up to the table, announcing what it is. He may pick any suit, but must lead the lowest he has of it. For this purpose cards rank, from low to high, 2 3 4 5 6 7 8 9 T J Q K A. Whoever holds the next higher card of the same suit must play it against the first, also announcing what it is; and so on. A player holding more than one card in ascending sequence may play them all.

A player who plays a card matching one of the boodle cards promptly collects all the chips staked on it in the layout.

Play continues until a stop is reached—whether because an Ace has been played, or because the next card up is in the widow, or because it has already been played. The player of a stopped card, when certain no one can follow, then starts another sequence by leading the lowest card he holds of any different suit from the one just stopped. If he can't change suit, the turn to start passes to the left until someone can play. If no one can play, the hand ends—or (*variant*): whoever played the stopped card leads the lowest card he has.

161

Misère

Play ends as soon as one player runs out of cards, and he collects from each other player one chip for each card remaining in his hand (two, in the case of unplayed boodle cards).

Misère

French for 'poverty': equivalent card terms in other languages include *bettel*, *contrabola*, *devole*, *null*, *nullo*, *pobre*. Tricks are played, usually at no trump, and the aim is to win none at all, or as few as possible. This does not allow sufficient variety to constitute a game in its own right, but it is the basis of such trick-avoidance games as Hearts and Black Maria, and provides an optional contract for most games involving an auction.

Monte

Gambling game

1. Also called Monte Bank. A Spanish, especially Mexican, gambling game played with the 40-card Spanish pack. Two cards dealt from the bottom of the pack form the bottom layout, then two from the top form the top layout. Punters individually stake on either layout. The top card of the pack is then turned face up and placed between them. This is called the 'gate'. The dealer pays all stakes set against a layout containing a card matching the suit of the gate, and collects all stakes set against a layout not containing a card of matching suit. These five are discarded, five more are dealt, and so on until all cards have been used.

2. Monte also denotes a variety of other gambling games, especially any form of three-card Poker.

3. Three-card Monte is a sideshow guessing game of dubious propriety.

Mouche

An eighteenth-century French game much like Five-Card Loo but lacking 'Pam'.

Mus

Spanish gambling game of Basque origin, of the Poker family but played by four in partnerships.

My Ship Sails

Collecting game: 3–7p, 52c

A children's game, possibly related to an early seventeenth-century gambling game recorded (but not described) as 'My Sow Pigg'd'.

Deal 7 cards each and leave the rest out of play. The aim is to get seven of a suit. All play simultaneously by repeatedly giving a card face down to his left-hand neighbour and receiving one from his right. The winner is the first to get seven alike, lay his hand down, and call 'My Ship Sails'.

Nain Jaune

Or Yellow Dwarf: relative of Pope Joan (q.v.).

Nap

Plain-trick game: 3–7p, 28–52c

Or Napoleon: a simplified relative of Euchre played widely, and with many variations, throughout Northern Europe. Despite its title and allusions, it is not recorded before the last third of the nineteenth century, and may have been first named after Napoleon III. It is best for four to five players using a stripped pack.

Deal 5 cards each, either in 1s or as batches of 3 and 2, from a 52-card pack ranking A K Q J T 9 8 7 6 5 4 3 2. Eldest bids or passes first, and each in turn thereafter must bid higher or pass. A bid is an undertaking to win at least the number of tricks stated, using a trump suit of one's own choice. From low to high, the bids are: two, three, miz (lose every trick), four, Nap (five), Wellington (five, for double stakes), Blücher (five, for redoubled stakes). Wellington may only follow a bid of Nap, and Blücher a bid of Wellington.

The highest bidder leads to the first trick. The suit of the card led is automatically trump—except in a bid of miz, if players have previously agreed that miz is played at no trump. Subsequent players must follow suit if possible, but otherwise may play any card. The trick is taken by the highest card of the suit led, or by the highest trump if any are played, and the winner of each trick leads to the next.

If successful, the bidder wins from each opponent 2—4 units for bids of two to four respectively, 3 for miz, 10 for Nap, 20 for Wellington, 40 for Blücher. If not, he pays the same amount to each opponent, though it may be agreed to halve it in the case of Nap, Wellington, and Blücher.

The turn to deal passes to the left, and it is customary not to shuffle the cards until a bid of five has been won.

There are many variations on the basic theme. The skill factor may be increased by stripping the pack of lower numerals so that the number of cards in play is from six to eight times the number of players. Four would therefore use 28 or 32 cards (Eight or Seven low), five 36 or 40 cards (Six or Five low). A Joker may be added, counting as the highest trump—or, in miz, as the only trump. Many other variations may be encountered or invented.

Notes. Skill, both in assessing the hand and in playing the cards, is at a premium when four or five play with 28 or 36 cards respectively, and diminishes significantly as the number of players or cards increases. The average bid of three requires at least three trumps of which at least one is higher than Ten, and either two side-suit Aces or a suit headed A K or A Q. If the trump lead holds, it is as well to press trumps before leading side suits. Non-trump cards that are probable losers should be lost early rather than late, being preferably discarded when unable to follow suit.

Neuner

Matching game: 2–5p, 33c

Or 'Nines': the Austrian equivalent of the game known elsewhere as Eights, Crazy Eights, or Swedish Rummy. Its forerunner, Mau Mau, became a national craze in Germany in the 1960s, and is also described below. For an English equivalent, see Switch.

Neuner

From a 32-card pack (A K Q J T 9 8 7), plus Joker, deal 5 cards each, turn the next face up to start a sequence, and stack the rest face down. The aim is to run out of cards.

Each in turn must play to the sequence either a wild card or one which matches the previous card by rank or suit. A wild card is the Joker or any Nine.

If the starter is the Joker, any card may follow; if it is a Nine, the next must follow suit or itself be wild. Thereafter, a wild card may be played at any time without restriction, and its player names any desired suit as the one to be matched by the following card.

Only one card may be played to the sequence at each turn. If unable or unwilling to match, the player may continue to draw cards from stock (so long as any are left) until he is able and willing to play.

If the next in turn cannot make a legal play, and the stock is exhausted, the turn to play passes to the left until someone can continue. If no one can continue, the original player may play any card.

The first to play the last card from his hand wins, and play ceases immediately. The winner scores the total value of all cards left in other players' hands, counting Joker 20, each Nine 15, Ace 11, King 4, Queen 3, Jack 2, Ten 10, Eight 8, Seven 7. The overall winner is the first to reach an agreed target, typically 100 or 150.

Notes. The main improvement on Eights is that you are allowed to draw cards even if you can play. Although this enlarges your hand, it reduces your opponents' ability to follow, and in the long run may get you out more quickly.

Mau Mau

From three to five players each receive 5 cards from a 32-card pack, the next is turned as a starter, and the rest are stacked face down. Each in turn must match the previous card by rank or suit, or play a Jack. A Jack entitles its player to name the suit to be followed, which need not be that of the Jack itself. A player unable to follow may draw one card from stock (so long as any remain). If he still cannot follow, the turn passes to the left. The first to play out all his cards ends the round by announcing 'Mau Mau'. The others are then penalized by the total face value of cards left in their hands, counting Ace 11, Ten 10, King 4, Queen 3, Jack 2 (or 20), others zero (or face value). The whole game ends when someone reaches 100 penalty points.

Newmarket

Stops game: 5–8p, 52c

A sociable and family gambling game ultimately derived from seventeenth-century Comet. Rules vary. The following are as played at the author's local community centre in south London.

Each player deals in turn and the turn to deal passes to the left. The four Kings are placed in the centre as a staking layout. The remaining cards are dealt round one at a time, the last card of each round going to a dead hand. It doesn't matter that some players may get one more card than others. Everybody stakes an agreed amount on each King and to a separate kitty.

A game consists of several deals and ends when all the Kings have gone.

One player may 'buy' the spare hand in exchange for the hand dealt him. Dealer has the first option, which passes to the left until someone exercises it. Whoever buys pays a fixed stake to the common kitty, except the dealer, who exchanges free.

Cards rank A 2 3 4 5 6 7 8 9 T J Q. Whoever holds the lowest diamond starts by playing it face up to the table. The holder of the next higher consecutive diamond plays it, then the next, and so on for as long as the sequence continues. Cards are played face up in front of their holders, not to a spread on the table.

Eventually the sequence will come to an end, usually because the next higher diamond is in the dead hand. In this case a new sequence is started by the player of the last card. That player must start with a suit of different colour, and with the lowest card held of it.

Example. A leads ◆3–4, C plays 5, B adds 6–7. No one has the Eight. B, holding ♠3–9–J ♥A–2–9–Q ♣8–Q ◆2, must play either ♠3 or ♣8.

If that player has none of the required colour, the turn to start a new sequence passes to the left until someone can change colour. If no one can, the round ends and the next deal ensues.

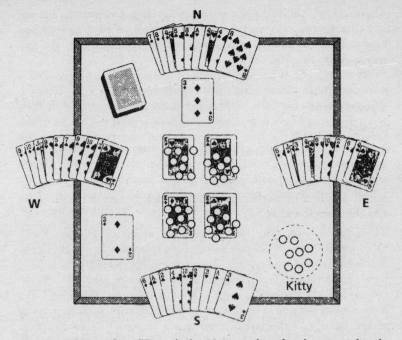

FIG. 16. **Newmarket.** West dealt. No one bought the spare hand, though South should have, holding too many low cards and an imbalance of black and red suits. The lowest diamond was led by West and followed by North, who played ♣4 when the ♦4 failed to appear. The play continued: ♠4–Q, ♦5–Q, ♣5, ♥A–3, ♣A–4, 'No red', ♥9–10, ♣Q, ♥6 and East is out. It is unusual for three Kings to be dismissed in one deal.

Alternatively, the sequence ends when someone plays a Queen. That player immediately wins everything staked on the King of that suit, and starts a new sequence with the lowest card held of a different colour. The stripped King is then removed, and remains out of play till the end of the game. In subsequent deals, whoever plays the Queen of an absent King has nothing to win, and merely starts a new sequence.

The deal ends in either of two ways. Whoever plays the last card from their hand thereby ends the play and wins the common kitty.

Alternatively, it ends when a sequence has been finished and no one can change colour to start a new one, though all have at least one card in hand. In this case the common kitty is carried forward and increased on the next deal.

When only one King remains, a new rule applies. A player who is dealt the Queen of that King's suit says 'Bury the Jack' (or 'Johnny'). Whoever holds the Jack, if it is not in the dead hand, must then swap their hand for the dead one, free of charge. If the holder of the Queen also holds the Jack, or any longer sequence, they order the burial of the next lower card. For example, the holder of T J Q says 'Bury the Nine'.

The game ends as soon as someone plays the Queen matching the fourth and last King, thereby winning both the stake on the King and the common kitty.

The book version. The staking layout consists of an Ace, King, Queen, and Jack, of different suits, taken from another pack. Cards are dealt around evenly, any remainder being added to the dead hand. Eldest leads. The starter of a new sequence need not change colour, but in some circles must at least change suit. Whoever plays a card matching one in the layout by rank and suit wins everything staked on it, but the layout card is not removed from the table. Whoever plays their last card ends the current deal and wins one chip from each opponent for each card left in hand.

Nines

See Neuner.

Ninety-Nine

Plain-trick game: 2–4p (3 best), 36c

Invented by the present author in 1968 in response to a need for a plain-trick game of skill for three players, Ninety-Nine has since been published in many languages and may now be regarded as well established. It also exploits the historically recent idea of bidding to take an exact rather than a minimum number of tricks (see also Oh Hell!). The original form is described first, and is followed by variations.

Three players use a 37-card pack consisting of A K Q J T 9 8 7 6 in each suit and a Joker. A game is nine deals. Deal 12 each in 1s and turn the next face up to establish trumps. If the turn-up is the Joker or a Nine, the game is no trump. The Joker has no permanent value of its own but adopts the identity of the card turned for trump: whoever holds it treats it exactly as if it were that card.

Each player discards three cards face down and plays the other nine to tricks. The aim is to win exactly the number of tricks indicated in code by the suits of the three discards. For this purpose

Each discarded diamond represents 0 tricks bid
                spade   1
                heart   2
                club   3

(*Example*: A bid to win three tricks may be made by discarding ♣ ♦ ♦ or ♥ ♠ ♦ or ♠ ♠ ♠. Nine tricks is represented by ♣ ♣ ♣, none by ♦ ♦ ♦.)

After the discard, but before the opening lead, each in turn from the dealer's left may offer to 'declare' or 'reveal', thereby increasing his potential bonus or penalty. To declare is to turn one's bid-cards face up so that the opponents know how many tricks are wanted; to reveal is the same, but also playing with one's hand of cards face up on the table. Only one player may declare or reveal. Priority goes to the player nearest the dealer's left, but an offer to reveal takes priority over an offer to declare. Players may not change their bid-cards once anyone has stated that they will or will not declare or reveal.

Eldest leads to the first trick. Subsequent players must follow suit if possible, but otherwise may play any card. The trick is taken by the highest card of the suit led, or by the highest trump if any are played, and the winner of each trick leads to the next.

At end of play, anyone who has taken exactly the number of tricks he bid must turn his bid-cards up to prove it. (Anyone who failed is not obliged to show them.) Each player scores 1 point per trick taken, regardless of his bid. For succeeding in one's bid, the bonus is

               10 each if all succeed
               20 if only two succeed
               30 if only one succeeds

(a)

(b)

FIG. 17. Ninety-nine. (a) Each suit, by its shape, encodes a number of tricks bid. (b) Five reasonable ways of bidding the hand shown, one for each trump situation.

There is a bonus of 30 for a declaration and 60 for a revelation. This goes to the declarer if he succeeds, or to each opponent if he fails. (The maximum possible score is 99, made when the only player to succeed bid and made nine, and he or another player revealed.)

Variant 1 (Sphinx). There is no Joker. The deal is followed by a round of bidding. Anyone who offers to declare or reveal chooses trumps (or no trump), and discards are made accordingly. If no one bids, the trump suit remains that of the previous deal, or none in the case of the first.

Variant 2 (Pennycook's). Declarations and revelations are ignored, and the game is played to a target of 150 points.

Variant 3 (Elegant Variation). There is no Joker. The first deal is played at no trump. Thereafter, the trump suit is determined by the number of players who succeeded in their bids on the previous deal: diamonds if none, spades if one, hearts if two, clubs if three. Play ends when someone reaches or exceeds 100 points. If the runner-up reaches 100, he gains one game point (or stake) and the winner two; if not, the winner gains three.

Notes. Since the shape of the hand is affected by the bid-cards, the aim is not so much to think of a number and bid it as to bid a reasonable number (three, if in doubt) and then make it. Since the number of tricks to be won is the nines-complement of the number to be lost (e.g. a bid to win four is also a bid to lose five), it is important to keep Aces and Kings for winning tricks, and Sixes and Sevens for losing them; therefore, the ideal discards are from Nines to Queens, and especially Tens and Jacks. Since the average bid is three, the nine discards are likely to include more diamonds than spades, spades than hearts, and hearts than clubs. This means that diamonds are the most 'unreliable' suit, as there will probably be few in play, with the danger that one's diamond lead will be trumped if the trick is wanted, or discarded to if not. Similarly, if diamonds are trump, the top trumps may well be discarded, leaving the Jack or Ten unexpectedly the best in play. Conversely, clubs are the most 'reliable' suit, followed by hearts. In play, concentrate first on making high cards in unreliable suits, then in getting rid of dangerous middling cards that risk winning unwanted tricks. When someone declares or reveals, it is in the scoring interests of the two

171

opponents to co-operate in beating him before trying to succeed in their own bids.

Ninety-Nine for two

Use 24 cards (Nine low, Joker optional) and deal 12 each. One player may reveal; a mere declaration is not admitted. The bonus is 10 if both succeed, 20 if only one, 30 for a revelation. The target is 100.

Ninety-Nine for four

Use 52 cards (Joker optional) and deal 13 each. A discard of three diamonds may be used to represent a bid of either no tricks or all ten: there is, of course, no need to say which was intended. If the Joker is not used, follow the rules of Variant 3, with no trump on the first deal or in any following one in which all four succeeded. There are no declarations or revelations, and if all succeed there is no bonus for doing so.

Naughty Nun

A radical variant for two to four players using a pack of 24, 36, or 52 cards with no Joker. Nine deals are played, with a different trumping arrangement in each. In all deals, suit must be followed if possible, otherwise any card may be played. A higher suit means one higher in bidding value.

1. Diamonds trump.
2. Spades trump.
3. Hearts trump.
4. Clubs trump.
5. Nuns (no trump).
6. Rondo: The trump varies at each trick according to the suit led: spades trump diamonds, hearts spades, clubs hearts, and diamonds clubs.
7. Whistle and flute (best suit): The trick is taken by the highest card of the highest suit played.
8. Top Dog: The trick is taken by the card of highest rank, or, if tied, by the tied card of the highest suit.
9. Snap: The trick is trumped by playing a card of the same rank as the one led and calling 'Snap!' (No call, no win.)

This is best played without declarations or revelations, and a player who fails to reach 100 points over nine deals loses double.

Ninety-Nine

Adding-up game: 3–6p, 52c

An adding-up game reportedly popular with gypsies.

Deal 3 cards each in 1s and stack the rest face down. Play starts in a clockwise direction, but may change. Each in turn plays a card face up to the table, announcing the total face value of all cards so far played, and draws a replacement from stock. The total may not exceed ninety-nine. The first player unable to play without busting loses a life. The first to lose three lives is the overall loser.

Cards count as follows:

Black Ace	*Any*	Seven	7
Red Ace	1	Eight	8
Two	2	Nine	*makes* 99
Three	0	Ten	*minus* 10
Four	0	Jack	10
Five	5	Queen	10
Six	6	King	10

A black Ace brings the total to anything its player chooses, from 0 to 99.

A Nine automatically makes the total 99, and can therefore be followed only by a Three, Four, Ten, or black Ace.

A Jack, besides counting 10, reverses the order of play—that is, the next card is played by whoever played the card preceding the Jack.

Noddy

Sixteenth-century ancestor of Cribbage; presumed extinct, but recent reports suggest it is still played in parts of Lancashire. Two or four players—the latter presumably partners—received 3 cards each from a 52-card pack counting as at Cribbage. The next was turned face up, scoring 2 to the dealer if a Jack ('Knave Noddy'). Each scored for any four-card combination he could make, using the turn-up as the fourth in his hand. The scores were 4 for a pair, 12 for a prial (three of a kind), 24 for a pair taunte (four of a kind), 2 for a fifteen, 2 for a twenty-five. Cards were then played out to 31, with scores for pairs as above, 1 for making fifteen, 1 for twenty-five, and 1 for last, or 2 if it made 31 exactly. Certain other cards had names and scores: 'Flatback' (♠K) 6, 'Countenance' (♥Q) 4, 'Roger' (♥J) 5, 'Knave Noddy' 2. No further details are furnished by the only description I know, in Randle Holme's *Academy of Armory*, 1688.

Nomination Whist

Plain-trick game: 4p, 52c

This relative of Solo Whist is said to be, or have been, popular in the Royal Navy. Its title is also used of Oh Hell!, and the equivalent at Bridge is called Pirate.

Deal 13 each from a 52-card pack ranking A K Q J T 9 8 7 6 5 4 3 2. Each in turn bids or passes. The lowest bid is seven, and each subsequent bid must be higher than the previous one. A bid is the number of tricks a player undertakes to win in exchange for naming trumps and playing either alone against the other three or with a temporary ally against the other two. The highest bidder then announces trumps and names a card, e.g. 'Hearts, Ace of spades'. The holder of the named card becomes his ally, but says nothing, revealing himself only by playing that card or obviously supporting the bidder by his play. The bidder may name a card in his own hand, in which case he is playing alone; but this fact, too, will only become known from the play.

The bidder wins from each opponent if successful, or pays to each opponent if not, one unit for each trick bid. A successful slam (13 tricks) wins or pays 26, but if the slam is made when not bid (e.g. 11 bid, 13 taken) the bidder pays 13 instead. If there was an ally, he and the bidder win from or pay to one opponent each.

Norwegian Whist

Plain-trick game: 4pp, 52c

Norwegian Whist may well be authentically named, as trumpless trick games are typical of Scandinavian card-play.

Four players sitting crosswise in partnerships receive 13 each from a 52-card pack ranking A K Q J T 9 8 7 6 5 4 3 2. Each in turn, starting from the left, may pass or bid. There are only two bids, and the first to name one establishes the contract for himself and partner. If the bid is 'grand', each partnership's aim is to win most tricks (seven or more); if 'nullo', it is to win fewer tricks (not more than six). If three pass, dealer must bid.

At grand, the opening lead is made by the player at bidder's right; at nullo, it comes from his left. Subsequent players must follow suit if possible, but otherwise may play any card. The trick is taken by the highest card of the suit led, and the winner of each trick leads to the next.

At nullo, the side taking fewer tricks scores 2 points per trick taken by the other side.

For a successful grand, the bidding side scores 4 points for each trick taken in excess of six. If unsuccessful, the other side scores 8 for each trick taken over six. (*Variant*: If the bidding side succeeds, it scores 5 for *every* trick it took; otherwise, the other side scores 6 for every trick it took.)

Game is 50 up.

Obstacle Race

Adding-up game: 3–6p, 32c

Or Hindernislauf: an adding-up game I know only from Jürgen Göring, *Stich um Stich* (Berlin, 1977), who says nothing of its background. Perhaps he invented it. It has some nice points, and can be made even more interesting with a little more creative thought.

For adding-up purposes, cards count as follows:

Ace	1	Ten	10
King	4	Nine	9
Queen	3 or −3	Eight	8
Jack	2	Seven	7

Note the Queens' unique ability to reduce the current total.

Deal the cards out evenly. If other than four play, the two left over are laid face up on the table to start the sequence, and the dealer announces their combined point-total.

Each in turn plays a card face up to the sequence, announcing the combined total of all cards so far played. The 'obstacles' are 55, 66,

Oh Hell!

77, 88, 99, and 111. A player scores one point for bringing the total to exactly an obstacle number, but loses a point for skipping over one without making it exactly. These apply whether the obstacle is reached forwards or, by the play of a Queen, backwards.

Play continues until the total reaches or exceeds 120, then starts again at zero. The winner is the player with the highest score when all cards have been played.

Oh Hell!

Plain-trick game: 3–7p, 52c

Also called Blackout, Botheration, Jungle Bridge, Nomination Whist, Oh Well!, Oh Pshaw!, etc., the following party game for otherwise serious card-players first appeared in the early 1930s and is sometimes credited to Geoffrey Mott-Smith. It explores the unusual idea of bidding to take an exact number of tricks (see also Ninety-Nine), and works best for four or five players.

Use a 52-card pack ranking A K Q J T 9 8 7 6 5 4 3 2 and appoint a scorekeeper, who should rule a sheet into as many columns as there are players and note the name or initials of one player at the head of each column. The number of deals to a game depends on the number of players.

Whoever cuts or draws the lowest card deals first. Cards are always dealt face down and one at a time. On the first deal, deal the cards round as far as they will go so that everyone receives the same number. If any remain, leave them face down to one side but turn the top card to establish trumps. If none remain, play at no trump.

Starting with Eldest, each in turn examines his hand and announces how many tricks he proposes to take, from 'none' to the maximum possible. The scorekeeper notes that number down in the appropriate column, as well as the total number of tricks to be played in that deal, and announces whether the total number of tricks bid fall short of, equals, or exceeds the number to be played. Each player's object is to take exactly the number of tricks he bid, neither more nor fewer.

Eldest leads to the first trick. Subsequent players must follow suit if possible, but otherwise may play any card. The trick is taken by the highest card of the suit led, or by the highest trump if any are played, and the winner of each trick leads to the next.

A player who took what he bid scores that number plus 10. One who failed scores nothing for that deal. The scorekeeper notes each player's total in the appropriate column, and on subsequent deals sums the score totals as he goes along.

Each subsequent deal is made after thorough shuffling by the next in turn to deal, and is played in exactly the same way as described above. However, the number of cards dealt decreases by one at each deal, so that on the last deal (seventeenth if three play, thirteenth if four, etc.) only one card each is dealt and only one trick played.

The winner, of course, is the player with the highest score at the end of the one-card deal.

Variants. The following variations may be encountered in various combinations:

1. One card is dealt on the first round, 2 on the second, and so on as far as possible.
2. No-trump hands may be avoided by not dealing all cards out when they could go round exactly, but, where necessary, leaving out of play as many cards as there are players.
3. The dealer, as last to bid, may be prohibited from bidding a number which would bring the total bid to the number of tricks in question, so at least one player is bound to fail.
4. Scoring: (*a*) Score 1 point per trick taken, whether bid or not. (*b*) A successful bid of zero scores 5 points, or (*c*) 5 plus the number of tricks played in that deal. (*d*) In any deal consisting of five or more tricks, there is a bonus of 50 for successfully bidding a slam (winning every trick), or 25 for a small slam (all but one).
5. Originally, the number of cards dealt was always as many as possible, and the game was played up to 100 points. Somewhere along the way Oh Hell! seems to have hybridized with Knockout Whist to produce the format described above.

Notes. Don't bid too high. It is easier to lose tricks than win them.

Oklahoma
Rummy game: 3–5p, 2 × 52c

One of the few species of Rummy worth retaining from the Rummy explosion of the 1930s and 40s, Oklahoma (also called Arlington) has the rare merit of being good for three players.

Oklahoma

Shuffle together two packs and (optionally) a Joker. The turn to deal and play passes regularly to the left. Deal 13 cards each one at a time, turn the next face up (the up-card) to start a wastepile, and stack the rest face down beside it to form the stock.

The aim is to make melds consisting of (a) three or four cards of the same rank—not more, and not necessarily of different suits; or (b) three or more cards in suit and sequence. For this purpose, cards rank A 2 3 4 5 6 7 8 9 T J Q K A. Ace may count high or low (A 2 3 or A K Q), not both (K A 2 illegal), but a sequence may be extended to fourteen cards with an Ace at each end. The Joker and all Deuces are wild, and may be used to represent any desired card in a set or sequence. Deuces, however, are 'natural' if forming part of a sequence between Ace and Three, or if melded together as a set of three or four.

Each in turn, starting at Dealer's left, has one opportunity to take the upcard, which he may do provided that he immediately incorporates it in a valid meld laid face up on the table with two or more cards from his own hand. If so, he ends his turn by replacing the upcard with a face-up discard, and play continues from his left.

If no one takes the first upcard, each in turn, starting at Dealer's left, does the following:

(a) Draws the top card of stock and adds it to his hand, or draws the top card of the wastepile and uses it immediately in a meld. This may be a new meld, or the card may be added to a meld he has already made, either continuing the sequence, or being the fourth of a set of three. Having taken and used the upcard, he must then take the whole of the wastepile into hand.

(b) Starts one or more new melds of three or more cards each, or lays off one or more cards to melds he has already made.

(c) Ends his turn by making one discard face up to the wastepile. He may not discard a ♠Q unless he has no other card. The wastepile is kept squared up, not fanned out.

When a wild card is used in a meld, the player must state exactly what it represents, and may not later change it.

Whoever melds the Joker may later replace it with the natural card it represents, taking the Joker back into hand for future use or discard. This may only be done by the player who melded it, and Deuces may not be so replaced at all.

Play ceases the moment someone runs out of cards, whether or not he makes a final discard. The player who went out scores a bonus of 100. Alternatively, it ends when someone takes the last card of the stock and reaches the end of his turn, in which case there is no bonus (unless the last player goes out).

Each player then scores plus for cards he has melded and a minus for cards left in hand, as follows:

	Plus if melded	Minus if in hand
Joker	100	200
♠Q	50	100
Ace	20	20
Deuce (unmelded)	—	20
K Q J T 9 8 (except ♠Q)	10	10
7 6 5 4 3 (and 2 if natural)	5	5
Deuce (as Eight or higher)	10	—
Deuce (as Seven or lower)	5	—

A player counting more against than for will get a negative score, which is deducted from his running total. The overall winner is the first to reach 1000 points over as many deals as necessary.

Notes. Work on sets and let sequences come as they will. There are more chances of matching a pair in the hand than extending a two-card sequence. Having matched a pair, meld three of a kind rather than four: the fourth may turn out to be needed in a sequence and, if not, can always be laid off in order to go out or to avoid being penalized when someone else looks on the point of doing so. So long as either ♠Q is unaccounted for, keep hold of spare Queens or high spades with which to meld a ♠Q if you draw one, as they cannot be discarded.

Old Maid

Going-out game: 3–10p, 52–104c

A popular Victorian game, often played with proprietary cards specially designed for children. Almost certainly deriving from an ancient gambling game in which the loser pays for the drinks, it is known in Germany as *Schwarzer Peter*, 'Black Peter', and in France as *Vieux Garçon*, 'Old Boy', the odd card being a Jack. You could add a Joker instead of removing a card, and then call it 'Old Joke'.

If more than six play, use two packs shuffled together. Remove ♥Q from the pack and deal the rest around as far as they will go. It doesn't matter if some players have one more card than others. The aim is to get rid of all your cards, and especially to avoid being left over with an odd Queen—the 'old maid'—in your hand.

Each player starts by examining his hand and discarding, face down, any pairs of cards of the same rank he may hold (two Sevens, two Jacks, etc.). This done, Dealer starts by offering his hand of cards face down to his left-hand neighbour, who draws one and adds it to his hand. If this gives him a pair, he discards it. Whether he discarded or not, he then offers his hand face down to his left neighbour. As players empty their hands by discarding pairs, they drop out of play. Eventually there will be only one player left, holding an unpaired Queen. He is the loser, and pays a forfeit. Or (to drag it out) loses a life, a forfeit being paid by the first to lose three lives.

Ombre

Pronounced 'Umber': English version of Hombre (q.v.).

Pan

Pan, originally Panguingue, is a casino variety of Rummy much played in the American west, especially Reno and Las Vegas. It requires eight 40-card packs (A 2 3 4 5 6 7 J Q K), with ten or more spades stripped out. This and other complexities render it unsuitable for detailed description here. See Mac James, *Pan: The Gambler's Card Game* (Las Vegas 1979).

Pandur

See Jass.

Patience

A large family of games mainly designed for one player, hence also known as Solitaire. In most, the player thoroughly shuffles a pack of cards and then seeks, by following a given set of playing rules, to get it back into perfect order, with cards running regularly A 2 3 4 5 6 7 8 9 T J Q K in each suit. Typically, the Aces are put out as the bases of thirteen-card suit-sequences, and cards turned from the pack are then built on them if they continue the sequence, or discarded to a wastepile if they do not. When the stock is exhausted, the wastepile is turned over and play proceeds again, until it either 'comes out' (you win) or 'blocks' (you lose). Often, there is a tableau or layout into which cards are temporarily stored in partial order until ready to be built in perfect order on the final piles. What distinguishes one game from another is the size and pattern of the layout (if any), how often the wastepile may be turned for replay (if at all), and the particular rules of partial and final ordering.

Like all card games, Patience is always based on chance but may also engage from little to a high degree of skill. In 'closed' or 'mechanical' games the player has absolutely no choice of move but must follow a given procedure blindly: whether or not the cards come out depends entirely on how they lie after the shuffle. In 'open' games, or games of 'perfect information', all cards are on display from the outset and the player can, in principle, work all his moves out in advance: whether or not they *can* come out depends on the lie of cards; whether or not they *do* depends very largely on the player's skill in calculation and foresight. Between these two extremes lie games which start off blind but gradually increase the amount of information presented as play proceeds.

Here are ten Patiences typical of various kinds and appealing to different temperaments. Some are selected as being the quickest to explain and follow of their respective types, others as being too well-known to ignore.

See also Cribbage Patience (under Cribbage), Poker Patience, Racing Demon, and Spite and Malice.

Accordion

From a single pack, start dealing cards in a row from left to right. Whenever the rank or suit of a dealt card matches that of its left-hand neighbour, or of the next but two to the left, place it on top of the matching card. Piles of cards so formed are to be treated as if they were single cards, and moved first or third left whenever the position allows. If very lucky, you will end up with all 52 cards in a single pile. Count half a win for two piles, an infinitesimal win for three.

Auld Lang Syne

From a single pack, remove the Aces and lay them in a row at the top of the board. The aim is to build them up into four thirteen-card suit sequences headed by their Kings.

Deal 4 cards face up in a row from left to right. If they include a Two, build it on its Ace; a Three may then go on the Two; and so on. This done, deal 4 more across, either covering previously dealt cards or filling gaps, pause, and build again if possible. Keep building when possible, and dealing 4 more across when not. A card once covered by another only becomes available for building when exposed by the building of the card that covers it. As described, the game almost never comes out, but its chances can be increased by dealing (say) 6 cards across instead of 4.

Canfield

Alternative name for Demon and Klondike (see either below).

Cromwell

A two-pack game of skill by Charles Jewell, based on the more traditional Belle Lucie, Fan, and House on the Hill.

Deal all cards out face up in 26 fans of 4. Overlap the cards of each fan so that all are visible but only one uncovered.

The aim is to release the Aces, as and when they become available, and to build each one up in suit and sequence to its King. Before play, examine the layout to ensure that there is at least one fan with a King at the bottom, covered by three cards. If not, exchange any King with the bottom card of any fan, otherwise the game will never come out.

At any time, the uncovered card of each fan is available for setting out (if it is an Ace), for building on a main sequence based on an Ace, or for packing elsewhere in the layout. Packing takes place in suit and descending sequence—e.g. ♠7 on ♠8. A whole sequence of properly packed cards may be packed elsewhere provided that the join follows the rule. A space made by emptying a fan is not to be refilled.

The game has reasonable chances of success, and offers one 'grace' or escape route. This consists in exchanging the positions of any two cards in the layout, whether covered or exposed. The grace may be taken at any time, but once only, and then not if it was used initially to get a King to the bottom of a fan.

(*a*) Accordion

(*b*) Demon (Canfield)

Bases

The Demon

Wastepile

FIG. 18. **Patience.**
(*a*) *Accordion* If the next card is a club, a Five, a heart, or an Ace (but not a diamond or a Queen), it goes on whichever of the previous cards it matches.
(*b*) *Demon* A lucky start: play Ace to Two, King to Ace, Queen to King, and fill gaps from the top of the demon. The bases are to consist of Tens and be built up to the Nines.

Demon (= American Canfield)

From a single pack, deal 13 cards face down in a pile and turn the top one face up. These constitute the demon. Whenever the top card is played, turn the next face up.

Deal the next card face up at the top of the board as the 'first base', then 4 more face up in a row beneath it to start the layout. The aim is to set out the other three cards of the same rank as the first base and to build all four up in suit and sequence until they contain thirteen cards each. (For example, if the base card is Ten, the sequence continues J Q K A 2 3 4 5 6 7 8 9.)

If the layout contains two cards of adjacent rank and opposite colour, pack the lower on the higher (e.g. red Ace on black Two, black King on red Ace). A whole sequence of properly packed cards may go on an exposed card in the layout, provided that the join follows the rule. A space made in the layout is immediately filled with the top card of the demon, or, if this is empty, from the top of the wastepile.

Turn cards from the stock in sweeps of three at a time and place them face up on a single wastepile. If the top card of the wastepile can be built on a base or packed in the layout, do so, thus releasing the next card down for play.

Having run out of stock, turn the wastepile face down and go through it again. Continue until the game either comes out or blocks. Lose no opportunity to play the top card of the demon. The game rarely comes out, and one measure of success—a score or handicap—is the number of cards left in the demon when you can play no further.

Golf

From a single pack deal 7 cards face up in a row, 7 more overlapping them, and so on, five times in all. Regard the resultant layout as seven columns of five cards each.

Deal the next card face up to one side as a base. The aim is to get all 52 cards built up in a pile with the base card at the bottom. (Or to regard the base card as a 'hole' and 'putt' the remaining 51 cards into it.)

Upon the base card, and subsequently upon on the top card of the pile as it grows, may be played a card either next higher or next

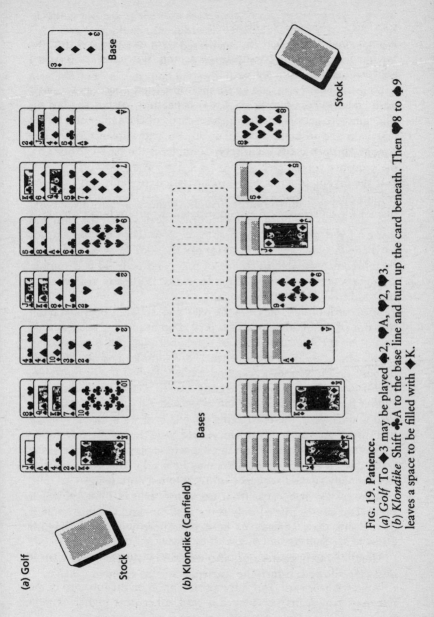

(a) Golf

Stock

Base

(b) Klondike (Canfield)

Bases

Stock

FIG. 19. Patience.
(a) *Golf* To ◆3 may be played ♠2, ♥A, ♥2, ♥3.
(b) *Klondike* Shift ♣A to the base line and turn up the card beneath. Then ♥8 to ♠9 leaves a space to be filled with ◆K.

lower in rank, regardless of suit. Aces and Kings are not consecutive. Thus, if the base is a Three, the sequence could go 2 A 2 3 4 3 etc., but not 2 A K etc. The uncovered card of any column in the layout may be taken for building on the pile. The removal of such a card releases the one below it for building, and so on. When a column is cleared, it is not re-formed. When no more cards can be built from the layout, turn the next card from stock, place it on the pile, and continue play from there.

Klondike (= English Canfield)

One of the best-known Patiences on both sides of the Atlantic.

From a single pack, deal 7 cards face down in a row. Deal a second card face down on the first six of them, a third on the first five, and so on, with one card less at each deal, so that the 28th and last card is dealt only to the first in the row. Turn the top card of each pile face up. The aim is to set out the four Aces, as and when they become available in course of play, and to build each one in suit and sequence up to its King. If an Ace is already visible, set it out, and turn up the card beneath.

Turn cards one by one from the pack and, so far as possible, build it to one of the building piles if it is next up in suit and sequence, or pack it on the top card of one of the layout piles if it is of opposite colour and next down in sequence. (For example, a turned ♥7 may be built on the ♥6, or packed on a black Eight.) If it is unusable, play it face up to a wastepile. At any time in course of play, the top card of the wastepile may be built or packed if it fits. So may any top card in the layout, thereby freeing the one beneath it for play, being first turned up if currently down. A card from the layout may not be moved to the wastepile. When the last card is played from one of the seven piles in the layout, its place may be filled with a King, or with any properly packed sequence of cards based on a King.

Some players turn cards from stock in sweeps of three, of which the second can be played only if the first can, and the third only if the second. This appears to be a later borrowing from English Canfield, or Demon.

Klondike rarely comes out, and would not always do so even if one were allowed to turn the wastepile and go through it again.

Miss Milligan

An infuriating two-pack classic which rarely comes out. The aim is to set up all eight Aces as and when they become available, and to build each one up in suit and sequence to its King.

Deal 8 cards face up in a row. If they include an Ace, set it out, and start building on it if possible. Otherwise, if any two are adjacent in rank and opposite in colour, place the lower on the higher (e.g. a red Jack on a black Queen).

When stuck, now and at any time in course of play, deal 8 more cards in a row across the layout, covering existing cards or filling gaps as the case may be. Then pause, do any building that can be done, and pack cards in the layout on one another in opposite colour and descending sequence. A whole sequence of properly packed cards may go on an exposed card in the layout, provided that the join follows the rule. A space made in the layout may be filled with a King from another part of the layout, or with a packed sequence founded on a King.

Keep going until no cards remain in hand and all cards have been built from the layout onto the eight piles.

When stuck, you may attempt the following escape route known as 'weaving' or 'waiving'. Remove any exposed card in the layout, set it to one side, and do any building or packing possible, starting from the card this leaves exposed. Continue until you either get stuck (in which case the game is lost) or can return the odd card into play by building it or packing it on a card in the layout in accordance with the rules of following. You may weave as often as you like, but with only one card at a time.

Quadrille

Remove the Queens from a single pack and arrange them symmetrically in the middle of the board. Around them, in a circle, place all four Fives and four Sixes alternately.

The aim is to build on the Sixes upwards in suit to the Jacks, and on the Fives downwards in suit to the Kings (going 4 3 2 A K).

Turn cards from stock one by one, and build them if possible or else discard them face up to a single wastepile. The stock exhausted, you may turn the wastepile upside-down and go through it again. The game always comes out if you turn the wastepile often enough,

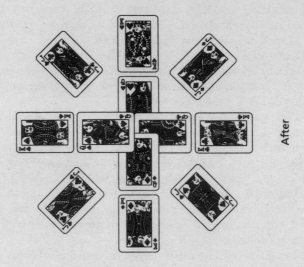

After

Before

(a) Quadrille

(b) Terrace

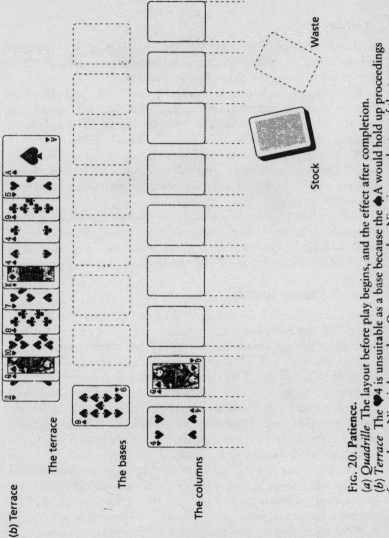

The terrace

The bases

The columns

Stock

Waste

FIG. 20. Patience.
(a) *Quadrille* The layout before play begins, and the effect after completion.
(b) *Terrace* The ♥4 is unsuitable as a base because the ♠A would hold up proceedings for too long. Nine is better than Queen, as another Nine is near the top of the terrace.

but the usual allowance is three such turns, giving a roughly 50–50 chance of success.

Strategy

Invented by Morehead and Mott-Smith, Strategy is a modern improvement on either Sir Tommy or Grandfather's, each of which lays claim to being the oldest known Patience.

From a single pack, turn cards face up one by one and play them face up to any of eight wastepiles. Place each Ace, as it appears, at the top of the board. The piles may be spread towards you in columns so that the contents of each are always visible.

When done, the aim is to build each Ace up in suit and sequence to its King. At each turn, only the top (uncovered) card of any column may be taken. Cards may not be transferred from one column to another.

Skill consists in selecting which pile to play to when dealing from the pack, so as not to trap lower cards beneath higher ones of the same suit. With accurate play, Strategy comes out more often than not. For greater challenge, reduce the number of wastepiles.

Terrace (Queen of Italy)

From a doubled pack of 104 cards deal 11 face up in a row at the top of the board to form the 'terrace'. These should overlap one another so that all are visible and all but one are covered.

Turn the next three cards from the pack face up and choose one of them to act as the 'first base'. Place this at the start of a row beneath the terrace. As the other seven cards of the same rank become available, they will be placed in this row to act as further bases. The object is to build each base card up in suit and sequence until it contains thirteen cards in all. Thus, if the base is a Ten, the sequence will continue J Q K A 2 3 4 5 6 7 8 9.

Place the other two turned cards face up in a row beneath the base, and deal seven more cards face up in a row to their right (not overlapping). These nine are the first row of the layout. If these include a base card, move it up into the base-card row and replace it. If the uncovered card of the terrace is a base, move it down into the base-card row, but do not replace it. If, now and in subsequent play, any two uncovered cards in the layout are adjacent in rank and of opposite colour, pack the lower on the higher (e.g. black Two on red Three). For building and packing purposes, King and Ace are adjacent, King being lower.

Turn cards from the stock and either build them on a main sequence or pack them in the layout, following the appropriate rule. If not, discard them face up to a single wastepile, of which the top card may always be taken for subsequent building or packing. Cards may only be packed one at a time, not in sequences. A space made in the layout must be filled with the top card of the stock or the wastepile, not from another column or from the terrace.

The uncovered card of the terrace may only be taken for building on a main sequence: it may not be packed on the tableau or discarded to the wastepile.

Although the wastepile is not to be turned and redealt, the game should still come out more often than not. Examine the cards of the terrace carefully before choosing the first base.

Pelmanism
Memory game: 2–5p, 52c

A children's game, also called Memory.

Shuffle the cards and deal them face down at random all over the table. The aim is to collect pairs of matching ranks (two Kings, Fives, or whatever). Each in turn picks up two cards and looks at them without letting the others see. If they form a pair, he wins them; if not, he replaces them face down in the same positions. The player with the best memory, or concentration, or both, will usually win. A score or pay-off can be devised based on the number of pairs collected, their ranks, or both. An optional rule is that winning a pair entitles the player to an immediate second turn. Another is that cards are shown to all when turned.

Penchant

A late nineteenth-century Bezique derivative that looks suspiciously like a one-off invention by an idiosyncratic enthusiast. (See *Foster's Complete Hoyle*.)

Persian Rummy

Rummy game: 4pp, 52c + 4 Jokers

Few Rummies are designed for partnership play. This is one of the best. It dates from the 1930s, and may be regarded as a relatively sober forerunner of the more hysterical Canasta.

Partners sit crosswise. A game is two deals. Use a 56-card pack, including four Jokers with backs identical to one another and the rest of the pack. Deal 7 each one at a time. Turn the next face up to start the discard pile, and stack the rest face down beside it.

The aim is to collect and display melds. A meld is three or four cards of the same rank, or three or more cards in suit and sequence from 2 3 4 5 6 7 8 9 T J Q K A. Ace counts only high. Jokers are not wild, but may only be melded together as a set of three or four.

Each in turn, starting from the player left of Dealer, must draw, may meld, and must then discard.

Draw. The top card of stock may always be drawn and added to the hand. The top card of the discard pile (which should be fanned slightly so that all remain visible) may be taken, provided that the taker immediately uses it to start a meld or add to an existing meld. In this case he must also take all the other cards of the discard pile, and may meld as many of them as he can and will. Any which he cannot meld are not taken into hand but left face up on the table before him—where, however, they still belong to his hand and may therefore be melded or discarded as if actually held.

Meld. Each player in turn may make as many melds and lay-offs as he can, laying all such cards face up on the table before him. A new meld must contain at least three of a kind or three in suit and sequence. If four of a kind are melded at once, they count double. This is indicated by squaring them up instead of fanning them out. A player may lay off a card that matches any meld on the table, regardless of who made it, but places any such lay-off on the table before him as part of his own scoring cards. This requires him to state which meld it ex ends. For example, if there are melds of three Fives and of ♣6 7 8 o the table, a player laying off ♣5 must state whether it extends the set or the sequence. If the sequence, any player may subsequently lay off ♣4 to it, otherwise not.

Discard. A player ends his turn by making one discard face up to the discard pile—unless he has none left to discard, in which case play ceases.

Play continues until one player goes out by melding, laying off or discarding his last card. If the stock runs out, players continue by drawing from the discard pile as long as they can and will. Play ceases when the player in turn goes out, or cannot legally draw, or will not do so.

Score. Cards count at face value from Two to Ten, courts 10 each, Aces 15, Jokers 20. Each player scores these values for all cards in his melds (remembering that immediate fours of a kind count double), and from this total subtracts the total face value of all cards left in hand, even if forming or usable in melds.

A partnership's score is that of both its members added together. If one member ended the play by going out, his side counts 25 extra. At the end of the second deal (dealt by the player to the left of the first dealer), the side with the greater total scores, for settlement, 50 plus the margin of victory.

Notes. A nice feature of this game is the possibility of signals, or conventional plays. Early on, the discard of an Ace—unless immediately following a meld—asks one's partner to discard a Joker if possible; similarly, discarding a card worth 10 calls for an Ace.

Phat

Point-trick game: 4pp, 52c

This game, first described by Arthur Taylor in 1976, was found by him 'played on a highly organized league basis in and around Norwich', where it was 'instantly recognizable because of its unusual, and enormous, pegging board'. It would be fascinating to attempt to trace the route by which it derives, as it obviously does, from All Fours. (The published description contains gaps which I have filled in on general principles.)

Four play, sitting crosswise in partnerships. Points are recorded on a yard-long board resembling a Cribbage board (or an actual Crib board, if no Phat board is available). The turn to deal and play passes always to the left.

From a 52-card pack deal 13 cards each, one at a time. Cards rank A K Q J T 9 8 7 6 5 4 3 2, except in trumps, which is headed by the Nine, the Five, then Ace and so on downwards.

Eldest leads, and the suit of his lead is automatically trump for the deal. Subsequent players must follow suit if possible, but otherwise may play any card. The trick is taken by the highest card of the suit led, or by the highest trump if any are played, and the winner of each trick leads to the next.

During play, the following cards won in tricks entitle the trick-winner to peg his side forward as follows:

Nine	18 trump, 9 non-trump
Five	10 trump, 5 non-trump
Trump Ace	4
Trump King	3
Trump Queen	2
Trump Jack	1

Trick-play ended, each side counts the card-point value of all counting-cards it has won in tricks on the following basis:

Each Ace	4
Each King	3
Each Queen	2
Each Jack	1
Each Ten	10

The side having the greater aggregate value pegs eight holes on the Phat board.

Continue until one side wins by reaching or exceeding a score of 181.

Picquet

Or Picket: see Piquet.

Pink Nines

Stops game: 2–6p, 52c

Another pub game collected by Arthur Taylor (see also Phat), this time in Bletchley. Related to Newmarket, it more closely resembles the original seventeenth-century French game of Comet.

Everyone stakes an agreed amount to a pool. Deal 13 cards each if two or three play, and stack the rest face down. (They are not used.) If more play, deal 4 face down to one side and the rest around as far as they will go.

The aim is to run out of cards by playing them to a single sequence on the table. The running order for this purpose is A 2 3 4 5 6 7 8 9 T J Q K A 2 . . . etc.

Eldest leads by playing out his longest sequence of cards, regardless of suit. When unable to continue, the next in turn carries on, if he can, from the next numeral in sequence. For example, if the first played J Q K A 2 and stopped, the next in turn would start with Three. If the next player cannot continue, the turn keeps passing until someone can. If no one can, the person who played last may play any card or sequence ad lib.

'Pink Nines' are ♥9 and ♦9. These are wild, and can be used to represent any desired card.

First out of cards wins the pool.

Pinochle

Point-tricks and melds: 2–4p, 2 × 24c

Pinochle (the spellings Penuchle, Pinocle died out at the end of the nineteenth century) is a game of American perfection deriving from an early European relative of Bezique called Binocle, or, in its German spelling, Binokel. The latter remains a popular family game in Württemberg and parts of Switzerland, despite the note in *Culbertson's Card Games Complete* (New York, 1952) averring that Binokel is unknown in Germany.

Two-hand Pinochle is virtually Bezique (q.v.) played without the Sevens and Eights. Auction Pinochle (q.v.) is generally considered the best three-handed form, if not the best version altogether. As adaptations for more than five seem somewhat artificial, the four-hand partnership game is worthiest of description here. This, too, comes in several basic forms, each with its own local variant rules. In the simplest, the last card is turned for trump and each side plays to take what it can get. More favoured now is

Partnership Auction Pinochle

Four players sit crosswise in partnerships. The turn to deal and play passes always to the left. The 48-card pack is a double pack of 24, with no cards lower than Nine. The rank of the cards for trick-taking purposes, and their point-values when captured in tricks, are:

	Modern	*Traditional*
Ace	10	11
Ten	10	10
King	5	4
Queen	5	3
Jack	0	2
Nine	0	0

Decide first whether to follow the modern American or traditional European count. Then deal 12 cards each, 3 at a time.

Each side's aim is to score 1000 or more points over as many deals as necessary. Points are scored for cards captured in tricks, at the rates shown above, plus 10 for winning the last trick, making 250 in all. Extra points may be scored in advance of play by individual players (on their partnership's behalf) for holding any of the following card melds:

Flush (A T K Q J in trumps)	150
Royal marriage (K Q in trumps)	40
Plain marriage (K Q in non-trump suit)	20
Hundred Aces (four Aces, one per suit)	100
Eighty Kings (four Kings, likewise)	80
Sixty Queens (four Queens, likewise)	60
Forty Jacks (four Jacks, likewise)	40
Pinochle (♠Q ♦J)	40
Dix ('deece') (= trump Nine)	10

(*Note*: If a flush is scored, the royal marriage it contains may not be scored in addition.)

An auction follows the deal. A bid is the minimum point-score a player declares that his partnership will make from melds and tricks if allowed to name trumps. Eldest is obliged to make an opening bid of at least 100. (*Variant*: 200.) Each in turn may pass or name any higher bid that is a multiple of 10. A player who has once passed may not bid again. A bid followed by three passes becomes the contract, and the declarer then names trumps.

Eldest leads to the first trick. (*Variant*: Declarer leads first.) As each person plays to the first trick, he announces, shows, and scores for any melds that he may have and wish to count. Subsequent players must follow suit and head the trick if possible; if unable to follow, they must play a trump, and beat any trump already played if possible. The trick is taken by the highest card of the suit led, or by the highest trump if any are played. Of identical winning cards, the first played beats the second. The winner of each trick leads to the next.

The bidding side counts its score first. If they took at least the amount bid, they score whatever they make; if not, the amount of their bid is deducted from their score. If the bidding side thereby reaches or exceeds 1000, they win, and the opponents do not then score. Otherwise, the opponents score everything they make—unless they fail to win a single trick, in which case their melds are annulled and they score nothing.

Notes. Most hands are worth opening for the minimum 100. By convention, an average-looking hand would be opened at 100 plus the value of melds it contains—for example, 120 shows a plain marriage held, 140 a trump marriage. Another convention is to bid an odd number of tens (e.g. 250, 270) to show a flush held, an even number (e.g. 180, 200) to deny this. As in all point-trick games, players will seek every opportunity to 'stuff' tricks their partners are winning by throwing high counters to them.

Pip-Pip
Point-trick game: 4–10p, 2 × 52c

A party game for players with sound experience of trick-play, Pip-Pip first appeared in the 1920s. Despite a thoroughly English title, its structure suggests a curiously imperfect acquaintance with some central European game such as Tyzicha (q.v.).

Use two 52-card packs shuffled together. Each deal is complete in itself. Deal 7 cards each, turn the next for trumps, and stack the rest face down on top of it. The aim is to score points for (*a*) changing the trump suit when possible and (*b*) capturing card-points in tricks.

Cards rank for trick-taking purposes in the following order, the top five carrying point-scores thus:

Deuce	A	K	Q	J	T	9	8	7	6	5	4	3
11	10	5	4	3	—	—	—	—	—	—	—	—

Eldest leads to the first trick. Subsequent players must follow suit if possible, but otherwise may play any card. The trick is taken by the highest card of the suit led, or by the highest trump if any are played. Of identical winning cards, the second played beats the first. The winner of each trick draws the top card of stock (so long as any remain), waits for the others to do likewise—each in turn starting from his left—then leads to the next trick.

Immediately before the first card is led to any trick, a player holding a King and Queen of the same suit other than trump may change the trump suit to that of the marriage by laying it face up on the table before him and calling 'Pip-pip!', thereby scoring 50 points. The two cards remain on the table but continue to belong to his hand until played to tricks. Neither of them may be used to 'pip' a second time, but there is nothing to stop the same suit from being pipped again when the other King and Queen are both shown together. If two players pip before the same trick, both score 50, and the suit is changed to that of the second one called. (*Variant, or if called simultaneously*: It is changed to that of the player nearest the Dealer's left, Dealer counting as furthest from his own left.)

When the last card is drawn from stock, play continues until everyone has played out all their cards. It doesn't matter if some players have one fewer card than others and so cannot play to the last trick.

Each player scores for all the pips he has made, and adds to this total that of all counting-cards contained in the tricks he has won.

Note. Players may prefer to adopt the more natural schedule:

A	T	K	Q	J	9	8	7	6	5	4	3	2
11	10	4	3	2	—	—	—	—	—	—	—	—

Piquet

Plain-tricks and melds: 2p, 32c

Piquet, or Picket, goes back to the early sixteenth century and has long been been regarded as one of the all-time great games for two players. It has also been regarded as of French origin and the national card game of France, though the origin is debatable and the French now prefer Belote (q.v.). The fact that rules vary but slightly from country to country is remarkable, given the many centuries over which it has been played throughout Europe. What follows is English 'Rubicon Piquet' as defined in the late nineteenth century by London's Portland Club.

A game, or *partie*, is six deals. If the loser fails to reach 100 points by the end, he is 'rubiconed' and loses extra. Higher cut deals first and the deal alternates. Deal 12 each in 2s or 3s. (Not 2s and 3s mixed, and whichever you choose on the first deal you must stick to throughout the partie.) The remaining eight form the 'talon' and are fanned out, face down, between the two players. Cards rank A K Q J T 9 8 7 in each suit.

In each deal, players discard and draw in quest of scoring combinations, then play to twelve tricks at no trump. Scores are carried forward in writing at the end of each deal, but as they are made little by little it is convenient to use a mechanical marker or Cribbage board.

Blank (carte blanche). If either player has been dealt all numerals (no courts), he may score 10 for a blank. He must declare it immediately, and subsequently prove it by dealing his cards rapidly face up to the table. However, if Younger (Dealer) has the blank, he need not prove it until Elder has exchanged.

The exchange. Elder must discard, face down, at least one card and not more than five. He then replenishes his hand by drawing the same number from the top of the talon. If he exchanges fewer than five, he may peep at the cards up to five which he did not take. Younger may then (but need not) discard any number of cards up to as many as remain—usually three, sometimes more. If he leaves any untaken, Younger may either show them to both players or leave them unseen, but may not see them alone.

Declarations. Players then score for combinations in each of three classes in the following order. Only the player with the best in any class scores for it. If there is a tie for best, neither scores: second best is not taken into account. The combinations are:

1. *Point.* The total point-value of cards in any one suit, counting Ace 11, courts 10, numerals as marked. The player with the highest

point scores one per card held of that suit. If equal, neither scores.

2. *Sequence.* Three or more cards in suit and sequence. The player with the longest sequence (or, if equal, that with the higher top card) scores for it and any other sequences he may declare. If still equal, neither scores. The sequences and their scores are, from three cards upwards: *tierce* 3, *quart* 4, *quint* 15, *sixième* 16, *septième* 17, *huitième* 18.

3. *Set.* A *trio* is three or more cards of the same rank, Tens or higher, and scores 3. Four or more is a *quatorze*, worth 14. Whoever has the higher-ranking quatorze, or, if neither has one, the higher trio, scores for it and any other sets he may declare.

Any point or sequence scored by either player must be fully identified and shown on request, though this is often unnecessary as most of an opponent's hand can be deduced from one's own. Trios and quatorzes are not shown, and it is not required to state which suit is missing from a trio.

Not every combination held need be claimed. Any may be 'sunk' in whole or part to disguise the fact that a certain card or cards are in play. But only what is declared is scorable, and only what is scorable need be shown.

Repique. If either player reaches a score of 30 for combinations alone before the other has scored anything, he adds a bonus of 60 for *repique.* For this purpose, combinations are counted strictly in order—blank, point, sequence, set. (Example: Younger scores 10 for a blank, neither scores for point because equal, Younger scores 15 for a quint and two tierces for 3 each, Elder scores a trio. Younger wins the repique for having reached 31 before Elder's trio took effect, counting not 31 but 91 to Elder's 3.)

Pique. If Elder reaches 30 upon or after leading to the first trick, and Younger has not yet scored anything for combinations or tricks, he adds a bonus of 30 for *pique.* Younger cannot score pique, as Elder automatically scores 'one for leading'.

Tricks. Elder leads to the first trick. Follow suit if possible, otherwise play any card. There is no trump. The trick is taken by the higher card of the suit led, and the winner of each trick leads to the next. In play, either player scores 1 for leading to a trick, and 1 for capturing a trick led by the opponent. The winner of the last trick scores 1 more.

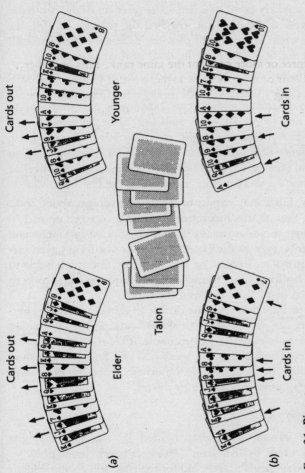

Piquet

FIG. 21. Piquet.

(a) Elder keeps his diamond point and hopes for the fourth King. Younger, having to keep his King and Queen suits guarded and wishing to retain three Tens for a possible fourth, could discard three hearts, or an Eight and two Sevens.

(b) After an unhappy draw, Elder calls first. E: Point of five. — Y: Worth? — E: 47. — Y: Not good. — E: Three Kings. — Y: Not good of five. — Y: Point of five. E: Point of five. — Y: A. Younger declares 'Point of five, 5; (sequence of) three in spades 8; fourteen Tens 22' and follows suit. Elder's bare ♠K causes him to lose seven tricks, leaving him a net score for the hand of 8 to Younger's 22 plus 8 for tricks and 10 for cards, total 40.

Labels within figure (a): Cards out, Younger, Cards out, Elder, Talon

Labels within figure (b): Cards in, Cards in

201

Cards and capot. A player winning seven or more tricks scores 10 'for cards'. For winning all twelve, he scores an additional 30 (40 in all) for *capot*.

Game. In the unlikely event of a tied score after six deals, two more deals are played. If the loser has reached the rubicon of 100, the winner's final game score is 100 plus the difference between their two scores. If not, it is 100 plus the *total* of their two scores.

Variants. (*a*) Instead of six deals to a partie, the game may be played up to a target score—originally 100 (*Piquet au Cent*), often 150. (*b*) *Carte rouge* is a hand in which every card forms part of a scoring combination, and scores 50. (*c*) A void suit, after the discard, may be submitted as a 'point of nought' counting 50½ and scoring 10, and as a 'sequence of nought' ranking between a King-high and an Ace-high quint, scoring 15. (*d*) Trick-play is considerably enlivened by awarding not 1 but 10 points for winning the last trick.

Notes. In play, Elder may expect to make, on average, about 26 to Younger's 18, though it is theoretically possible to score up to 170 in one deal. Elder should normally keep his best point suit intact and discard five cards, even at the expense of an Ace or King unless it is needed for a quatorze. In play, he will generally find it advisable to keep pressing his long suit. Younger's main requirement is to keep himself guarded in all suits to avoid the capot.

If Younger in the sixth and last deal is in danger of being rubiconed—having, say, 80 or less—he should sink part of a winning combination so as to equalize. For example, if Elder declares a point counting 49 and Younger has 50, he should say 'Equal' rather than 'Not good', since the 5 he would otherwise score for point will count in Elder's favour in case of a rubicon.

Auction Piquet

A worthwhile variant somewhat limited by the fact that the standard work on it, by 'Rubicon' (1920), is barely intelligible.

In each of the six deals players bid for the right to become 'Elder', thereby exchanging up to five cards and making the opening lead. Non-dealer bids first; the lowest bid is 'seven'; and each new bid must be numerically higher up to a maximum of twelve. Any bid may be made 'plus' or 'minus'. The aim in a plus contract is to win at least the number of tricks bid; in a minus contract, it is to *lose* at least the number bid. A bid may be doubled, in which case the bidder may not pass: he must either bid higher (which cancels the double) or else redouble, which makes him 'elder' and ends the auction.

Elder may discard and draw up to five cards, and younger up to as many as remain; but neither is obliged to discard any.

Combinations are declared and scored as at ordinary Piquet, except that:

1. Carte blanche is ignored.
2. In a minus contract, each player scores everything 'good' in his *opponent's* hand. ('Sinking', therefore, is not allowed.)
3. Pique and repique are made by reaching, before the opponent has scored anything, 29 points in a plus deal or 21 in a minus.

Each won trick scores 1 point: there is no point for leading or for winning the last.

Winning seven to eleven tricks in a plus deal, or losing them in a minus deal, earns 10 'for cards'. Winning all twelve tricks in a plus deal, or losing them in a minus deal, earns 40 for capot. These scores are not affected by doubling unless the contract was for twelve tricks, when capot scores 80 or 160 accordingly.

If Elder wins more tricks than he bid (or loses more, in a minus contract), he adds 10 per overtrick. If he fails to make his contract, Younger scores 10 for each trick by which elder fell short. These scores are affected by doubling and redoubling; furthermore, Elder scores an additional 20 for fulfilling a doubled contract, or 40 for a redoubled one.

After six deals, the player with the greater total scores 150 plus the difference between their two totals; or, if the loser fails to reach 150 points, 150 plus the sum of the two totals.

Note. 'Rubicon' says younger can score for pique in a minus deal but not in a plus. As this rule does not follow logically, it is presumably arbitrary (being modelled on original Piquet, where it is logical), and should therefore be ignored. Players may also wish to reset the target for pique and repique as 30 in a plus deal and 20 in a minus.

Pirate

Plain-trick game: 4p, 52c

A defunct variety of Bridge which replaces fixed partnerships with differing, *ad hoc* partnerships made from deal to deal, so that each person plays for himself in the long run. First published in 1917, it was favoured, if not invented, by R. F. Foster. Critics say the players with the best-matched hands in each deal will always find each other and usually make their contract, but players who dislike fixed partnerships may wish to make up their own minds about this. The following outline of basic essentials assumes a knowledge of Bridge.

Dealer bids first. If all pass, the hands are thrown in. When a bid is made, each in turn thereafter must either accept it, thereby offering himself as dummy in partnership with the bidder, or pass. If no one accepts, the bid is annulled, and the turn to bid passes to the left of the player who made it. There is no need to overcall an unaccepted bid. For example, if South opens 'two diamonds', and no one accepts, West may call anything from 'one club' upwards. If no one accepts any bid, the hands are thrown in.

Once a bid is accepted, players to the left of the accepter may bid higher, double, or pass. If all pass, the accepted bid becomes the contract. A new bid need not differ in suit from an accepted bid, and may itself be accepted by its previous bidder or accepter, thereby denying the originally proposed alliance. An accepted bidder may himself try to break an alliance by naming a new contract when his turn comes round; but that alliance stands if no higher bid is accepted.

A double reopens the bidding, giving the would-be allies a chance to bid themselves out of the alliance by naming another bid in the hope that someone will accept it. Or they can stay with the accepted bid, and redouble if confident enough to do so.

A contract established, declarer leads to the first trick, his partner lays his hand down as a dummy, and play proceeds as at Bridge. Auction or Contract scoring may be followed, the score being noted above or below the line in the column of each of the players involved.

Pishti

Fishing game: 2–4p, 52c

A reportedly Turkish member of the fishing family, also called Pashta. Closely related is a Greek game described by Robert Harbin (*Waddington's Family Card Games*, London, 1972) under a title translated by him as the Dry Game.

Pishti

Deal 4 cards each, 4 face down in a pile, and turn the top card of the pile. Each in turn plays a card face up to the pile. If it matches the top card by rank (not suit), that player wins all the cards in the pile, leaving the next player with no option but to start a new one by playing any card. When each has played four cards, 4 more are dealt, and so on until all cards have been played and won. Capturing a pile consisting of a single card ('pishti') scores 10 points immediately. At end of play, each player sorts through his won cards and additionally scores as follows:

For having most cards	3
For having ◆ 10	3
For having ♣2	2
For each Ace taken	1
For each Jack taken	1

The winner is the first to reach 100.

Optional bluffing rule. When a pile contains only one card, the next to play may play a card face down and claim 'pishti'. If unchallenged, he wins it and scores 10. Otherwise, the card is revealed. If it matches, he wins both and scores 20; if not, the challenger wins them for 20.

Dry Game

From two to four players receive 6 cards each dealt in 3s from a 52-card pack, and 4 are dealt face up in a pile. Each in turn plays a card to the pile, capturing the pile if the card he plays matches the top card or is a Jack, and leaving it on top if not. After a capture, the next in turn can only start a new pile with a single card. If the following player captures the single card, he is said to win a 'dry' trick, and scores 10.

Pitch

Whenever all have played six cards, 6 more are dealt. (In some circles, 4 more are also dealt to the top of the pile.) Continue until not enough cards remain for a full deal. A pile left at end of play remains untaken.

Players then sort through their cards and score as follows:

For having most cards	3
For having most clubs	3
For having ♦10	2
For having ♠2 (*sic*)	2
For each Jack taken	1

Game is 25, 50 or 100 up. Four may play as partners.

Pitch

A multi-player version of All Fours. See Auction Pitch.

Plain-trick games

Games in which all tricks are of equal value, so that win or loss depends solely on the number of tricks taken. The term is used in contrast to 'point-trick' games, q.v.

Poch

Gambling game: 3–8p, 32 or 52c

Poch, or Pochen, is a popular German family game of exceptionally ancient date, being first mentioned at Strasbourg in 1441. It has always been played in various ways, but its most constant feature is a distinctively tripartite structure. The first stake goes to whoever has been dealt the highest cards, or certain specified cards. The second is won by successfully vying or bragging (*pochen*) as to who holds the best combination. The third is won for either drawing to 31 or, at a later date, playing the cards to a sequence as at Newmarket. This structure underlies such other historic games as Belle, Flux, et Trente-et-Un and the original three-stake form of Brag. The second element, that of vying or bragging, has since become isolated as the sole mechanism of modern Brag and Poker, which latter derives its name from *pochen*, 'to knock', via the French game of Poque.

Poch involves a circular board of traditional design containing several staking compartments, one for each winning card or combination. (See also Pope Joan.)

From two to four players use a 32-card pack (A K Q J T 9 8 7); more than four use 52.

In Part 1, players dress the board by placing chips in the first seven of eight compartments labelled Ace, King, Queen, Jack, Ten, Marriage, Sequence and Poch. Five cards each are dealt and the next is turned for trump. The stakes for Ace, King, Queen, Jack, and Ten

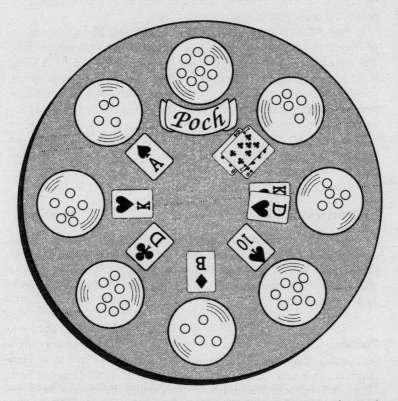

FIG. 22. **Poch.** A Poch board, with staking compartments for Poch, sequence, marriage, and five top trumps from Ten to Ace.

go respectively to the players dealt those particular trumps. That for marriage goes to the holder of both King and Queen of trumps, in addition to the individual stakes for King and Queen. Sequence is won by anyone dealt the 7 8 9 of trumps. Unclaimed stakes are carried forward to the next deal.

In Part 2, players vie as to who holds the best combination. A quartet beats a triplet, a triplet a pair, and a pair an unpaired hand, with ties determined by the highest card. The first to bet places a stake in the poch compartment, saying 'Ich poche eins' ('I bet one', or however many). Each in turn must either add the same amount or drop out of this phase of play. The opener may raise it when his turn comes round again. When he does not, there is a showdown and the best hand wins everything staked on poch.

In Part 3 the cards are played out in sequences. The winner of the previous round starts by playing the lowest card of his longest suit. The next higher card of the same suit (in order 2 3 4 5 6 7 8 9 T J Q K A) is then played by whoever holds it, and the next, and so on, until the sequence ends either because the Ace is played or because the next card up has not been dealt. The player of the last card then begins a new sequence (and, in some circles, receives one chip from each opponent). This continues until a player wins by playing out the last card from his hand. The others pay him one chip for each card left in hand.

Point-trick games

Games in which win or loss depends on the point-value of certain cards captured in tricks, rather than on the mere number of tricks taken. An obvious schedule is Ace 4, King 3, Queen 2, Jack 1 (Reversis); a far commoner one is Ace 11, Ten 10, King 4, Queen 3, Jack 2 (Skat, etc.).

Poker

Vying game: 3–8p, 52c

Poker was born in or around New Orleans in the 1820s, of an ancestry including Primero, Brag, Bouillotte, Poch, Poque, and others. The basis of modern Poker evolved by about 1870, and it has since become virtually America's national card game. Unlike most great games, especially Bridge, it is played in a many different forms—often deliberately, at the same table and in the same session—which can disconcert the beginner. Poker is a game of skill, in that it offers the player considerable choice of play. The chance element of the deal can be negated, in the long run, by a conscious or intuitive grasp of mathematical principles, the accurate management of financial resources, and the application of practical psychology. The mark of Poker's greatness, like that of Bridge, is not that some people play it very well, but that so many play it very badly.

This entry can only cover the most basic forms of Poker: Draw, Stud, and one or two variations applicable to them all. Other possibilities are outlined, and with prior experience of the basic forms it is a simple matter to work ways of putting them into practice. For this purpose it helps that Poker does not have official rules, only basic principles.

Basic principles

Two sets of basic principles must be understood first: (*a*) Poker hands, which represent the fixed values on which players set their stakes, and (*b*) the mechanics of staking and betting.

Poker hands. In all forms of Poker, players bet as to which of them has the best hand. A Poker hand, by definition, is five cards. More may be dealt or held, but only five count in a showdown. These five may be totally unmatched, or may form one of the following universally recognized combinations. (Other combinations can be invented.) The value of each type of hand is indicated by the odds against receiving one when dealt five cards from a thoroughly shuffled pack. Figures above 100 are rounded to the nearest 50.

1. *High card.* No combination. Of two such hands, the one with the higher top card wins, or second higher if tied, etc. Odds: 1–1 (evens). Cards rank (high–low) A K Q J T 9 8 7 6 5 4 3 2.
2. *One pair.* Two of the same rank, the rest unmatched. Of two such hands, the one with the higher-ranking pair wins. If equal, go by highest top card. Odds: 1½–1.
3. *Two pair(s).* Self-explanatory. Of two such hands, the one with the higher-ranking pair wins; if equal, that with the higher-rank-

ing second pair; if still equal, go by the higher odd card. Odds: 20–1.

4. *Three of a kind (triplets, trips).* Three of the same rank, two unmatched. Of two such hands, the higher-ranking triplet wins. Odds: 46–1.

5. *Straight.* Five cards in numerical sequence, but not all in one suit. Ace counts high (A K Q J T) or low (5 4 3 2 A). Of two straights, that with the higher-ranking cards wins. Odds: 250–1.

6. *Flush.* Five cards of the same suit, but not all in sequence. Of two flushes, that with the higher top card wins, second higher if tied, etc. Odds: 500–1.

7. *Full house.* A triplet and a pair. Of two fulls, that with the higher triplet wins. Odds: 700–1.

8. *Four of a kind (fours).* Four cards of the same rank, the fifth irrelevant. Odds: 4150–1.

9. *Straight flush.* Five cards in suit and sequence, Ace counting high (A K Q J T) or low (5 4 3 2 A). An Ace-high straight flush, known as a royal flush, is unbeatable, but can be tied, as no suit is better than another in orthodox Poker. Odds: 65,000–1.

Betting procedure. Play does not take place with cards but with money, or with chips representing money, which are bought from a 'banker' before play. Chips should be of at least three different colours. Typically, whites count as one agreed monetary unit, reds as two, blues as five. (Other possible scales begin 1, 5, 10; 1, 5, 20, etc, and additional colours may be used.) To bet, a player moves one or more of the chips from the 'stack' in front of him towards the centre of the table, where they become part of the pool or 'pot' being played for. Chips once staked cannot be retrieved, except by winning the pot. Throughout play, individual players' stakes must be kept separate from one another and not physically combined into a single pile of chips, as it is essential to know exactly how much each one has staked.

In all forms of Poker, someone makes the first or opening bet. Rules vary as to (*a*) who has the first chance to open, (*b*) what minimum combination, if any, he must hold in order to open, and (*c*) the least and greatest amount he is allowed to make as his opening bet. If no one opens the pot, the hands are thrown in and there is a new deal. Before the pot is open, each in turn may bet

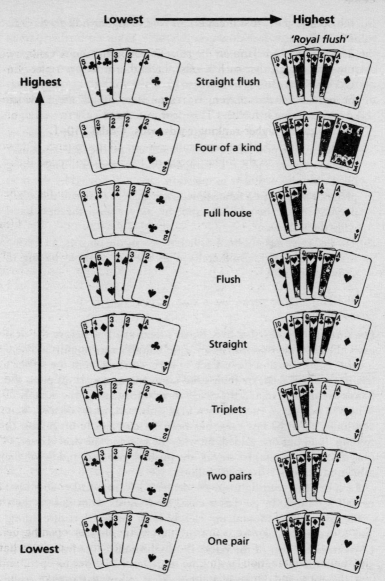

FIG. 23. **Poker.** Poker hands from lowest to highest.

(thereby opening it), pass ('check'), or fold (drop out). A player who folds lays his cards face down on the table, takes no further part in the deal, and has no claim on the current pot. Once the pot is open, each in turn must either match, raise, or fold, but may not pass. To match ('stay' or 'call') is to increase his stake so that it matches that of the previous active player. To 'raise' is to match the previous stake and increase it further. This continues until either:

(*a*) The player who last raised has been called by the other players still left in the pot. All bets now being equal, the last raiser may not raise again, and the 'betting interval' is at an end. Depending on the variety of Poker in question, this is followed by the next phase of play or by a final showdown. In a showdown, those still playing reveal their hands, and the player with the best hand wins the pot. Or:

(*b*) The last raise has not been called by any of the players, all having folded. The last raiser thereby wins the pot without having to show his hand.

Draw Poker

For three to six, best for five. Players deal in turn. Before the deal each player stakes one chip as an 'ante'. Shuffle thoroughly and deal 5 cards each, one at a time. Each in turn, starting from the dealer's left, may open, pass, or fold, until someone opens. If all pass, the hands are thrown in and the pot is carried forward to the next deal. With the pot open, each in turn may only call, raise, or fold. Play continues until the last raise has been followed only by calling or folding. If all but one folded, he wins the pot and the deal is over. If not, all the chips staked so far are pushed into the middle of the table and there is a draw, as follows.

Each in turn, starting from the dealer's left, may either stand pat or call for cards. In the latter case, he discards from one to three cards face down, announcing clearly how many he is discarding, and is promptly dealt by way of replacement the same number of cards from the top of the pack. Dealer himself is the last to draw, and must himself state clearly how many he is discarding.

A second betting interval follows. First to speak this time is the player who opened the pot on the first round. Each in turn may check (pass, indicate by knocking on the table) or bet until someone bets. If all check, the original opener must open up again. Each in turn thereafter may 'call' (match the previous stake), raise, or fold.

This continues until the last raise has been followed by calls for a showdown, in which case the player with the best hand wins the pot, or until all but one have folded, in which case the last in wins without showing his hand.

The following rules also apply unless otherwise agreed.

In the first round, no one may open the pot unless he has a pair of Jacks or better (a higher pair or a higher combination). If no one opens, the hands are thrown in. If someone opens and subsequently discards one of his qualifying pair, he must, when the pot is won, prove from his hand and discard that he was entitled to open.

Lower and upper limits should be set on the amount of any opening bet or raise. A logical lower limit is one white. The upper limit may be a fixed amount (e.g. five), or it may be set at the whole or half the amount currently in the pot.

The best way of ending the game is to agree a time limit and to finish at the end of the hand being played when that limit is reached. A player who runs out of chips must either buy more to continue, or drop out, in which case he loses all claim to the pot. (But he may be allowed to 'tap out'—i.e. pay as much as he has to the pot, any extras by other players then going to a side pot won by the second-best hand if the tapped-out player wins the main pot.)

Notes. When five play, at least one player can be expected to hold Jacks or better to open. It is not usual for much betting to be done before the draw, as the strong hands will naturally not want to frighten the weak ones out of the pot. It is not worth drawing one card to an inside straight (e.g. 5 6 7 x 9), and rarely worth attempting to fill a four-flush. Drawing three cards to a pair gives away so much information as to be pointless. Most hands are eventually won on two pairs or three of a kind, and straights and flushes will turn up occasionally, but it is possible to pass several hours without sight of a full house—except in a game where the players are sufficiently loose to bet on anything, when they will sometimes fall lucky to a foolhardy draw. Skill at play demands (*a*) an either mathematical or intuitive understanding of the chances of improving a given hand, (*b*) the ability to 'read' opponents' hands from the way they look or speak, (*c*) ability to play with such apparent inconsistency as to be unreadable by anyone else, (*d*) self-control.

Poker

Hi-Lo Draw. The only variation much in use today. The pot is split evenly between the holders of the highest and the lowest hands. For the latter purpose, a hand lacking any combination obviously beats a pair or better. As between two low hands, decide which is the higher on a high-card basis, and the other one is automatically lower. The lowest possible hand is a Seventy-Five (7 5 4 3 2 of mixed suits), unless it is agreed to count Ace low, in which case it is a Sixty-Four (6 4 3 2 A).

Lowball. In this variety, the pot is won exclusively by the lowest hand. Straights and flushes are then ignored, so the lowest possible is 5 4 3 2 A, known as a 'wheel' or 'bicycle'.

Seven-Card Draw. Poker does not work well for fewer than four players. Two may work out their own rules for Strip Poker, and three may play Seven-Card Draw. In this case each player is dealt 7 cards. In the draw, each must discard at least two, and receives as many as necessary to restore his hand to five.

Stud Poker

Stud Poker livens the game up by increasing the amount of information available and the number of players to eight. In Five-Card or 'Short' Stud, the dealer antes as many chips as there are players and deals each player 1 card face down (his 'hole'-card) and one face up. Everyone examines his hole-card and places it face down and half covered by his up-card. First to speak is the player showing the highest card or, if equal, the matching player nearest from the dealer's left. When bets have all been equalized, a second card is dealt face up, then a third, and finally a fourth, with a betting interval after each. At each deal the opening bet is made by the player showing the best combination (pair, three of a kind, etc), or, if none, the highest card or cards, or, if equal, by the player nearest from the dealer's left. If all pass on the last round there is a show-down, at which everyone reveals their hole-card and the best hand wins.

Seven-card or 'Long' Stud. Deal 2 cards face down and 1 face up. After a betting interval, deal a second, a third, and a fourth face up, then a third face down, with a betting interval after each. In a showdown, each player selects the best five of his seven cards as his final hand.

English Long Stud. A hybrid of Stud and Draw. Play as above until each has been dealt 5 cards and that betting interval is closed. Each in turn may then either stand pat or make one discard in return for a replacement. The replacement is dealt face down or up depending on whether the abandoned card was down or up. A betting interval follows. Anyone who discarded on the previous round may then either stand pat or make one more discard, which again matches up or down the card it replaces. A final betting interval follows.

Variants. Any form of Stud may be played Hi-Lo or Lowball as described for Draw Poker. Also appropriate are wild-card variants, the most basic being Deuces wild.

Other forms of Poker

Spit Poker. Any form of Poker in which one or more cards dealt face up to the table are counted by each player as if they were part of his own hand. The ancestral game, called Spit in the Ocean, is basically a form of Draw designed for up to eight players. Each receives four cards, the next is dealt face up to the table, and everyone counts this—the 'spit'—as his fifth card. For fun, the spit itself, or all four cards of the same rank, may be designated wild.

Wild Poker. A wild card is one which its holder may count as any natural card lacking from his hand. Any form of Poker may be played with one or more wild cards. The purpose is to increase the chances of making the higher and more interesting combinations, such as four or five of a kind and a straight flush. Which cards are made wild depends on how many are wanted: the more there are, the higher the winning hands, and the more incalculable the mathematics involved. For one wild card, add a Joker; for two, specify 'one-eyed Jacks'; for four, any given rank; for eight, any two ranks; and so on. Even wilder are variable wild cards, as exemplified by the Stud rule that any card subsequently dealt to a player that matches the rank of his hole-card is wild, but for that player only.

Although wild cards alter the mathematics, they do not normally change the relative ranking of hands. They do, however, introduce a new hand consisting of four of a kind and a wild card counting as the fifth. By agreement, 'five of a kind' either beats everything or is beaten only by a royal flush. Of tied hands, one with fewer wild cards beats one with more.

Poker Patience

Freak hand Poker. Freak hands, nowadays not so popular, are additional combinations designed to spice up games like basic Draw in which most winning hands are low. Widely recognized in the late nineteenth century was the *blaze*—any five court cards other than four of a kind, ranking below it but above a full house. The self-explanatory four-flush, if recognized, ranks between two pair and triplets.

Short-pack Poker. Poker is often played with short packs where these are customary—32 in France, 40 in Italy, Spain, and South America, and so on. Like wild cards, short packs change the mathematics but not the relative ranking of hands.

Poker Patience

Patience game: 1–Np, 52c

Poker Patience is the best known of a group of one-player games following a similar format, which can easily be extended to almost any game with distinctive scoring combinations. (See also Cribbage.)

Turn 25 cards one by one from a shuffled pack and place each one face up on the table in such a way as gradually to build a square of five rows and columns. Cards once placed may not be moved in relation to one another. At end of play score for each row and column (ten in all) according to the Poker combination it makes, regardless of the actual order of cards within the line. There are two possible scoring schedules, of which the American is more natural, the English more accurate:

	English	American
One pair	1	2
Two pair	3	5
Triplet	6	10
Straight	12	15
Flush	5	20
Full house	10	25
Four of a kind	16	50
Straight flush	30	75
Royal flush	30	100

The target score is 70 by the English system or 200 by the American.

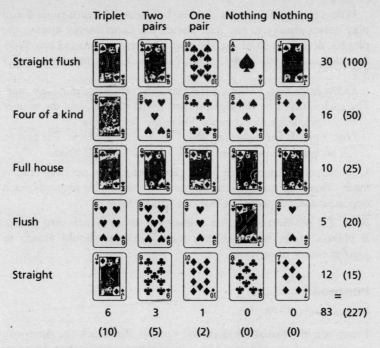

FIG. 24. **Poker Patience.** This Poker square contains one of each combination, scoring a total of 83 by the English count, or 227 by the American.

When played competitively, each player has a complete pack and arranges the cards in order for ease of identification. One person has a shuffled pack and plays any game of Poker Patience, calling out the name of each card as he turns it. Everyone else picks out the same card and arranges it in their own square. Whoever makes the highest-scoring square wins.

Polignac

Trick-avoidance game: 3–6p, 32c

A French game, probably eighteenth-century and ancestral to Hearts and Black Maria. See also Slobberhannes.

217

Pontoon

Unless four play, remove the black Sevens. The turn to deal and play passes always to the left. Divide the cards evenly among the players, dealing in 2s or 3s. The aim is to avoid capturing any Jacks in tricks, and especially ♣J, called Polignac. Cards rank K Q J A T 9 8 7.

Eldest leads first. Follow suit if possible, otherwise play any card. The trick is taken by the highest card of the suit led, and the winner of each trick leads to the next. There are no trumps.

Lose 2 points for capturing ♣J, 1 for each other Jack. The first to reach an agreed total of penalties—10 or 20—is the loser.

Optional rule. Anyone may bid capot before the opening lead is made. This is an undertaking to win every trick. If it succeeds, each opponent loses 5 points; if not, the bidder loses 5.

Note. The position of the Ace is common to old French card games. If players prefer to make Ace high, penalties should attach to Queens rather than Jacks.

Pontoon

Banking game: 3–10p, 52c

Pontoon is the British or domestic version, Blackjack the American or casino version, of Vingt-Un, a French game popular at the court of Louis XV and, later, much favoured by Napoleon, especially at St Helena. In the twentieth century it became the most popular game of the armed forces of English-speaking nations. The basic home game is described first, together with some common but optional extras. Pontoon, unlike casino Blackjack, has no official rules and varies widely from school to school.

Pontoon

Each player should start with at least twenty chips, counters, matchsticks, or other objects of unitary value. Pontoon is an arithmetical game. Cards Two to Ten count 2 to 10 respectively, courts 10 each, Aces 1 or 11 as their owners may freely declare. It is also a banking game. The banker is the dealer and has considerable advantages in play. For this reason the first dealer should be picked at random, such as by dealing cards around face up until someone receives a Jack.

In each deal, the punters' aim is to receive cards totalling more in face value than the banker's—but not exceeding 21, otherwise he is 'bust' and loses. A 21 consisting of an Ace and a card worth 10 is a 'pontoon', and pays extra, but banker's pontoon is unbeatable, as he always wins in cases of equality.

Shuffle the cards thoroughly at start of play. Thereafter, they are not shuffled before each deal but only after one in which a player gets a pontoon.

The banker deals one card face down to each player including himself. Everyone except the banker examines his card and stakes one or more chips on it, up to a previously agreed maximum. The banker then deals a second card to each, but does not yet look at his own. If anyone has a pontoon, he turns the Ace face up and stakes nothing more.

The banker then addresses himself to each player in turn and asks whether he wants more cards. That player may do one of the following.

1. *Stick*, i.e. decline extra cards, provided that he has a count of 16 or more.
2. *Buy*. In this case he increases his stake and is dealt another card face down. The amount staked for each new card must be not less than that staked for the previous one, nor more than the total amount he has staked so far. *(Variant:* Each new buy may be for less but not more than the previous one.)
3. *Twist*. In this case he is dealt one card face up, free of charge. Having once twisted, he may twist further cards but may not subsequently buy.

Buying or twisting continues until the punter either sticks or busts. Having bust, he loses his stake and hands his cards to the banker, who places them at the bottom of the pack.

When all have been served, the banker turns his two cards face up, and may, if he wishes, turn more cards face up until he is satisfied with his count, or busts. If he gets:

A pontoon, he wins all the stakes.

Twenty-one on three or more cards, he pays double to anyone with a pontoon, but wins all the others' stakes.

Under twenty-one, he pays anyone with a higher count (double for a pontoon) but wins all the other stakes.

Pontoon

A *bust*, he keeps the stakes of those who also bust, but pays anyone with a count of 16 to 21 (double for a pontoon).

When a punter gets a pontoon and the banker does not, the bank passes to the pontoon holder, who may play it or sell it to the highest bidder. (*Variant*: Each banks in turn, and the bank is held for as many deals as there are players.)

The following optional extras may be included.

Five-card trick. No one may receive more than five cards. A five-card hand worth 21 or less beats everything except a banker's pontoon, and is paid double.

Royal pontoon. A hand consisting of three Sevens beats everything except a banker's pontoon, and is paid treble.

Splitting. A punter (but not the banker) whose first two cards are of the same rank may split them and play each one as a separate hand, buying a second card for each and generally acting as if he were two people. Some permit only Aces to be split, others permit anything *but* Aces to be split. (In fact, Aces are the only rank worth splitting. It is certainly unwise to split Twos, Threes, Fives, Tens, or courts.) Some, if a split Ace becomes a pontoon, do not pay it double or permit that player to take the bank.

Blackjack

A twenty-one is called a 'natural'. Before dealing second cards, the dealer may look at his first and call for double stakes. Punters must then double their stakes, or redouble, or throw the hand in.

A second card is dealt face up to everyone. A punter with a natural is paid double by the dealer, unless he also has one, in which case he wins single from the holder of a natural and double from everyone else.

If the first two cards are a pair they may be split into two hands, as in Pontoon.

If a punter's first two cards total 11, he may 'double down'—that is, turn one face up, double his stake, receive a third card face down, then stick.

There is no buying. A punter may call for more cards dealt face up ('hit me') until he busts or stands, which he may do with any total.

Extras: A five-card trick or a 6 7 8 pays double, a 7 7 7 triple, a six-card trick quadruple.

Footnote: Casino Blackjack is generally more restrictive than the domestic and informal version described here.

Pope Joan

Stops game: 3–8p, 52c

A once popular Victorian family game, since replaced by its less elaborate relative Newmarket (q.v.). See also Comet, and Yellow Dwarf.

A staking board is required, with eight compartments labelled Ace, King, Queen, Jack, Game, Pope (♦9), Matrimony (K Q of trumps), Intrigue (Q J of trumps). Each player is equipped with a number of chips or counters, and ♦8 is removed from the pack.

The dealer 'dresses the board' by placing a stake of six counters in the compartment labelled Pope, two each to Matrimony and Intrigue, and one to each of the others. He then deals the 51 cards round as far as they will go, but to one more hand than there are players. It doesn't matter if some have one more card than others. The last card dealt to the dead hand is turned for trumps. If it is

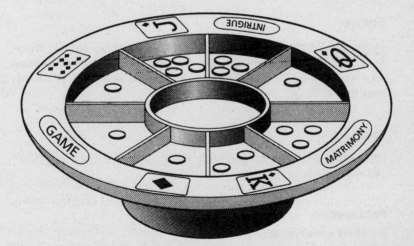

FIG. 25. **Pope Joan.** A Pope Joan board with staking compartments for the various contingencies of the game.

Poque

Pope, or the Ace, King, Queen, or Jack, Dealer wins the contents of the appropriate compartment.

Play begins, the aim being to run out of cards before anyone else.

Eldest plays a card face up to the table. It may be of any suit, but must be the lowest he has of it. For this purpose, cards run A 2 3 4 5 6 7 8 9 T J Q K. If he has the next higher card of the same suit, he plays this too, and so on until he can go no further. The sequence is then continued by the player who holds the next card up.

If no one can play the next card up because it is in the dead hand, or because a King has been reached, a new sequence is started by the person who played the last card (the 'stop'). As before, it may be of any suit, but must be the lowest he has of it.

The content (if any) of the Ace, King, Queen, and Jack compartments goes to the person playing the said trump card, as does that for Pope. That for Intrigue can only be won if the same person is able to play Queen and Jack, as does Matrimony for King and Queen. If any stake is not won, it is carried forward to the next deal.

The first to play out all his cards wins the stake for Game, plus one chip from each other player for each card remaining in his hand—except that anyone holding the Pope is excused payment.

Poque

Eighteenth-century French gambling game, probably derived from Poch, and itself the source of Poker's name and the idea of betting on a five-card hand, though only pairs, triplets and fours of a kind were counted.

Post

Fifteenth-century English gambling game, later called Post and Pair, and ancestral to Brag.

Preference

Plain-trick game: 3p, 32c

A classic three-hander popular in Eastern Europe, especially Austria, since the late 18th century. Its failure to penetrate the

English-speaking world is surprising, as it has much to offer Bridge or Solo players when lacking a fourth. Preference has enjoyed a considerable revival in Russia since the fall of the Communist regime, but there are several different versions of it and all are extremely complex. The following variety, based on a description published by Piatnik, the Austrian card-makers, takes less space to explain and is relatively easy to follow.

Preliminaries. Although three take part in each deal, the game is often played by four, each dealing in turn and sitting his own deal out. It may be played for a hard or soft score (cash or writing): if hard, players should agree a basic stake consisting of a multiple of ten units.

The 32 cards rank A K Q J T 9 8 7 in each suit. The turn to deal and play passes always to the left. If playing for hard score, the dealer places a single stake in the pot, then deals (face down) 3 each, 2 to the table, 4 each, and again 3 each, so that everyone receives 10 cards. The two odd cards constitute the talon.

Auction. An auction determines who will play alone against the other two. The soloist will name trumps, may take the talon and discard two cards, and must then win at least six tricks in play.

The basic bids are from one to four. 'One' entitles the bidder, if he becomes the soloist, to name any suit as trump. 'Two' prevents clubs from being named, 'three' prevents also spades, and 'four' prevents diamonds, automatically making hearts trumps.

Each in turn, starting with Eldest, may pass or bid, and, having passed, may not come in again. The first bid is 'one'. Each thereafter must either pass or bid one higher — 'jump-bidding' is not allowed. However:

1. An earlier player may 'hold' the bid of a later player. *Example*: If Abel bids 'one', Baker must pass or bid 'two'. If he bids 'two', Charlie must pass or bid 'three'. Baker and Charlie may not hold the previous bid, as they speak later in the auction. Abel, however, may then hold Charlie's bid of three, as he is the earlier of two players willing to bid the same amount. If Abel passed, Baker would be able to hold Charlie's three, and Charlie would then have to bid 'four' or pass.
2. Any player in turn to bid may declare 'hand' or 'preference'. 'Hand' is an undertaking to play with the hand as dealt, without

first seeking to improve it by taking the talon and making two discards. If two players are willing to bid 'hand', they name their suits, and the higher-ranking wins the bid. For this purpose, hearts beat diamonds beat spades beat clubs. 'Preference' is a bid of hearts, hand, which cannot be overcalled.

Play. Unless playing from the hand, the soloist then picks up the talon, adds it to his hand, discards any two cards face down, and announces trumps.

Before leading, he asks the player to his left, then to his right, whether they will stay in or drop out. A player who stays in must win at least two tricks, or else will be penalized. If one drops out, the other plays alone against the soloist. If both drop out, the soloist wins without playing at all.

The soloist now leads to the first trick—unless he thinks his game unwinnable, in which case he can throw it in. Subsequent players must follow suit and head the trick if possible; if unable to follow, they must play a trump, and beat any trump already played if possible. The trick is taken by the highest card of the suit led, or by the highest trump if any are played, and the winner of each trick leads to the next.

An additional rule of trick-play is important and unusual enough to require special attention. When three are active, and the soloist leads, the second must—if possible—win the trick with the *lowest* card that will do so. This is called 'indulging' (*largieren*), its purpose being to enable the partner to take his requisite two tricks. Failing to indulge when able to constitutes a revoke. (*Variant*: Some schools suspend this rule when the second partner has already taken his two tricks.)

Score. A player taking the requisite minimum of tricks—soloist six, partner two—wins one-tenth of the pot, or scores 1 point, for each trick taken. If a partner fails, he doubles the pot or loses 10 points. If the soloist fails, he triples the pot or loses 20 points. If he threw the hand in before the first trick, he pays each opponent the equivalent of three-tenths of the pot, or five-tenths if only one was active, and the pot remains unchanged.

If anyone revokes—i.e. fails to obey any of the rules of trick-taking, including 'indulging', when able to do so—play ceases and settlements are made without recourse to the pot. If the soloist revokes, he pays the others the equivalent of three-tenths of the pot, or five-tenths if only one opponent was playing. If an opponent revokes, he pays the soloist the full amount of the pot, and his partner (if active) the equivalent of four tenths.

When scoring in writing, for 'tenth' read 'point', and ignore references to the pot. (Pot scoring is, in fact, so unwieldy that complicated rules obtain to prevent anyone from winning too much after the pot has been fattened by a series of losses.)

Variants. If one partner drops and the other plays alone, the lone partner must take four tricks to avoid penalty.

If one wishes to drop, the other may invite him to stay. If, then, they fail to take four tricks between them—not necessarily two each—the one who issued the invitation will pay the dues from both.

Some schools pay the soloist a bonus, independent of the pot, for playing with, or (more rarely) without, all four Aces in hand.

Bettel is a bid to lose every trick. There is no trump, but players must still head the trick if possible. It usually outbids 'four', but its bidding position and value are variable. It may be played with exchange or from the hand, and 'open' (face up) for a higher score.

Mord, or *Durchmarsch*, is a bid to win every trick, following the same rules as Bettel.

Sans atout appears in one account (Claus D. Grupp, *Kartenspiele*, Wiesbaden, 1975) as a bid in which the soloist, playing at no trump, must win at least six tricks in succession. If they are the first six, the seventh must be won as well.

In these additional bids, some schools forbid either opponent to drop out, but allow them to double the value of the game, which the soloist may then redouble.

Another optional feature is that, when a player has made an ordinary suit bid, taken the talon, and discarded, an opponent may then take over as soloist by bidding one of the higher games, taking the new talon, and discarding in its place.

Notes. A basic game requires five certain or four-and-a-half probable tricks in hand. For example, ♥A 8 ♦K J 7 ♠A Q T 8 ♣9 allows a bid of 'two' (spades, possibly converting to diamonds); ♥K ♦K Q J 9 7 ♠K J T ♣9 8 allows 'three' (diamonds). With these cards, if well ahead, you could chance a 'hand' bid, hoping for a lucky break, or that the Ace of hearts or spades or the Queen of spades is in the talon. The normal requirement for a hand bid is, obviously, six fairly certain tricks. If not playing from the hand, use the exchange of two cards with the talon to void a suit, if possible.

The obligation to head the trick, combined with the 'indulging' rule, has some nice repercussions on the play. Suppose, as soloist, you lead the Queen from ♥Q J T 9; second hand, with ♥K 9, must play the King; third, with ♥A 7, must likewise play the Ace. The rules of following thus make your heart sequence good for three tricks once the Queen has gone. But reverse the holdings of second and third hand. Now second must play the Ace, but third can discard low, thus retaining the King and leaving your hearts good for only two tricks.

Primiera

Vying game: 4–8p (4 best), 40c

A 'prime' is a four-card hand containing one card of each suit, and hence the exact opposite of a 'flush' in Poker. The major gambling game based on this combination goes back to the sixteenth century, being known to Cardano as Primiera, Rabelais as Prime, and Shakespeare as Primero. It is still played in central Italy—with Italian-suited cards, of course—under such names as Goffo or Bambara.

The turn to deal and bet passes to the left. Each player stakes a previously agreed amount (the ante) and receives 4 cards dealt in 2s from a 40-card pack ranking K Q J 7 6 5 4 3 2 A.

Anyone dealt a winning combination calls for an immediate showdown, and the player with the best hand wins the pot. From lowest to highest, the winning combinations are:

1. *Primiera*. One card of each suit.
2. *Fifty-five*. Seven, Six, Ace of the same suit, the fourth card any.
3. *Flush*. Four cards of the same suit.

As between equal combinations, the best is that totalling the greatest point-value, counting for this purpose

Each Seven	21
Six	18
Ace	16

Five	15
Four	14
Three	13
Two	12
K, Q, J	10

If still equal, the deal is annulled and the pot carried forward to the next. (*Variant*: Flushes and fifty-fives may be decided on a best-suit basis: hearts highest, then diamonds, clubs, spades.)

Example. Aldo declares a primiera: ♠K ♥Q ♣3 ♦3. Bruno counters with a fifty-five: ♠7 6 A ♦A. This is beaten by Carlo's flush, ♣7 2 Q J. Dino, however, sweeps the pool with ♥6 5 4 3, counting 60 to Carlo's 53. Four such hands are, of course, most unlikely to occur in a single, honest deal.

If no one has a winning combination, each in turn makes one or more discards and receives the same number from the top of the pack. An additional stake may be required at this point. If there is still no claim, there is a showdown, and the pot is won by the player with the best 'point', i.e. highest value of cards in one suit. (*Example*: ♥7 4 ♣A ♠K, counting 35 in hearts, beats ♦K Q 4 ♠7, counting 34 in diamonds.)

In some schools, the period between a draw and final showdown may be filled with a round of stake-raising as at Poker, or there may be further draws until a win is claimed or the pack runs out.

Note. Pairs and sequences do not count, but three or four of a kind will often win as a primiera. In Cardano's treatise the best hands are: *chorus* (four of a kind), *fluxus* (flush), *supremus* (fifty-five), *primiera*, and *numerus* (point).

Punto Banco

See Baccara.

Put

Plain-trick game of bluff: 2–4p (2 best), 52c

First recorded in the sixteenth century as a tavern game of ill repute, in the seventeenth as played only by menials, and now long defunct,

Quadrille

Put is still quite amusing if not played too seriously. It clearly relates to the more elaborate French game Truc (q.v.), and so belongs to a very ancient family.

Cards rank 3 2 A K Q J T 9 8 7 6 5 4 (Three high, Four low). Players deal alternately, shuffling thoroughly before each deal. Whoever cuts the higher Put card deals first. They put up equal stakes, and are dealt 3 cards each, one at a time.

The aim is to win more tricks than one's opponent, thereby winning the stake. If neither wins outright, points may be scored, and the stake is eventually won by the first to reach 5 points over as many deals as it takes.

Non-dealer leads to the first trick. Either player, when about to lead, may throw his hand in, or 'put' it to his opponent that he should throw his in. If either throws it in, the other marks a point, and the next in turn to deal does so. If not, the trick is played.

Any card may be played: suit need not be followed, and there are no trumps. The higher card takes the trick, and the winner of one trick leads to the next. If both play equal cards, the trick is tied: neither wins it, and the same leader leads again.

If one player wins more tricks than the other, he wins the stake. Otherwise, it is a tie, and there is another deal. The commonest result is a draw by 'trick and tie'—that is, one trick each and one tied.

Old texts say Put can be played by three or four, the last in partnerships. Details are not recorded, except to note that, in the partnership game, each player passes his highest card across to his partner before the opening lead.

Quadrille

See Patience.

Quadrille

Plain-trick game: 4p, 40c

This classic game, directly ancestral to Boston and Solo Whist, was devised in early eighteenth-century France as a four-handed version of Hombre, and remained popular for over a hundred years in

France and England until it was ousted by partnership Whist. Modern taste will revolt against its irregular ranking of cards (an ancient inheritance), its excessively complicated pay-off schedule, and its total lack of standardization. This is a great pity, as the underlying game is remarkably varied and well designed. I append a suggested system of written scores to this entry in hope of making Quadrille more palatable.

Format. Four play, each for himself in the long run, though temporary alliances may be made from deal to deal. Each should start with an equal number of chips or counters, not fewer than forty.

Rank of cards. Use a 40-card pack lacking Eights, Nines, and Tens. In trick-play, the basic ranking of numeral cards is 'high in black, low in red', i.e.

$$\text{in } \spadesuit, \clubsuit, \quad K\ Q\ J\ 7\ 6\ 5\ 4\ 3\ 2$$
$$\text{in } \heartsuit, \diamondsuit, \quad A\ K\ Q\ J\ 2\ 3\ 4\ 5\ 6\ 7$$

The current trump suit, however, has further peculiarities. The highest trumps rank downwards and bear names as follows:

1. *Spadille*, $\spadesuit$A
2. *Manille*, the nominally lowest trump (Two if black, Seven if red)
3. *Basto*, $\clubsuit$A

These three are called 'matadors' and have special powers in play. When a black suit is trump, the fourth highest is King, and so downwards to the Three (Two being Manille). When a red suit is trump, the fourth highest is Ace (called Punto or Ponto, but not a matador), and so downwards to the Six (Seven being Manille). Note that the black Aces are always the first and third highest trumps, regardless of the nominal trump suit.

Deal. A game consists of any number of deals divisible by four. The turn to deal and play passes always to the right. Before each deal, each player stakes one chip to the pot. (Or the dealer stakes four, if preferred.) Deal 10 cards each in 3s and 4s, either 4 3 3, 3 4 3, or 3 3 4.

Auction. An auction to determine who will become *Hombre*, or principal player, is opened by Eldest hand, the player at Dealer's right. Each in turn may pass or bid, and, having passed, may not come in again.

The lowest bid is 'Ask-leave'. This is an offer to win at least six tricks after naming trumps, calling for a partner, and playing with him or her against the other two. Ask-leave is so called because the bidder is asking leave to seek a partner, which any later player can deny by bidding 'solo'. (Compare 'prop and cop' in Solo Whist.)

Solo, the principal bid, is an offer to win at least six tricks after naming trumps and playing alone against the other three. The first player to bid solo is on, and names trumps immediately.

If an ask-leave is not overcalled by solo, the game played is 'alliance'. Before play, Hombre names trumps and nominates the King of any non-trump suit which he does not hold himself. If he holds all three, he calls a Queen instead. The holder of the called card automatically becomes the other partner, but does not announce that fact, which can only be established when the called card is played to a trick, or when its holder makes some other play obviously advantaging the bidder.

If all four pass, the game is 'forced Spadille'. It means the player holding ♠A is obliged to play alliance by calling a King, or Queen if necessary. In this case, however, he may either name trumps himself, or invite his partner to do so. (Sources do not remark on the conflict of this rule with that forbidding partner's self-declaration. But it is a nice point—perhaps intentional—that the caller should either name trumps, or know his partner immediately, but not both.)

Play. The game established, Eldest leads to the first trick. Subsequent players must follow suit if possible, but otherwise may play any card. The trick is taken by the highest card of the suit led, or by the highest trump if any are played, and the winner of each trick leads to the next.

Reneging. An exception to the rules of trick-play concerns matadors. If an ordinary trump is led, a player holding a matador is not obliged to play it, but may, if lacking other trumps, 'renege' by playing from another suit. The same applies to the holder of a higher matador if a lower one is led. However, if a higher matador is led, and another player has no trump but a lower matador, then he may not renege, but must play it. In brief: A matador is not forced by the play of a lower trump or matador, but only by a higher one.

Premiers and the vole. If Hombre wins the first six tricks straight off, he gains a bonus for 'premiers', and may claim a win without further play. If, however, he leads to the seventh trick, this automatically counts as a bid to win all ten (the 'vole'), which carries an additional bonus if successful. If unsuccessful, it reduces but does not entirely cancel his basic win. In an alliance, the same rule applies to the partnership if they take the first six between them, and they must (obviously) discuss whether or not to lead to the seventh.

Settlements if contract won. For a successful solo, Hombre wins the stake. If, in addition, any of the following bonuses apply, they are paid to him by each opponent. A 'unit' means one quarter of the current stake. The stake may be greater than four chips, as it is carried forward when a game is lost.

Hombre held three matadors	1 unit
Hombre held all three plus Punto	2
Hombre won premiers	1

(Punto, or Ace, only applies when a red suit is trump.)

Settlements for the vole varied enormously. The following is suggested. Having won the game and premiers, and gone for the vole, Hombre receives an additional 2 units from each opponent if successful, otherwise pays 2 units to each for the loss.

In an alliance or forced Spadille, the stake is divided between the allies, and each opponent pays each partner any of the relevant bonuses listed above. In this case 'matadors held' means 'held between the allies', not necessarily in one hand.

Settlements if contract lost. If Hombre wins only five tricks, the loss is a 'remise'; if four or fewer, it is a 'codille'; and the same applies to an alliance.

Given remise, Hombre doubles the stake—which is carried forward to the next deal—and, if applicable, pays each opponent for any matadors held by the contracting side.

Given codille, the stake is won by and divided between the two or three opponents of the contracting side (unless there are three and the stake is not exactly divisible), and twice the amount of that stake is paid by Hombre to be carried forward to the next deal.

In an ordinary alliance, the loss is borne entirely by the player who called a partner, as the latter had no say in joining the partnership. In forced Spadille, however, it is shared, as both played on equally involuntary terms.

Point-score. The following is a suggestion. Points for matadors held are ignored. If Hombre has an ally, the appropriate winning score is credited to each, but a losing score is only deducted from the ally's in the case of forced Spadille:

	Forced	Alliance	Solo
Won	3	5	10
Won with premiers	6	10	20
Won with vole won	12	20	40
Won with vole lost	1	2	5
Lost remise	−6	−10	−20
Lost codille	−12	−20	−40

If a game is lost (remise or codille), the following game is won or lost double. If two are lost in succession, the next is trebled in value; if three, the next quadrupled; and so on, until a game is won, when the next counts singly again.

Optional extras. Countless variations were played on this basic theme, all devoid of standardization.

By 'preference', a suit was fixed on in advance—usually that of the trump of the first deal—such that future bids in that suit overcalled the same in another, and were won or lost double.

By 'vole announced', Hombre could declare in advance of the first trick his intention of winning all ten. This increased the game value but, if lost, lost the whole game.

One comprehensive list of bids ran, from low to high:

Forced Spadille.

Alliance.

Médiateur (Dimidiator). Soloist plays after calling for a King (or Queen if four held) and taking it into his own hand in exchange for any unwanted card.

Casco (Respect). A player holding both black Aces makes an alliance by calling a King and allowing his partner to name trumps.

Solo.

Grandissimo. A solo with no trump suit, apart from the two black Aces, which Hombre does not necessarily hold.

Devole (Nemo). Hombre undertakes to lose every trick, playing at no trump except for the black Aces.

Quintille

Five-hand adaptation of Quadrille (see above). Each receives eight cards, and Hombre aims to win at least five tricks, either alone or with the aid of a partner found by calling a King.

Quinto

Point-trick game: 4pp, 52c + Joker

Invented by 'Professor Hoffman' (Angelo Lewis) within sight of 1900, Quinto has too many points of interest, and is too finely structured, to be omitted on grounds of mere artificiality.

Players sit crosswise in partnerships established by any agreed means. The turn to deal and play passes always to the left. From a 53-card pack ranking A K Q J T 9 8 7 6 5 4 3 2, and including one Joker, deal 12 cards each and leave the other five face down on the table as a talon (or 'cachette', according to Hoffman).

Each side's aim is to score 250 points over as many deals as necessary. Points are scored for winning tricks (5 each) and especially for any 'quints' contained in them. The best quint is the Joker, or 'Quint royal', scoring 25 points. Additional quints are the Five of each suit, and two cards of the same suit totalling five (Ace and Four, Three and Two) falling to the same trick. A quint in hearts scores 20, diamonds 15, clubs 10, spades 5.

Before play, each has one turn in which to pass, double, or redouble an opponent's double. A double increases the value of won tricks from 5 to 10 points in the current deal, a redouble further increases them to 20 each.

Eldest leads to the first trick, and the winner of each trick leads to the next. Suit must be followed if possible, otherwise any card may be played. There is no single trump suit. Instead, the suits rank in order from low to high: spades, clubs, diamonds, hearts. A player unable to follow suit to the card led may discard from a lower suit (if any) or 'trump' by playing from a higher suit (if any). The trick is therefore taken by the highest card of the highest suit played. The Joker may not be led to a trick, but otherwise may be played at any time, whether or not its holder can follow suit. It cannot win a trick.

During play, the side winning a trick containing a quint scores immediately for the quint (Joker, Five, A + 4, 3 + 2), according to its suit. If this brings them to the 250-point target, they have won, and play ceases immediately.

Otherwise, the side winning the last trick wins also the talon, which counts as a thirteenth trick, and scores for any quint or quints it may contain.

If neither side has reached or exceeded 250, the thirteen tricks are then counted at 5, 10, or 20 each, depending on any doubling. If both sides are still under 250, or both are over but tied, there is another deal.

(Hoffman does not cover the remote possibility that the holder of the Joker may eventually be forced to lead it. I suggest the trick be taken by the highest card played. Pennycook suggests the trick go by default to the opposing side.)

Notes. Clearly, doubling will be exercised by a player with a strong hand—such as lots of red cards and a short black suit. A neat effect of doubling/redoubling is that it increase the value of tricks, and hence of trick-play, relative to that of quints, which are not affected by it. It will be noted that a side winning all thirteen tricks, redoubled, thereby gains 260 points and the game. A player not holding the Joker will naturally seek to win an early trick in second position, even if it means playing an inordinately high 'trump', in case his partner has it. On the other hand, the holder of ♥A will try to keep it for as long as possible in order to win the last trick, which is worth two. Other points of strategy will soon suggest themselves.

Quinze

Gambling game: 2p, 52c

An old two-player equivalent of Pontoon. Players match stakes and receive one card each. Cards count Ace 1, numerals face value, courts 10 each. A hand counting more than 15 is bust. Non-dealer draws further cards, one at a time, until either satisfied with his hand or bust. Dealer then does likewise. The player with the higher non-bust total wins. If one busts, the other wins. If both tie or bust, the stake is doubled and a new deal played.

Rams

Plain-trick game: 3–5p, 32c

A widespread European drinking game related to Nap and Loo; also called Rounce. The basic idea is fairly constant, but scoring systems vary.

Each player starts with five, seven, or ten counters (or marks drawn on paper), and the general aim is to lose counters by winning tricks. Each player drops out as he pays his last counter, and the last left in is the overall loser. Alternatively, the first to run out of counters is the overall winner.

The 32 cards rank A K Q J T 9 8 7 in each suit. A first dealer is selected at random, and the turn to deal and play passes to the left. Deal 5 cards each, in batches of 3 and 2, including an extra hand or 'widow' face down. Turn the next card up for trumps.

Anyone who thinks he can win all five tricks immediately announces 'General Rams'. No one may then drop out, and play begins. Otherwise, each player in turn from Dealer's left announces whether he will pass, i.e. throw the hand in without penalty, or play, thereby undertaking to win at least one trick. Another option is to throw the hand in and take the widow in its place. Only the first player to bid this may do it, and he must then play.

There must be at least two active players. If all pass up to the player at Dealer's right, both he and the dealer must play. The dealer may not pass if only one previous player has undertaken to play.

Before play, dealer may take the trump turn-up and throw out any unwanted card face down. The opening lead is made by the player at dealer's left, unless anyone declared a General Rams, in which case the declarer leads. Subsequent players must follow suit and head the trick if possible; if unable to follow, they must play a trump, and beat any trump already played if possible. The trick is taken by the highest card of the suit led, or by the highest trump if any are played, and the winner of each trick leads to the next.

Each player removes a counter for each trick he wins. Anyone who played but failed to win a trick is saddled with five more. The declarer of a General Rams loses five counters if successful, and everyone else takes five more. If unsuccessful, the declarer takes five

Ranter-go-Round

more, the others drop one counter for each trick they have won, and a player who took none is exempt from penalty.

Alternative scoring. By another method, the dealer puts five chips in the pool, and each player takes a counter for each trick won, or adds five to the pool for taking none.

Bierspiel is a variant in which ♦7 is the second best trump.

Rounce is an American variety played with 52 cards.

Ranter-go-Round

See Chase the Ace.

Reunion

Point-trick game: 3p, 32c

The point-trick equivalent of Euchre, Reunion is an eighteenth-century Rhenish game too interesting to omit even if now defunct. It is a nice three-hander, and makes a good springboard for more complex games like Skat.

Cards rank from high to low in the following order, and bear the stated point-values:

trJ	J	A	T	K	Q	J	9	8	7
12	12	11	10	4	3	2	—	—	—

The highest trump is the Jack of trumps, or Right Bower; the second highest is the other Jack of the same colour as trumps, or Left Bower; these count 12 each. Non-trump Jacks rank between Nine and Queen, and count 2 each. With an additional 10 for the last trick, the total number of points in play is 150. A game is three deals, one by each player. The aim is to take most points in the partie, and especially to avoid taking fewer than 100.

The player cutting the lowest card deals first, and the turn to deal and play passes to the left. Deal 10 each in batches of 3 4 3, and turn the second of the final two for trump. The dealer then makes two face-down discards, which may not include an Ace or a Bower. Any card-points they contain will count for him at end of play as if he had won them in tricks. The two undealt cards belong to him, and he may take the face-down card immediately, but must leave the turn-up in place until the second trick is over.

Eldest leads to the first trick, and the winner of each trick leads to the next. A player unable to follow suit must play a trump if possible. The trick is taken by the highest card of the suit led, or by the highest trump if any are played. If both Bowers fall to the same trick, the holder of the Left Bower immediately pays one unit to whoever played the Right.

At the end of the game, an opponent with 100–149 points pays the winner one unit. One with 150 or more pays nothing, but the other then pays double. Anyone with under 100 pays double, under 50 triple. If two tie for most, the loser pays each one accordingly.

Reversis

Trick-avoidance game: 4p, 48c

A classic game, the ancestor of Hearts and Black Maria, Reversis was popular with the French aristocracy in the seventeenth and eighteenth centuries, and was much played elsewhere, though not in Britain. It has some novel features and is interesting and exciting to play. Unfortunately, it involved vast quantities of counters and sported so complex a system of pools and side-payments as to require a disproportionate amount of space to detail. Rather than omit it on those grounds, I offer it here with simplified point-scores loosely based on the original rules. For authenticity, see the article by John McLeod in the *Journal of the Playing-Card Society*, May 1977.

Four players use a 48-card pack ranking A K Q J 9 8 7 6 5 4 3 2 (no Tens). Play any number of deals which is a multiple of four. The turn to deal and play passes to the right.

Deal. The dealer deals, in 3s and 4s, 11 cards to each player and 12 to himself, then one odd card face down before each other player, who may not yet look at it. All examine their hands and make any single discard, which may not be ♥J, and (except for the dealer) replace it with the odd one. This leaves everyone with eleven cards in hand. The four discards constitute the talon, which is not looked at until end of play.

Object. The primary aim is to avoid capturing point-cards contained in tricks. An Ace taken in a trick counts 4 against, King 3, Queen 2, Jack 1 point. The player taking fewest card-points wins the deal; the player taking most loses.

Additional aims are:

(a) to discard the ♥J (called *Quinola*) to a trick led in a suit other than hearts;

(b) to discard Aces, particularly ♦A, to tricks led in other suits;

(c) given a suitable hand, to lose every trick ('espagnolette').

(d) given a suitable hand, to win every trick ('reversis').

Tricks. Dealer's right-hand neighbour leads to the first trick. Subsequent players must follow suit if possible, otherwise may play any card. The trick is taken by the highest card of the suit led, and the winner of each trick leads to the next. There are no trumps.

Premium cards. Certain cards have special values when played to tricks. They are ♥J (Quinola) = 5; ♦A = 2; each other Ace = 1 point.

If the holder of such a card throws it to a trick when unable to follow suit, he immediately scores its value, and the trick-winner deducts it from his own score.

If the holder is forced to play it to a trick (having no other card of the suit led), he loses that amount, and the player who led to the trick scores it.

If the holder leads it to a trick, he loses that amount, and the same amount is added to the score of the eventual winner of the deal.

These premiums, plus or minus, are doubled if the two players concerned are placed opposite each other, or if the event occurs in the last two tricks. (Quadrupled, if both.)

Espagnolette. An attempt to lose every trick may be undertaken by a player who holds all four Aces, or three Aces and Quinola. This player has the special privilege—called the espagnolette—of not being required to follow suit in any of the first nine tricks. Not following when required to do so is deemed to represent a bid to lose every trick. Only in the tenth trick must he follow suit if possible.

Reversis. A player who wins the first nine tricks is deemed to have undertaken the reversis. This obliges him to win the other two or lose the game.

Scoring. If no espagnolette or reversis was undertaken, each player totals the value of counting-cards contained in the tricks he won. The player with fewest wins, the player with most loses. The amount added to the winner's score and deducted from the loser's is 4 plus the value of any counting cards contained in the talon, for which purpose ♦A counts 5 instead of 4. A tie for winner or loser is decided in favour of the player who took fewer tricks or, if equal, of the player in the best position. For this purpose, Dealer is best placed, and the player at his right worst placed, priority diminishing clockwise around the table.

If espagnolette was attempted and won, its player takes absolute precedence as winner, and scores as described above. If lost, he is the absolute loser, and pays the winner as described above. He also deducts from his score 50 points plus twice the value of any premiums he scored in course of play.

If the reversis was attempted and won, its player scores 30, and the player sitting opposite loses 30. If lost, its player loses 30, and 30 is scored by the winner of the tenth trick, the eleventh being then not played.

If both espagnolette and reversis were attempted and won, the reversis takes precedence. In this case, the 30-point penalty attaches to the espagnolette player, not necessarily to the one opposite the reversis player.

Rockaway

Same as Crazy Aces; see Switch.

Rolling Stone

Going-out game: 3–6p, 32 or 52c

A simple, but maddening, nineteenth-century European game known in French as *Enflé* and in German as *Schwellen*—i.e. 'inflation', from the way one's hand tends to grow in size. More advanced relatives include Durak and Svoyi Koziri.

Cards rank A K Q J T 9 8 7 6 5 4 3 2. Ideally, the number of cards in the pack is eight times the number of players, so strip out as many lower numerals as necessary to produce this effect. Then shuffle thoroughly and deal 8 each in 1s. The turn to deal and play passes to the left.

The aim is to be the first to run out of cards.

Eldest hand leads any card face up. Each in turn thereafter must play a card of the same suit if possible. Whoever plays the highest card wins the trick (worthless in itself) and leads to the next. A player who cannot follow suit takes all the cards so far played, adds them to his hand, and leads to the next.

Play ceases the moment anyone plays the last card from his hand, and that player wins.

Variant. A full pack may be used. Each receives 10 cards and the rest are stacked face down. A player unable to follow suit must draw from stock until able. When the stock is empty, a player unable to follow suit takes the cards so far played, and the game continues as before.

Rouge et Noir

Or 'R. & N.': see Trente et Quarante.

Rounce

See Rams.

Rubicon

Tag denoting any variety of game (though chiefly Bezique and Piquet) in which the losing player or side is penalized more heavily for failing to 'cross the Rubicon' of a stated minimum point-score. (Compare the 'lurch' at Cribbage, 'schneider' at Skat etc.)

Ruff

In Ruff, a sixteenth-century relative of Trump (ancestor of Whist), each player received 12 cards and there was a stock of four, one of them turned for trump. Whoever held the trump Ace could 'ruff' by taking these four cards in hand and discarding any four in their place. In Ruff and Honours, its seventeenth-century derivative, the Deuces were omitted, 12 cards each were dealt, and extra payments were made for holding certain high cards or 'honours'. In Whisk and Swabbers, its eighteenth-century derivative, 13 each were dealt, and the 'swabbers' (honours) were ♥A, ♣J, and the Ace and Deuce of trumps.

Rummy

Rummy game: 2–8p, 52 or 104c

'Rummy' denotes a large family of games based on the same principle. The principle consists of a method of play called 'draw and discard', and a twofold objective, to collect sets of cards of the same sort and to eliminate them from the hand in matching sets or 'melds'. Play ceases when one player 'goes out' by playing his last card. In early Rums (notably Gin) melds themselves have no scoring value: the main aim, therefore, is to go out first, and those who have not done so are penalized for cards left unmelded in their hands. In later forms (notably Canasta), melds carry positive scores: the main aim, therefore, is to meld as much as possible, and to delay going out until it can be done with most profit.

Rummy probably originated in China as a card or tile game (compare Mah Jong). The earliest Western form was a nineteenth-century Mexican game, Conquian (q.v.). A vast expansion of Rummy games took place during the first half of the twentieth century, culminating in the highly elaborate partnership game of Canasta in the 1950s. The bubble now seems to have burst, leaving different groups of players—blamelessly ignorant of the historical background—practising a variety of informal games under an equal variety of interchangeable rules and titles. To some, all forms of Rummy are 'Gin', to others, they are 'Kalookie'; and so on (just as there are those who call all forms of card-solitaire 'Patience', 'Klondike', 'Canfield', or whatever.)

The most basic form of Rummy is described below. There are typical variations which players may adopt or adapt to suit their own tastes. Separate entries will be found for these more specialized members of the family: Canasta (including Bolivia, Samba, etc.),

Conquian, Contract (and Continental) R., Czech R., Gin, Kaluki, Michigan R., Oklahoma, Persian R., Vatican. Also relevant are Calypso and so-called Whisky Poker.

Basic Rummy

Two to four players use one 52-card pack, five to eight use two packs shuffled together. Thorough shuffling is essential before each deal in all Rummy games. Decide first dealer by any agreed means. The turn to deal and play passes always to the left.

Deal 7 cards each in 1s, and stack the rest face down in the middle of the table to form the stock.

The first player draws the top card of stock, adds it to his hand, and discards one card face up beside the stock to start the discard pile. The top card of the discard pile is called the 'upcard'. Each in turn thereafter must draw either the top card of stock or the upcard, add it to his hand, and discard one face up to the discard pile.

The aim is to be the first to go out by eliminating all the cards in one's hand. This is done by collecting sets of matching cards and laying them face up on the table in 'melds'. A meld may be a *set* or a *sequence*. A set is three or more cards of the same rank (Aces, Sixes, Jacks, or whatever). A sequence is three or more cards of the same suit and in numerical order. For this purpose, cards run A 2 3 4 5 6 7 8 9 T J Q K. Cards once melded may not be moved from one meld to another, and no card may belong to more than one meld.

A player with a meld lays it face up on the table after drawing a card but before discarding one. Having made at least one meld, a player may subsequently get rid of single cards from the hand by matching them to melds already made, whether by himself or someone else. For example, ♦7 could be laid off to a set of Sevens, or ♦Q to a set of Queens, or either attached to such a sequence as ♦8 9 T J. As many melds and lay-offs as possible may be made between drawing and discarding in a single turn.

Play ceases the moment someone goes out by playing the last card from his hand, whether as part of a new meld, a lay-off, or a discard. That player wins, and scores (or is paid) by the other players according to the face value of cards left unmelded in their hands. Numerals count at face value from Ace 1 to Ten 10, and court cards 10 each.

Russian Bank

A two-hand competitive Patience. See Spite and Malice.

Samba

An elaboration of Canasta (q.v.).

Sant

Or Saunt, Cent, etc: old name for Piquet (q.v.).

Scarto

Tarot game: 3p, 78c

Scarto, meaning 'discard', is played in Piedmont, especially Pinerolo and Turin. It is less complicated than most Tarot games, and probably differs little from the fifteenth-century ancestor of them all. The following description is based on Michael Dummett, *Twelve Tarot Games* (London, 1980).

It should be played with a Tarocco Piemontese pack, in which the Angel trump, No. 20, is actually the highest, beating No. 21. If such is not available, any 78-card Italian-suited pack will do, and the 21 can then resume its normal high position.

The pack consists of

1. The Fool (*Matto*).
2. Twenty-one trumps, headed by the Angel (20), followed by 21, 19, 18, and so numerically down to No 1, the *Bagatto*.
3. Fifty-six plain cards, fourteen in each of the four suits, swords, batons, cups, and coins. The highest cards are King (*Re*), Queen (*Dama*), Cavalier (*Cavallo*), Jack (*Fante*). These are followed by the ten numerals. In swords and batons they rank downwards from Ten high to Ace low. In cups and coins they rank in reverse order from Ace high to Ten low.

A game is three deals, one by each in turn. Points are scored for capturing certain cards ('counters') in tricks, namely, the Angel, Bagatto, Fool, and all sixteen courts. Each plays for himself, and whoever has the lowest cumulative score after three deals is the loser.

Choose first dealer by any agreed means. The turn to deal and play then passes regularly to the right. Deal all the cards around in 5s, Dealer himself taking the remaining three.

Dealer examines his hand and discards three cards face down, which will count for him at end of play as if he had won them in tricks. He may not discard the Angel, the Fool, or any King, and may only discard the Bagatto if he holds no other trump or the Fool. Every player now has twenty-five.

Eldest leads to the first trick, and the winner of each trick leads to the next. Suit must be followed if possible; if not, it is obligatory to play a trump if possible; if not, any card may be played. The trick is taken by the highest card of the suit led, or by the highest trump if any are played. It is not necessary to keep tricks separate: each player simply makes a single pile of all the cards he wins.

Whoever holds the Fool may play it at any time, in contravention of any of the above rules. It cannot win the trick, but neither can it be lost. Instead, its player simply shows it as his played card, then adds it to his own pile of cards won in tricks, where it stays for the rest of the deal. It is legal, if pointless, to lead it to a trick. In this case, any card may be played second, and the third player must follow suit to that.

At end of play, each player sorts through his won cards and reckons their values in batches of three at a time. The counting cards and their values are:

The Angel (20)	5
The Bagatto (1)	5
The Fool	4
Each King	5
Each Queen	4
Each Cavalier	3
Each Jack	2

A batch of three counters scores 2 less than the total value of its counters. Two counters and a blank score 1 less than the two counters together. One counter and two blanks score just the value of the counter, and three blanks score exactly one. Whoever played the Fool counts 4 for it without including it in a batch. Whoever won the trick to which the Fool was played will have two odd cards left over. He counts these exactly as though they were three, the third being a non-counter.

No matter how the cards are batched in threes, the total of points distributed between the three players will always be 78. Since the average score is 26, each player counts towards game the difference between 26 and the points he took. Thus, if the counters divide 30 27 21, the respective scores are 4, 1, and −5.

The player with the lowest score after three deals pays a small stake to each of the others.

(If the point-counting seems difficult, it is nevertheless typical of all Tarot games. There are two ways of simplifying it. One is to try to make all batches of three contain at least two blanks, as these give the simplest scores, namely, 1 point or the value of the single counter. The other is to assume a notional value of 1 point per blank, in which case any three cards count 2 less than their total face value. For example: Angel, Cavalier, Ten counts $(5 + 3 + 0) - (1) = 7$ by the first method, and $(5 + 3 + 1) - (2) = 7$ by the second.)

Notes. All Tarot games are deep and subtle, and an ounce of play is worth a pound of book. Suffice here to say that the dealer will use the discard to bury a vulnerable counter, or to create a void suit; and, since he has this advantage, the other two may find it mutually profitable to play to some extent as if they were partners against a soloist. Much of the interest centres on saving or capturing the Bagatto, as it counts 5 points and is vulnerable as being the lowest trump. If the dealer has it, he cannot (by law) save it by putting it in his discards, unless it is the only trump he holds. One of his aims in voiding a suit as soon as possible will be to enable him to win the trick with the Bagatto when that suit is led. Conversely, this is one good reason for his opponents not to lead a King until they have discovered, by playing lower cards, in which suit the dealer may have voided himself. A player holding the Bagatto may, if he holds significantly more than the average of seven trumps, try to save it by drawing his opponents' trumps whenever possible, either by leading trumps, or by leading suits in which they are void, as they are then obliged to trump if possible.

Schafkopf

Point-trick game: 4p, 32c

The national card game of Bavaria is popularly (but questionably) supposed to have derived its name—meaning 'sheep's-head'—at a time when it was played up to nine points, which were marked as nine lines on a board gradually building up to the stylized representation of a sheep's head. First recorded in the first decade of the nineteenth century—with numerous variations, even then—it evidently borrowed from Quadrille and Tarock, contributed to Skat, and is the immediate ancestor of the far more complex Doppelkopf (q.v.). Unlike Doppelkopf, it is usually played with German-suited cards.

There are versions for three and four players, with many variations of detail. The following four-hander is taken from Claus D. Grupp, *Schafkopf, Doppelkopf* (Wiesbaden, 1976), which is stated to be 'current in Upper Franconia, in Coburg and its surroundings'. This makes it royally appropriate for an English readership; even so, it should not be undertaken without previous experience of simpler 'Ace-11, Ten-10' games, such as Klaberjass, Skat, or Pinochle.

Cards. Use should properly be made of the 32-card German-suited pack, but this is not assumed in the following account.

Format. Each plays for himself in the long run, though *ad hoc* partnerships are formed from deal to deal. Each deal is settled immediately in coins or counters. A game consists of any number of deals which is a multiple of four. Choose the first dealer by any agreed means. The turn to deal and play passes always to the left. Deal 8 cards each in 4s.

Cards. Cards have point-values as follows: Ace 11, Ten 10, King 4, Queen 3, Jack 2, Nine, Eight, Seven 0 each. Note that the total value of card-points in the pack is 120.

For trick-taking purposes, cards rank from high to low:

Trumps	♣Q ♠Q ♥Q ♦Q ♣J ♠J ♥J ♦J ♥A T K 9 8 7
Plain suits	A T K 9 8 7

Note that no fewer than fourteen of the 32 cards in play are trumps. Queens and Jacks, collectively known as *Wenz* or *Wenzel*, belong not to the suits marked on their faces but to a single trump 'suit', which includes also all the hearts.

Object. One player undertakes to capture in tricks cards totalling at least 61 of the 120 card-points available. He may do this playing alone against the other three (solo), or—more commonly—with the aid of a temporary partner against the other two. The game value is doubled for taking 90 or more (*schneider*), or trebled for winning all eight tricks (*schwarz*).

Bidding. Starting with Eldest, each in turn may pass, call (for a partner), or bid one of several varieties of solo. If everyone passes, the cards are thrown in, reshuffled, and dealt by the next in turn. In this event, each player adds one unit to a kitty, which eventually goes to the winner of a solo bid.

The lowest bid is 'call'. If not overbid, the caller finds a partner by naming an Ace which he does not hold. Whichever player holds that Ace becomes the partner, revealing himself only by playing that Ace as soon as the named suit is led. The called Ace may be neither of hearts nor of a suit in which the caller is void. (A Queen or Jack does not save a suit from being void, as the Wenzel do not belong to their nominal suits.) A player unable to fulfil these conditions—holding three Aces, or being void in the only suit(s) in which he lacks an Ace—is therefore not permitted to 'call'. His options then are (*a*) to pass, hoping he will himself be called; (*b*) to call himself—i.e. to name an Ace in his own hand, thereby playing a 'secret solo', or (*c*) to bid solo openly. Note that a declared solo stands to win or lose much more than a secret solo.

A solo bid rates higher than a call, and gives the soloist a choice of trumps. If more than one wish to play a solo, the bids run from low to high as follows:

Wenz solo: Only Jacks are trumps, with ♣J highest as usual. Queens belong to their nominal suits, ranking between King and Nine, and hearts form an ordinary plain suit.

Suit solo: One of three suits other than hearts ranks below the Wenzel as additional trumps. A diamond solo overcalls a Wenz solo, but is overcalled by a spade solo, and that in turn by a club solo.

Trump solo: The highest bid restores the basic situation, with hearts as trumps below Wenzel.

Doubles. An opponent who thinks the contract can be beaten may announce 'double'. This increases the game value, but obliges his side to take at least 61 in order to beat the contract. (The soloist would then need only 60 to win.) The soloist or his partner, if any, may in turn 'redouble'; in which case they must again make 61. (Some circles impose no limit on doubles, redoubles, etc; but whichever side doubled last must always make 61 or more to win.)

High bid. In a solo game, the soloist may, before playing to the first trick, bid 'Du' (literally 'thou', a play on the French word 'tout'). This is an undertaking to win all eight tricks, and wins or loses extra. It may be doubled, redoubled, etc.

Play. Eldest leads to the first trick. Subsequent players must follow suit if possible, but otherwise may play any card. The trick is taken by the highest card of the suit led, or by the highest trump if any are played, and the winner of each trick leads to the next.

In a partnership or secret solo, the holder of the called Ace (a) must play it when its suit is led, (b) must lead it the first time he elects to lead from its suit, and (c) may not discard it when unable to follow. Despite (b), however, he may underlead the Ace if dealt four or more in its suit, and doing so absolves him from subsequently complying with (a) and (c). (Other variations may be encountered.)

Settlement. 'One unit' means any agreed basic stake.

For a successful 'call', each partner wins one unit from one opponent, or two for making *schneider* (90+ card-points), or three for *schwarz* (all eight tricks). If unsuccessful, the same amount is paid by each to one opponent. If the soloist 'called' himself (to a secret solo), he wins the same amount from or pays it to each opponent. These basic values are doubled, quadrupled, etc., depending on how many doubles were applied.

A solo wins or loses 4 units per opponent, or 5 if hearts were trumps. This amount is doubled for *schneider*, trebled for *schwarz*, quadrupled for a 'Du' bid. These values are also further increased by any doubles that may have been applied.

The kitty. The winner of a declared solo, as opposed to a secret one, also wins the kitty. The kitty is empty to start with. Whenever a deal is passed out, everyone adds 1 unit to the kitty. A losing soloist not only pays each opponent individually but also doubles the kitty.

Optional extras. These are many and various. The commonest is to strip the pack to 24 cards by omitting Sevens and Eights. Each then receives 6 cards in 3s, and trumps consequently account for more than half the cards in play.

If all pass, the holder of ♣Q (the top trump) is obliged to bid. If he has the top three trumps, he must call an Ace, but it may be one of a suit in which he is void. Such a bid may not be doubled. If not, he may either call an Ace or bid 'ramsch'. In ramsch, each plays for himself with a view to avoiding card-points. Whoever takes most card-points loses, paying each opponent 15 units, or 30 to anyone who took no trick at all. A player winning all eight tricks, however, instead receives 15 units from each opponent.

Premiums may be payable to or by the soloist, depending on the outcome, in respect of *matadors*, or 'runners' (*Läufer*). Matadors are consecutive trumps from the top downwards. If the soloist himself, or the bidding partners between them, held the top three trumps, then they afterwards receive 1 unit for each matador held in play. Having, for example, held all four Queens but not ♣J, they would receive 4 units. The same applies if matadors were held against them. Thus if they held between them nothing higher than ♦Q, they would have been playing without, or against, three matadors, and so receive or pay a premium of three.

Notes. With trumps accounting for half the cards in play, a bidder needs a good quarter of them (at least four) to 'call', as there is no guarantee that the Ace-holder will have any. A suit solo requires at least five, including three Wenzel and the trump Ace or Ten. In practice, the number of trumps held is less significant than their power (three Queens is better than five low hearts), the relative positions of the call partners (neighbouring or crosswise), and how they are distributed between the four hands. In a called game, it is usual to lead trumps if you are the soloist or a called partner, otherwise the called suit, in order to clarify who the partners are. The soloist should make early trump leads to clarify the trump distribution and to draw adverse trumps to clear the way for side-suit Aces. With only six cards in a plain suit (four in the 24-card game) it is only likely to go round once, if that. Partners will seek in play to throw high-scoring cards on tricks being, or likely to be, won by their own side. It is theoretically possible to capture 44 card-points in a single trick, and to make or defeat the contract by winning three or even two of the eight tricks played.

Schieber

See Jass.

Schmaus

See Mauscheln.

Schnapsen

Or Schnapser: see Sixty-Six.

Schnipp-Schnapp-Schnurr-Burr-Basilorum

See Snip-Snap-Snorem.

Schwellen

See Rolling Stone.

Scopa

Fishing game: 2–3p, 40c

Scopa and Scopone are two of Italy's major national card games. They are also the most distinctly Italian of all card games, as the principle of play involved is not widespread elsewhere in the West. The only one commonly recorded in English-language game books is the excessively elaborated Cassino (q.v.).

Two or three players use a 40-card pack with A 2 3 4 5 6 7 J Q K in each suit. Decide first dealer by any agreed means. The turn to deal and play passes always to the right.

Deal 3 cards each in 1s, and 4 face up to the table. When all have played their cards, deal 3 more each from stock. Continue until all cards have been used and captured.

Each in turn plays a card from hand with a view to capturing one or more table cards. Table cards may be captured in two ways:

1. By *pairing*. An Ace takes an Ace, a Two a Two, and so on. Only

one card may be paired in one turn, and if the hand-card can capture in either way it must do so by pairing. For example, with 3 4 7 on the table, the play of a Seven captures only the Seven, not the Three and Four.

2. By *combining*. A hand-card takes two or more table cards totalling the same as itself. For this purpose, cards count at face value from Ace 1 to Seven 7, followed by Jack 8, Queen 9, King 10. Thus a Seven will capture two or more cards totalling 7 (A + 6, 2 + 2 + 3, etc), a Jack two or more totalling 8, and so on. Only one such combination may be made at a time. Thus, with 1 2 4 5 on the table, a Six will capture either 1 + 5 or 2 + 4, but not both.

The captured and the capturing cards are stacked face down in front of the successful player, whose turn then ends. If the capture results in a sweep, so that no cards remain to be captured, the capturing card is left face up in the player's pile and will count one point at end of play.

A player must capture if possible, otherwise he must 'trail' by playing one of his cards to the table. (This is inevitable after a sweep.)

When no cards remain in stock, the last to make a capture (not necessarily the last to play, since he may be forced to trail) takes all the other table cards with it. This does not count as a sweep, even if, technically, it happens to be one.

Players then sort through their won cards and score as follows:

1 for taking the most cards. If tied, no score.
1 for having captured ◆7, or *sette bello*.
1 for taking the most diamonds. If tied, no score.
1 for *primiera* (see below).
1 per *sweep*, as indicated by face-up cards.

For *primiera*, each player extracts the highest-scoring card he has in each of the four suits, and the player whose four have the highest combined value scores the point. A player who took only three suits cannot compete. For this purpose only, cards count as follows: Seven 21, Six 18, Ace 16, Five 15, Four 14, Three 13, Two 12, courts 10 each. (Swiss variant: King 10, Queen 9, Jack 8.)

The winner is the player with the highest score at the end of the deal in which anyone reaches 11 points.

Scotch Whist

Variants. Scopa is rich in alternative rules and optional extras.

In *Scopa d'assi*, an Ace from the hand sweeps all the cards from the table. This may or may not be permitted if the table cards include an Ace, and may or may not score as a sweep.

In *Scopa de quindici*, a card from the hand may capture one or more cards on the table which, together with the capturing card, total fifteen. For example, with A 3 7 K on the table, a Five could be played to capture the 3 + 7 (or, less profitably, the King). In some versions, point-count captures may be made only in this way, to the exclusion of other forms of addition.

Scopa de undici is the same, but with 11 as the key total.

Some start by dealing 9 cards to each player. When both (or all three) players have had a turn, they draw a replacement card from stock before playing again, so long as any remain in stock.

Points may be scored for capturing particular cards in addition to ◆7, notably ♠2; and for capturing a sequence of three cards, typically ◆A 2 3, ♠A 2 3, or ◆J Q K.

In some circles, points are remembered as they accrue, and the winner is the first to claim correctly that he has reached 11. A false claim loses the game.

Some use a 52-card pack, and count Jack 11, Queen 12, King 13.

Scopone

The four-hand partnership form of Scopa differs in the following respects. Players sitting opposite each other are partners. Each receives 9 cards, and 4 are dealt face up to the table. Alternatively, each receives 10, and the first player can only trail. Both versions have staunch devotees. Beginners will probably be happier with the former.

Scotch Whist

See Catch the Ten.

Sechsundsechzig

See Sixty-Six.

Sedma

Point-trick game: 2 or 4p, 32c

Sedma, the Czech for 'Seven', is an appropriate title for this Bohemian game with rules both simple and highly unusual. The four-hander is described first, as seeming more natural.

A game is typically twelve deals. Although each plays for himself in the long run, the players sitting opposite each other at each deal are partners. Partners are changed after every four deals, so that everyone partners everyone else an equal number of times throughout.

A 32-card pack is used, with cards ranking A T K Q J 9 8 7 in each suit. Deal 8 cards each, one at a time. The aim is to win Aces and Tens in tricks, each counting 10 points. A further 10 for winning the last trick makes 90 in all and so prevents ties.

Eldest leads to the first trick, and the winner of each trick leads to the next. Any card may be played: suit need not be followed. All Sevens are trumps. A trick is taken by the last played card of the same rank as the one led, or by the last played Seven if any are played.

Examples. (*a*) The cards played are 9 J A J. The Nine wins, having been neither matched nor trumped, and the trick counts 10 for the Ace. (*b*) 9 A A 9: the second Nine wins a trick worth 20. (*c*) 9 7 J T: the Seven trumps a trick worth 10. (*d*) A 7 7 A: the second Seven wins a trick worth 20. (*e*) 7 7 7 7: the last-played Seven wins.

Each player scores the points made by his own partnership. These scores are carried forward, and the winner is the player with the highest total after 12 deals, or any other agreed number.

Sedma for two

Deal 4 cards each and stack the rest face down. Non-dealer leads first, and the winner of each trick leads to the next. A trick may contain any even number of cards, each playing alternately. The follower may play any card. If it fails to match or trump the lead, he says 'Pass', and the leader wins the trick without further play. If it does match or trump, the leader must himself then either match or trump—unlike his opponent, he may not play a losing card. If he passes, the follower wins the trick.

This continues until an even number of cards have been played, and the original leader has either won the trick or passed. The trick is taken by the last played card of the same rank as the one led, or by the last played Seven if any are played.

Each in turn, starting with the winner, then draws from stock until he has four cards again, and the previous trick winner leads to the next. The stock exhausted, continue until all cards have been played.

Setback

See Auction Pitch.

Seven Up

American name for All Fours (q.v.).

Sextille

Six-handed Quadrille.

Shanghai Rummy

Form of Contract Rummy (q.v.).

Shasta Sam

See California Jack.

Sheepshead

Point-trick game: 3–4p, 32c

American equivalent of Schafkopf. The following versions, from Joseph Petrus Wergin, *Skat and Sheepshead* (McFarland, Wis., 1975), are typical.

Cards count Ace 11, Ten 10, King 4, Queen 3, Jack 2, Nine, Eight, and Seven 0. Permanent trumps, from highest to lowest, are

♣Q ♠Q ♥Q ♦Q ♣J ♠J ♥J ♦J ♥A T K 9 8 7

In plain suits, cards rank A T K 9 8 7.

Three players

Each receives 10 cards and 2 are dealt face down as a blind. Eldest has first choice of taking the blind, making any two discards, and playing against the other two with the aim of taking at least 61 card-points in tricks (including also any that may be contained in the blind). If he passes, second hand has the same choice, then Dealer. If all pass, a 'leaster' is played, in which each plays for himself with the aim of taking fewest card-points in tricks, the blind going to the winner of the last trick. Eldest leads to the first trick and the winner of each trick leads to the next. Follow suit if possible—noting that all fourteen trumps belong to the same 'suit'—otherwise play any card. The trick is taken by the highest card of the suit led, or by the highest trump if any are played. The bidder wins 2 units from each opponent for taking 61+, 4 for 91+ (*schneider*), or 6 for winning every trick (*schwarz*). If unsuccessful, he pays each according to the same schedule. In a leaster, the player taking fewest card-points wins 2 of each opponent, or 4 if he takes no trick. An improved schedule, proposed by Wergin, is 3 4 5 for a positive game and 2 3 for a leaster.

A solo bid may be included, ranking higher than an ordinary game. In this case the soloist aims to take 61 or more card-points without using the blind, except at end of play to score for any counters it may contain. The appropriate pay-offs are 4 5 6.

Four players

Partnership game. Each receives 8 cards and there is no blind. Ties are avoided by counting an additional point for winning the ♦A in a trick. This is known as 'catching the fox'.

Solo game. Remove the black Sevens, deal 7 each and 2 to the blind. Whoever takes the blind (Eldest having first choice, and so round the table), aims to take 61+ either alone or with the aid of a partner. If he holds ♦J he must play alone, but does not announce that fact.

Shep

If not, the holder of ♦J automatically becomes his partner, without announcing that fact—unless the soloist prefers to play alone, in which case he must say so immediately.

Shep

Alternative name for Sheepshead.

Short Whist

Partnership Whist played up to five points, as opposed to the the now defunct ten of Long Whist.

Sift Smoke

Plain-trick game: 3–6p, 52c

Also called Lift Smoke (mistakenly) and Linger Longer (appropriately), this nineteenth-century game is simple, fun, and not devoid of depth.

Cards rank A K Q J T 9 8 7 6 5 4 3 2 in each suit. Deal, 1 at a time, 10 each if three play, 7 if four, 6 if five, or 5 if six. Turn the dealer's last card for trump, and stack the rest face down.

Eldest leads to the first trick, and the winner of each trick leads to the next. Follow suit if possible, otherwise play any card. The trick is taken by the highest card of the suit led, or by the highest trump if any are played.

Tricks are of no account in themselves; but the winner of each trick, and he alone, draws the top card of stock and adds it to his hand before leading to the next. As players run out of cards, they drop out of play, and the winner is the last player left with any card in hand. If all play their last card to the same trick, its winner wins the game.

If the stock runs out before anyone wins, the won tricks are gathered up, shuffled, and laid down as a new stock.

The winner scores a point for each card remaining in his hand. Credit is sometimes given for tricks won. For example, each may score 1 per trick taken, the winner's trick-score being then multiplied by the number of cards left in hand.

256

Six-Bid Solo
Point-trick game: 3p, 36c

An American invention deriving ultimately from an eighteenth-century German game based on Tarock, but dispensing with the tarock suit. The latter reached the United States in the 19th century under the name Frog (from German *Frage*), and underwent a variety of local modifications under such names as Solo, Slough, and Sluff. Six-Bid Solo was first recorded in 1924 and associated with Salt Lake City.

Three players use a 36-card pack ranking A K Q J T 9 8 7 6 in each suit. Cards captured in tricks have point-values as follows: Ace 11, King 4, Queen 3, Jack Two, Ten 10, others zero.

Each player starts with 120 chips, or scores may be kept in writing and settled up later if desired. Choose first dealer by any agreed means. The turn to play and deal passes always to the left. Deal 11 cards each in batches of 4 3 4, with an extra batch of 3 face down to the table as a blind (or skat, widow, slough, etc.). The blind remains untouched throughout play.

There is an auction to decide who will play alone against the others. Each in turn, starting with Eldest, must pass or name a higher bid than any previous one. From low to high, the six bids are:

1. *Solo*. The bidder will name a trump suit other than hearts and aim to take at least 60 card-points in tricks.
2. *Heart solo*. The same, but with hearts as trump.
3. *Misère*. Playing at no trump, the bidder aims to take no counting cards in tricks. (He may take tricks, provided they count for nothing.)
4. *Guarantee solo*. The bidder will name any suit as trumps and guarantee to take at least 80 in tricks, or 74 if hearts are trump.
5. *Spread misère*. As misère, but the bidder will lay his hand of cards face up on the table immediately before he plays to the first trick.
6. *Call solo*. The bidder will name trumps and aim to win all 120 points in tricks (not necessarily all eleven tricks). Before choosing trumps, he 'calls' any card, the holder of which must give it to him in exchange for any discard. If the called card is in the blind, there is no exchange. (*Variant*: he may call a different card.)

Eldest leads to the first trick, and the winner of each trick leads to the next. Follow suit if possible, otherwise trump if possible, otherwise play any card. The trick is taken by the highest card of the suit led, or by the highest trump if any are played.

At end of play, in a positive bid, the blind is turned face up and any card-points it contains count for the soloist.

In a solo game, the soloist scores, or wins off each opponent, 2 units for each card-point he took over 60, or 3 in a heart solo. A 60–60 outcome is a tie. The other bids have fixed values: misère 30, guarantee solo 40, spread misère 60, call solo 100, call solo in hearts 150.

If the contract fails, he deducts from his score, or pays each opponent, 2 or 3 units per point taken short of 60 in a solo, or the prescribed amount for any other bid.

Frog

The same, but with only three bids:

1. *Frog.* Hearts are trump; the bidder takes the blind before play and makes any three discards face down.
2. *Chico.* The bidder names any suit but hearts as trump, and plays without taking the blind.
3. *Grand.* The same, but with hearts as trump.

In each case the bidder aims to take at least 60 card-points in tricks, including any that may be contained in the blind or discard. He wins or loses the amount taken above or below 60 in frog, doubled in chico, quadrupled in grand.

Sixte

Plain-trick game: 6p, 36 or 52c

An eighteenth-century French game worth mentioning because simple to play and uniquely designed for six players. Sizette is the partnership version.

Cards rank A K Q J T 9 8 7 6 (5 4 3 2) in each suit. The turn to deal and play passes to the right. Deal 6 cards each in 1s. If 36 cards are used, turn the dealer's last card for trump; if 52, stack the rest face down and turn the topmost card for trump.

Eldest leads to the first trick, and the winner of each trick leads to the next. Follow suit if possible, otherwise play any card. The trick is taken by the highest card of the suit led, or by the highest trump if any are played.

One point is scored by the first player to win three tricks, or, if everybody wins one trick, by the winner of the first; otherwise there is no score. The overall winner is the first to reach six game points; but winning all six in one deal wins the game outright.

Sizette

There are two partnerships of three each, and each player is flanked by two opponents. Deal 6 cards each from a 36-card pack, turning the last for trump. Play as described above. The first side to win three tricks scores 1 point, or 2 if it wins all six. More interesting scoring schedules are easily devised.

Also recorded is a variant in which all the players of a side sit consecutively—i.e. A A A B B B instead of A B A B A B. Equally playable would be a three-partnership version, with players sitting A B C A B C.

Sixty-Six

Point-tricks and melds: 2p, 24c

Deservedly popular German game said to have been invented at Paderborn in 1652. Also called Mariage; probably ancestral to Bezique; see also Gaigel and Tute. An excellent two-hander, its omission from English game-books is inexplicable.

Cards rank and count in each suit as follows:

A	T	K	Q	J	9
11	10	4	3	2	0

The deal alternates, and the winner is the first to reach 7 game points over as many deals as it takes. Deal 6 each in 3s; turn the next for trumps; stack the remainder face down on top of but not completely covering it.

Object. Players keep mental count of card-points won in tricks and other scoring features. The first to claim (correctly) to have reached 66 scores one or more game points.

Tricks. Elder leads to the first trick, and the winner of each trick leads to the next. Suit need not be followed. The trick is taken by the higher card of the suit led, or by the higher trump if any are played.

Trump Nine. A player holding or drawing the trump Nine may exchange it for the turn-up at any time, provided he has won a trick.

Marriages. A player holding King and Queen of a suit may score for a marriage — 40 in trumps, 20 otherwise — by showing both when leading either of them to a trick (but not when following). If a marriage is declared on the opening lead, and the leader never takes a trick, it is annulled.

Last six. When the last card of stock (the turn-up) has been taken, the last six tricks are played to different rules. Follow suit if possible, otherwise trump if possible; and in either case beat the card led if possible. Marriages may no longer be declared. The winner of the last trick scores 10.

Shut-out. Before the stock is exhausted, either player, if he thinks he can win with the cards remaining in hand, may shut the game by turning the turn-up face down. The last six (or five) are then played as above, but without 10 for last.

Score. Play ceases when the last trick has been taken, or when either player claims to have reached 66. If both have 65, or if it is found that one player reached 66 without declaring, it is a draw, and the next deal carries an extra game point. A player correctly claiming 66 scores

1 game point, or
2 if the loser failed to reach 33, (*schneider*), or
3 if he took no trick (*schwarz*).

If a player claims 66 incorrectly, or fails to reach 66 after shutting, the opponent scores 2 game points, or 3 if he took no trick.

Notes. Keep track of the other player's points as well as your own throughout play. Don't lead an Ace in the first half, unless you can think of a good tactical reason for wanting it trumped. The trump Ace is best reserved for capturing an Ace or Ten rather than for drawing a Nine. Trumps in general are best not led before the last six tricks. Keep careful track of the Kings and Queens played, so as to know whether or not it is worth aiming for a marriage. The main point of the game is to know when to shut it. Expert players conclude more games by shutting than by playing them through to the bitter end.

Schnapser

The Austrian national two-hander. Play as above, but deal 5 each from a 20-card pack lacking Nines. The trump Jack may be exchanged for the turn-up.

American Sixty-Six

The last six tricks are played with obligation to follow suit but not necessarily to head the trick or to trump if unable to follow. Marriages remain declarable throughout.

Auction Sixty-Six

American four-player partnership version. Game is 666 points over as many deals as necessary, compiled from the actual point-scores made for counting-cards, marriages and last tricks. Deal 6 each, leaving no stock. Each in turns bids for the right to name trumps: the lowest is 60, and a suit is not named until a contract is established. Tricks are played to Whist rules. If the bidding side takes at least what it bid, it scores what it makes. If not, the other side scores what it makes plus the amount of the bid. The maximum bid of 130, whether won or lost, counts 260 to the scoring side.

Tausendeins

Tausendeins, or Thousand-and-one, is nominally the target score of this Austrian two-hander played also in Switzerland under the name Mariage. Deal 6 cards each from a 32-card pack ranking A T K Q J 9 8 7, and stack the rest face down. Play as at Sixty-Six, but at no trump until a marriage is declared. This is done by leading a King or Queen to a trick and showing its partner. The first marriage establishes a trump suit, and each subsequent marriage changes it. The score for a marriage is 40 in diamonds, 60 in hearts, 80 in spades, 100 in clubs. Cards captured in tricks count Ace 11, Ten 10, King 4, Queen 3, Jack 2, others 0. Marriages may not be made in the last six tricks, and there is no score for winning the last. The winner is the first to reach 1001 over as many deals as it takes, and play ceases the moment either player correctly claims to have done so.

Mariage

As above, but: Deal 5 cards each from a 24-card pack ranking A T K Q J 9. Regardless of suit, the first marriage declared scores 20, the second 40, the third 60, and the fourth 80. There is a bonus of 100 for winning the last five tricks. Actual scores are divided by ten with remainder ignored, and the winner is the first to reach 100.

Sixty Solo

Same as Six-Bid Solo.

Skat

Point-trick game: 3p, 32c

Skat, one of the world's great card games, and certainly the best for three players, originated at Altenburg, near Leipzig, in the early nineteenth century, and has long been Germany's national card game. The following account incorporates changes to the official rules that came into effect on 1 January 1999.

Basics. There are three active players, but often four play together, each in turn sitting out the hand to which he deals. A 32-card French- or German-suited pack is used. A game is any number of deals exactly divisible by the number of players. Choose first dealer by any agreed means. The turn to deal and play passes always to the left.

Deal 10 cards each in batches of 3 (2) 4 3. The (2) denotes 2 cards dealt face down to the table immediately before the first 4. These constitute the *skat*.

In trump bids, the four Jacks are always the four highest trumps, regardless of the suits marked on them. The rank of cards for trick-taking purposes, and their point-value when captured in tricks, is as follows:

Trumps	♣J	♠J	♥J	♦J	A	T	K	Q	9	8	7
Point-value	2	2	2	2	11	10	4	3	0	0	0
Non-trumps					A	T	K	Q	9	8	7

The total number of card-points in play is 120.

Object. An auction determines who will play alone against the other two. The soloist's aim is normally to capture at least 61 card-points in tricks, but he may aim to capture at least 90, or to win all ten tricks, or to lose every trick, depending on his bid.

There are three types of game:

1. *Grand.* Only Jacks are trumps, forming a fifth suit of four cards, such that the lead of a Jack requires Jacks to be played if possible. The other four suits rank A T K Q 9 8 7 each.
2. *Suit.* A suit is named as trump. The entire trump suit then contains eleven cards, headed by the four Jacks, and followed by A T K Q 9 8 7.
3. *Null.* This is a bid to lose every trick. There is no trump, and cards rank A K Q J T 9 8 7 in every suit.

Any game may be undertaken in either of two ways:

1. *With the skat*: the soloist, before play, adds the skat to his hand and makes any two discards face down;
2. *From the hand*: the skat is not turned until after the last trick.

Either way, any card-points contained in the skat count for the soloist at end of play, if needed.

Game values. Players bid by announcing not the *name* of the game being offered but its *value*, the score to be made by the bidder if he successfully undertakes the game, or lost by him if he fails. Whoever bids highest becomes the soloist. Except for nulls, which have invariable scores, games are valued as follows.

Trump games are valued by taking the *base value* of the suit selected as trump and multiplying this by a number of additional factors called *multipliers*. The base values are:

diamonds 9, hearts 10, spades 11, clubs 12
grand 24 (also grand ouvert, which is no longer valued at 36)

The multipliers are:
1 per matador (always)
+1 for game (always)
+1 for *schneider* (taking at least 90 card-points)

+1 for *schwarz* (winning every trick)
+1 for playing from the hand (if bid)
+1 for *schneider* declared (hand only)
+1 for *schwarz* declared (hand only)
+1 for playing a suit game *ouvert* (with schwarz declared)

'Matadors' means consecutive top trumps from ♣J down. If the soloist holds ♣J, he is playing 'with' as many matadors as he holds. (e.g. holding ♣J but not ♠J = 'with 1'; ♣J ♠J but not ♥J = 'with 2'; and so on, to a maximum of 'with 11' in a suit game or 'with 4' at grand). If lacking ♣J, then he is playing 'without' as many matadors as lie above the highest trump he holds (e.g. if ♥J, then 'without 2'; if ♦J, 'without 3'; if trump Ten, then 'without 5'; and so on, to a maximum of 'without 11 in suit' or 'without 4' at grand). Game value is affected only by the *number* of matadors involved: whether 'with' or 'without' is irrelevant.

To this number is added 1 factor if the soloist merely reckons to win at least 61 card-points, or 2 for schneider if he thinks he can take 90+ card-points, or 3 for schwarz if he thinks he can win every trick.

If, and only if, playing 'from the hand', the soloist may further increase his game value by declaring that he will win schneider or schwarz, for 1 or 2 extra factors respectively—these in addition to the 1 or 2 for actually winning it.

If, and only if, playing from hand and declaring schwarz, he may further increase his game value by playing with his cards face up on the table (*ouvert*). This adds a final multiplier, whether in a suit game or, since 1999, at grand. (Formerly, it increased the base value of grand from 24 to 36.)

The lowest possible game value is therefore 18 (diamonds, with or without 1, game 2, × 9 = 18); the highest 360 (grand ouvert with 4, game 5, hand 6, schneider 7, declared 8, schwarz 9, declared 10, × 36 = 360).

Negative or null games have invariable values as follows:

Null (with skat)	23
Null hand	35
Null ouvert	46
Null ouvert, hand	59

Auction. From Dealer's left, the players are identified as Forehand, Middlehand, Rearhand. Middlehand starts by bidding against Forehand, and Rearhand takes over when either of them passes. A player having passed once may not bid again.

The bidding takes place by naming successive game values from the lowest up, i.e. 18, 20, 22, 23, 24, 27, 30, 33, 35, 36, etc. To each of these, Forehand says 'Yes' if he is prepared to play a game of equal or higher value. When one passes (either Middlehand because he will not make a higher bid, or Forehand because he can't accept the last bid named), Rearhand may then in like manner continue against the survivor by naming the next higher bid. When one of them passes, the survivor becomes the soloist, and must play a game at least equal in value to the last bid made. If neither Middlehand nor Rearhand will open at 18, Forehand may play any game; but if he also passes, the deal is annulled and the next in turn to deal does so (unless it is agreed to play *Ramsch*: see below).

Game announcement. If playing with skat exchange, the soloist adds the skat to his hand, makes any two discards face down, and then announces his game—grand, a suit, null, or null ouvert. He need not announce the game he had in mind, so long as what he does announce is worth at least the amount he bid. If playing from hand, he announces his game, adding 'hand' and any other declaration that may be applicable (*schneider, schwarz, ouvert*). If playing ouvert, he lays his hand of cards face up on the table before the opening lead.

Conceding. The soloist may concede the game at any time before he plays to the first trick. The commonest reason for conceding is when, playing with skat exchange and *without* two or more matadors, he finds one or more higher matadors in the skat. For example, suppose he won the bid at 22, intending to play in hearts 'without 2, game 3, × 10, = 30'. He turns the skat and finds the club (or spade) Jack. This revalues his game at 'with (or without) 1, game 2, × 10 = 20', which is lower than the 22 he bid. He now has several options:

(*a*) He may announce hearts as intended, and, secretly, attempt to win schneider for the extra multiplier which will bring his game value to 30.

(*b*) He may attempt a different game—perhaps spades (22), null (23), clubs (24), or even grand (48).

If none of these is playable, he will (*c*) concede, announcing (of

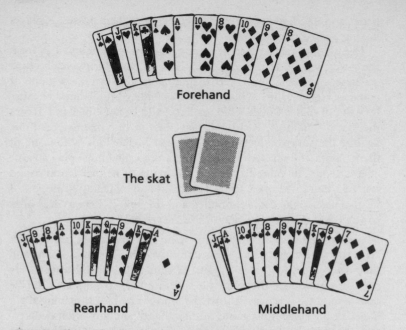

Forehand

The skat

Rearhand   Middlehand

FIG. 26. Skat. The skat holds two Queens. Forehand can certainly think of a game in a red suit with skat exchange (worth 18 or 20), and might consider grand for 48. Middlehand bids up to 23 for a null, which Forehand accepts with grand in mind. Middlehand passes, not being prepared to play from the hand or to chance a good enough skat to play it open. Rearhand is willing to play in spades and bids up to 44, which Forehand accepts. He then decides to play from the hand, worth 55 (trusting that the skat will not contain a devaluing Jack). If Forehand passes at 50, it is touch and go whether Rearhand will finish with more than 59 card-points including the Queens. If he accepts Rearhand's 55 and goes for a grand hand, he should win by leading one Jack and holding the other back until he has shed his worthless cards.

course) the lowest possible game consistent with his bid—in this case spades.

Play. Forehand leads to the first trick, and the winner of each trick leads to the next. Follow suit if possible, otherwise play any card. The trick is taken by the highest card of the suit led, or by the highest trump if any are played. (*Note*: At grand, a Jack led calls for

Jacks to be played. In suit, any trump led calls for the play of any other trump, not necessarily a Jack for a Jack.) Cards won by the partners are kept together in a single pile. All ten tricks must be played — except at null, if the soloist wins a trick — and the skat then faced to ensure that the game is correctly valued.

Won game. The soloist wins if (a) he took at least 61 card-points, or 90 if he bid schneider, or every trick if he bid schwarz, or no trick if he bid null; and (b) the game as revalued after play is worth at least the amount bid. If successful, the bidder's actual game value is added to his aggregate score.

(*Note*: (*a*) a hand game played 'without' two or more matadors may be reduced in value if the skat is found to contain a matador, and may therefore be 'lost' by default; (*b*) the skat counts as part of the hand for game valuation purposes, so it is possible to be 'with' or 'without' eleven even though only ten cards are actually held.)

Lost game. If a lost game is worth at least the amount bid, its full value is first doubled and then deducted from the soloist's aggregate score. (This since the 1999 revision. Previously, lost hand games were not doubled.) If the game value is less than the bid, the amount to be doubled is the nearest appropriate multiple of the relevant base value that equals or exceeds the bid. *Note*: If the soloist is schneidered, by failing to take at least 31 card-points himself, there is no extra penalty — in other words, his lost game value is not increased by an extra multiplier for the schneider.

Variants. It may be agreed: (*a*) To value grand at 20 (ouvert 30) instead of 24 (36); (*b*) to permit either partner to double the announced game, and the soloist to redouble, before the first trick has been led to. In this case the score or penalty, as detailed above, is doubled or quadrupled before being applied; (*c*) in the event that all three pass, to play ramsch instead of annulling the hand. At ramsch, there are no partners and no winner, only a loser, and cards rank and value as at grand (Jacks trump). There are several versions, the commonest being push ramsch. Forehand takes the skat and passes two cards face down to Middlehand, who passes any two face down to Rearhand, who discards any two to the skat. (The passing of Jacks may be agreed illegal.) The winner of the last trick adds the skat to his won cards, and whoever takes the most card-points has that number deducted from his score.

Notes. Use the skat to create a void suit or to lay away a vulnerable Ace or Ten. A suit game normally requires at least five trumps, including the Ace or Ten, and not more than four losers. Given also a void suit or bare Ace, play from hand; with slightly less, take the skat. A grand normally requires five of the following nine power factors: Jacks, Aces, and the lead. It is sometimes quite possible to bid a grand 'without four', and a suit game 'without' four or more. Do not declare schneider unless confident of winning nine tricks. In play, the soloist should normally lead trumps at every opportunity, and each partner should throw a high counter, especially a vulnerable Ten, to a trick being won by the other. At null, every suit should contain a Seven, or an Eight if holding not more than two of the suit. A bare Nine or higher is risky unless there is a chance of throwing it to a lead in a void suit. A suit containing J 9 7 is impregnable, unless the soloist is Forehand and has to lead from it.

American Skat

American and modern German Skat both derive from a late-nineteenth-century original which offered three types of suit-game: with skat exchange, tourné, and hand. German Skat has retained the first and dropped the second, but American has retained the tourné and dropped the skat-exchange bid (except at grand). The hand bid, here called *solo*, remains unchanged. The games and base values of American Skat are:

Tourné. Diamonds 5, hearts 6, spades 7, clubs 8, grand 12. The soloist takes one card of the skat and may accept its suit as trump, in which case he shows it, adds the other card to his hand without showing it, and discards two to the skat. If it doesn't suit him ('Paßt mir nicht')—either because he hasn't enough of that suit, or because its value is lower than his bid—he adds it to his hand without showing it, and *must* then turn up and accept the suit of the second card as trump. In either case, if the turn-up is a Jack, he may either entrump the suit it shows, or play at grand.

Solo. Diamonds 9, hearts 10, spades 11, clubs 12, grand 20, grand ouvert 24. The soloist announces trump and plays without taking the skat first. There is no extra multiplier for this, the base values being higher instead. Extra multipliers may be added for making or declaring schneider and schwarz. Suit solos are not playable ouvert.

Guckser. The soloist may only start by taking both cards and discarding two in their place when playing grand. The bid is called *guckser* and has a base value of 16.

Null. Null may only be played solo, without skat-exchange. It counts 20, or 40 ouvert.

Ramsch. If Middlehand and Rearhand make no bid, Forehand may announce 'ramsch'. The skat is untouched, Jacks are trumps, and the player taking the fewest card-points scores 10, or 20 if he took no trick. A player careless enough to win every trick loses 30 instead of the others winning 20.

As in German Skat, game value is found by multiplying the base value by: 1 per matador, plus 1 for game (61+), or 2 for schneider (91+), or 3 for schwarz (win every trick), plus another 1 or 2 for schneider or schwarz declared.

Auction, rules of play, and scoring are basically as for German Skat. But note: (*a*) the bid values begin 10 (diamonds, tourné, with or without 1), 12, 14, 15, 16, 18, 20, 21, 24, 25, 28, 30 . . . ; (*b*) to win schneider, the soloist needs at least 91 card-points, not 90 as at German Skat; and (*c*) the value of a lost guckser is doubled before being deducted, and so is that of a tourné if the soloist played *second turn*, having rejected the first suit as trump.

A tourné bid normally requires at least two Jacks, one of them black, and three biddable suits.

Slapjack
Testing game: 2–6p, 52c

A children's game that tests reaction speed.

Deal all the cards round as far as they will go. Each player keeps his cards in a neat pile face down on the table before him. Each in turn, as fast as possible, takes the top card of his pile and plays it face up to a pile in the middle of the table. Whenever a Jack appears, the first player to slap his hand over it wins the central pile. He shuffles it in with his own pile to make a new one of his own, which he then places face down before him before playing a card out to start a new central pile.

A player who slaps a card other than a Jack must lose one of his own cards to the person who played the card he wrongly slapped. A player who runs out of cards is allowed one opportunity to win a pile by correctly slapping a Jack, but if he fails to do so he is out of the game. Play continues until only one player remains, or utter boredom sets in, whichever is the sooner.

Slobberhannes

Trick-avoidance game: 4–6p, 32c

A simple German game of the Hearts family, similar to the French game of Polignac. The name means 'Slippery Jack', though the card in question is a Queen.

The 32 cards rank A K Q J T 9 8 7 in each suit. If five or six play, remove the black Sevens. The turn to deal and play passes always to the left. Deal all the cards out one at a time. The aim is to avoid winning the first trick, the last trick, and the trick containing the ♣Q.

Eldest leads to the first trick, and the winner of each trick leads to the next. Follow suit if possible, otherwise play any card. The trick is taken by the highest card of the suit led: there are no trumps.

A player loses 1 point for winning the first trick, 1 for winning the last, and 1 for winning the ♣Q in a trick. A player winning all of these loses 4 points (or, as an interesting variant, *wins* 4 points). The overall winner is the player with the fewest penalty points when someone reaches a previously agreed total. If played for hard score, everyone starts with (say) ten units, and pays the appropriate penalty into a pool immediately upon incurring it. The pool is divided equally among the winners when one player goes broke.

Slough

Or Sluff: see Six-Bid Solo.

Smoojas

A nineteenth-century Flemish forerunner of Klaberjass, Clobiosh, or Belote, in which two play a form of Bezique (q.v.) using the card-point system of Jass (q.v.). The name means 'Jewish Jass'.

Snap

Testing game: 2–5p, 52c

Those who maintain that Snap is the only card game of pure skill should note that the skill here tested is not that of card sense but that of reaction speed, which is nowadays more often exercised by a computer. Snap stands in its own right as an excellent and classic game for children, without need of such spurious rationalization.

Deal all the cards around as far as they will go. Each player keeps his cards face down either on the table before him, or held in hand. Each in turn, as fast as possible, plays the top card of his pile face up to the middle of the table. When the card played matches the rank of the previous card (Ace on Ace, Jack on Jack, etc), the first player to call 'Snap!' wins the central pile and adds it to his own pile. A player who runs out of cards drops out of play. The winner is the player who ends up with all 52 cards.

If one player snaps mistakenly, or two or more snap simultaneously, the central pile is placed to one side as a pool (or on top of an existing pool) and a new one is started. Whenever a card played to the main pile matches the top card of the pool, the pool is won by the first player to call 'Snap pool!'

Variant. There is no central pile. Instead, each plays his cards face up to a pile in front of himself on the table. Whenever a card played matches the rank of any other player's face-up pile, the first to call 'Snap!' wins his own and the other player's pile and adds them to his playing pile. Whenever a player runs out of face-down cards, he takes his face-up cards, turns them down, and continues playing from them.

Snip-Snap-Snorem

Matching game: Np, 32 or 52c.

Snip-Snap-Snorem (or -Snorum) heads a range of children's games which certainly go back to the eighteenth century and probably derive from a more ancient and bibulous gambling game.

A pool is formed and the pack dealt round as far as it will go. The turn to play starts at dealer's left and passes to the left. The first person plays any card face up to the table. Each in turn thereafter must play a card of the same rank if possible, otherwise pass. The first to match ranks says 'Snip', the second 'Snap', and the third 'Snorem'. The third then discards the quartet face down and leads any card to the next round. Anyone unable to match pays one counter to whoever played the previous card. If two or more match consecutively, the first of them is 'snipped' and pays 1 counter to the pool if he was the leader, or 'snapped' for 2 counters if he played the second card, or 'snored' for 3 if the third. The pool goes to the first out of cards, who also receives one counter from everyone else for each card left in hand.

Earl of Coventry is the same, but played without counters for a simple win. The leader says 'There's as good as [King] can be' (or whatever rank it is); the second player 'There's a [King] as good as he'; the third 'There's the best of all the three'; the fourth 'And there's the Earl of Coventreeee'.

A related game called Jig is a cross between Snip-Snap and Stops, in that the aim of succeeding players is not to match rank but to play the next higher card of the same suit, from Ace low to King high. The leader plays any card and says 'Snip', and the next four able to continue the sequence announce respectively 'Snap', 'Snorum', 'Hi-cockalorum', 'Jig'. The last turns down the five-card sequence and starts a new one. When a sequence cannot be continued because the last card was a King or the next card has been played out, the last player says 'Jig' regardless of position, and leads to the next round. As before, the first out of cards receives 1 counter for each card left in other players' hands.

Almost identical is the German game of Schnipp-Schnapp-Schnurr-Burr-Basilorum, except that Kings are not stops but are followed by Ace, Two, etc.

Solitaire

See Patience.

Solo

Solo is basically a bid in which a player declines to improve his hand by exchanging cards with a blind or widow, believing he can win the required number of tricks solely with the cards he has been dealt. By extension, it denotes any game in which a player aims to take a given number of tricks by playing alone against the combined forces of his two or more opponents. See also German Solo, Six-Bid Solo, Solo Whist, Spanish Solo.

Solo Whist

Plain-trick game: 4p, 52c

English Solo derives from an early variety of Boston Whist (q.v.) through a Flemish form of the game called Ghent Whist, and became popular in Britain as a relaxation from the rigours of partnership Whist in the 1890s, just as Bridge was appearing on the scene. Were it not for the phenomenal expansion of Bridge, Solo might have developed further and occupied the social position now claimed by Contract. In the event, it remains an essentially informal game of home and pub, and is played for the direct interest of small stakes rather than for the more arcane pleasures of ingenious coups and complex scores. A potentially deep and subtle game, it remains sadly underestimated. It is particularly recommended to players who prefer to play without the encumbrance of a permanent partnership. (See also Nomination Whist and Pirate Bridge.)

Four players use 52 cards ranking A K Q J T 9 8 7 6 5 4 3 2 in each suit. Solo is usually played for hard score, each deal being complete in itself and settled as such, rather than forming part of an overall game structure with a final settlement at the end. But a written score is easily kept if preferred. Choose first dealer by any agreed means; thereafter, the turn to deal and play passes regularly to the left. Deal 13 cards each in three batches of 3 and one of 4 cards. The dealer's last card is dealt face up and establishes a preferred suit as trump. There is an auction to determine who will be the soloist and which game will be played. The possible games are, from lowest to highest:

Proposal ('prop and cop'). The soloist undertakes to win at least eight tricks, using the turned suit as trump, and playing in partnership with anyone who accepts his proposal.

Solo. A bid to win at least five tricks, using the turned suit as trump, and playing alone against the other three.

Misère (mis). A bid to lose every trick, playing at no trump.

Abondance (a bundle, or bunny). A bid to win at least nine tricks alone, after naming as trump any suit other than the one turned.

Royal abondance. The same, but accepting the turned suit as trump.

Misère ouverte (spread). As misère, but playing with his hands of cards exposed to view on the table after the first trick has been quitted.

Abondance déclaré (slam). A bid to win all thirteen tricks, playing at no trump, and leading to the first trick.

The auction proceeds as follows. Each in turn, starting with Eldest, may bid or pass, and, having passed, may not come in again. Each bid must be higher than the preceding one. If an earlier player proposes ('Prop'), a later one may accept ('Cop'), provided that no higher bid has intervened. As an exception to the rule of passing stated above, Eldest hand is permitted to accept a proposal even if he passed on the first call.

Note 1. The question may arise whether a player whose proposal has been accepted and not overcalled may himself then break the contract by raising his bid. I have never seen or heard the point discussed, but suspect that it would be frowned on.

Note 2. A player bidding abondance does not yet state his proposed trump suit, and need only specify 'royal abondance' if necessary to overcall another bid of abondance.

If all four pass, a 'general misère' may be played. There is no trump, and whoever wins the last trick loses. (*Variant*: Whoever takes the fewest tricks wins.) Alternatively, the cards are thrown in and the next in turn to deal does so.

Eldest leads to the first trick—except in a slam, which is led to by the soloist regardless of position—and the winner of each trick leads to the next. Follow suit if possible, otherwise play any card. The trick is taken by the highest card of the suit led, or by the highest trump if any are played.

In a spread misère, the hand is not exposed until the first trick has been taken. In an abondance, many follow the practice of playing the first trick at no trump, and only then declaring which suit is trump.

Typical pay-offs are as follows.

Prop and cop pays 10 for the bid and 2 per overtrick, or a flat 20

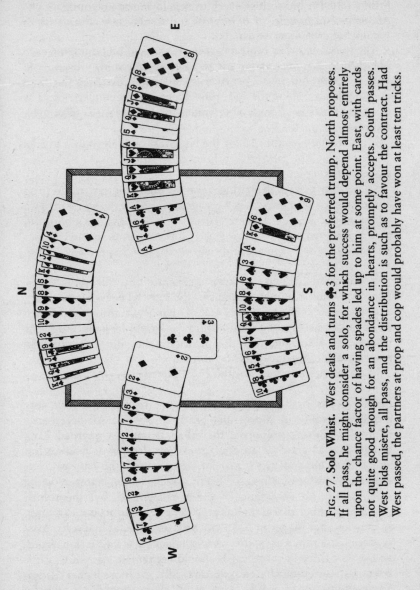

FIG. 27. Solo Whist. West deals and turns ♣3 for the preferred trump. North proposes. If all pass, he might consider a solo, for which success would depend almost entirely upon the chance factor of having spades led up to him at some point. East, with cards not quite good enough for an abundance in hearts, promptly accepts. South passes. West bids misère, all pass, and the distribution is such as to favour the contract. Had West passed, the partners at prop and cop would probably have won at least ten tricks.

if the partners win all thirteen. This is paid by one opponent to one partner, and by the other to the other. If the bid fails, the loss is 10 for the bid plus 2 per undertrick.

The soloist in other contracts receives the said amount from each opponent if he wins, or pays it to each opponent if he loses. Solo pays 10 for the bid, plus 2 per over or undertrick, or 20 for the slam; an abondance 30 for the bid, plus 3 per over or undertrick. The other contracts have invariable values, such as mis 20, spread 40, slam 60.

A general misère costs 10 for the last trick; or, if the aim is to take fewest tricks, the player(s) taking most tricks pays 10 to the player(s) taking fewest.

Scores may be kept in writing. I use the following system. At prop and cop, each partner scores 1 per trick taken between them; solo scores a basic 10, plus 1 per overtrick; abondance scores a basic 20, plus 5 per overtrick. For losing any of these games, deduct 10 per undertrick. Misère, spread, and slam win or lose respectively 20, 40, 50.

It is common practice to keep a separate kitty for abondances. Everybody stakes a fixed amount to the kitty whenever it is empty, and whenever everyone passes and the hands are thrown in. When an abondance is bid, the soloist takes the kitty if he wins, otherwise increases it. Associated with this practice is that of not shuffling the pack until an abondance has been won.

Many other variations will be encountered.

Notes. A proposal requires four or more trumps and four sure tricks, preferably in short suits headed by Aces. An acceptance requires plain-suit support rather than trumps, a guarded King being often as good as an Ace. Solos are deceptive: it is all too tempting to bid solo with only four sure tricks, and easy to over-estimate the value of a long plain suit, which is often trumped on the second lead. An abondance is easily recognized, but the soloist should remember that if he has great length in his proposed trump, so may another player in his own, with unpredictable results. Misères are harder than they look. Any suit lacking a Two is dangerous, and one of three or more cards should contain at least three cards below Seven—in which case, paradoxically, the more higher cards it also contains, the safer it is. Spreads and slams should only be bid if unbeatable by almost any freak distribution of cards. Remember that apparently freak distributions are common when the cards are not shuffled between deals.

Auction Solo

Introduced in the 1920s under the influence of Auction Bridge, this form of Solo sought to expand the skill and interest by increasing the range of bids, but has signally failed to displant the original game.

The bids are: five, six, seven, eight, mis, nine, ten, eleven, twelve, spread mis, no trump slam (soloist leads), trump slam (Eldest leads). Bids of five to eight are solos, and win or lose 1 unit per trick actually bid, regardless of over- or undertricks. Bids of nine to twelve are abondances, and win or lose from 15 to 18 units respectively. Mis counts 10, spread mis 20, slams 25 or 30. Any solo or abondance can be overcalled by the same number in the turned suit, but no trump suit is named before play unless necessary to distinguish a 'royal' from an ordinary trump bid.

Solo for three

The usual method is to play with a 40-card pack (Five low), dealing 13 each and leaving the last face up for trumps. There is no prop and cop (of course), and misère and spread misère should overcall abondance royale and a slam, respectively, as they are more difficult to make against two than against three opponents. Even so, the game is rather unsatisfactory, and a better option for three is to play Preference instead.

Solo for five

A very playable form of Solo is easily devised for five along these lines. Deal 10 each and 2 to the table, one up and one down. The upcard offers a trump suit.

In a *proposal*, the bidder and partner aim to take at least six tricks with the turned suit as trump. Before play, the bidder takes the upcard and his partner the other, and both make one discard face down. Score 1 per trick taken, or lose 10 per undertrick

All other contracts are played one against four. In each case, the

Špády

soloist may first take the odd two cards and discard any two face down in their place. If he does not, he wins or loses double.

The bids are:

Mis: to lose every trick at no trump (win or lose 10);

Solo: to win more tricks than any single opponent, using the turned suit as trump (score 10 plus 1 per trick taken, or lose 20);

Spread: a misère with the hand exposed (win or lose 20);

Abondance: to win at least six tricks with any suit as trump (win 20 plus 1 per trick taken, or lose 30);

Slam: to win all ten tricks at no trump (win or lose 50).

Špády

See Trappola.

Spanish Solo

Point-trick game: 3p, 36c

A cross between Hombre and Malilla (see Manille), Spanish Solo remains more popular in South America than in its country of origin.

Three players use a 36-card pack, typically A K Q J 7 6 5 4 3 in each suit. Choose first dealer by any agreed means. The turn to deal and play passes to the right. It is customary to shuffle at the start of a game, but not between deals. Deal 12 cards each in 4s.

The top cards in each suit rank and count as follows:

$$7 \; A \; K \; Q \; J$$
$$5 \; 4 \; 3 \; 2 \; 1$$

The Seven is called *malilla* ('imp', more or less). The other numerals (6 5 4 3 2 or 9 8 6 5 4), have no point-value. In addition, each trick counts 1 point, bringing the total available to 72.

Each in turn, starting with eldest, must pass or make a higher bid than any gone before. A player who passes adds a chip to a pool, and is then out of the auction. The bids are:

Juego (solo): To take at least 37 points in cards and tricks, or 36 if bid by Eldest. Game value 2, or 4 in diamonds.

Bola (slam): To win every trick, after first naming a wanted card and receiving it from its holder in return for any unwanted card. Value 8, or 12 in diamonds.

Bola sin pedir (no-call slam): A bid to win every trick without first calling a wanted card. Value 16, or 20 in diamonds.

The highest bidder becomes the soloist and names a trump suit. No suit is named while bidding unless the proposed trump is diamonds, as this always beats the same bid in a different suit.

If all pass, the dealer names trumps, each plays for himself, and whoever takes most points wins.

Eldest leads to the first trick, and the winner of each trick leads to the next. Follow suit if possible, otherwise play any card. The trick is taken by the highest card of the suit led, or by the highest trump if any are played.

The appropriate amount is paid by each opponent to the soloist, or by him to each opponent.

Spanish sources do not state what happens to the pool. Probably it goes to the soloist if successful, and is doubled by him if not. Nor do they state the pay-off for the case when all pass and each plays for himself. A reasonable arrangement is for whoever takes fewest points to pay 2 to whoever takes most.

Nor do the sources adequately detail two optional misère bids. In *bola pobre*, the soloist aims to lose every trick after first calling a wanted card in exchange for an unwanted one; *bola pobre sin pedir* is the same, but without calling a card. It is unstated where these fit into the bidding hierarchy, whether they are played with or without trumps, and how they are valued.

Spinado

Stops game: 3–6p, 52c

A simple family game lying about half-way between Pope Joan and Newmarket. It is marginally more subtle than it may appear.

Remove ♦8 and all four Deuces from the pack. Make a layout with three compartments labelled Matrimony, Intrigue, and Game. Dealer stakes twelve counters on Matrimony, six each on Intrigue and Game, other players three each in every compartment. Deal the rest round as far as they will go, with an extra, 'dead' hand left face down on the table. Cards rank A 3 4 5 6 7 8 9 T J Q K.

Eldest starts a sequence by playing a card face up to the table. It may be of any suit, but must be the lowest he holds of it. Whoever holds the next higher card of the same suit adds it to the first, and so on, so that a numerical sequence of cards is built up in the same suit. Eventually a card will be played which no one can follow. Aces are all stops, because the Twos are out; ◆7 is a stop because the Eight is out; Kings are all stops because there is nothing to follow them; and others may be stops because the following card lies in the dead hand. The player of a stop then starts a new sequence, again with the lowest card he holds of any suit he pleases.

Anyone who succeeds in playing a King receives immediately 1 counter from each opponent, or 2 in the case of ◆K.

The pool for Intrigue goes to whoever plays ◆J Q in one turn; that for Matrimony similarly goes to the player of ◆Q K, in addition to the side payment for playing ◆K. A player holding ◆J Q K can, of course, win both; but it is equally possible that no one can win either, in which case the stakes are carried forward to the next deal.

The ◆A, known as Spinado or 'Spin', has a special power. The player holding it may, on playing any card in the normal course of events, play Spin at the same time, announcing (for example), 'Seven and Spin', or whatever rank it may be. Besides earning him an immediate 3 counters from each opponent, this has the effect of making the Seven (or whatever) a stop, and so entitling him to start a new sequence.

Play ceases when one player plays his last card. He thereby wins the stake for Game, and is exempt from staking in the next deal.

Spit in the Ocean

A variant of (Draw) Poker (q.v.).

Spite and Malice
Competitive patience: 2p, 2 × 52c + Jokers

Bridge expert Easley Blackwood first published in 1970 a description of this game, which he says he discovered 'several years ago' being played by various schools in various ways. His suggested standard version is described below. Derived from a late nineteenth-century Continental game variously called Crapette, Cripette, Robuse, Rabouge, Russian Bank (etc.), Spite and Malice is easier to learn but deeper to play than may appear at first sight. It is certainly fun to play, and has the sort of addictive potential which should require it to be the subject of a government health warning.

Preliminaries. Use two packs of the same size but different back colours or designs. One contains 52 cards, the other 56 by the addition of four Jokers. (But three or even two will suffice.)

Shuffle the 52-card pack very thoroughly and deal 26 each. Each player's 26 cards form his 'riddance pile' and are placed face down on the table in front of him with the top card turned face up (the 'upcard').

Shuffle the 56-card pack very thoroughly, deal 5 each to form a playing hand, and place the remainder face down and squared up as a common stockpile.

Cards rank A 2 3 4 5 6 7 8 9 T J Q K. The player with the higher upcard goes first. If equal, bury the upcards and turn the next ones up.

Object. The aim of the game is to play out all twenty-six cards from one's riddance pile. The first to do so wins. As each one is played, the one beneath is turned face up. Riddance cards may only be played to one of eight piles which are gradually built up in the centre of the table. Each centre pile starts with an Ace, on which is built any Two, then a Three, and so on, until it contains thirteen cards headed by a King. Suit need not be followed. When a centre pile is completed, it is turned face down and put to one side.

Play. A turn consists of one or more of the moves described below. On your turn to play, the following rules apply.

If your upcard is an Ace, you must play it to the centre to start a pile. If it is a Two, and an Ace is in position, you must play it to the Ace. If it is any higher playable card, you need not play it if there is any reason why you may prefer not to.

If in your hand you hold an Ace or a card playable to a centre pile, you may play it to the centre, but are not obliged to. Playing to a centre pile entitles you to another move. If you play off all five cards

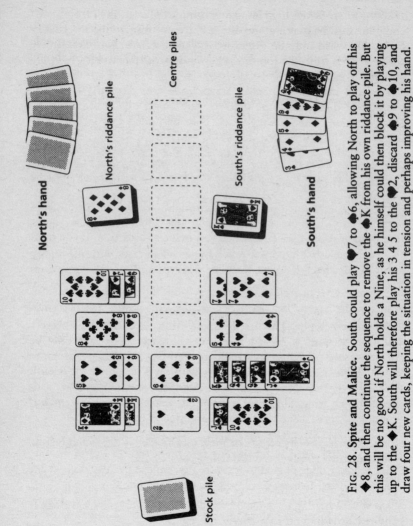

Fig. 28. Spite and Malice. South could play ♥7 to ♣6, allowing North to play off his ♦8, and then continue the sequence to remove the ♠K from his own riddance pile. But this will be no good if North holds a Nine, as he himself could then block it by playing up to the ♦K. South will therefore play his 3 4 5 to the ♥2, discard ♦9 to ♠10, and draw four new cards, keeping the situation in tension and perhaps improving his hand.

to centre piles, you draw five more from the common stockpile and continue play.

Discard piles. When unable or unwilling to play to the centre, you end your turn by making one discard face up from your hand to the table. Any card may be discarded except an Ace. You then draw enough cards from the top of the common stockpile to restore your hand to five.

The first discard you make starts your first discard pile. Each subsequent discard may be used to start a new pile, up to a maximum of four. Alternatively, each may be added to the top of a discard pile, provided that it is either equal to or one card lower in rank than the card beneath. (For example, if the top discard is a Jack, you may play to it any Jack or any Ten.) You may never play to or from your opponent's discard piles.

To keep your turn going, you may at any time play off the top card of a discard pile to a centre pile.

End of turn. Your turn ends when you make a discard, or if you find you can neither play to a centre pile nor make a legal discard. In the latter case, your hand is said to be 'frozen'.

Frozen hands. If one player's hand is frozen, the other keeps playing even after he has made a discard, and continues in this way until the first player announces after a discard that he can now continue.

If both players freeze, there is a redeal. All the cards in play *except the riddance piles* are gathered up, and shuffled and reshuffled very thoroughly together. Then 5 more each are dealt, the remainder are stacked face down, and play starts again from the beginning.

Jokers. A Joker may be played to a centre pile at any time and counted as the required card. For example, it may be called an Ace and used to start a pile, or it may be played as a Two to an Ace, a Three to a Two, and so on. It may not, however, be played onto a King. A Joker once played to a centre pile cannot then be removed.

Alternatively, it may be played to a discard pile and counted as any legal card without being identified until it is necessary to do so. (Thus if two Jokers are played to a Ten, they may be followed by a Ten, Nine, Eight, or Seven.) Although Aces themselves may not be discarded, any number of Jokers may be discarded on a Two, since they can all be counted as Twos. What a Joker stands for on top of a discard pile does not have to be kept when it is played to a centre pile: it can be played off as anything required.

Forced moves. Most moves are optional, and if both players decline to make any move from a given position then it is the same as if both hands were frozen, and a redeal is made as described above. There are, however, two exceptions:

1. If your upcard is an Ace, you must play it to the centre. If there is a bare Ace in the centre, and you have a natural Two showing as your upcard or on the top of a discard pile, then you must play it to that Ace. (But: a Joker is not so forced, even if it logically counts as a Two; and if you also hold a Two you may always play it from hand instead.)
2. If both hands are frozen, or both refuse to play, the next in turn must play an Ace or a Two from hand to the centre if he legally can, and his opponent must then do likewise.

End of stock. When the common stockpile is reduced to twelve or fewer cards, there is a pause while a new one is formed. This is done by taking all the centre piles which have been built up to the King, adding them to the existing stock, shuffling the whole lot very thoroughly indeed, and then laying them down as a new stockpile. Incomplete centre piles are not taken for this purpose, unless *all* are incomplete, in which case *all* are taken.

End. The game ends as soon as one person has played off the last card from his riddance pile. The winner scores a basic 5 points, plus 1 for each card left unplayed from the loser's.

Spoil Five

Plain-trick game: 3–10p (5 best), 52c

Spoil Five is the traditional book version of the Irish national card game usually called Twenty-Five, and underlies the Canadian game of Forty-Five. It is extremely old. Charles Cotton described it in 1674 as 'Five Fingers', a nickname applied to the Five of trumps; its sixteenth-century ancestor, Maw, was the favourite game of James VI of Scotland (I of England); and it exhibits several distinctive features which, shared also by Hombre, certainly go back to the fifteenth century. For all its initial complexity, it is a fascinating game, which undoubtedly explains its longevity. From the fact that the Irish word for 'trick', *cuig*, also means 'five', one may suspect that five was originally considered the ideal if not the statutory number of players.

Cards. The 52 cards rank for trick-taking purposes in various ways according to the suit, whether red or black, trump or plain:

Top trumps	tr5	trJ	♥A	trA
In ♥♦	K Q J T 9 8 7 6 <u>5</u> 4 3 2 A
In ♣♣	K Q <u>J</u> <u>A</u> 2 3 4 <u>5</u> 6 7 8 9 T

In other words:

In red suits, cards rank in their 'natural' order, from Ace low to King high.

In black suits, numerals rank upside down, from Ten low to Ace high.

In trumps, the best card is always the Five, followed by the Jack, followed by ♥A, followed by the trump Ace when hearts are not trump.

Preliminaries. Each player starts with 20 chips or counters, and adds one to the pool at the start of each deal. Choose first dealer by any agreed means. The turn to deal and play passes to the left. Deal 5, each in batches of 2 and 3. Stack the rest face down, turning the topmost card for trumps.

Object. The aim is to win at least three tricks, and all five if possible. Alternatively, it is to 'spoil' the five tricks by playing in such a way as to prevent anyone else from taking three or more.

Robbing. If the turn-up is an Ace, the dealer may 'rob the trump' by taking it in exchange for any unwanted card from his hand, which he discards face down. Otherwise, a player dealt the Ace of trumps may himself rob the trump at any time before playing to the first trick. If the holder of the trump Ace does not wish to rob, and does not announce the fact that he holds it before playing to the first trick, then, whenever he does play it, it counts as the *lowest* trump.

Play. Eldest leads to the first trick, and the winner of each trick leads to the next. Rules of trick-play vary as follows:

1. If a plain suit is led, players may either follow suit or trump, as preferred, but may only renounce if unable to follow suit.

285

2. If a trump is led, players must follow suit if they can, otherwise may play any card. However:

3. The top three trumps (tr5, trJ, ♥A) confer the privilege of *reneging*. To explain this, we will refer to them as 'matadors' (as in related games). If a trump is led, and a player holds no trump other than a matador, he need not trump but may play from a different suit. But this does not apply to the holder of a lower matador if a higher one is led. Thus, if the trump Five or Jack is led, and a player has no trump other than the Jack or ♥A, then he must play it.

(Remember, though, that if hearts are trump and the holder of ♥A failed to announce it, it loses its status as a matador and becomes the lowest ordinary trump instead.)

Jinking. If a player wins the first three tricks straight off, he may claim the pool without further play. If, however, he leads to the fourth trick (which is described as 'jinking'), he thereby obligates himself to win all five.

Pay-off. If no one wins three tricks, or if a player jinked and failed to win all five, the game is 'spoiled'. Everyone then adds another chip to the pool, which is carried forward to the next deal. Otherwise, whoever took three tricks wins the pool, with an additional chip from each opponent if he took all five.

Notes. Decide from the outset what your aim is. With four trumps, or three including two matadors, you can reasonably go for three tricks; with three you should wait and see how things develop; with two or under, if not matadors, you should aim to 'spoil five'. High cards in plain suits, even Kings, are not very useful in early tricks, because they can be trumped at will; but they can come into their own in later tricks if trumps are drawn early on. The 'wait and see' strategy is particularly encouraged in this game by the amount of choice you have in early tricks, in that a plain lead invites you to follow suit or trump, and a trump lead to follow suit or renege. Having decided to spoil, do everything possible to ensure that each player wins one trick, and that a player who wins two does not get a third.

Postscript. The interest of Spoil Five is itself spoiled by the complexity of upside down ranking, which has no significant bearing on the strategy, merely imposing, as one writer puts it 'an irrelevant strain on the attention'. Unless you are superstitious about flouting tradition, there is no serious reason why cards in all suits but trump should not rank A K Q J T 9 8 7 6 5 4 3 2.

Forty-Five

A point-scoring variation for two players, or for four or six in two partnerships. The player or side first reaching 45 points wins. Score 5 points for winning three or four tricks, or 10 for all five. Alternatively, the winners score five times the difference between the number of tricks taken by each side. The game is called Twenty-Five when 25 is set as the target.

Auction Forty-Fives

A partnership extension of Forty-Five played in the more Scottish parts of Canada, and especially in Nova Scotia. Four players each receive five cards dealt 3–2 or 2–3. Bidding, initiated by Eldest, is made in increasing multiples of five up to a limit of thirty. Dealer has the exclusive privilege of saying 'I hold' to the previous bid, thus taking it over without having to increase it. Declarer names trumps, and each in turn from Dealer's left then discards as many as he likes and receives replacements from the top of stock. Each side scores 5 per trick, the side holding the highest trump gets 5 extra, and the winning side adds the amount of their bid, making the highest possible score 60. If the contract fails, the opponents score as above, but the amount taken by the declarers, plus the amount of their bid, is subtracted from their current total. Game is 120 points. A side standing at 100 or more may not bid less than 20.

Stops

A family of going-out games in which cards are played to a common sequence and the first player to run out of cards wins. Their defining feature is that not all cards are dealt out, and those lying out of play create 'stops' in the sequence. See Comet, Epsom, Michigan, Newmarket, Pink Nines, Pope Joan, Spinado.

Strip Poker

A mythical game. In the straight version, bets are made by raising the amount of promised divestiture. In Hi-Lo, the best hand specifies one such item on the part of the loser, or on the part of everyone else if all have folded. Each of these may be played by two (Honeymoon Poker) or more (Orgy Poker). The problem with the former is that it is hard to tell who has won and why; in the latter, everyone is past caring.

Stuss

A variety of Faro (q.v.).

Sueca

Point-trick game: 4pp, 32c

A Portuguese game of obvious Germanic origin (the name means 'Swedish', and the game is virtually identical with an old German one called Einwerfen) Sueca forms an excellent beginners' introduction to point-trick games.

Four players sit crosswise in partnerships and receive 10 each from a 40-card pack ranking and counting

A	7	K	Q	J	6	5	4	3	2
11	10	4	3	2	0	0	0	0	0

(The Seven is called *manilha*. It may be replaced by a Ten if preferred.)

The last card is shown and its suit establishes trumps. If dealer forgets to turn it, Eldest may declare any suit trumps upon leading to the first trick. Each side's aim is to capture the greater value of counting-cards in tricks—i.e. at least 61 of the 120 available.

Eldest leads to the first trick, and the winner of each trick leads to the next. Follow suit possible, otherwise play any card. The trick is taken by the highest card of the suit led or by the highest trump if any are played.

A side scores one game point for taking 61 or more card-points, 2 for taking 90 or more, or 3 for winning every trick. A 60–60 tie doubles the value of the following game. If two successive rounds are tied, the next is quadrupled. Play up to four game points.

Notes. As in all point-count games, players will try to throw high-scoring cards to tricks being won by themselves or their partners, and worthless cards to those won by their opponents. (The German name, 'Einwerfen', means 'to throw [points] in'.)

Variant. Players may agree to follow the practice of Einwerfen, whereby the suit of the first deal remains 'favourite' for the rest of the game, and whenever the favourite suit is entrumped again the score for that deal is doubled.

Svoyi Koziri

Going-out game: 2p, 24–52c

Svoyi Koziri ('Personal Trumps') is an old Russian game related to Dudak. The two-player version of it first described in English under the name 'Challenge' by Hubert Phillips in *The Pan Book of Card Games* (London, 1953) is described below. It is unusual in being a card game of material equality and perfect information, each player's hand being a mirror image of the other's. This feature, however, seems to have been added by players at Cambridge University in the 1950's.

Svoyi Koziri may be played with any number of cards which is a multiple of four. They rank A K Q J T 9 . . . in each suit, as far as it goes. Phillips regarded 32 as standard (Seven low), and this is assumed below.

To start, each player chooses two suits as 'his' and nominates one of them as his personal trump. Assuming Dealer chooses black suits, with spades trumps, and non-dealer red suits, with hearts trumps, the former deals out half the pack (16 cards) face up in a row, extracts from them those of his own suits, and discards the rest. This gives him approximately half his playing hand. He then distributes to non-dealer, as the first half of his hand, all the red cards which exactly reflect the dealer's black cards. Example:

Dealer	♠ K J 9 7	♣ A Q J
Non-dealer	♥ K J 9 7	♦ A Q J

To complete both hands, Dealer takes all the remaining red cards and non-dealer all the remaining black ones. Each player's hand is therefore a mirror image of the other's, and neither has a strategic advantage other than that of the lead—if such it be. Each hand should include at least two cards in every suit. If not, a redeal is desirable.

The aim of the game is to be the first to play out all one's cards.

At each turn, one player leads a card of his choice. The first lead is made by the non-dealer. The second must then either play a better

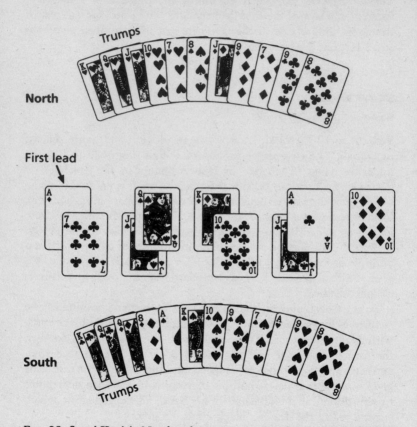

FIG. 29. Svoyi Koziri. North, whose trump suit is hearts, leads ◆10 to the fifth 'trick'. South could play ◆Q or another of his own trumps (clubs). Instead, he takes all the cards so far played and will make the next lead. This gives him a larger but more powerful hand. Whether or not it will pay off remains to be seen.

card, in which case he leads next, or else take up all the cards so far played and add them to his hand, in which case his opponent leads next. A 'better' card is a higher one of the same suit as the one led, or any card of one's own personal trump (if different from the suit led). Note that any card may be led at each turn: it need not relate in any way to the previous card played.

The first to play his last card wins. As this can take hours, it may be agreed that a player who falls asleep during play loses by default, unless the other is also asleep, in which case it is a tie.

Swedish Rummy

See Switch.

Switch
Going-out game: 2–5p, 52c

Switch, also called Two Four Jack, or Black Jack (as opposed to the quite different Blackjack), is an extension of Eights (Crazy Eights, Rockaway, Swedish Rummy, etc.) that became popular in pubs and schools during the 1970s. It is related to the Continental game of Mau Mau (q.v.), and spawned a proprietary version, with specially designed cards, called Uno. As it is essentially a folk game rather than a book game, the version described here has probably undergone many changes since.

Choose first dealer by any agreed means. Thereafter, the turn to deal passes to the left. The turn to play also starts by passing to the left, but (as described below) may be 'switched' to the right and back again as play proceeds. Deal 12 each if two or three are playing, otherwise 10. Stack the rest face down, turn the top card face up, and place it next to the stock as the start card of a sequence.

The aim is to be the first to play out all one's cards.

Each in turn, starting with Eldest, continues the sequence by adding to it, from his hand, a card of the same rank or suit, or any Ace. An Ace entitles him to specify what suit must next be followed, which need not be that of the Ace itself.

A player unable to do any of these must draw cards from the top of the stock until he can. When the stock is empty, all the cards of the sequence except the last one played are gathered up, shuffled, and laid down as a new stock next to the last card, which of course continues the sequence. The player who exhausted the stock, if still unable to play, must continue drawing until he can.

The game described so far is virtually identical with Rockaway — or (with Eights wild instead of Aces) with Crazy Eights or Swedish Rummy.

Switch itself has special rules relating to Twos, Fours, and Jacks.

Playing a Two forces the next in turn either to play a Two himself, or, if unable, to draw two cards from stock and miss a turn. If he draws and misses a turn, the next after him may play in the usual way; but if he does play a Two, the next after him must either do likewise or draw four cards and miss a turn. Each successive playing of a Two increases by two the number of cards that must be drawn by the next player if he cannot play a Two himself, up to a maximum of eight.

Fours have the same powers, except that the number of cards to be drawn is four, eight, twelve, or sixteen, depending on how many are played in succession.

Playing a Jack reverses ('switches') the direction of play and forces the preceding player to miss a turn, unless he, too, can play a Jack, thus turning the tables.

Twos, Fours, and Jacks operate independently of one another. You cannot escape the demands of a Two by playing a Four instead, or of a Jack by playing a Two, and so on.

The game ends when a player wins by playing his last card. A player with two cards in hand must announce 'One left' as soon as he plays one of them; otherwise, he must miss his next turn and draw one from stock instead.

The winner scores the face value of all cards left in other players' hands, with special values of 20 per Ace, 15 per Two, Four, or Jack, and 10 per King and Queen.

Play up to any agreed total, or settle each deal in coins or counters.

Tablanette

Fishing game: 2–4p, 52c

Tablanette was first described by Phillips and Westall in 1939 and said to be of Russian provenance, which is plausible but lacks evidence. The name presumably derives from French *table nette,* or 'clean table', which is how it is left when it has been swept. Four may play individually, or (better) in partnerships.

Choose first dealer by any agreed means. Thereafter, the turn to deal and play passes to the left. Deal 8 cards each if two play, otherwise 4. Then deal 4 cards face up to the table, and stack the rest face down. If the table cards include a Jack, bury it in the pack and replace it with the top card of stock.

The aim is to capture Aces, Tens, Jacks, Queens, Kings, ♣2, and ♦T. Table cards are captured by matching them with cards played from the hand. Points are also scored for 'sweeps'. A sweep, or *tablanette,* is the capture of all the table cards in one turn.

Each in turn, starting with eldest, plays a card face up to the table. It may capture one or more table cards in the following ways:

1. *Pairing.* An Ace captures one or more Aces, a Two one or more Twos, etc.
2. *Combining.* A played card captures two or more table cards which together total the value of the capturing card. To this end, numerals bear their face value, Aces count 1 or 11 as the player wishes, Queen counts 13 and King 14.

Examples. An Eight will capture two or more cards totalling eight, such as A 7, 2 3 3, etc. A Queen could capture A 3 9 (Ace=1) or A 2 (Ace = 11), and an Ace (= 11) could capture A(= 1) 4 6.

3. *Jacking.* The play of a Jack captures all the cards on the table in one turn, but this does not count as a sweep. Jacks have no numeral value and cannot be involved in combining.

A single card may make all possible captures in a single turn. For example, if the table cards are 3 5 8 10 Q, the play of a Queen will capture the Queen by pairing, and the 3 10 and 5 8 by combining, thus making a sweep. A player making a sweep scores *immediately* the total face value of all cards involved, including the capturing card.

Both captured and capturing cards are stored face down in front of the player who made them.

A player unable or unwilling to make any capture must 'trail' by adding one card face up to the table cards. If the discard is capable of capturing, it must do so.

When players have run out of cards, the same dealer deals from the top of the stock the same number to each player as he received in the beginning, but does not deal any more to the table.

The game ends when no cards remain in hand or stock. The player of the last card automatically wins it and all the cards left on the table, but this does not count as a sweep unless it happens to be one by definition.

Each player sorts through his won cards and scores, in addition to any sweeps he may have made:

3 for taking the greatest number of cards (0 if tied)
1 per Ace, Ten, Jack, Queen, and King
2 for ♦T instead of 1
1 for ♣J

Game is 251 up if two play, or four in partnerships. If three or four play as individuals, a better target is 151.

Notes. The play largely hinges on sweeps. After a sweep, the next player can only trail. Ideally, the best trailer is a rank of which the other three have already gone, so that the next in turn to play cannot make a one-card sweep. Otherwise, a lower rather than a higher card should be trailed, so as not to give the next in turn too high a score for making a one-card sweep. A Jack is not a bad trailer, as it gives the next in turn only 2 points if he captures it, and makes further sweeps impossible until another Jack has been played and a new card trailed.

Variants. Some accounts specify a deal of 6 cards each when two play. One authority advocates the following scoring system for cards reckoned at end of play: each captured Ace counts 11, Ten 10, King 4, Queen 3, Jack 2, others nil.

Tapp

See German Tarock.

Tapp Tarock

Tarot game: 3p, 54c

Tapp Tarock, extensively played in Austria, makes a good introduction to the general principles of Tarot play and serves as a springboard to more advanced 54-card, French-suited games such as Point Tarock and Königsrufen. The following account is based on Michael Dummett, *Twelve Tarot Games* (London, 1980) and F. Babsch, *Original Tarock* (Vienna, 1975); but rules will be found to vary from place to place.

Cards and point-values. The Austrian Tarock pack contains 22 trumps ('tarocks') and 32 plain cards divided equally between four suits.

The highest tarock is the unnumbered *Sküs* ('Excuse'), bearing the figure of a Fool or Joker. Second highest is that numbered XXI, called *Mond* ('Moon', though from French *monde*, meaning 'world'). Others follow in descending order (XX, XIX, XVIII, etc.) to the lowest trump, I, called *Pagat*. The Sküs, Mond, and Pagat form a trio called the 'trull' (from French *tous les trois*, meaning 'all three').

In plain suits, cards rank downwards as follows:

In spades and clubs	King Queen Cavalier Jack T 9 8 7
In hearts and diamonds	King Queen Cavalier Jack A 2 3 4

Deal. Whoever cuts the highest card deals first (trumps beat plain suits). The deal and turn to play then pass regularly to the right. Deal a talon of 6 cards face down to the table in 3s, the second batch lying crosswise atop the first, then 16 cards to each player in 8s. Anyone who receives a hand completely devoid of tarocks may demand that all hands be thrown in and a new deal made by the same dealer.

Object. There is an auction to decide who will play alone against the other two. The soloist's primary aim is to win, in tricks, cards totalling at least 36 of the 70 points available. For this purpose, cards count as follows when taken in tricks:

Sküs	5
Mond	5
Pagat	5

Each King	5
Each Queen	4
Each Cavalier	3
Each Jack	2
All others	1 each

This gives a theoretical total of 106. However, won cards are reckoned in batches of three, and each batch is actually counted as 2 less than its face value. As there are 18 batches (54/3), the final total is 70 (106 − 36), of which the 36-point target represents a clear majority, i.e. one more than half.

Each player should mentally note whether he holds two or three cards of the trull, or all four Kings, as he may claim a score or payment for such at end of play.

Games. There are basically only two types of game that may be bid. In an exchange game, the soloist turns up the six cards of the talon, adds either the top three or the bottom three to his hand, and discards three cards face down in their place. His three discards may not include a King or a card of the trull. They may only include other tarocks if he has no other legal card(s) to throw out, and in this case he must show his opponents which tarocks he has discarded. These three discards will count for him at end of play as if he had won them in tricks, while the other three, which are turned face down again, will similarly count for the opponents. In a solo game, he leaves the six cards of the talon unturned, and all six will count for the opponents at end of play as if they had won them in tricks.

Bidding. Although exchange and solo are the only two biddable games, the lower of them (exchange) can be bid at three different levels, namely 'threes' (*Dreier*) for a score of 3, 'lowers' (*Unterer*) for 4, and 'uppers' (*Oberer*) for 5 points. (So called because they originally referred to which of the two batches of three cards, lower or upper, the soloist was obliged to take. Nowadays he has a free choice.) These bids must be made in order. That is, 'lowers' may only be bid to overcall 'threes', and 'uppers' to overcall 'lowers'. Solo, however, may be bid at any time, and cannot be overcalled.

Each in turn, starting with Eldest, must pass or bid. A player who has once passed may not come in again. The first bid must be either 'threes' or 'solo'. If it is 'threes', the next must be 'lowers' (or solo).

'Lowers' may be overcalled by 'solo' from either opponent, 'uppers' from the third player, or 'hold' from the first. This is because a player who comes later in the bidding order can only overcall by raising the bid, whereas one who comes earlier can overcall by agreeing to raise his previous bid to the new level, which he does by saying 'hold'. Similarly, a bid of 'lowers' is overcalled by a bid of 'solo' from either opponent, or 'uppers' from a later bidder, or 'hold' from an earlier one. 'Uppers' can only be overcalled by 'solo', or by 'hold' from an earlier bidder. Solo itself can theoretically be 'held' by an earlier player, but it is extremely unlikely that two players would both have hands strong enough to contest it.

Announcements. Unless the highest bidder is playing a solo, he next turns up the six cards of the talon, takes either the top or the bottom three, and discards as described above. Before a card is led, any of the following announcements may be made:

(*a*) The soloist may announce 'Pagat', thereby undertaking to win the last trick with the lowest trump (I). In this case, he is not allowed to lead or play Pagat to any earlier trick if he has any other legal choice of card, even if he might wish to do so in order to save his basic contract.

(*b*) The soloist may announce 'Valat', thereby undertaking to win every trick.

(*c*) Either opponent may announce 'double the game', 'double the Pagat', 'double the Valat' (as the case may be) if he believes the soloist will not fulfil his contract or achieve whatever feat he announced. In return, the soloist may announce 'redouble' to anything that was doubled. These announcements respectively double and quadruple whatever scoring feature is won or lost by the soloist.

Play. Eldest leads to the first trick, and the winner of each trick leads to the next. Suit must be followed if possible; if not, it is obligatory to play a tarock if possible; otherwise any card may be played. The trick is taken by the highest card of the suit led, or by the highest tarock if any are played. Tricks needs not be stored separately, and all cards won by the two partners are thrown face down to a single pile.

Score. Each side counts the card-points it has won as described above under 'Object'. If the soloist has reached his 36-point target he scores the appropriate game value, or is paid it by each opponent; if not, each opponent scores the appropriate game value, or receives it from the soloist. The basic game values are:

Threes	3
Lowers	4
Uppers	5
Solo	8

These amounts are doubled or quadrupled if the game was respectively doubled or redoubled.

If the soloist wins every trick, he scores the above amount fourfold, or eightfold if he previously announced 'Valat'. But if he announced Valat and failed to win every trick, he loses the above amount eightfold, regardless of how many card-points he took. This amount is doubled or quadrupled if the announcement was respectively doubled and redoubled.

If the soloist wins the last trick with Pagat, he scores 4 points, or 8 in a solo bid. Conversely, if he leads Pagat to the last trick and loses it—or, having announced it, plays it to any earlier trick—he is deemed to have been attempting to make the bonus, and the appropriate 4 points (8 in a solo) is scored by each opponent. These amounts are doubled, won or lost, if he previously announced his intention of winning the last trick with Pagat, and further doubled or quadrupled if the announcement was respectively doubled or redoubled. Note that the score for Pagat obtains independently of the main contract: it is possible for the soloist to score for game and the partners for Pagat, or vice versa.

Finally, any player whose original hand contained one of the following features may now claim and score for it:

(a) the three cards of the trull: 3 points;
(b) any two cards of the trull: 1 point;
(c) all four Kings: 3 points.

(In some circles, these scores are doubled in a solo game.)

Play continues for any agreed number of deals, which should be a multiple of three.

Variants. Many variations of procedure and scoring will be encountered. Some permit additional redoubles, and some credit any player with a score of (say) 2 points for capturing trump XXI with the Sküs. Of greatest interest is that whereby the holder of Pagat may bid to win the last trick with it even though he is not the soloist. In this case:

1. The soloist may double the announcement, and its maker or his partner may redouble.
2. The Pagat announcer may not lead or play it to any earlier trick than the last if he can legally avoid doing so.
3. If the Pagat holder plays it to the last trick and loses it to an opponent—or, having announced it, plays it to any earlier trick—he is deemed to have been trying to win the last trick with it, and the other side scores the appropriate bonus. (Four points, doubled in a solo, doubled if announced, and doubled or redoubled as the case may be.)
4. Prior agreement must be made as to what happens if, in the above case, one of the partners plays Pagat to the last trick, and the other partner wins it. Strictly, the Pagat-player has lost it, and the soloist scores; but it may be agreed to call it a stand-off, and leave the bonus unearned.

Notes. The game is often won on tarocks, plain cards being used to pad out the value of tricks rather than intentionally to win them. In assessing a hand for the bid, think first of the possible split of the tarocks and then of the seven 5-point cards (Kings and trull). The most even split is about seven tarocks in each hand and one in each half of the talon. A minimum bid of threes therefore requires at least eight tarocks, including several high ones and at least one card of the trull. Higher bids require correspondingly higher strength. A very short side suit is a possible strength factor, as one aim of taking the talon is to create a void. Solo should not be bid with fewer than three of the 5-point cards, eleven good tarocks, and at least void suit or singleton King.

In play, the soloist will start by leading tarocks in order to draw two for one from the partners; conversely, the partners will lead long plain suits to force out the soloist's tarocks. A key point occurs when one of them is out of tarocks and can throw high-counting cards to tricks being won by his partner. As in any three-hander, it is always desirable to keep the soloist in the middle, i.e. playing second to the trick.

Winning the last trick with the Pagat should not be bid (or

attempted) unless at least ten tarocks are held, and they of above average strength. In playing against this feat, one's main aim is to get rid of all plain-suit cards before the last trick, as a diminished hand consisting entirely of tarocks is then bound to capture the Pagat.

Tarot

The pack which English-speakers call by the French name Tarot (there being no English tradition of Tarot play) is called Tarocco in Italian, Tarock in German, and various similar words in other languages. Contrary to popular belief, Tarot cards did not precede ordinary playing cards, and they were invented not for occultic but for purely gaming purposes.

The Tarot was invented in Italy in about 1430–40 by adding to the existing four-suited pack a fifth suit of 21 specially illustrated cards called *trionfi*, and an odd card called the Fool—which, despite appearances, is *not* the origin of the modern Joker. From *trionfi*, or 'triumphs', comes the English word 'trumps', their original purpose being to act as cards that would beat any ordinary card played to the same trick. Only later was the word *trionfi* replaced in Italian by the inexplicable *tarocchi*, and the idea of having a special suit of trumps replaced in ordinary packs by that of turning a card and simply entrumping whatever suit it happened to be.

Tarot games subsequently spread to most parts of Europe (notable exceptions being the British Isles, the Iberian peninsula, and the Balkans), and still thrive in Italy, France, Austria, Hungary, Czechoslovakia, and parts of Switzerland and southern Germany. Most follow the same underlying pattern, being trick-taking games for three to five players in which win or loss is determined by the value of counting-cards captured in tricks.

For a complete and authoritative survey of Tarot games, see Michael Dummett, *The Game of Tarot* (London, 1980), and for a representative selection the same author's *Twelve Tarot Games* (London, 1980). From the latter I have selected for inclusion in this book three still current games suitable for beginners: Tarot as now played in France with the 78-card French-suited pack; Scarto, a Piedmontese game using the 78-card Italian-suited pack; and Tapp Tarock, an Austrian game using the 54-card French-suited pack.

Tarot (French)

Tarot game: 3–4p, 78c

French Tarot has been gaining in popularity in France during the latter part of the twentieth century, helped largely by the fact that there is basically only one main French game, despite (or perhaps because of) the complaints of authoritarians that no official standard is universally adhered to. The following account is based on Dummett (see previous entry), with reference to Patrick Arnett, *Le Tarot* (Paris, 1977) and Claude-Marcel Laurent, *Le Jeu de Tarots* (Paris, 1975). As usual, the following rules are typical rather then definitive.

Cards. Four players use a 78-card French Tarot pack, consisting of

1. the Fool, or 'Excuse';
2. 21 trumps numbered 1–21;
3. 14 cards in each of the plain suits, spades, clubs, hearts, diamonds, ranking from high to low: King (R), Queen (D), Cavalier (C), Jack (V), 10 9 8 7 6 5 4 3 2 1.

Of these, the lowest and highest trumps (1 and 21) and the Excuse are specially designated *bouts* (or *oudlers*). As *bouts* means 'ends', I will use the cognate English word 'butts'.

Play centres on the winning of tricks containing counters or scoring-cards, these being the three butts and 16 courts. All other trumps and plain cards are non-counters, or blanks. Aces, numbered '1', have no special value. The total value of all tricks and counters is 91.

Deal. The first deal is made by whoever draws the lowest card, trumps counting higher than plain suits. The turn to deal and play then passes to the right.

After cutting to the left, deal 18 cards each and 6 to the table, all face down, in the following way: 3 to the right, 3 to the player opposite, 1 to the table, 3 to the left, 3 to the dealer; and the same again five more times. The six down-cards constitute *le chien*, 'the dog'.

If the player dealt trump 1 holds no other trump, nor the Excuse, he may annul the deal, and the next in turn to deal does so. (Other options are open to him, but the relevant rules are more complicated than the rarity of the event justifies detailing here.)

Object. There is an auction to determine who will play alone against the other three. The soloist's aim is to win a minimum number of points which varies with the number of butts contained in his won tricks, viz.

3 butts	36 points
2 butts	41 points
1 butt	51 points
0 butts	56 points

(It will be noted that the missing value, 46, is one point more than half the total available).

Auction. Each in turn, starting with Eldest, must pass or name a higher bid than any gone before. A player having passed may not come in again. The bids from lowest to highest are:

1. *Prise* (Take). The soloist will turn the dog face up, add it to his hand, and make any six discards face down before play. These discards will count for him at end of play as if he had won them in tricks. He may not discard a butt or a King, and may only discard trumps if he hasn't enough plain cards; in this case, he must say how many he has discarded, but need not say which ones.
2. *Pousse* (Push). Same as prise, but for a higher score.
3. *Garde sans le chien* (Without the dog). The soloist will play with the hand as dealt, and leave the dog untouched; but those six cards will still count for him at end of play as if he had won them in tricks.
4. *Garde contre le chien* (Against the dog). As above, but those six cards will count to the opponents as if they themselves had won them in tricks.

Declarations. Each player, just before playing to the first trick, may make one or more of the following applicable declarations:

1. Any player holding ten or more trumps may declare a *poigne*, or bunch (literally 'fist'). The possible declarations are 'Ten', 'Thirteen', 'Fifteen' or 'Eighteen' trumps. Such a declaration must be supported by showing the stated number of trumps. The Excuse does not count as a trump unless the hand is one short of a declarable number, in which case it may be used to make it up. A player holding a bunch is not obliged to declare it; nor, if he holds

cards in excess of a bunch, need he state whether or how many extra he holds; but it is not legal to declare a smaller relevant number than actually held. (*Example*: You may declare 'Ten' if you hold ten, eleven, or twelve trumps; but if you hold thirteen, or twelve and the Excuse, you must declare, if anything, 'Thirteen'.) A bunch declared by the soloist will score for him alone if he wins, or by each opponent if he fails. One made by any partner will be credited to *each* of them if they beat the contract, or to the soloist if he wins.

2. A partner may declare 'No trumps' if he holds neither any trump nor the Excuse; 'No courts', if he holds no court card; or 'Misère', if he has either of the above but prefers not to say which. This earns him a private and personal bonus at end of play.
3. The soloist may declare 'Slam' or 'Little slam'. A little slam is an undertaking to win at least seventeen tricks, a slam to win all eighteen. (*Variant*: In some circles, a slam bid overcalls a bid 'Against the dog'.)

Play. The soloist either takes the dog and discards, as detailed above under 'Auction', or moves it to his side of the table if playing 'without', or to the opposite player's side if playing 'against'.

Eldest leads to the first trick, and the winner of each trick leads to the next. Subsequent players must follow suit if possible, otherwise must play a trump if possible. In playing any trump—whether to a plain-suit or a trump-suit lead—it is obligatory, if possible, to play a higher trump than any so far played to the trick, even if it is already being won by a partner. The trick is taken by the highest card of the suit led, or by the highest trump if any are played. All tricks won by the partners are kept together in a single pile.

The Excuse. The holder of the Excuse may play it at any time and in contravention of any rule stated above. If it is led, the suit to be followed is that of the second card played. The Excuse normally loses the trick. If, however, it is led to the last trick, and its holder has won all 17 previous tricks, then it wins.

If the soloist plays the Excuse, he may, when the trick has been taken, retrieve the Excuse from the won trick, and replace it with any card (preferably worthless) that he has himself already won in a trick. If he has not yet won a trick, he lays the Excuse face up before him, and, upon winning a trick, passes one of its cards to the opposing side. In either case, the Excuse is then incorporated into one of his tricks, and cannot be played again.

If a partner plays the Excuse to a trick, and it is taken by the soloist, he has exactly the same privilege of retrieving it in exchange for a card from a trick won by his own side, and of retaining it for this purpose if his side has yet to win a trick.

Obviously, if the partners (or, improbably, the soloist) win not a single trick, they cannot reclaim the Excuse.

Last trick. There is a bonus for winning the last trick if it contains *petit,* the lowest trump ('1'). If the soloist plays it to the last trick, he gains the bonus from each opponent if he wins the trick, or pays it to each opponent if not. If a partner plays it to the last trick and wins, the bonus is paid by the soloist to each opponent; but if a partner loses it in the last trick, then each partner pays the soloist, even if it was a partner who captured it. (This makes it a penalty rather than a bonus.)

Score. At end of play, the opponents count the value of all the tricks and counters they have won, including the six dog cards if the soloist played 'against'. For this purpose, cards count as follows:

Each butt	5 (trump 21, trump 1, Excuse)
Each King	5
Each Queen	4
Each Cavalier	3
Each Jack	2

Cards are counted in pairs, each pair consisting of two blanks or a blank and a counter. A pair of blanks counts 1 point; a blank and a counter take the value of the counter.

Whatever the partners count is subtracted from 91 to yield the soloist's count. As stated above, he needs 36, 41, 51, or 56 to win, depending on whether he took three, two, one, or no butts. If he wins, he is paid the appropriate amount by each opponent; if not, he pays it to each of them. If scores are kept in writing, it is only necessary to record the amount as won or lost in the soloist's own score column, as a settlement properly made on the basis of the final scores will come to the same thing as if each deal had been settled in coins or counters as it occurred.

Scoring systems, although following the similar basic principles, vary greatly in detail. Dummett recommends the following:

For the main contract, the score won or lost is a basic 10, plus 1 for each point by which the soloist exceeded or fell short of his required count. This total is then doubled in a 'push' contract (*pousse*), quadrupled at 'no dog' (*garde sans*), or octupled at 'against the dog' (*garde contre*).

Example. The soloist bid 'push' and took two butts for 52 points, or 11 over the target. He scores $(10 + 11) \times 2 = 42$. With two butts and 40, he would have been one short, and lost $(10 + 1) \times 2 = 22$ points. With three butts and 40, he would have been four over, and scored $(10 + 4) \times 2 = 28$ game points.

The score for a misère (no trumps or no courts) is 10, for a bunch of Ten 10, of Thirteen 20, Fifteen 30, and Eighteen 40. This is scored independently of winning or losing the main contract; it is not multiplied according to the bid made; and it goes to the soloist if he declared it, or to each opponent if one of them did.

The score for *petit* (the lowest trump in the last trick) is 10. This is scored independently of the main contract; and goes to the soloist or to each opponent as described in the appropriate paragraph. Some make it a fixed score; others multiply it by two, four, or eight, according to the contract.

The score for a declared slam may be set at 500 for a little slam and 750 for a grand, and is won or lost as a fixed amount.

Notes. The first two players should bid cautiously, especially the second as he hasn't even the advantage of the lead. The third and fourth may be bolder if the first two pass. The average number of trumps dealt is about five; no bid should be undertaken with less. A simple bid may be undertaken if holding the highest trump, or the lowest and a good chance of making it. A push bid requires length in trumps or strength in every suit, and the promise of making two butts. A bid 'without' would be undertaken on such a hand as:

tr 21 17 16 14 12 11 5 4 X (X = Excuse)
♠ —
♣ K C J 10 4 2
♥ J 3
♦ 7

Tausendeins

and a bid 'against' on:

> tr 21 19 18 16 14 10 9 8 1 X
> ♠ Q 2
> ♣ K 6
> ♥ K Q 3
> ♦ K

The interest of the play rests as much on the outcome of *petit*, the lowest trump, as on the main contract, since it both counts as a butt and carries weight in the last trick. If you hold it, decide from the outset whether or not to save it for the last trick. As soloist, try to ensure its safety by leading trumps whenever possible so as to draw them all and leave the lowest safe. A partner holding the highest trump (21) should lead it as soon as possible in case another partner holds the *petit*, as this will notch up the soloist's target to 51 points and perhaps thereby defeat a risky hand.

The game for three

The same, but with these variations. Deal 24 cards to each player in 4s, and 6 to the dog. The lowest declarable bunch is Thirteen (score 10), the highest Twenty-one (score 40). A little slam is 22 or 23 tricks. If an odd card remains after counting in pairs, ignore it.

Tausendeins

See Sixty-Six; also Tyzicha.

Terziglio

See Tressette.

Thirty-Five

Gambling game: 2–5p, 40 or 52c

This American game, described by Morehead and Mott-Smith in *Culbertson's Card Games Complete* (New York, 1952), is said to be of Italian origin (*Trentacinque*). As it does not appear in any Italian book consulted, I follow *Culbertson* entirely.

From two to four players may use the Italian 40-card pack lacking Eights, Nines, and Tens; five need all 52. The turn to deal and play passes to the right. Players each contribute five chips, or any other agreed number, to a pool. Deal, face down and one at a time, 4 cards to each player and to a widow (spare hand), then 5 more to each player.

The aim is to get a hand containing four or more cards of the same suit totalling 35 or more points, counting courts 10 each and numerals at face value (Ace 1 only, not 11). Any player dealt such a hand may show it and claim the pool, thus ending the round. If more than one player can show 35 or more in a suit, they share the pool equally, regardless of their actual totals.

Failing that, each in turn, starting with Eldest, then bids for the right to discard four cards from his hand and replace them with the four cards of the widow, thereby aiming to acquire cards totalling 35 or more in a suit. Each bid must be higher than the last, but none may exceed the total in the pool. Bidding ends when all but one have passed, or when this limit is reached.

The highest bidder then discards four and takes the widow. If he can then show 35 or more in a suit, he wins from the pool the amount of his bid; if not, he pays that amount into the pool, which (in either case) is carried forward to the next deal. (*Variant*: If successful, the bidder wins the whole pool.)

Optional extras. A bonus of 2 chips may be claimed from each opponent by any player able to show a 'beggar' (a hand consisting entirely of numerals) or a 'royale' (K Q J of the same suit). This is said to be claimable only by someone who has not passed, and only after the highest bidder has been determined. But since it is only by everybody's passing that the highest bidder is determined, this proviso seems to contradict itself. Perhaps the privilege may be exercised by (*a*) those who have not passed, but have been excluded from the auction by a preceding maximum bid, or (*b*) those who made at least one bid before passing.

Thirty-One

Drawing cards to a total of 31—counting Aces 1 or 11, courts 10, and numerals at face value—has formed the whole or part of

Towie

various games since the fifteenth century. See, for instance, Commerce, Cribbage, Trentuno, and Wit and Reason.

Towie

An adaptation of Contract Bridge for three players, invented by Replogle and Fosdick in 1931. The basic idea is that four hands are dealt, six cards of the dummy are turned up, and players bid for the right to partner it. See also Booby.

Trade or Barter

See Commerce.

Trappola

Point-trick game: 2–4p, 36c

This early sixteenth century Venetian game spread to other European countries and survived, under various names and in various forms (Trapulka, Bulka, Hundertspiel, Špády, Sestadvacet, etc.) until perhaps the middle of the twentieth century. All versions were played with a special pack of Italian-suited cards, last reported to have been manufactured in Prague in 1944. The distinctive feature of this delightful and intelligent game, no doubt accounting for its extraordinary popularity in so many different societies, is that of leading a Deuce, the lowliest card, and winning the trick because no one can follow suit.

A special study of Trappola has been independently made by Michael Dummett (*The Game of Tarot*, London, 1980) and Robert Kissel (*Journal of the Playing-Card Society* 17/1 (London), August 1988). Described here are Dummett's reconstructions of (*a*) the original two-hander outlined by the 16th-century scholar Girolamo Cardano, and (*b*) the four-hand partnership game of Špády outlined in *Hráčy Karty: Karetní Hri* (Prague, 1969).

The 36-card Trappola pack, lacking numerals from Three to Six inclusive, was a specialized version of the Italian pack featuring suits of swords, batons, cups, and coins, and courts of King, Cavalier, and Footsoldier. These are here translated into (respectively) spades, clubs, hearts, diamonds; King, Queen, Jack.

Trappola (2p)

Cards rank and count as follows:

$$A \quad K \quad Q \quad J \quad T \quad 9 \quad 8 \quad 7 \quad 2$$
$$6 \quad 5 \quad 4 \quad 3 \quad — \quad — \quad — \quad — \quad —$$

The aim is to score points for (*a*) combinations held before play, (*b*) point-cards won in tricks, (*c*) winning the last trick, and (*d*) winning any trick with a Deuce, especially the last trick or the last successive tricks.

Deal 9 cards each in batches of 4 then 5, and lay the remaining 18 face down as a stock. Non-dealer, if unsatisfied with his hand, may discard it face up and take in its place the first nine cards of stock. If still unsatisfied, he may do the same again, but must then play with the last nine cards taken from stock. If he leaves any, Dealer may then exercise the same option either once or twice, depending on how many remain. Faced discards may not be taken up.

A player holding three or four Aces, Kings, Queens, Jacks, or Deuces may declare them any time before playing one of them to a trick (provided that, having three only, he has not already captured the fourth in a trick). He need say no more than 'three' or 'four' as the case may be, unless they are Aces, when he must add 'Aces'. The appropriate scores are not made until the trick-play is over.

Elder leads to the first trick, and the winner of each trick leads to the next. Follow suit if possible, otherwise play any card. A trick is taken by the higher card of the suit led, there being no trump.

A player who wins a trick with a Deuce scores 10 points immediately, and the winner of the last trick scores 6 points. These are superseded by winning the last one, two, three, or four successive tricks with Deuces, the respective compound scores being 26, 52, 78, and 104.

Each player then adds in the value of counting-cards taken in tricks, and finally the value of any three- or four-card combination declared at start of play. The respective scores are:

	Aces	*Kings*	*Queens*	*Jacks*	*Deuces*
Three held	12	6	6	6	10
Four held	24	12	12	12	20

The winner receives an amount proportional to the difference.

Trappola

Špády (4pp)

Four players sit crosswise in partnerships. The player cutting the highest card deals first, and the suit he cuts is trump for the deal. The turn to deal and play passes to the left. In subsequent deals, the dealer cuts a trump after shuffling but before dealing.

Deal 9 cards each in 3s. The rank and value of cards and the general aim of play is as for Trappola (above), but now complicated by the existence of a trump suit.

After the first card is led, each in turn, starting with Eldest, may claim and score for holding three or four Aces, Kings, Queens, Jacks, or Deuces, the score being 5 for a trio and 10 for a quartet. In each case the rank must be stated, but the cards claimed need not be shown; nor, if three are held, need their suits be identified. A score of 5 may also be claimed for a *blanche* (a hand containing no courts), or 10 for a *bianca* (no courts or Aces). For each 5 or 10 scored by one side for declarations, the other marks an equivalent −5 or −10, so that all scores sum to zero.

Eldest leads to the first trick, and may not lead trumps (unless he has no other suit). Follow suit if possible, otherwise trump if possible; and in either case beat the highest card so far played to the trick if possible. The trick is taken by the highest card of the suit led, or by the highest trump if any are played, and the winner of each trick leads to the next.

Points are scored by one side (and correspondingly recorded minus by the other) for each of the following feats:

Winning the first trick with the trump Deuce	20
Winning the last trick with any Deuce	10
Winning the last two tricks with Deuces	20
Winning any other trick with any Deuce	5

(Winning the last trick with Deuce is called a Twenty-Six, and winning the first with the trump Deuce is called a Fifty-Two, reflecting a now defunct scoring tradition.)

A score for 'game' is made by whichever side takes 40 or more of the 78 card-points available for capturing counters in tricks (each Ace 6, King 5, Queen 4, Jack 3), plus 6 for winning the last trick. The score is 10 for game, the other side correspondingly marking −10. It is made quite independently of any score for declarations or Deuce-tricks.

If hearts are trumps, the scores for game and for tricks taken with Deuces are doubled, but not those for declarations.

If both sides take 39 of the 78 for game, settlement is made only for declarations and Deuce-tricks, but in the following deal all scores (for declarations, game, and Deuce-tricks) are doubled, or redoubled if hearts are trump.

Trédrille

An eighteenth-century adaptation of Quadrille for three players—just as Quadrille itself had been an adaptation for four players of the previously three-handed Hombre.

Trente et Quarante
Gambling game: Np, 6 × 52c

Or Rouge et Noir: Traditional French casino game not favoured elsewhere because of its low house percentage. Essentially, the banker deals cards into two rows notionally labelled 'black' and 'red', stopping as soon as each has reached a count of at least 31 (and not over 40, whence the title). Punters bet, for even money, on whether the *rouge* or *noir* row will finish closer to 31, or that the first card dealt will be of the same (*couleur*) or opposite (*inverse*) colour to the winning row. A tie is a stand-off. On a 31-point tie, player may 'double or quit' on the next coup or immediately lose half their stake.

Trentuno

See Commerce.

Tresillo

Later name for Hombre.

Tressette
Point-trick game: 3p, 40c

One of Italy's major national card games, together with Scopone and Briscola, Tressette is recorded only from the early eighteenth century, though greater antiquity is suggested by its trumplessness—compare, for example, Piquet, Truc, and Trappola, all of which can be traced back a further two centuries. The name of the game, literally 'three Sevens', may refer to a scoring combination no longer recognized, or to the fact that it is played up to twenty-one.

Tressette is played in a full range of formats, with versions for any given number of players from two to eight, including a non-partnership version for four (Mediatore), a trick-avoidance variety (Rovescino), and the intriguing Madrasso, which is a hybrid of Tressette and Briscola apparently unique to Venice. Described below are the standard partnership game for four and a classic three-hander popular in Lombardy under the name Terziglio, sometimes called Calabresella. Sources: Giampaolo Dossena, *Giochi di Carte Italiani* (Milan, 1984); Rino Fulgi Zaini, *Giochi di Carte* (Milan, 1934–77); Anon., *Giochi di Carte* (Milan, 1969).

Partnership Tressette

Four players use a 40-card pack (no Eights, Nines or Tens) and sit crosswise in partnerships. A stake is agreed, and a first dealer chosen by any agreed means. The turn to deal and play passes to the right. Deal 10 cards each in 1s (some say in 5s). A player whose point-cards total less than 1 point (see below) may demand a fresh shuffle and deal from the same dealer.

Each side's overall aim is to reach a score of 21 over as many deals as necessary. Points accrue for winning counters in tricks, for which purpose cards rank and count as follows:

$$3\ 2\ A\ K\ Q\ J\ 7\ 6\ 5\ 4$$
$$\tfrac{1}{3}\ \tfrac{1}{3}\ 1\ \tfrac{1}{3}\ \tfrac{1}{3}\ \tfrac{1}{3}\ 0\ 0\ 0\ 0$$

In practice, complications are avoided by reckoning $\frac{1}{3}$-point counters at the rate of 1 point for every three taken and ignoring fractions. This gives a total of 6 for honours, which, with 1 per Ace and 1 for winning the last trick, makes 11. (Some accounts rate counters at 1 each, Aces and last trick at 3 each, making 35 in all; but as they are still counted in batches of three, and odd ones are ignored, it comes to the same thing in the end.)

Eldest leads to the first trick, and the winner of each trick leads to the next. Follow suit if possible, otherwise play any card. The trick is taken by the highest card of the suit led. There are no trumps.

Each player, upon leading to a trick, may make one of the following conventional announcements or signals to his partner. False signals are illegal.

Busso (or bunch one's fist on the table): 'If possible, win the trick and return the same suit.'

Volo (or slide the card slowly onto the table): 'This is the last or only card I have of its suit.'

Striscio (or skim the card rapidly onto the table): 'This comes from my best suit.' (This convention is not always admitted.)

The side winning the last trick scores an additional 'one for last' (*dietra*).

Normally, the game ends as soon as one side claims to have reached 21, any remaining cards being left unplayed. That side wins the fixed stake—or loses it, if the claim proves mistaken. Alternatively, any of the following special events ends the game:

1. *Cappotto*. One side wins all ten tricks in a deal. This wins a double stake.
2. *Cappottone*. A single player wins all ten tricks. This wins sixfold.
3. *Stramazzo*. One side takes all the counters, but not all the tricks. This wins treble. Its also prevents the losing side from scoring a point for winning the last trick, as also does:
4. *Strammazzone*. A single player takes all the counters, and the opposing side wins at least one trick. This wins eightfold.

Honours (optional). If so agreed, a player dealt a particular combination of cards may announce *buon gioco* before the first trick is played, then declare and score it to his partnership's credit when that trick is over:

Four Threes, Twos, or Aces	4 points
Three Threes, Twos, or Aces	3
3 2 A of same suit (*napoletana*)	3

The suit of a napoletana must be stated, as must the suit *missing* from three of a kind. When honours are included, the game is played up to a higher target, such as 31 or 51.

A player dealt all ten of a suit, or *napoletana decima*, wins the game outright for his side. This win is called *collatondrione* and receives a sixteenfold stake.

Notes. The challenge of Tressette, and that which most needs getting used to, is its absence of trumps. This increases the incidence of 'squeezing', whereby players unable to follow suit may be uncertain which other suits to discard and which to keep guarded. It also tends to reduce the amount of information obtainable by conventional play, and it is to compensate for this deficiency that partners are instead allowed to give information by means of conventional announcements. Scoring for honours, if admitted, also contributes to the amount of information available, and is thus significant to the game in a way that scoring for honours in Whist and Bridge is not.

Terziglio (Calabresella)

Three play as above, but with these differences:

Deal 12 cards each and spread the remaining four face down, forming a *monte*.

The overall aim is to be the first to make a score of 21. In each deal, one person plays against two with the aim of capturing in tricks cards totalling at least 6 of the 11 points available for counters and the last trick. The soloist is determined by auction. Each successive bid must be higher than the last, and a player who has once passed may not come in again. The bids from low to high are:

Chiamo (Call). The soloist plays after calling for a card lacking from his hand, and receiving it from its holder in exchange for any card he does not want—unless the called card is in the monte, in which case he does not get a second call. Having called, he turns the monte face up for all to see, adds it to his hand, and makes any four discards face down to restore his hand to twelve.

Solo. The soloist does not call a card, but simply takes the monte and discards as explained above.

Solissimo. The soloist plays without calling a card or taking the monte, which remains face down and out of play.

Solissimo aggravato. The soloist not only plays without the monte, but even allows the opponents to use it. If he says 'half each' (*dividete*), each of them takes two cards without showing them, and makes any two discards face down, also without showing them. If he says 'you choose' (*scegliete*), they turn the four face up and may agree to split them 2 2, 3 1, or 4 0, in which each discards (face down) as many as he took.

Eldest leads to the first trick, except in a bid of *solissimo,* when players may have agreed to follow the alternative rule permitting the soloist to lead. The rules of trick-play are as for four, except that the two partners may not communicate with one another unless so agreed beforehand.

The winner of the last trick, besides scoring one for last, also wins the *monte* as if it were an extra trick. The soloist counts the points he has won in tricks, as described above, and ignoring fractions. If he has taken at least 6 points, he scores the appropriate amount, or is paid it by *each* opponent; if not, each opponent scores the appropriate amount, or is paid it by the soloist. The appropriate amounts are: call 1, solo 2, solissimo 4, aggravato dividete 8, aggravato scegliete 16. The appropriate score is trebled for taking all 11 points but not every trick, or quadrupled for winning every trick.

Game is normally 21 points, but may be made 31 or 51 if preferred.

Optional extra. If all pass without bidding, the monte is left intact and the hands are gathered up and redealt by the same dealer without being shuffled. This time, the lowest permissible bid is solo. (Sources do not state what happens if this also is passed out. It would be reasonable to force Eldest to play a simple 'call'.)

Notes. The main aim in exchanging through the monte is to secure guards for your Aces and only secondarily to replace low cards with high ones. If you haven't the lead to the first trick, you need at least all four suits headed by 3, or 2 A, or A x x, or three suits headed 3 2. Given the lead, a single suit will do, if it is long enough and headed by top cards. Play centres largely on the trapping or saving of Aces and winning the last trick. The partners must study each other's play carefully to discover which suits they are strong in.

Triomphe

Early sixteenth-century name applied to several games, not all closely related. The most characteristic form is now best represented by Écarté (q.v.).

Triumphus Hispanicus

'Spanish Trump': a sixteenth-century game ancestral to Hombre and related to Trump, the ancestor of Whist.

Trouduc

Going-out game: 4p, 52c + Joker

This unusual game has appeared only recently in the West. It may be of Oriental provenance, as substantially similar games are played in China (*Zheng Shàngyóu*, or '[Social] Climbing') and Japan (*Dai Hin Min*, 'very poor man'). At the same time, it looks like a logical extension of such eastern European games as the Russian Durak and Svoyi Koziri. The unusual feature is that players form a social hierarchy and actually change their seating positions from deal to deal according to the level they occupy. In the Japanese game, for instance, the relative positions are designated king, noble, poor man, and very poor man, or down-and-out. Such a game appeared in France in the 1980s under the name Trouduc, the relative positions being *patron*, 'boss'; *contremaître*, 'foreman'; *ouvrier*, 'worker'; and *trouduc*, literally 'arsehole'. The following account is from a French newspaper article (Daynes, in *Sud-Ouest Dimanche*, 27 December 1987). A substantially similar game has since been reported played by English schoolchildren under the name 'Arsehole'. I have bowdlerized 'arse-hole' to 'bum' partly for its appropriate alternative meaning ('tramp').

Four players use a 53-card pack ranking 2 A K Q J T 9 8 7 6 5 4 3 in each suit. The Joker may be used to represent any card.

From the second deal onwards, the players form a hierarchy from highest to lowest ranged around the table in a clockwise direction. The first player is the Boss; to his left sits the Foreman, to his left the Worker, and to his left the Bum. At the end of a deal they may have undergone reversals of fortune, so causing them to move up or down the hierarchy and to change seats accordingly. For this purpose it is helpful to designate the appropriate positions (which themselves remain unchanged) by means of distinctive seating. The Boss position may, for instance, be furnished with a comfortable armchair, the Foreman's with a wooden armchair with cushion, the

Worker's with a kitchen upright, and the Bum's with a broken-down stool or rickety orange-box — if, indeed, with anything at all.

In the first deal all players are equal, so the seating and first to deal may be determined by any agreed method. Shuffle the cards thoroughly and deal them around one at a time, starting with Eldest, who (since there are 53 cards in the pack) will start play with 14 cards to everyone else's 13.

The aim is to play all one's cards out as soon as possible. Play consists of an indefinite number of rounds, and ends when only one player has any card(s) left in hand.

Eldest leads to the first round by playing face up to the table from one to four cards of the same rank. Each in turn must then either pass or else play the same number of cards as the leader, but of a higher rank than any so far played. (*Example*: A pair of Eights are

Fig. 30. **Trouduc.** Possibly the only game in which players may change seats and social classes from deal to deal.

led. If the second player passes and the third plays an Ace and the Joker, equivalent to two Aces, the fourth must either pass or play a pair of Twos. Note that if a single card is led, a Joker may be played as a Two, but it cannot beat a Two played by anyone else.)

Whoever plays the highest card or cards turns all the played cards face down to a common wastepile. He then leads to the next round, unless he has run out of cards, when the lead passes to the first player from his left who is able to make it. The leader may always play any number of cards—he is not constrained in any way by the number played in the previous round—but the followers must always play the same number as the leader. One cannot, therefore, beat a singleton by playing a pair, a pair by a triplet, etc.

Play ceases as soon as three players have played out all their cards. The first who did so scores 4 points and becomes the Boss in the next deal, occupying the appropriate chair accordingly. The second scores 3 and occupies the Foreman's chair, and the third scores 2 and occupies the Worker's. The last player—the Bum— scores nothing, even if he could have played his last card or cards to the same round as the third who went out.

From Deal 2 onwards, it is always the Bum who deals (after a shuffle and cut) and therefore the Boss who receives 14 cards and leads to the first round. Before doing so, however, the Boss must pass to the Bum the two lowest-ranking cards in his hand and receive in exchange the two highest-ranking cards in the Bum's hand. Similarly, the Foreman gives his single lowest card to the Worker and receives the Worker's highest in exchange. The exchanged cards must be the lowest and highest held, even if this breaks up a desired pair. The Joker, however, is exempt from exchange, and is retained by the player to whom it was dealt. Note that card-exchange does not take place in the first deal.

Play up to any agreed target, e.g. 50 points for about an hour-and-a-half of play, or for any previously agreed length of time.

Notes. The spice of this game lies in the fact that, once the relative positions are established at the end of the first deal, it is not easy to dislodge the Boss or to rise from the Bum's position, as each player's hand is either improved or weakened by the exchange of cards. This is designed to favour the Boss most and the Bum not at all—just like life, really, only fairer.

It is desirable to arrange all one's cards not by suit but by the number of each rank held—ranging, for example, from the highest quartet at one end of the hand to the lowest singleton at the other. In play, it is essential to get rid of low cards as soon as possible.

Truc

Plain-trick game: 2p or 4pp, 32c

This delightful game of bluff and counterbluff has been reasonably likened to Poker for two. With slight variations, it is played in south-western France, especially Roussillon and Pays Basque. More elaborate versions are played in Uruguay and Argentina under such names as Truco, Truque and Truquiflor. The nearest English equivalent is Put.

Two players use a 32-card pack ranking 7 8 A K Q J T 9 in each suit. A rubber is the best of three games, and a game is 12 points, which may require several deals to reach. Players deal in turn, the first being chosen by any agreed means.

Deal 3 cards each in 1s. The aim in each deal is to win two tricks, or to win the first trick if each wins one and the third is tied.

Non-dealer may propose a redeal. If Dealer agrees, the hands are put to one side and each receives 3 new cards. Only one such redeal may be made, and only if both agree to it.

Non-dealer leads to the first trick, and the winner of each trick leads to the next. Any card may be played by either player. There is no trump, and the trick is taken by the higher-ranking card regardless of suit. If both play equal ranks, the trick is 'spoilt' and belongs to no one, and the same leader leads to the next. Note that Sevens are highest, then Eights, Aces, etc.

Theoretically, the winner scores one game point. Either player, however, before playing to a trick, may offer to increase the score for a win by saying 'Two more?' The first such increase raises the value from 1 point to 2, and subsequent increases add 2 more each, raising the game value from 2 to 4, then 6, and so on. If the other says 'Yes', play continues for the increased score; if not, he throws his hand in, play ceases, and the challenger scores whatever it was worth before he offered to raise. It is possible for both to raise in the same trick—the leader before leading and, if accepted, the follower before replying. It is also legal to concede at any time, even if the other has not just offered to double.

An even more drastic raise may be made as follows. Either player, on his turn to play, may declare 'My remainder' ('*Mon reste*') — thus jump-raising the game value to whatever he needs to make 12, with a view to winning the game outright. To this, however, the opponent may either concede, in which case the increase does not take effect, or may himself announce 'My remainder', in which case whoever wins the deal wins the game.

The round finishes when one player concedes or when three tricks have been completed. Whoever took two tricks, or the first if each took one, scores the game point, or whatever value it may have been increased to. If all three tricks were spoilt, neither scores.

Variant. Sid Sackson, who was the first to describe this game in English (*A Gamut of Games*, New York, 1969; London, 1972), proposed a variation which has since been followed by others, including myself, viz. Each increase doubles the game value (2 4 8 . . . , not 2 4 6 8 . . .), but neither player may double if this would give him more points than he needs for game. For example, a player with 5 may double from 1 to 2 points, or from 2 to 4, but not from 4 to 8, which would make him 13 if he won. In this case he must, instead, bid 'My remainder'. Conversely, a player may not bid 'My remainder' if he could instead legally double it, though this constraint does not apply to the second player if the first one bids 'My remainder' legally. I do not now consider this an improvement; it is certainly more cumbersome to explain.

Partnership Truc

Four players sit crosswise in partnerships, the turn to deal and play passing to the right. Play as above, but with these differences.

The dealer acts as the governor for his partnership, and Eldest hand as governor for his. Only Eldest may propose an exchange, and only Dealer may accept or refuse it. Eldest leads to the first trick, and each subsequent trick is led by the winner of the last, or by the previous leader if the trick is spoilt. Only the governor of each side may propose an increase in the game value, and then only when himself about to play to the trick. Similarly, only the governor may accept or concede when an increase is proposed.

Throughout play, the governor's partner may indicate what card or cards he holds by means of a conventional code of gestural signals, and the governor for his part may tell his partner what to play. (They may not reverse these roles.) The holding of a Seven is indicated by a grin, an Eight by a wink, an Ace by a shrug. Naturally, the signaller will attempt to signal when his governor is looking and his opponents are not. An instruction may take the form: 'Play the Seven', 'Play low', 'Leave it to me', and so on. Signals must be truthfully made, and instructions obeyed.

Sackson states that a trick is spoilt if (and, by implication, only if) the highest card played by one side is matched in rank by the highest played by the other. Neither he nor Pierre Berloquin (*Cent Jeux de Cartes Classiques*, Paris, 1975) comments on the case where tied winning cards are played by two partners. Presumably they win the trick, and whichever of them led to it leads to the next. But what happens if neither of them led? I would suggest that if two partners tie for highest then the trick is spoilt, just as if one of the tied cards were played by the other side.

Trump

Ancestor of Whist.

Tute

Point-tricks and melds: 2p, 40c

Tute (pronounce both syllables) has replaced Tresillo in the card-playing affections of Spain and Latin America. It is said to be of Italian origin and to come from *tutti*, meaning all, or everyone, though it is quite obvious that games with this scoring schedule derive from Central European games played with packs containing Tens. It is played in many forms by two, three, or four players. I here describe the two-hander known as Tute Habañero, but must point out that no two Spanish accounts even of this specific form appear to be identical.

Tute

Two players use a 40-card pack lacking Eights, Nines, and Tens. Cards rank and count as follows:

A	3	K	Q	J	7	6	5	4	2
11	10	4	3	2	—	—	—	—	—

(Players may prefer to replace Threes with Tens.)

Points accrue for winning counting-cards in tricks and for declaring certain combinations. These must be totalled and remembered as play proceeds, not written down. The winner is the first to announce (correctly) that he has reached 101 points, which may take one or two deals.

Choose first dealer by any agreed means. Deal 8 cards each in 1s. Turn the next for trump, and lay the rest face down as a stockpile on top of but not entirely covering the turn-up.

If the turn-up is a Jack or higher, either player may take it in exchange for the Seven, but not before he has won a trick. Similarly, if it is a Seven—whether dealt or exchanged for a Jack—it may be taken in exchange for the Two. Exchanging is optional, not obligatory.

Eldest leads to the first trick, and the winner of each trick leads to the next. Second to a trick must follow suit if a trump is led, but otherwise may play any card. If unable to follow to trumps he must lay his hand of cards face up on the table and keep it there until he draws a trump, when he may take it up again. The trick is taken by the higher card of the suit led, or by the higher trump if any are played. The winner of a trick draws the top card of stock, adds it to his hand, and waits for the other to do likewise.

Before leading, the trick-winner may show and score for a marriage or a tute. A marriage is a King and Queen of the same suit and scores 20, or 40 in trumps. A tute is all four Kings or all four Queens, and wins the game outright. A combination may only be declared upon winning a trick, and only one may be declared per trick.

When the stock is exhausted and the turn-up taken in hand, the last eight tricks are played to different rules. Combinations may no longer be declared. Second to play must follow suit and head the trick if possible. If unable to follow, he must trump if possible. Winning the last trick scores 10 extra. Before the last eight are played, either player may declare capote, thereby undertaking to win them all. If successful, he wins the game outright; if not, he loses.

Play ceases with a tute or capote, or when one player claims to have reached or exceeded 101 points, or when either player is found to have reached 101 points but has failed to claim it. A correct claim of 101 wins the game, a false claim or failure to claim loses. If neither has claimed 101 by the end of play, but it transpires that both have made it, the game is won by whoever took the last trick.

If none of these applies, there is another deal, which must be made by the winner of the last trick.

Variants. Some accounts give the target score as 121. One states that the tute declaration wins outright and that capote can be won without being declared, another that capote is valid only if declared and a tute does not count at all.

Notes. Tute will be easily followed by anyone acquainted with Bezique or Sixty-Six, and has some nice points of its own which make it a pleasant change from these better-known games—especially, of course, the 'sudden death' win for a tute (compare gaigel in the game of that name). It sometimes happens that a player falls only a few points short of the target score at the end of the first deal. That player should seek to win the last trick, for by so doing he will be the next dealer and so be in a better position to win the first trick with a high counter.

Twenty-Five

See Spoil Five.

Twenty-Nine

Adding-up game: 2–6p, 52c

Of relatively recent origin, Twenty-Nine is classed as a children's game, but perhaps only because its potentially interesting premiss has not been adequately developed: there are so many obvious ways of improving it that they may safely be left to discover themselves. Any number may play. Four is most convenient, playing either individually or in partnerships.

From a 52-card pack, remove (unless four play) as many Tens as necessary to ensure that everyone receives the same number of cards. Deal all the cards around in 1s.

Eldest plays any card face up to the table and announces its face value, for which purpose Aces and courts count 1 each. Each in turn contributes a card to the count and announces the new total. The count may not exceed 29: if it is less, and the next in turn cannot play without going over 29, he misses a turn. Whoever makes it exactly 29 wins the cards so played and turns them face down like a won trick. The player at his left then leads to the next 'trick'.

The winner is the player (or partnership) who has captured most cards.

Notes. When four play, the total pack value is 232, or 8 × 29. Eight 'tricks' will therefore be taken, each containing anything from three to a theoretical 21 cards. If other than four play, the last trick will count less than twenty-nine. The earliest source (Albert A. Ostrow, *The Complete Card-Player*, New York, 1945) states that the last trick remains untaken, though no one else seems to follow this rule.

Twenty-One

See Pontoon.

Two-Four-Jack

See Switch.

Tyzicha
Point-trick game: 3p, 24c

An unusual but challenging three-hander, Tyzicha is short for *tyzicha odin*, which is Russian for the game's target score of one thousand and one. Several games of this type, all derived from Mariage or Sixty-Six, are played in various parts of Central and Eastern Europe—see, e.g. the Austrian two-hander called Tausendeins. Tyzicha itself was first described in English in *Games and Puzzles* magazine by Don Laycock, an Australian games expert with a Ukrainian mother-in-law. My account is based on his (or, rather, her) rules, but with modifications taken from Czech and German sources.

Three players use a 24-card pack ranking and counting as follows:

A   T   K   Q   J   9
11 10 4   3   2   0

Points accrue for winning counters in tricks (120 in all) and for declaring marriages, a marriage being the King and Queen of the same suit. The winner is the first to reach 1001 points over as many deals as it takes.

Choose first dealer by any agreed means; thereafter, the turn to deal and play passes to the left. Deal 3 cards to each player, then 3 face down to the table to form a widow, then 4 more each in 1s.

An auction determines who will play alone against the other two. The first bid is made by the player at Dealer's right (not by Eldest), who must bid at least 110 or pass. Higher bids are made in multiples of 10. When two have passed, the third is the soloist. If the first two players pass, Eldest may not pass but must either bid 110 or more, or play a 'forced' game worth a nominal 100.

The soloist turns the widow up for all to see, except in a forced game, when he takes it up without showing it. He may, given a bad pick-up, now throw the hand in by announcing 'Forty each', in which case each opponent scores 40 and the soloist subtracts from his score the amount of his bid. Alternatively, given a good pick-up, he may raise his bid to any higher multiple of ten. Whether he raises or not, he then passes one card from his hand face up to each opponent, and leads to the first trick.

There is no trump at first, but, as play proceeds, a trump suit may be established and changed up to three times. If the leader to a trick has a marriage, he shows both cards and leads one of them. The suit of this marriage thereby becomes the trump and remains so to the end of the game, unless it is changed by another marriage. Whoever declares a marriage scores for it according to its suit as follows:

♦ = 40, ♥ = 60, ♠ = 80, ♣ = 100

A marriage may not be declared when following to a trick, but only when leading to it. The soloist may do so upon leading to the first trick.

Players are obliged to follow suit if possible, otherwise to play a trump if possible. The trick is taken by the highest card of the suit led, or by the highest trump if any are played, and the winner of each trick leads to the next.

Each opponent scores whatever he has made for counters and marriages, unless this brings him to more than 1000, in which case his score remains pegged at 1000. The soloist either adds or subtracts the amount of his bid, depending on whether or not he has taken at least as many points as he bid. The game can only be won by a successful soloist, and that when his score exceeds 1000.

Variants. Players often round scores off to the nearest five—though, of course, the soloist may not round up if he took less than he bid. An opponent's score is then pegged at 995 or 1000 as the case may be, but the soloist wins by exceeding 1000, if only by one point.

Laycock gives the marriage scores as spades 40, clubs 60, diamonds 80, hearts 100; but in the above account I have preferred the schedule of the equivalent Czech game, Tisíc a Jedna.

Notes. Tyzicha should not be undertaken without experience of something similar, such as Sixty-Six, Pinochle, Clobiosh, or Belote. Even then it is difficult to bid effectively until sufficient practice has been acquired. Bear in mind that, given an even distribution, the soloist can expect more than his fair share (40) of the 120 available card-points, as his advantage of the pick-up and the lead should give him something in the region of 50 to 60, and more if he can quickly establish a good trump suit. A marriage in hand will add to this anything from 40 to 100, thus explaining the minimum forced bid of 100. Multiple marriages are not advantageous, as the card led from one generally loses the trick, and it may then be impossible to get back in again to declare the next—especially if another suit is entrumped, or one of the marriage partners is lost under the obligation to follow suit. Given four marriage partners of different suits, the chances of mating one of them from the widow are better than even; with three, they are less than even, but worth taking if you are either sufficiently in the lead to be able to afford the risk, or sufficiently behind not to be able to afford not to. Having overcome the hurdle of accurate bidding, the actual play should be relatively straightforward for a skilled soloist, as it is difficult for the two partners to play with effective co-operation. The soloist often thereby ends up with considerably more than he bid—which is a good reason for allowing him only to score what he bid, thus exerting even greater pressure to bid up to the full potential of the hand. The game can get very exciting when someone is close to 1000 points, as careless bidding at this critical point may induce irrecoverable reversals of fortune.

Ulti

Point-trick game: 3p, 32c

Hungary's national card game is named from the winning of the last trick with the lowest trump, a feature perhaps derived from such games as Trappola and Tapp Tarock, though the game as a whole must have grown naturally out of the Czech Mariáš (q.v.), as suggested by its alternative title Talonmariáš. Though virtually unknown outside its home borders, Ulti is well worth exploring, as it offers some unusual and intriguing features. The following account is based on the only authoritative English-language description available, by John McLeod in the *Journal of the International Playing-Card Society* (May, 1976).

Preliminaries. Three players use a 32-card pack basically ranking A T K Q J 9 8 7 (Ten high). Choose first dealer by any agreed means; thereafter, the turn to deal and play passes to the right. Deal a batch of 5 cards to each player, lay the next 2 face down as a talon, then deal another batch of 5 each.

Object and contracts. In each deal the highest bidder becomes the soloist and plays alone against the other two with a view to fulfilling whatever contract he bid. In trump games, Aces and Tens captured in tricks count 10 points each, and winning the last trick counts 10 more, making a possible total of 90. In addition, the declaration of a marriage (King and Queen of the same suit), scores 20 points, or 40 in trumps, bringing the maximum possible total to 190. In no-trump contracts card-points and marriages do not count, and cards rank A K Q J T 9 8 7 (Ten low).

The basic contracts are listed below. Any one of them, if involving a trump suit, may be increased in value by adding 'ulti' to the basic bid. Ulti is an undertaking to win the last trick with the trump Seven. This adds 4 points to the game value, or 8 with hearts trump.

1. Simple: the soloist undertakes to win a majority of points for Aces, Tens, and marriages. It is bid by naming the intended trump, 'spades', 'hearts', etc., and is worth 1 game point, or 2 with hearts trump.

2. Hundred: The soloist, holding a marriage, undertakes to win at least 100 points in play including the score for marriage. Only one marriage may be scored. It is bid by announcing the intended trump and adding either '40-hundred' or '20-hundred', depending on whether the marriage concerned is in trumps or not. (It will be noted that in a 20-hundred he can afford to lose only one Ace or Ten, whereas in a 40–100 he can afford to lose three.) This is worth 4 game points, or 8 in hearts.

3. Bettel: The soloist undertakes to lose every trick, playing at no trump, and with Tens ranking low. There are three such bids: single bettel for 5, double bettel for 10, and bettel ouvert for 20. The first two are identical, except for the scores. In bettel ouvert, he lays his hand of cards face up on the table after the first trick has been played.

4. Plain durch: The soloist undertakes to win every trick, playing at no trump, and with Tens ranking low. As with bettel, there are three such bids: single durch for 6, double durch for 12, and durch ouvert for 24.

5. Trump durch: the soloist undertakes to win every trick, using a trump suit of his own choice, and with Tens ranking high. This may not be bid alone, but must be combined with an ulti, a hundred, or both. Like plain durch, it may be bid single for 6, double for 12, or ouvert for 24, but the score will be increased by the appropriate bonus for ulti or hundred.

In the auction, a 'higher' bid is one worth the greater number of game points if successful. As some bids are of equal value, it may be helpful to list all possible bids in ascending order of value and precedence as follows:

1 Simple in spades, clubs, diamonds
2 Simple in hearts
4 Hundred
5 Ulti (1 + 4)
5 Single bettel
6 Single durch (NT)

  8 Ulti/100. Hearts 100.

10 Hearts ulti.

10 Double bettel. Single durch ulti or 100 (6 + 4).

12 Double durch (NT).

14 Single durch ulti/100 (6 + 4 + 4).

16 Hearts ulti/100 (8 + 8). Double durch ulti or 100 (12 + 4).

20 Bettel ouvert. Double durch ulti/100 (12 + 4 + 4). Double durch ulti or 100 in hearts (12 + 8).

22 Single durch ulti/100 in hearts (6 + 8 + 8).

24 Durch ouvert (NT).

28 Durch ouvert ulti or 100 (24 + 4). Double durch ulti/100 in hearts (12 + 8).

32 Durch ouvert ulti/100 (24 + 4 + 4). Durch ouvert ulti or 100 in hearts (24 + 8).

40 Durch ouvert ulti/100 in hearts (24 + 8 + 8).

Note that 'Ulti/100' denotes a combined bid of ulti *and* 100, as opposed to 'ulti or 100'. Normally, a bid can only be overcalled by one of greater value. Exceptionally, ulti is overcalled by single bettel, and hearts ulti by any other bid worth 10.

Auction. The auction is conducted in an unusual way which is virtually unique to Ulti. Eldest starts—he may not pass—by naming a possible trump suit, taking the talon and adding it to his hand without showing it. He is then obliged to make a bid either in the suit he named or at no trump. He concludes the opening bid by laying any two unwanted cards face down on the table to form a new talon.

    Thereafter, each player may pass or else pick up the talon and bid. Passing does not of itself prevent him from bidding again later. A player who takes the talon must make a higher bid than the previous one, then lay any two cards face down to re-form the talon. This continues until two players pass in succession. The third player thereby becomes the soloist. He must state whether or not the talon contains any Aces or Tens, but need not specify how many or which ones.

Conceding, doubling. In a simple suit bid with no extras, the soloist may throw his hand in before the first trick is led. This prevents the opponents from doubling and so restricts him to a 1-point loss (2 in hearts). Otherwise, either opponent may, upon playing to the first trick, announce 'double' to the soloist's basic bid, or to his additional ulti, or both. If the soloist thinks he can still make it, he may announce 'redouble' upon playing to the second, thus quadrupling the appropriate score. Similarly, and finally, either opponent may then announce 'surdouble' upon playing to the third trick, thus octupling it. A double or surdouble made by one partner is binding upon the other, except in respect of a bettel or durch bid. In these cases only, one or both partners may double, and any such double is binding only upon its maker's final settlement with the soloist.

Play. The soloist leads to the first trick, and the winner of each trick leads to the next. Follow suit if possible, otherwise trump if possible; and in either case beat the highest card so far played to the trick if possible. The trick is taken by the highest card of the suit led, or by the highest trump if any are played.

In a trump contract, any player having a marriage to declare does so upon playing to the first trick. If this is one of the partners, the points for the marriage are marked or remembered to the credit of the partnership. In a hundred contract, the soloist may declare only the marriage whose value he stated when bidding.

In an ulti contract, the soloist may not lead or play the trump Seven before the last trick, unless forced by the rules of following.

Score. The soloist wins his basic contract if he takes a majority of points for cards and marriages (a tie is impossible because of the odd '10 for last'), or if he takes at least 100 in a hundred bid, or loses every trick in a bettel, or wins every trick in a durch. For winning, he receives the stated amount from each opponent; for losing, he pays it to each. If written scores are kept, it is sufficient to add or subtract the value from the soloist's score alone. (*Note*: Although most scores and bonuses are doubled in hearts, this does not apply to a bid of durch in hearts.)

Ulti, if bid, is won or lost independently of the basic contract—i.e. the soloist may score positively for fulfilling his contract and at the same time negatively for failing to win the last trick with the trump Seven, or vice versa. A failed ulti bid pays 4 to each opponent (8 in hearts), plus another 4 (hearts 8) if the Seven was captured in the last trick. If the ulti bid was doubled, redoubled, etc., such doubling affects only the basic 4 (hearts 8) for losing, the additional penalty for its capture remaining undoubled.

The following bonuses also obtain:

1. *Unbid ulti.* Ulti may be won or lost without having been bid, and that by either side. If the soloist or a partner plays the trump Seven to the last trick, and it wins, he scores 2 points (4 in hearts) for himself or his side. If the soloist so plays, and it loses, he pays the same amount to each opponent. If a partner does so, each opponent pays the soloist, even if the trick was won by the other partner.

2. *Unbid hundred.* If the soloist takes 100 points or more without having bid it, he gains a bonus of 1 unit from each opponent (2 in hearts). If the opponents take 100 or more, he pays them the same amount. An unbid 100 may include more than one marriage.

3. *Unbid durch.* If the soloist wins every trick without having bid durch, he gains a bonus of 3 points or units.

Play up to any agreed target or for any agreed length of time.

Notes. Beginners' greatest problems with Ulti lie in grasping the details and relative values of the various contracts. Once these are overcome, the play of the game, though requiring much skill, offers a greater degree of clarity than most three-handers of the same format, such as Skat, Tyzicha, Jass, and so on. Its greatest and most original feature is the fact that the talon changes from bid to bid. As McLeod points out, players get to see and even use one another's discards, and genuine or misleading information can be conveyed by means of them. With helpful discards, it may be possible to build up a stronger hand, which in turn tends to increase the competitiveness of the bidding.

Uruguay

See Canasta.

Van John

See Pontoon.

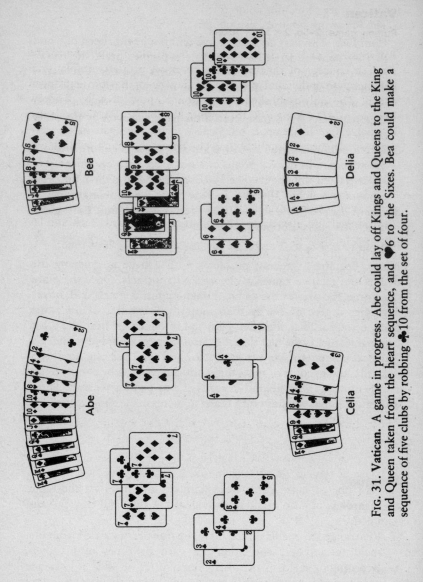

FIG. 31. Vatican. A game in progress. Abe could lay off Kings and Queens to the King and Queen taken from the heart sequence, and ♥6 to the Sixes. Bea could make a sequence of five clubs by robbing ♣10 from the set of four.

Vatican

Rummy game: 2–5p, 2 × 52c + Jokers

An unusual and challenging form of Rummy, embodying the modern concept of making melds common property rather than belonging to individual players. It may be of Eastern European origin. The only published description I know of is by Andrew Pennycook (*The Book of Card Games*, St Albans, 1982), who learnt it from a Czech national; but it also forms the basis of the proprietary tile game Rummikub, which was certainly first published in the East.

Though playable by two to five, the game is best for three or four. Shuffle together two 52-card packs and two Jokers, making 106 cards in all. Choose first dealer by any agreed means; thereafter, the turn to deal and play passes to the left. Deal 13 cards each and lay the rest face down as a stockpile. (*Note*: After being shuffled, the pack should be cut by the player at dealer's right. If he cuts a Joker, he may keep it, and is then dealt 12 more cards instead of 13.)

The aim is to be the first to go out by playing all one's cards from hand to table.

Each in turn takes a card from stock and adds it to his hand. He does not discard, but may, if able, take a suit-sequence of three or more cards from his hand and lay it face up on the table. For this purpose, cards run A 2 3 4 5 6 7 8 9 T J Q K A. Ace counts high or low but not both at once (K A 2 is illegal).

Once a player has made an initial meld, he may on each subsequent turn play out as many cards as he can. If unable to do so, he must draw an extra card from stock and end his turn. In playing out, he may now do any of the following:

1. Make another meld, which need not be a sequence but may be three or four cards of the same rank and different suits.
2. Add one or more cards from hand to any meld on the table, regardless of who made it, provided that they still leave a valid meld;
3. Rearrange any melds on the table, by transferring cards from one meld to another, and adding a card or cards of his own. Rearranging melds is permissible only if (*a*) he adds at least one card from his hand, and (*b*) at the end of his turn all cards left on the table form valid melds of three or more each.

Vingt-Quatre

A Joker may be used to represent any desired card. Subsequently, it may be replaced by the card it represents, but must then be shifted to another meld in place of any card that would legally complete it. Once played, a Joker may not be taken into hand.

The first to play out all his cards ends and wins the game.

If the stock empties before anyone has gone out, each in turn must continue to play if possible, but otherwise must pass.

Vingt-Quatre

See Imperial.

Vingt-Un

So called, even by the French, instead of the strictly more correct Vingt-et-Un (Twenty-One). See Pontoon.

Vint

Plain-trick game: 4pp, 52c

Vint is the Russian equivalent of Bridge. Like Bridge, it evolved in the nineteenth century from an apparent grafting onto partnership Whist of bidding principles developed in such games as Boston and (especially in Russia) Preference. Its early forerunners were Yeralash and Siberia; Vint as such is mentioned several times in the writings of Chekhov from the early 1880s. Also like Bridge, it has evolved considerably since then. The game described below—for the first time in English, I believe—differs markedly from that of E. Hoffmann and A. von Rennenkampff in *The Laws and Principles of Vint* (London, 1900), though something like it appears in the later chapters of that unbearably dull and dreary tome. Vint means 'screw', and is so called (if that tome is right) from a metaphorical resemblance between raising the bidding and tightening a screw. This account is taken from a Swedish book (Einar Werner and Tore Sandgren, *Kortoxen*, Helsingborg, 1975), where it is recorded as both 'Skruv' and 'Vint', with a note to the effect that if you want to know more, you must first learn either Finnish or Estonian, in which all the literature on it appears. Whether it is still popular in Russia I do not know, but it evidently remains a significantly Baltic game.

Four players use a 52-card pack ranking A K Q J T 9 8 7 6 5 4 3 2 in each suit. A session consists of three rubbers, one for each combination of two players sitting crosswise in partnerships from each other, so that the final result is an individual rather than a partnership score or settlement. A rubber consists of an indefinite number of preliminary deals, followed by four final deals, which are played to different rules and begin when one of the partnerships has scored two games below the line. Each rubber is recorded on a scoresheet divided into a column for each partnership and bisected by a horizontal line. Below the line are recorded scores counting towards the winning of each game, above the premiums and bonuses.

Choose first dealer by any agreed means; thereafter, the turn to deal and play passes to the left.

Preliminary deals. Deal 12 cards each in 1s and lay the last 4 face down on the table, forming a talon. There are two stages to the auction. Dealer bids first, and each bid must be higher than the last. As in Bridge, the number stated in a contract is the number of tricks to be taken in excess of six.

The lowest bid is 'four nullos'. This is an undertaking to *lose* at least ten tricks, playing at no trump. The next higher bid is four spades, then four clubs, four diamonds, four hearts, and four grands, each of which is an undertaking to win at least ten tricks using the stated suit as trump—except for 'grand', which means no trump. Any four bid is overcalled by a bid of five, then six, then seven, the last being a bid to win—or, in nullos, to lose—all thirteen.

Passing does not prevent a player from bidding again. The first auction ends when everyone has passed twice—that is, after *eight* consecutive passes. If no one bids at all, a 'pass-misère' is played, as described later.

Whoever bid last is the declarer. He turns up the four cards of the talon for all to see, adds them to his hand, then passes any four cards face down to his partner. The latter selects any three discards, and passes one face down to each other player, so that everyone now has 13 cards in hand.

Declarer then begins the second stage of the auction, which takes place only between himself and his partner. The first bid need not be in the same suit as the provisional contract, but it must be higher, as, of course, must each subsequent bid. Stage two ends when both players have passed twice, i.e. after *four* consecutive passes. The last bid made becomes the final contract. Note that bidding is not compulsory—both players may pass immediately; also that bidding may result in the original declarer's partner becoming the new declarer.

Before play, the opponent at declarer's left passes a card secretly to his partner, who, after adding it to his hand, passes any card over in return. This privilege is annulled, however, if the declaring side reached a contract of at least six tricks (or grand) in the first stage of the auction.

Final deals. When one side has won two games, the last four deals are played as follows. Deal 13 each in ones, leaving no talon. The lowest bid is six, and a nullo bid now overcalls its numerical equivalent in hearts. As before, eight passes end the auction, and if all pass immediately a pass-misère is played. Otherwise, the declarer passes four cards face down to his partner, who then passes any four back to declarer before the second bidding round. The non-declarers do not exchange cards.

Pass-misère. If all four pass immediately, Dealer deals the talon around so that everyone has 13 cards. The aim is to avoid winning tricks, playing at no trump. Before play, each in turn, starting with Dealer, passes any card from his hand face down to his partner.

Doubling. Any game may be doubled by one side and redoubled by the other. First to speak is the player at declarer's left, or at Dealer's left in the case of pass-misère. Doubling doubles, and redoubling quadruples, whatever scores are made by either side, but only those recorded above the line. (*Note:* It is often agreed beforehand that if a contract of four is not doubled, it is not played out, but promptly scored by the declarers as if its win were a foregone conclusion—as, indeed, is usually the case.) Doubling is normally indicated by knocking.

Play. The opening lead comes from declarer's left, except in a bid misère, when it comes from his right. Follow suit if possible, otherwise play any card. The trick is taken by the highest card of the suit led, or by the highest trump if any are played, and the winner of each trick leads to the next.

Above-line scoring. Scores are made above the line for the contract, any overtricks, and for honours. The contract score is determined solely by the number of tricks contracted, regardless of whether made in suit, nullos or grands. The contract scores are:

	Won	*Lost*
Four	1000	400 p.u.
Five	2000 + 200 p.o.	500 p.u.
Six	3000 + 200 p.o.	600 p.u. + 400 for the contract
Seven	4500	700 p.u. + 1000 for the contract

(p.u. = per undertrick, credited to the opposing side; p.o. = per overtrick.)

Overtricks are not rewarded in a contract of four. Remember that in a bid misère, an over-trick means an extra trick lost, an under-trick its opposite.

Honours are the four Aces and top five trumps (if any). Whichever side held the majority of honours between them after the card exchanges (if any) scores—regardless of who made the contract and whether they won or lost—the number of honours they held, multiplied by ten times the number of tricks contracted. For this purpose the trump Ace counts once as an Ace and again as a trump.

Example: One side held three Aces including that of trumps, plus K Q T of trumps, in a contract of six. They score (3 Aces + 4 trumps) × 60 = 420 points.

Additional scores are made by a partnership for any of the following held in one of its hands when play began:

Three Aces	200
Four Aces	400
Trump A K Q	200, plus 200 for each lower card in sequence
Non-trump A K Q	100, plus 100 for each lower card in sequence

At grand, only Aces are honours. A side holding three or four adds 1 and multiplies by ten times the contract value. Three or four held in one hand count 400 or 800, and suit-sequences headed A K Q count 200 per card involved.

At nullos, honours do not count as such, but either side scores for any Ace which it succeeds in discarding to a trick. This scores 100 times the number of the trick in which it was taken. For example, if a player unable to follow suit in the ninth trick discards an Ace to it, and the trick is won by an opponent, his side scores 900, or 1800 if his partner manages to do the same.

At pass-misère, the side taking fewer tricks scores 100 times the difference in tricks won between the two sides—six tricks 100, five tricks 300, etc. Either side also scores for discarding Aces when unable to follow suit, as in a nullo bid.

Below-line scoring. Regardless of whether the contract was won or lost, each side scores below the line (except in pass-misère) an amount found by multiplying the number of tricks it took by the value of the contract. For example, if one side bid six and took eleven tricks (one short) it scores $6 \times 11 = 66$ to the other's $6 \times 2 = 12$ below the line. Each time a side wins a game by reaching 60 below the line, it adds a bonus and draws another line, and a new game is started (from zero). A side's second won game earns a bonus of 400, and at this point the last four deals begin. The bonus for a side's third game is 600, its fourth 800, and so on in increments of 200 until the rubber ends. (*Note*: (*a*) A pass-misère does not score below the line, as no contract was named. (*b*) Below-line scores are not affected by doubling.)

Notes. It would be facile to dismiss Vint as a souped up version of Bridge in which the minimum four-bid (10 out of 13 tricks) is secured by, in effect, stacking the pack. A few rounds of play should suffice to reveal the game's potential. Extensive bidding conventions, which there is not space to outline here, take full advantage of the fact that eight passes precede the establishment of a provisional contract.

Vira

Swedish national card game, a three-handed cross between Hombre and Boston Whist. See Göran B. Nilsson, *Handbok i vira* (Stockholm, 1973).

Vying games

Skilled gambling games in which players vie with one another as to who holds the best hand by progressively raising the stakes. The pot is won either by the player with the best hand or by the player who, by convincing others that he has the best hand ('bluffing'), forces them all to concede rather than pay for a showdown. See Bouillotte, Brag, Poch, Poker, Primiera.

Watten

Plain-trick bluffing game: 2–4p, 32c

An eccentric Bavarian gambling game typifying an ancient family that includes Put (q.v.), Truc (q.v.), Aluette, and Karnöffel (q.v.). They are characterized by the fact that suit need not be followed, and certain specified cards count as trumps rather than a particular suit. Despite its eccentricities, Watten is fun to play and not too hard to learn. (Source: Claus D. Grupp, *Kartenspiele*, Wiesbaden, 1975.) It is normally played with German-suited cards, but French (international) cards will do.

If four play, they sit crosswise in partnerships. Choose first dealer by any agreed means; thereafter, the turn to deal and play passes to the left. Deal 5 cards each (3 + 2) from a 32-card pack basically ranking A K Q J T 9 8 7 in each suit, and stack the rest face down.

The aim is to score one or more game points, either by winning three tricks or by bluffing the other side into conceding defeat. Game is 15 points over as many deals as necessary.

Three cards are permanent highest trumps. They are called *Kritischen,* which we may call 'matadors' by analogy with other games. From the top down, they are:

♥K, or 'Maxi'

♦7, or 'Belli'

♣7, or 'Spitz'

Eldest makes the first announcement by naming any rank of card. All four cards of that rank (or three, if one is a matador) count as the next highest trumps, and are called 'strikers' (*Schläge*).

Dealer makes the second announcement by nominating any suit as trump. The striker of the trump suit is thereby promoted to 'chief striker', ranking below the matadors as the fourth highest card. Below the other strikers, the remaining cards of the trump suit rank A K Q J T 9 8 7, omitting any that may be a matador or a striker.

Examples. (1) Eldest announces 'Jacks' and Dealer 'spades'. Trumps therefore rank ♥K ♦7 ♣7 ♠J (♥J ♣J ♦J) ♠A K Q T 9 8 7. (2) Eldest announces 'Kings' and dealer 'hearts'. Trumps now rank ♥K ♦7 ♣7 (♠K ♣K ♦K) ♥A Q J T 9 8 7. In this case there is no chief striker, as the heart King is always a matador. Cards in brackets are of equal rank.

Whisk

Eldest leads to the first trick and the winner of each trick leads to the next. Suit need not be followed except in one instance: if the chief striker is led, everyone else must play a trump if possible, and beat any others already played if possible. All matadors, strikers, and trumps count as trumps. The trick is taken by the highest trump played; or, if headed by equal strikers, by the one played first; or, if not trumped, by the highest card of the suit led.

The player or side who first wins three tricks gains one point, and the rest are not played. However, any player, at any time, may raise the value of the game. The first to do so says 'Double'; the next 'Three', then 'Four', and so on. If the other side concedes, play ceases and the challenger wins the value of the game as it was before being raised; if they accept, either verbally or by continuing play, then the increase applies to the score made by the eventual winner(s). (Source does not state what happens if, when three play, one player challenges and only one of the others accepts. Presumably the one who drops immediately concedes the old value to the challenger, and the other two fight the rest out between them.)

A player or side standing at 13 or more points may not challenge. If they mistakenly do so, they lose 2 points (or the other side scores 2, if so agreed).

When four play, partners may signal certain card holdings to each other by means of conventional signals. 'Maxi' is indicated by pursing the lips, 'Belli' by winking the right eye, 'Spitz' by winking the left.

Whisk

See Whist.

Whisky Poker

See Poker.

Whist

Plain-trick game: 4pp, 52c

The most prestigious card game of the Western world between about 1750 and 1900, when it was relegated by Bridge. It derives from the sixteenth-century English game of Trump or Ruff, via Ruff and

Honours, Whisk and Swabbers (probably a word-play on the former), Whisk, and, by about 1730, plain Whist. Starting as an 'alehouse game' with several complications but little strategic depth, it eventually became an upper-class game by shedding the complications and attracting much intellectual analysis—a practice brilliantly promoted by Edmond Hoyle in his *Treatise* of 1742. Intellectualism has subsequently transferred itself to Bridge, leaving Whist to be now peaceably and unpretentiously played by droves in drives.

Of many adaptations and varieties of the game, separate entries will be found for Boston, Bridge, Cayenne, Chinese W., Contract W., Dutch W., German W., Knockout W., Nomination W., Norwegian W., Scotch W., Solo W., and Vint. (Russian Whist is Vint, and Whist de Gand, or Ghent Whist, is Solo.)

Described below is the classical game of Short Whist, followed by some variants not covered in separate entries.

Short Whist

Four players use a 52-card pack ranking A K Q J T 9 8 7 6 5 4 3 2 in each suit and sit crosswise in partnerships. Determine partnerships, seating and first dealer by any agreed means; thereafter, the turn to deal and play passes to the left. A rubber is the best of three games. A game is 5 points, which may take one or more deals to attain.

Deal 13 cards each in 1s, turning the dealer's last card for trumps before taking it into hand.

Eldest leads to the first trick, and the winner of each trick leads to the next. Follow suit if possible, otherwise play any card. The trick is taken by the highest card of the suit led, or by the highest trump if any are played.

The side taking the majority of tricks scores 1 point per trick taken above six.

The first to reach five points scores a single game or stake if the opponents have 3 or 4, a double if they have 1 or 2, a treble if they have no points.

Honours. It may be agreed to score for honours. At end of play, a side which held most of the four highest trumps (whether or not in the same hand) adds 2 points if they held three, or 4 if they held four. A side standing at 4 points to game, however, may not score for honours.

Notes. Skill at play lies in communicating information to one's partner by choosing, when possible, leads and discards to which conventional meanings are attached. For example:

The leader to the first trick should lead trumps if he has five or more. From

A K Q J *lead* J, Q
A K Q   Q, K
A K   K, A if holding seven or more trumps, otherwise
               fourth best

Fourth best enables partner to calculate how many trumps are held between them by applying the 'rule of eleven', i.e. subtract from eleven the value of the card led: the residue indicates how many higher trumps are missing from the leader's hand, thus allowing further deductions to be made and inferences drawn.

If not trumps, lead from the longest or strongest plain suit according to its top cards as follows:

from A K Q J *lead* K, J
        A K Q   K, Q
        A K J   K, A
        A Q J   A, Q
        K Q J   J

From other holdings, lead the King if held, otherwise Ace (if held) then fourth best, otherwise fourth best.

The overall aim is to enable the partners to discover early on which is their best suit, so that they may seek to draw trumps and win subsequent tricks by leading it when the opponents can neither follow nor trump.

American Whist

As above, but playing up to 7 points and not scoring for honours, so that it is just possible to reach game in one deal—a self-evident improvement.

Long Whist

The game played up to 10 points, as it was before Short Whist was introduced in the early nineteenth century.

Progressive Whist

The version now played in Whist drives, whereby players change tables and partners from deal to deal, ultimately producing a single overall winner. No card is turned for trump; instead, the suits rotate in order hearts, clubs, diamonds, spades.

Bid Whist

No card is turned for trump. Instead, each in turn, starting with eldest, bids by stating the number of tricks above six he would contract to take with his partner if allowed to name trumps. Each bid must be higher than the last, and trumps are announced by the last bidder when three have passed. Score 1 point per trick taken above six, or lose 1 per trick short of the number contracted.

Whist for three

The classic game is Dummy, which may have originated the distinguishing feature of Bridge. Four hands are dealt, that opposite the dealer is turned face up and arranged into suits, and the dealer plays from it as if half of him were his own partner. It was usual for each player to partner himself for the duration of a rubber.

Sergeant Major. Deal 16 to each player and 20 to the dealer, turning the last for trumps. Dealer discards four. Each player scores 1 point per trick taken in excess of his quota, which is eight for dealer, five for eldest, and three for the other.

See also Dutch Whist ('Bismarck').

Whist for two

The classic game is German Whist (q.v). In both the following, the last card is turned for trump and play proceeds as in ordinary Whist.

Double Dummy. The two sit next to each other, the player cutting the lower card being to the right of the other. Deal four hands, that opposite each player being his dummy. Turn the dummies up and sort the cards into suits. Non-dealer leads and play goes clockwise, each playing alternately from his own and from his dummy's hand.

Humbug. The players sit opposite each other. Deal four hands, leaving the dead hands face down. Each has the option of playing with the cards as dealt, or throwing the hand in and taking the dead hand on his right instead. (*Recommendation:* If one plays the hand as dealt, all scores are doubled; if both, they are quadrupled.)

Yellow Dwarf

Or Nain Jaune (French), Gelber Zwerg (German): Continental forerunner of Pope Joan (q.v.).

Yeralash

Or Ieralasche (French, German): Forerunner of Vint (q.v.).

Yukon

Point-trick game: 2–5p, 52c

A peculiar and not too serious game said to have been popular in the Yukon Gold Rush—though it is not actually recorded before 1945, and looks like a whimsical hybrid of Scotch Whist and Skat.

Two to five may play, but the best format is four in partnerships. Use a 52-card pack, removing one or two Twos if three or five play. The turn to deal and play passes to the left. Deal 5 cards each and stack the rest face down.

The winning player or side is the first to take 250 in card-points over as many deals as necessary. For this purpose the Jacks, called Yukons, are the four highest cards. The spade Jack or 'Grand Yukon' is highest of all and counts 15 points, the other Yukons counting 10 each. The remaining cards rank A K Q T 9 8 7 6 5 4 3 2, each Ace counting 5 points, King 3, Queen 2, Ten 10, others 0.

Eldest leads to the first trick. Subsequent players must follow suit if possible (including that of a Yukon if led), otherwise must play a Yukon if possible, otherwise may play any card. The trick is taken by the Grand Yukon if played, or by the first played of two or more other Yukons, otherwise by the highest card of the suit led. The winner of each trick leads to the next, after first drawing the top card of stock, adding it to his hand, and waiting for the others to do likewise. When the stock is empty, play continues until all have run out of cards.

The points taken by each player or side are not counted until end of play. Play ceases when someone has reached 250 points, and the winner is the player or side that took most.

Zetema

Collecting game: 2–6p, 65c

Zetema was marketed by J. Hunt as a proprietary game in about 1870. It seems to have been soon forgotten, but (fortunately) not before making its way into *Cassell's Book of Indoor Amusements, Card Games and Fireside Fun* (1881), from which it was rescued, revised, and enthused over by Sid Sackson in *A Gamut of Games* (New York, 1969). It is in fact an excellent and unusual game, with reminiscences of Bezique and Poker, but less earnest and more fun than either. In the following account I incorporate Sackson's improvements to the scoring system. In addition, I dispense with the word 'trick', originally used to denote a set of five discards, as it gives the impression that Zetema is a trick-play game, which it emphatically is not. I now call such sets 'zetemas' in order to make use of the otherwise redundant and apparently meaningless title.

From two to six may play, three being an ideal number, and four or six playing best in partnerships. The 65-card pack is made by shuffling in a whole suit from a second pack of identical back design and colour. The duplicated suit—it doesn't matter which it is—is called the imperial suit.

The turn to deal and play passes to the left. Shuffle thoroughly, deal 6 cards each (or 5 if six play), and stack the rest face down.

Game is 300 points (200 if more than three play) over as many deals as it takes. Points are scored for declaring melds in the hand and for winning zetemas. A zetema is a set of five discards of the same rank.

Each in turn, starting with Eldest, draws a card from stock, adds it to his hand, may declare a meld if he has one, and (usually) ends by making one discard face up to the table. Discards are made in sets of the same rank—i.e. thirteen wastepiles are formed, one for each rank. The player adding the fifth card to a wastepile scores for a zetema and discards it face down to a common wastepile. A zetema of Kings or Queens scores 50, Jacks 20, Aces or Fives 15, other ranks 5 each.

Upon drawing a card, a player may show and score for one of the following combinations:

1. *Sequence* (scores 20): six cards in sequence, not all the same suit. For this purpose, cards run A 2 3 4 5 6 7 8 9 T J Q K.
2. *Flush* (scores 30): six cards of the same suit, not all in sequence.
3. *Flush sequence* (scores 50): six cards in suit and sequence.
4. *Assembly.* Five cards of the same rank. An assembly of Kings or Queens scores 130, Jacks 120, Aces or Fives 110, other ranks 100.

Having declared one of the above, the player ends his turn by discarding one of the declared cards to its appropriate wastepile.

5. *Marriages.* A marriage is a King and Queen of the same suit. They may both come from the hand, or one of them may come from the hand and its partner be taken from the appropriate discard pile on the table. Marriages may be saved up and scored simultaneously—the more the better. One marriage scores 10, two 30, three 60, four 100, all five 150. If fewer than five are declared, each marriage in the doubled suit counts an additional ten. Having declared one or more marriages, the player discards them face up to the common wastepile (they do not contribute to zetemas), and draws from stock to complete his hand to six cards. He does not make any other discard.

Note: Marriages may be scored both ways in the same turn (though, of course, an imperial King or Queen may only be partnered once), but it is not permissible to declare a six-card meld and marry the seventh in the same turn.

When the last card of stock has been drawn, players continue by discarding to the wastepiles and scoring for zetemas when made. When two play, a player completing a zetema is obliged to play another card, and so on until he fails to complete one.

It may happen that some players go out before others—if so, they simply stop playing. Overall play ceases the moment anyone reaches the target score of 200 or 300, even in mid-play. Otherwise, it ends, very neatly, when the last zetema has been taken and turned face down to the wastepile, leaving an otherwise empty table.

FIG. 32. **Zetema.** South discards the fifth Three and scores 5 for the zetema. If he is lucky enough to draw a King, he will have a sequence to score on his next turn.

Notes. The original scores for assemblies were 100, 90, 80, 60; but they are so difficult to acquire that even with the revisions quoted above they are rarely worth aiming for. The exceptionally high scores for King and Queen zetemas are somewhat academic, since the declaration of any marriage prevents either from being completed.

Zheng Shàngyóu

Zheng Shàngyóu

See Trouduc.

Zioncheck

See Contract Rummy.

Zwicker

Fishing game: 2–4p, 52c + Jokers

A simpler version of Cassino, Zwicker is described (by Claus D. Grupp, in *Schafkopf, Doppelkopf*, Wiesbaden 1976) as a long popular family game of Schleswig-Holstein.

From two to four players use a 52-card pack, to which it is now customary to add six Jokers of (preferably) the same back design and colour as the main pack.

The turn to deal and play passes to the left. Deal 4 cards each, and 4 face up to the table to form a pool. Stack the rest face down.

Each in turn, starting with Eldest, plays a card to the table, thereby capturing one or more pool cards if possible, otherwise leaving it there as part of the pool. When everyone has played four cards, 4 more each are dealt so long as any remain in stock, and play proceeds as before.

The aim is to capture Aces, the ♦7, the ♠7, and, especially, the ♦10, and to make sweeps. A sweep is the capture, in one turn, of all the cards left in the pool.

Each in turn, starting with Eldest, plays a card face up from hand to table. It may capture one or more pool cards by either:

matching—an Ace captures one or more Aces, a Seven one or more Sevens, etc; or

combining—a card captures two or more cards whose values add up to itself. For this purpose numerals Two to Ten count face value, Ace 11, Jack 12, Queen 13, King 14.

Example. The pool cards are 5 5 7 J. A Five may be played to capture both Fives. A Jack, on the other hand, will capture the Jack by matching and the Seven and one Five by combining, since 7 + 5 make the value of a Jack.

The capturing and captured cards are taken and laid face down before the player who took them like a won trick in other games. At any given time there may be anything from one to five or more cards in the pool. If all are taken at once, the sweep is indicated by leaving the capturing card face up in the pile of won cards. After a sweep, the next player has no option but to add a card to the pool.

A player unable to capture can only add a card to the pool. He may, however, arrange it as a separate card, or make a 'build' by placing it half over another card. In this case the build counts as if it were a single card of their combined value, and may be captured but only as a whole. For example, a Five played to a Seven makes a build of 12, which can later be captured by a Jack—or, if there is also a Two on the table, by a King in conjunction with the Two, since the Two and the 12-build are equalled by the value of the King. More discards may be added to a build, so long it does not exceed 14 in total.

Jokers may be captured by matching. In addition, a Joker counts as any desired value from 2 to 14, and may be played or captured accordingly. Of course, it may only count as one value at a time: it cannot capture two different cards, or builds of different values, in the same turn.

No cards are added to the pool when extra cards are dealt. On the last deal, it does not matter that there may not be enough cards to go round. The last person to play a card from the hand also wins any cards left in the pool, but this does not count as a sweep, unless it happens to be one as defined above.

At end of play each player sorts through his won cards and scores as follows:

♦7	1 point
♠7	1
Each Ace	2
Each sweep	3
♦10	10

Play up to any agreed target.

Variants. Various restrictions may be imposed on the power of Jokers. In some circles, for instance, a Joker in the pool may not be captured at all, thus preventing any more sweeps from being made.

Zwikken

Point-tricks and bluff: 3p, 20c

This old Dutch army gambling game, supposedly of ill repute, has a sufficient element of bluff to be interesting to play without serious gambling. Accounts vary; the following is typical.

Three players use a 20-card pack ranking and counting thus in each suit: Ace 4, King 3, Queen 2, Jack 1, Ten 0. The turn to deal and play passes to the left. Each player chips one to the pot and receives 3 cards dealt either 1 and 2 or 2 and 1. The next card is turned for trump. Anyone holding the Ten of trump may eventually exchange it for the turn-up, but for the time being keeps mum.

Each in turn has one opportunity to shoot for the whole or a portion of the pot—typically a third or a half—or to pass. If one player shoots for less than the total in the pot, a subsequent player can take it off him by offering to shoot higher, i.e. for a greater proportion of it.

The highest bidder becomes the shooter. His aim is either to have the best *zwik* (three of a kind), or to win two tricks, or one trick containing more card-points than the other two combined.

If all pass, the dealer may (but need not) require everyone to add a chip to the pool, and then turns the next card for trump. If all pass a second time, dealer has the same option. If he declines the option, or no one bids after three turns, the deal is annulled and the pool is carried forward to the next.

Otherwise, play begins as soon as someone offers to shoot. Now:

1. Anyone holding the Ten of trump may exchange it for the turn-up.
2. Anyone holding a *zwik* (three cards of the same rank) shows it and wins the pool. Of two *zwiks*, the higher-ranking wins. Otherwise:
3. Eldest leads to the first trick. Players must follow suit if possible, and otherwise must trump if possible. Any trump played must be higher (if possible) than any already played to the trick. The trick is taken by the highest card of the suit led, or by the highest trump if any are played, and the winner of each trick leads to the next.

The soloist wins by taking two tricks, or one trick counting more in card-points than the other two combined, equality being insufficient. If successful, he wins the amount he bid; if not, he adds it to the pot.

Notes. A wicked feature of the game is that exchanging the Ten may give a player a *zwik*. Equally crafty is the dealer's possibility of passing the first round with a good hand in the hope of shooting later when he has exercised his option of increasing the pool. It should be added that the card-points are virtually academic, as a single trick rarely counts enough to beat the other two. Sources vary as to the number of times the dealer may turn another trump, and whether turning the same suit as before counts as a separate turn.

Appendix: Terms used in card-play

Only terms used in this book are listed. Most are traditional. A few, such as 'alliance' in its special sense, are suggestions designed to serve particular purposes or to fill self-evident gaps.

alliance   A temporary partnership, lasting only for the current deal (as in 'prop and cop' at Solo Whist).

ante   In games, an obligatory stake made before play begins—usually by every player, sometimes only by the dealer.

auction   A period of bidding to establish the conditions of the game, such as who is undertaking to win, how many tricks constitute a win, which suit is trump, etc.

bettel   Same as misère.

bid   An offer to achieve a stated objective (e.g. a given number of tricks) in exchange for choosing the conditions of play (e.g. a trump suit). If the offer is not overcalled by a higher bid, it becomes a contract.

blank   (1) In card-point games, a card worth nothing. (2) A hand without courts, consisting only of numerals.

blind   (1) A dead hand or set of spare cards; same as 'widow'. (German *Blinde*.) (2) To bet on, select, exchange, or play a card, without knowing what it is.

carte blanche   Same as 'blank' (2).

carte rouge   A hand in which every card counts towards a scoring combination.

chicane   A hand which, as dealt, contains no trumps.

chip   A gaming counter, especially in Poker.

combination   A set of cards matching one another by rank or suit and recognized by the rules of the game as a scoring feature.

contract   See 'bid'.

counter   (1) An object representing a score or partially won game. (2) A card with a point-value, in point-trick games such as Skat and Pinochle.

court cards   (originally 'coat cards'; also called 'face cards'): King, Queen, Jack, and other personages, as opposed to numerals or 'pip' cards.

cut   To lift off the top portion of the pack and either (1) reveal its bottom card, so as to make a random decision such as who deals first; or (2) to replace it beneath the lower half, so as to ensure that no one knows what the bottom card is.

cut-throat   All-against-all; without partnerships.

dead hand   See 'widow'.

deadwood   (Rummy) Penalty cards remaining in opponents' hands when one player has gone out.

deal   (1) To distribute cards to the players at start of play. (2) The play ensuing between one deal and the next.

declare   (1) To announce the contract or conditions of play (number of tricks intended, trump suit, etc.). (2) To show and score for a valid combination of cards in hand.

declarer   The highest bidder, who declares and then seeks to make good the stated contract.

deuce   The numeral 'Two' of any suit.

discard   (1) To lay aside an unwanted card or cards from hand; (2) to throw a worthless or unwanted card to a trick; (3) the card or cards so disposed of.

doubleton   Two cards of the same suit in the same hand, no others of that suit being held.

draw   To take, or be dealt, one or more cards from a stock or wastepile.

drinking game   Typically, one that results in a loser rather than a winner, in order to decide who pays for the next round.

dummy   A full hand of cards dealt face up to the table (or, in Bridge, dealt to one of the players, who eventually spreads them face up on the table) from which the declarer plays as well as from his or her own hand.

earlier, -est   Same as Elder; see also 'priority'.

Elder, -est   The player with greatest priority in order of play; the one due to make the opening lead or bet. (See also 'Forehand', 'priority', 'Younger'.) In most games, Eldest is the player seated next to the dealer in rotation of play, and the dealer himself is Youngest.

exchange   (1) To discard one or more cards from hand and then draw or receive the same number from stock. (2) To add a specified number of cards to hand and then discard a like number. (3) To exchange one or more cards with a neighbour, sight unseen.

finesse   In trick games, to refrain from winning a trick with a card known to be the best in its suit, instead playing a lower but non-consecutive card in the hope that it will hold the trick, thereby yielding its player two tricks in the suit.

flush   A hand of cards all of the same suit.

follow   (1) To play second, third, etc. to a trick. (2) Follow suit: To play a card of the same suit as that led.

Forehand   Same as 'Eldest'. (German *Vorhand*.)

frog The lowest bid in certain games of German origin. From German *Frage*, 'request'.

game (1) A series of deals or session of play. (2) The contract, or conditions of the game; e.g. 'Solo in hearts'. (3) The target score; e.g. 'Game is 100 points'.

go out To play the last card from one's hand.

grand A bid equivalent to no trump in some games, a slam in others.

hand (1) The cards dealt to an individual player, which he either plays from or bets on, depending on the type of game. (2) Same as 'deal' (2).

hard score Scoring done with coins, chips or counters, as opposed to a written or 'soft' score. (See Introduction for conversion of one to the other.)

head To play a higher card than any so far played to the trick, especially in games such as Écarté where it is obligatory to do so if possible.

honours Cards attracting bonus scores or side-payments, usually to whoever holds and declares them, occasionally to whoever captures them in play.

lead To play the first card; or, the first card played.

line, above/below (Bridge) Scores made for tricks contracted and won are recorded below a line drawn half way down the sheet, and count towards winning the game; overtricks, honours, and other premiums are scored above it and mainly determine the size of the win.

marriage King and Queen of the same suit.

matadors Top trumps, sometimes with special privileges (especially in Hombre).

meld A combination of matching cards attracting scores or privileges, or winning the game; (2) to declare such a combination.

Middlehand In three-hand games, the player of intermediate priority. (German *Mittelhand*.) See also 'priority'.

misère A contract or undertaking to lose every trick.

miss A dead hand, especially in Loo; see 'widow'.

negative game One in which the object is to avoid taking tricks or penalty cards. (I prefer to call this an 'avoidance' game, and to use 'negative' for a game which results in a loser rather than a winner.)

null Same as misère (German).

numerals Number cards, as opposed to courts. Also called pip cards, spot cards, spotters, etc.

ouvert(e) A contract played with declarer's cards spread face up on the table for all to see.

overcall To bid higher than the previous bidder. (Suit overcall: bid to entrump a higher-ranking suit; majority overcall: to take a higher number of tricks; value overcall: to play a game of higher value or to capture a greater total of card-points.)

overtrick A trick taken in excess of the number required to win.

pair Two cards of the same rank.

partie A whole game, as opposed to a single deal, especially at Piquet.

partnership Two or more players whose interests are bound together as a team and who therefore play cooperatively rather than individually. A partnership may be either fixed in advance and last for the whole session, as at Whist and Bridge, or vary from deal to deal, as at Quadrille or Solo, in which case it is better referred to as an 'alliance'.

pass In trick-games, to make no further bid; in vying games, to pass the privilege of betting first but without dropping out of play.

pip A suitmark printed on a card, or the number represented—e.g. the Deuce shows two pips. (Originally 'peep'.)

plain suit (side suit): A suit other than trumps.

plain-trick games Those in which importance attaches only to the number of tricks taken, regardless of the cards comprising them, as opposed to point-trick games.

point (1) The smallest unit of value, score or reckoning. In various games distinctions may be drawn between card-points, which are notional values attached to certain cards, the object being to capture a minimum number of them; score-points, which are points credited to a player's account; and game points, which might loosely be described as 'bundles' of score-points and may be affected by other bonuses. (2) The total face value of all cards held of any one suit (Piquet).

point-trick games Those in which in which win or loss is determined not by the number of tricks taken but by the total value of counters contained in them, as opposed to plain-trick games.

pool, or pot A sum of money or equivalent, to which everyone contributes initially or throughout play, and which is eventually awarded (in whole or part) to the winner.

prial ('Pair-royal'): A triplet; three cards of the same rank.

priority The order in which players take precedence over one another when (for example) two or more wish to make bids of equal value. Typically, an 'older' or 'earlier' player has priority over a 'younger' or 'later'. Priority normally starts with the player sitting at the dealer's left in games played clockwise around the table, or at his right in games played counter-clockwise.

rank (1) The denomination of a card (e.g. Ace, Two, King), as opposed to its suit. (2) The relative trick-taking power of a card (e.g. 'Ace ranks above King').

Rearhand The player with least priority (q.v.), usually in three-hand games. (German *Hinterhand*.)

renege To fail to follow suit to the card led, but legally so, by exercise of a privilege granted by the rules of the game, as in Spoil Five.

renounce   Strictly, to play a card of any different suit from that led—the same as 'renege' if done legally, or 'revoke' if not. Loosely, to do so only from a non-trump suit, thereby renouncing all hope of winning the trick.

revoke   To fail to follow suit to the card led, though able and required to do so, thereby incurring a penalty.

riffle   A method of shuffling. The pack is divided into two halves which are placed corner to corner, lifted, and allowed to fall rapidly together so that they interleave.

rotation   The order in which play passes around the table, whether from right to left (clockwise) or left to right (counter-clockwise).

round   (1) A period or phase of play in which all have had the same number of opportunities to deal, or bid, play to a trick, etc. (2) Round game: one playable by an indefinite number of players, typically three to seven.

rubber   A contest won by the first side to win two games; i.e. best of three.

ruff   To play a trump to a plain-suit lead.

run   (Brag, Cribbage) Same as 'sequence'.

sans prendre   A bid to play with the hand as dealt, without benefit of exchanging, thereby increasing the difficulty and hence scoring value of the game. Also called 'solo'.

sequence   A scoring combination consisting of three or more cards in numerical sequence or ranking order

shuffle   To randomize the order of cards in the pack. See also 'riffle'.

side suit   (plain suit): a non-trump suit.

singleton   A card which is the only one of its suit in a given hand.

skat   Same as 'widow'. (German; from Italian *scarto*, 'discard').

slam   The winning of every trick, or a bid to do so.

small slam   As above, but every trick bar one.

soft score   Score kept in writing or on a scoring device, as opposed to 'hard score' of cash or counters. (See Introduction for conversion of one to the other.)

solo   (Trick games). (1) Originally, to undertake a contract with the cards as dealt, rather than seeking to improve the hand by exchanging any; same as 'sans prendre'. (2) A bid to achieve a given objective playing alone against the combined efforts of the other players.

soloist   One who plays a solo.

spread   Same as 'ouvert'.

squeeze   In trick-taking games, a situation in which a player cannot follow suit to the card led, but either cannot play without weakening himself in another suit, or cannot tell which suit is safe to play from.

stock Cards which are not dealt initially but may be drawn from or dealt out later in the play.

stops Cards which terminate a sequence, in games of the Stops family (Newmarket, Pope Joan etc.); or those which are not dealt initially and whose absence from play prevents the completion of sequences.

straddle An obligatory stake made, before any cards are dealt, by the second player around, the first having put up an ante.

straight In Poker, a five-card sequence.

suit A series of cards distinguished by the presence of a common graphic symbol throughout; or the symbol (suitmark) itself.

talon The stock, or undealt portion of the pack.

tourné(e) A contract in which the bidder turns the top card of stock and accepts its suit as trump.

trey The numeral Three of any suit.

trick A set of cards equal to the number of players, each having contributed one in succession.

trump (1) A superior suit, any card of which will beat that of any other suit played to the trick. (2) To play such a card. (From 'triumph'.)

turn-up A card turned up at start of play to determine the trump suit.

unblock To play a high card, even if it loses, to prevent it from impeding subsequent play from one's partner's (or dummy's) long suit.

undertrick A trick less than the number required to win the deal.

upcard A card lying face up on the table, or the faced top card of the wastepile at Rummy, Patience, etc.

void Having no card of a given suit (e.g. 'void in hearts').

vole A slam; the winning of every trick played. (French, from Spanish *bola*.)

vulnerable (Bridge) Describes a side which, having won one game towards the rubber, is subject to increased scores or penalties.

wastepile A pile of discards, usually face up, as at Rummy, Patience, etc.

widow A hand of cards dealt face down to the table at start of play and not belonging to any particular player. One or more players may subsequently exchange one or more cards with it. (Also 'blind', 'miss', 'skat'.)

wild card One that may be used to represent any other card, with or without stated restrictions. Typically the Joker in Rummy games, Deuces in Poker.

x a card whose precise rank is insignificant to the point at issue, as in Kx.

Younger, -est The player last in turn to bid or play at the start of a game. See 'Eldest', 'priority'.

Appendix

Solution to Eleusis problem (see Fig. 13, p. 101). The secret rule reads: 'If the last card played is higher than the previous one, play a red numeral; if lower, play a black numeral; if equal, play a court.' Since ♥2 is lower than ♣K, the next card must be a black numeral. Only ♠7 complies with the rule. (*Note:* Ace is always low in Eleusis.)

Bibliography

This list identifies only books specifically mentioned in the text. It is not a complete list of books consulted.

Abbott, Robert, *Abbott's New Card Games* (New York, 1963).

Andrews, J., *Win at Hearts* (New York, 1983).

Anon., *Cassell's Book of Indoor Amusements* . . . (London, 1881).

Anon., *The Royal Game of Costly Colours* (Shrewsbury 1805).

Anon., *Giochi di carte* (Milan, 1969).

Arnett, Patrick, *Le Tarot* (Paris, 1977).

Babsch, F., *Original Tarock* (Vienna, 1975).

Berloquin, Pierre, *Cent jeux de cartes classiques* (Paris, 1975).

Blackwood, Easley, *Spite and Malice* (New York, 1970).

Collinson, John (pseud.?), *Biritch, or Russian Whist* (1886; facsimile repr. Richmond-upon-Thames, 1977).

Cotton, Charles, *The Compleat Gamester* (London, 1674).

Culbertson, Ely: *see* Morehead and Mott-Smith.

Dossena, Giampaolo, *Giochi di carte italiani* (Milan, 1984).

Dummett, Michael, *The Game of Tarot* (London, 1980).

—— *Twelve Tarot Games* (London, 1980).

Egg, Gottfried, *Puur, Näll, As* (Neuhausen-am-Rheinfall, n.d. [1970.]).

Foster, R. F., *Foster's Complete Hoyle* (London, 1897).

Gerver, Frans, *Le Guide Marabout à tous les jeux de cartes* (Verviers, 1966).

Göring, Jürgen, *Stich um Stich* (Berlin, 1977).

Grupp, Claus D., *Schafkopf, Doppelkopf* (Wiesbaden, 1976).

—— *Kartenspiele* (Wiesbaden, 1975).

Harbin, Robert, *Waddington's Family Card Games* (London, 1972).

Hoffmann, E., and Rennenkampff, A. von, *The Laws and Principles of Vint* (London, 1900).

Holme, Randle, *The Academy of Armory* (1688).

James, Mac, *Pan: The Gambler's Card Game* (Las Vegas, 1979).

Kissel, Robert, 'Trappola', *Journal of the Playing-Card Society* 17/1 (London), Aug. 1988.

Laurent, Claude-Marcel, *Le Jeu de Tarots* (Paris, 1975).

McLeod, John, 'Reversis', *Journal of the Playing-Card Society*, May 1977.

——'Ulti', *Journal of the Playing-Card Society*, May 1976.

Morehead, Albert H., and Mott-Smith, Geoffrey, *Culbertson's Card Games Complete* (New York, 1952).

Bibliography

Nilsson, Göran B., *Handbok i vira* (Stockholm, 1973).

Omasta, V., and Ravik, S., *Hráčy Karty: Keretní Hri* (Prague, 1969).

Ostrow, Albert A., *The Complete Card-Player* (New York, 1945).

Parlett, David, *Original Card Games* (London, 1977).

Pennycook, Andrew, *The Book of Card Games* (St Albans, 1982).

Phillips, Hubert, *The Pan Book of Card Games* (London, 1953).

—— and Westall, B., *Card Games* (London, n.d. [1930s]).

Rubicon (pseud.), *Auction Piquet* (London, 1920).

Sackson, Sidney, *A Gamut of Games* (New York, 1969; London, 1972).

Taylor, Arthur, *Pub Games* (St Albans, 1976).

'Trumps' (pseud.), *The American Hoyle* (New York, 1880).

Wergin, Joseph Petrus, *Skat and Sheepshead* (McFarland, Wis., 1975).

Werner, Einar, and Sandgren, Tore, *Kortoxen* (Helsingborg, 1975).

Zaini, Rino Fulgi, *Giochi di Carte* (Milan, 1934; repr. 1977).